Collins

Atlas of
World
History

Collins

Atlas of World

History

First published in 2004 by
COLLINS BOOKS
HarperCollins*Publishers*
77–85 Fulham Palace Road
Hammersmith, London W6 8JB

The Collins website address is **www.collins.co.uk**

Collins is a registered trademark of HarperCollins Publishers

Copyright © HarperCollins*Publishers* Ltd 2004
Edited and designed by D & N Publishing, Marlborough, Wiltshire

ᴛh Library Cataloguing in Publication Data:
ᴊe record is available from the British Library

ted and bound in Italy by LEGO, Vicenza

ISBN 0-00-716640-0

The Collins Atlas of World History

HarperCollins*Publishers*
Editorial Direction: Philip Parker
Editorial and Picture Research: Céire Clark and Terry Moore
Cover design: David Wardle

Cartographic and Design Direction: Martin Brown

D&N Publishing
Editorial and Design Direction: David Goodfellow
Design: Shane O'Dwyer
Proof-reading: Michael Jones

Further proof-reading: Margaret Gilbey
Index: Chris Howes

The Collins Atlas of World History is an entirely new sort of history, taking as its starting point the visual representation of historical events and trends through maps. Covering the entire span of human history, from the first faltering steps of our ape-like ancestors to the recent conflicts in Afghanistan and Iraq, the present volume's scope is vast, but its fundamental premise is very simple. By actually seeing the boundaries of the Roman empire laid down just as they would be in a modern atlas, or tracing lines portraying the German advance in World War II, it is relatively simple to understand in graphic form what would otherwise take ten thousand words to describe.

A wide historical perspective is vital to understanding events which are unfolding in the world today. Without an understanding of the events leading up to the Partition of India in 1947, for example, the troubled relations between India and Pakistan might seem puzzling to an outsider. In just 192 pages, the reader can see the break-up of the Soviet Union visually represented, follow the campaigns of Napoleon, understand the religious divisions in Europe after the Reformation, trace the routes of the Crusades and follow the rise of the Roman Empire. Further afield, maps plot the rise of the Inca and Aztec empires, the territorial control of the ancient Egyptians, the Harappan cultures of India and all the principal dynasties of China. The French, Russian and Chinese revolutions find their place, together with the Industrial Revolution and the Information Revolution.

Although the maps are at the core of this book and its approach, they are supported by a comprehensive and analytical text which act as a companion to their coverage and together with them create a package of unrivalled breadth and accessibility.

If a knowledge of the history of the world, its peoples and cultures is almost a prerequisite for intelligent discourse on the problems of the contemporary world, **The Collins Atlas of World History** offers an easy, informed and pleasurable way into the subject. Particularly suitable for students, but intended to appeal to all lovers of history, this book truly brings the past into focus.

CONTENTS

PART I **THE PREHISTORIC WORLD**

In the vast time perspective of earth history the human species is a relative newcomer. The first life on earth of which we have any trace, simple single-celled organisms, date back some 4,600 million years. In contrast, fully modern *Homo sapiens sapiens* originated a mere 120,000 years ago. Yet within that short period of time we have become one of the most successful species ever, colonizing virtually every corner of the globe, increasing enormously in numbers and manipulating the earth's resources and environment in a way never attempted by any other organism on our planet.

Study of chromosomes shows that our nearest relatives in the animal kingdom are the African apes (gorillas and chimpanzees). With them we share a common descent from various ape-like species such as the *Dryopithecines* which lived in Africa, Europe and south Asia some 20–15 million years ago. The parting of the ways, when the human line diverged from that of the chimpanzees and gorillas, may have come as recently as eight million years ago, a tiny interval in the 4,600 million years of life on earth.

The earliest-known hominine remains come from the Afar region of Ethiopia, and it is here that the oldest remains have been found. These are of a small creature known as *Australopithecus* or 'southern ape', from the first discovery at Taung in South Africa in 1924. Between three and four million years ago, skeletal and fossilized remains of *Australopithecus afarensis* indicate small agile creatures, only around four feet tall, serviceable, if not fully bipedal, gait, hands still partly adapted for specialized tree climbing and a brain approximately one-third the size of ours. They lived almost exclusively on nuts, fruits and berries. But they already displayed some of the trends which were to lead to modern humans. The bipedal posture freed the hands for other tasks, in turn stimulating the development of a larger brain. At the same time, the jaw and snout became less prominent as hands could be used to break off foods and bring them to the mouth.

About three million years ago, *Homo* began to undergo important evolutionary trends, acquiring a larger brain and bipedalism. As larger brains need better diets to sustain them, the increase of brain size may have been accompanied by a move towards an energy-rich diet including animal proteins. Burnt bones found in southern Africa indicate that by 1.5 million years ago, hominines had learned to cook their food.

This pattern of development was the basis for the colonization by Homo erectus of areas outside sub-Saharan Africa around 1.8 million years ago. Then, a million years ago *Homo heidelbergensis* migrated into North Africa and the Near East, reaching northern Europe about 500,000 years ago. Both *erectus* and *heidelbergensis* probably shared a common African ancestor, *Homo ergaster*, best known from the Nariokotome skeleton. All three had brains of about 1,000 cubic centimetres and an adaptable stone technology; the weight and careful shaping of their distinctive hand axes, whether pointed or oval, made them effective tools for butchery.

NORTH AMERICA

North Atlantic Ocean

SOUTH AMERICA

South Atlantic Ocean

Swanscon
Pontnewydd
Paviland
Boxgrove
St Césaire
Steinhe
Cro Magnon
Atapuerca
La Chapelle Aux Saints
& La Ferrassie Zaffaray
Gibraltar
Sidi Abderrahman
Salé
Dar Es Soltan
Ternifi
Jebel Irhoud

Sahara Desert

A F

Sterkfont
Elandsfontei

1 Important fossils of human ancestors have been found at sites in Africa, Asia and Australia (map above). East Africa's Great Rift Valley is a crucial area since fossils found here in the stratified deposits can be reliably dated. The location of the remains suggests that these early humans lived away from the more densely populated forests and inhabited the grasslands where a different range of resources could be exploited with less competition. Even here, life was not without its dangers: some Australopithecine skulls found in southern Africa have leopard teeth-marks on them.

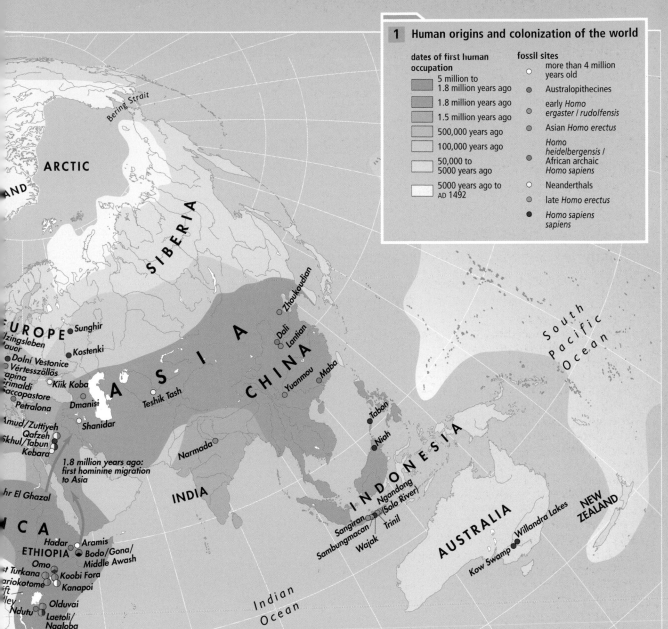

1 Human origins and colonization of the world

dates of first human occupation

- 5 million to 1.8 million years ago
- 1.8 million years ago
- 1.5 million years ago
- 500,000 years ago
- 100,000 years ago
- 50,000 to 5000 years ago
- 5000 years ago to AD 1492

fossil sites

- more than 4 million years old
- Australopithecines
- early *Homo ergaster / rudolfensis*
- Asian *Homo erectus*
- *Homo heidelbergensis /* African archaic *Homo sapiens*
- Neanderthals
- late *Homo erectus*
- *Homo sapiens sapiens*

ARCTIC

SIBERIA

ASIA

CHINA

Zhoukoudian

Dali
Lantian

Yuanmou
Maba

EUROPE

Bilzingsleben
Mauer
Sunghir
Kostenki
Dolní Vestonice
Vértesszöllös
Krapina
Grimaldi
Saccopastore
Petralona
Kiik Koba
Dmanisi
Teshik Tash
Shanidar
Amud/Zuttiyeh
Qafzeh
Skhul/Tabun
Kebara

1.8 million years ago: first hominine migration to Asia

Narmada

Tabon

Niah

INDONESIA

Ngandong (Solo River)

Sangiran
Sambungmacan   Trinil
Wajak

INDIA

Bahr El Ghazal

AFRICA

ETHIOPIA
Hadar
Aramis
Bodo/Gona/
Middle Awash
Omo
West Turkana
Nariokotome
Rift
Koobi Fora
Kanapoi
Valley
Ndutu
Olduvai
Laetoli/
Ngaloba

SOUTHERN AFRICA
Kabwe
Kromdraai
Makapansgat
Border Cave
Sterkfontein Swartkrans
Klasies River Mouth

AUSTRALIA

Kow Swamp
Willandra Lakes

NEW ZEALAND

South Pacific Ocean

Indian Ocean

Homo erectus survived for a million years or more, but some time after 500,000 years ago new types of hominine began to develop in Europe and Africa. In Europe, these changes led *c.*100,000 BC to the appearance of Neanderthal man, named after a skull found in the Neander valley in Germany in 1856. The line of development leading to modern humans, however, was based in Africa. Here, a little over 100,000 years ago, developed the first members of our own species, *Homo sapiens sapiens*: larger-brained creatures, able hunters and gatherers, equipped with sophisticated language and technology. From Africa the new species spread throughout the whole of the territory which had been occupied by *Homo erectus* and its descendants, and beyond into the hitherto unsettled regions of Australia and the Americas. For a while, Neanderthals hung on in parts of Europe, as the last Ice Age gathered pace; but their days were numbered. By 30,000 years ago, of the many species of hominine that had walked the earth during the past 5 million years of human development, only one, *Homo sapiens sapiens* was left.

the **ice age** world

We are well aware today that the earth's climate is not a stable, static phenomenon. Indeed, for at least 14 million years world climate has gradually been cooling. Around two million years ago this process intensified, and by 800,000 years ago the earth was in the grip of the first of the great Ice Ages which were to come and go roughly every 100,000 years, and to dominate human history until the last of them receded only 10,000 years ago.

The Ice Ages were periods of intense cold in northern and southern latitudes away from the equator. Temperatures fell by up to 15°C, and ice sheets advanced across the frozen wastes of northern Eurasia and North America. As more of the earth's water became locked into the growing ice sheets, sea levels fell, and even equatorial regions did not escape the effects of climatic adversity as rainfall diminished, turning half of all the land area between the tropics into desert.

The glaciers advanced and retreated several times, reaching a climax every 100,000 years but also giving way for short periods of 10,000 years or so to more temperate regimes. With each ice advance the plants and animals of the northern hemisphere withdrew before them to warmer latitudes, waiting for the ice's retreat to allow them to move northwards again. Yet despite the harshness of the coldest periods, the human species continued to develop during these millennia. It was indeed at this time that the human species spread from its original African homeland to east and south-east Asia and Europe. The mastery of fire and the invention of clothing and shelter were crucial to this achievement, but so were new social and communication skills. The human species as we know it today is the product of the long process of adaptation to the harsh conditions of the Ice Age.

The final phase of the Ice Ages began 75,000 years ago. By tying up water on a grand scale these reduced sea levels, and land bridges appeared, linking most of the major land areas and many present-day islands (including the British Isles) into one single continental mass. It was at this time, too, that a new species of human, fully modern *Homo sapiens sapiens*, began to spread from Africa, replacing or interbreeding with existing hominid populations in Europe and Asia. It was these modern humans that were able to take advantage of the short sea crossing caused by sea-level fall and colonize Australasia in about 50,000 BC. A little later, perhaps as early as 40,000 BC, humans also colonized America, either by crossing the land bridge which joined the two sides of the Bering Straits at certain periods or by use of boats. With the onset of warmer conditions some 10,000 years ago rising sea levels cut off these human communities in Australia and the Americas from further contact with Eurasia. Henceforward, these regions pursued their own independent lines of development.

Modern humans were relatively late arrivals in western Europe, replacing earlier Neanderthal populations only around 35,000 years ago. Yet here, as in Australia and South America, the new communities soon developed new levels of cultural expression. In the Dordogne area of southwest France, in the Pyrenees and in the Cantabrian region of northern Spain, hundreds of caves were decorated with paintings of symbols and animals. As hunting techniques and tool technology became more sophisticated, human communities became more and more able to cope with their environment. It was, however, change in the environment itself which was most important in opening up new opportunities. Around 10,000 years ago, the last Ice Age was in its closing stages. As temperatures rose, vegetation spread and animals began to recolonize the cold northern wastes. With them went the human hunters and gatherers. By 8000 BC, in certain crucial corners of the world such as Central America and the Near East, people had begun to move beyond their existing resources to investigate new ways of producing food, manipulating plants and animals in the first experiments in farming.

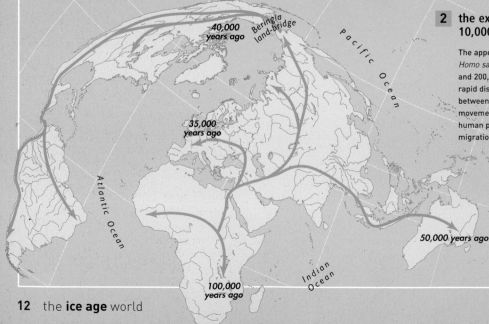

2 **the expansion of modern humans from 10,000 years ago**

The appearance of anatomically modern humans – *Homo sapiens sapiens* – in Africa between 150,000 and 200,000 years ago was followed by the relatively rapid dispersal of these new populations. However, between 100,000 and 50,000 years ago, population movements stopped. About 50,000 years ago, modern human populations began to grow again and migrations to many new areas of the world took place.

1 The height of the last Ice Age was reached about 20,000 years ago. Huge areas of the northern hemisphere were covered by ice sheets and much of the tropics had been turned into savannah. At the same time, with sea levels so much lower than today, land masses were much larger, creating sub-continents such as Sunda in south-east Asia. Humans were able to cross land bridges to areas such as Australia and the Americas.

Kanto Plain

Sokchang-Ni

Beringia land-bridge

Zhoukoudian Upper Cave

S I B E R I A

Salawusu   Tongliang

Malta   Buret

Arctic Ocean

Shestakovo   Shlenka

A S I A

Anyi

SUNDA

Sokchang-Ni   Kanto Plain

Pacific Ocean

Laharia-Dih

SUNDA

SAHUL

90°

Pushkari   Kostienki   Amvrosievka

INDIA

Nawamoyn

Krakow Spadzista

Puritjarra

E U R O P E

AUSTRALIA

WEST ASIA

Lake Mungo   Murray

Grotta dei Fanciulli

Koonalda

Lascaux   Kastritsa

Wadi Al-Hammeh

Kutikina

Altamíra   Paglicci   Kebara Cave

Wadi Jilat

Cueva Morin

Parpalló   Tamar Hat   Haua Fteah

Indian Ocean

Taforalt   Wadi Kubbaniya

Nile

60°

Sahara

Omo

A F R I C A

Ishango   Nasera

Depression Cave   Sehonghong

Klasies River Mouth
Boomplaas
Nelson Bay Cave

80°

150°

120°

1   the ice age world

maximum extent of ice caps	grassland scrub
mammoth steppe	temperate desert
savannah	loess
tropical deserts	ancient coastline
tropical forest refuges	modern coastline
forest steppe	■ cave art site
	■ other sites

from **hunting** to **farming**

Somewhere around 8000 BC human communities began to select, breed, domesticate and cultivate various species of plant and animal. This was the beginning of agriculture and is sometimes called the Neolithic or agricultural revolution. In fact, it was a slow and partial process which occurred at different times and speeds in different parts of the world and was never complete, if only because climatic and soil variations precluded agriculture in many areas. The arid zones were the home of mobile pastoralists who domesticated sheep and horses and colonized the grazing grounds of the steppes, while the densely afforested areas, in northern Europe and elsewhere, were inhabited, as earlier, by hunters. The result, following the spread of agriculture, was a differentiated world economy, with well-defined zones, cereal and root-crop cultivation being characteristic of the temperate and tropical regions respectively.

The transformation from a hunter and fisher to an agriculturist, and from a migratory to a sedentary life, was a decisive event in world history. The increase in food resources which followed made possible a spectacular growth of human population calculated to have multiplied 16 times between 8000 and 4000 BC. It also required co-operative effort, particularly after the introduction of irrigation c. 5000 BC, leading to the establishment of settled, organized societies, at first villages, then towns and cities. Urban civilization dates from c. 3500 BC, but already before 6000 BC there were 'proto-cities' covering extensive sites at Jericho in the Jordan valley and Çatal Hüyük in Anatolia. Here also there is evidence of long-distance trade.

There is no doubt that agriculture developed independently in different parts of the world, presumably in response to similar stimuli, but the beginnings of cereal cultivation are clearly associated with the Near East. Here, on the remote mountain uplands, were found the wild

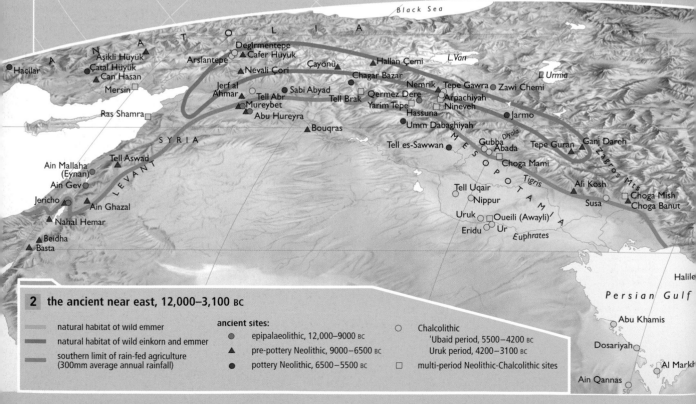

2 the ancient near east, 12,000–3,100 BC

	natural habitat of wild emmer
	natural habitat of wild einkorn and emmer
	southern limit of rain-fed agriculture (300mm average annual rainfall)

ancient sites:
- ● epipalaeolithic, 12,000–9000 BC
- ▲ pre-pottery Neolithic, 9000–6500 BC
- ● pottery Neolithic, 6500–5500 BC

- ○ Chalcolithic
  'Ubaid period, 5500–4200 BC
  Uruk period, 4200–3100 BC
- □ multi-period Neolithic-Chalcolithic sites

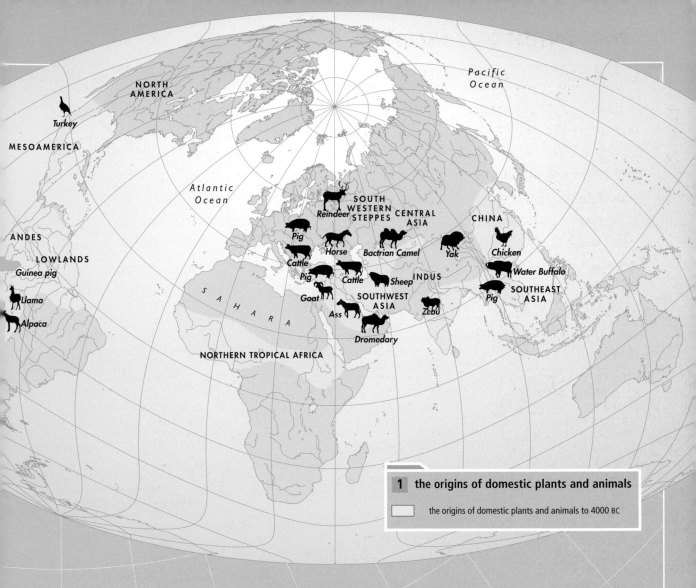

NORTH
AMERICA

Turkey

MESOAMERICA

ANDES

LOWLANDS

Guinea pig

Llama

Alpaca

*Atlantic
Ocean*

*Pacific
Ocean*

SOUTH
WESTERN
STEPPES

CENTRAL
ASIA

CHINA

Reindeer

Pig

Horse

Bactrian Camel

Yak

Chicken

Cattle

Pig

Cattle

Sheep

INDUS

Water Buffalo

SOUTHEAST
ASIA

Goat

SOUTHWEST
ASIA

Pig

S A H A R A

Ass

Zebu

Dromedary

NORTHERN TROPICAL AFRICA

1 the origins of domestic plants and animals

the origins of domestic plants and animals to 4000 BC

1 Most crops and animals were domesticated in a few 'core' areas (map above). The earliest and most important centres of domestication were southwest Asia, China and southeast Asia, tropical Africa north of the equatorial rainforest, Mesoamerica and northern South America.

2 The earliest known settlements are found within the Fertile Crescent, the broad arc running along the foot of the Taurus and Zagros mountains and on the nearby plains. Unlike the more southern lowland steppe, these areas have rainfall in excess of 300 mm a year. It was here that agriculture first developed, based on the wild ancestors of wheat (emmer and einkorn), barley, sheep, goats, cattle and pigs. The map (left) shows the primary distribution of the wild wheats.

ancestors of wheat and barley, and the villages where they were first cultivated (*c.* 8000 BC) grew up on the edge of this zone, within the critical rainfall limit of 300 mm (12 in) a year. Only with the introduction of irrigation was it possible to extend cultivation into the adjacent dry plains. This occurred during the fifth and fourth millennia BC. At about the same time, the ox-drawn plough began to be adopted throughout much of Eurasia, enlisting animal traction to increase the efficiency of farming. In much of the world, however, hoe agriculture persisted and human muscle power remained the basis of farming until relatively recent times.

Many other parts of the globe contributed their quota at different times to the supply of domesticated plants and animals. Their diffusion from their original habitat not only supplemented native food resources, but also affected human diet. Rice, which originated in South-East Asia and southern China, passed into the Near East and Mediterranean Europe, where it became a staple foodstuff. The yam and banana, later to be major African food crops, were introduced from Asia during the first millennium BC.

As farming spread, hunting and gathering was increasingly relegated to the more marginal world environments where agriculture was unable to secure a foothold. The gradual decline of hunters and gatherers can be traced across the centuries, until in recent times their sole surviving representatives have been found only in hot deserts such as the Kalahari and Australia, in the dense rainforests of the Amazon basin, central Africa and South-East Asia, and in the frozen wastes of the Arctic.

early **cultures** of **asia**

From an origin in Africa, *Homo erectus* or its close relatives had spread widely through Asia by the Middle Pleistocene period (400–200,000 years ago). It is not possible to establish the precise history of this colonization process, but it is reasonable to assume that these hominids first reached India, where hand-axes, chopping tools and flakes of the early Stone Age are found not only in the foothills of the Punjab but as far east as southern Bihar and northern Orissa and as far south as Madras. It was not long before *Homo erectus* also became established in both East and South-East Asia, as shown by skeletal remains from Java and China. Here they remained until replaced some 60,000 years ago by our own fully modern species *Homo sapiens sapiens*.

Comparatively little is known of the development of human societies in this part of the world until the advent of agriculture. At about the same time as farming communities were getting under way in western Asia, the first experiments in agriculture were also being made in East and South Asia. In China, the most important centre of early farming was the Yellow River valley in the north, where crops of millet were raised on the well-drained loess terraces of the river valleys from around 6000 BC. A little later, rice cultivation spread northwards from its original heartland in South-East Asia, giving a second productive staple crop. The early villages grew and prospered, and new technologies made their appearance: jade-carving, silk-weaving and very high quality pottery production using the fast wheel.

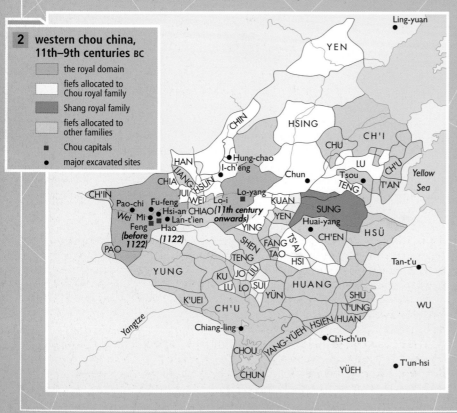

2 western chou china, 11th–9th centuries BC

- the royal domain
- fiefs allocated to Chou royal family
- Shang royal family
- fiefs allocated to other families
- ■ Chou capitals
- ● major excavated sites

1 The civilization of the Indus valley (map right) was centralized to a large degree. The major cities acted as centres of storage and distribution for the agricultural produce of the surrounding areas, mainly wheat and barley, but also rice. The annual flooding of the river produced fertile silts on which crops could be grown with little need for irrigation works.

2 The early Chou dominions comprised a large number of domains. Some remained under court control, others were granted as fiefs to supporters and servants of the Chou in a sort of feudal tenure. Much of the area shown on the map was still occupied by peoples of different ethnic origins who were gradually assimilated by the Chou and their vassals.

1 the indus civilizations of harappa

○ pre-Harappan settlements
● principal sites of Harappan civilization

Swastu

Mundigak

Zhob

Periano Ghundai

Jhelum

Chenab

Ravi *Sutlej*

Beas

Rupar
(Kojla Nihang Khan)

Kili Ghul Mohammad
Damb-Sadaat
Quetta
Rana Ghundai

PUNJAB

Harappa

Chak Purbane Syal

Togau
Dabarkot

Indus

Sandhanawala
Kalibangan

Alamgirpur

Siah Damb

Anjira
Judeirjo-Daro

11 sites in Bahawalpur State

Ganges

BALUCHISTAN

Nal
Kot Diji
Rohri

Mehi
Kotasur

Nokjo Shahdinzai
Mohenjo-Daro
Diji-li-Takri

Nundara
Nindowari
Lohumjo-Daro

RAJASTHAN

Shahi Tump
Pandi Wahi
Lohri

Kulli
Ali Murad
Ghazi Shah

Thar (Indian) Desert

Sutkagen-Dor
Mitha Deheno
Damb Buthi

Gorandi
Chanhu-Daro

Sotka-Koh
Dhal
Amri

Karchat
Shahjo-Kotiro

Bala-Kot
Kotrash
Othmanto Buthi

Allahdino
S I N D

Tharro

Desalpur

Dholavira

Arabian Sea

Halar

Amara
Rangpur
Lothal

Rojadi

Mehgam

Kinnarkheda
Telod

Narmada

Somnath
Bhagatrav

Tapti

In about 1800 BC the thriving villages and small towns which had developed in northern China gave rise to the first Chinese civilization. Early dynasties soon gave way to the Shang, who ruled much of the North China plain and parts of the Yangtze valley from the 16th to the 11th century BC. Great cities developed, notably at Cheng-chou and An-yang, and rulers were given lavish burial in royal tombs.

The first civilization of South Asia developed in the valley of the Indus river. Again, this was founded on a secure agricultural base which had been developing since *c*.6000 BC or earlier. Large-scale settlement of the fertile river plain seems to have occurred in the 4th millennium BC, and soon afterwards the first cities appeared, notably those of Harappa and Mohenjo-daro. These were highly-developed cities covering nearly 1,295,000 sq. km, and surviving for over 1,000 years. A standardized system of weights and measures was devised, and trade with the Persian Gulf brought Indus products to the great cities of southern Mesopotamia. Influences from South Asia also reached South-East Asia, where the distinctive Dong Son drums were produced by communities of village farmers from 1500–500 BC.

The Indus cities were abandoned soon after 2000 BC, overtaken perhaps by environmental change or natural disaster, and it was over 1,000 years before cities reappeared in the sub-continent. The focus had by this time shifted to the Ganges, where the historic cities and states of northern India began to form in about 500 BC. By that time China too was divided between a number of major kingdoms, as the unified rule of the Shang and their successors the Chou broke down and fragmented. Yet, despite the divisions, the basic foundations of Chinese and Indian civilization had been laid.

Climatic change, between 5,000 and 6,000 years ago, profoundly influenced the early history of Africa and Australasia. North Africa developed in close association with western Asia, and by 3000 BC an advanced civilization was established in Egypt. But Africa south of the equator, almost certainly the original home of humans, was cut off from the mainstream for centuries by the desiccation of the Sahara. Similar changes occurred in Australia which had been populated during the late Pleistocene Ice Age via the land bridge from New Guinea. Here the rise of the sea level drowned large areas of coastal lowland and severed the land link with New Guinea. The Australasian continent developed thenceforth in geographical isolation. The colonization of the islands of Melanesia occurred considerably later, when settlers from New Guinea, associated with the distinctive Lapita pottery, reached Fiji (c. 1300 BC) and then made their way into Polynesia via Tonga and Samoa, reaching the Marquesas Islands c. AD 300. From here they spread north to Hawaii (c. AD 800) and south-west via the Cook Islands to New Zealand between 850 and 1100.

Geographical isolation was an important factor in shaping the cultures of southern Africa and of Oceania. In much of Australia the aborigines remained hunters and gatherers and there was no use of iron, but they were prolific in their decoration of rock shelters with deeply symbolic designs. Elsewhere in Oceania, notably in New Zealand, a mixed hunting-farming society developed and settlement spread inland. But populations remained small, about 300,000 in Australia and 100,000 in New Zealand when the Europeans arrived. The isolation of southern Africa was never so complete. In East Africa settlers spread down the Rift Valley from Ethiopia during the first millennium BC, and trans-Saharan trade increased in importance after the introduction of the camel from Asia c.100 BC. This facilitated the spread of iron tools and weapons, introduced in the north by Greeks and Carthaginians in the eighth and seventh centuries. Aided by the new iron technology, Bantu-speaking farmers and cattle-herdsmen began to colonize southern Africa in the early centuries AD. By the 13th century powerful Bantu chiefdoms had emerged, such as that centred on the Great Zimbabwe enclosure, cattle-raising communities already engaged in trade when the Portuguese arrived at the close of the 15th century.

1 Africa's early farming and metal-working practices (map far right) were extremely diverse, reflecting the continent's varied environments and the life-styles of its inhabitants.

2 Most of the main groups of islands of Melanesia and western Polynesia were first settled over the last two millennia by maritime colonists bearing Lapita style pottery (map right). Between AD 400 and 1,000, Polynesian settlers travelling with crops and livestock in small double canoes and outriggers reached virtually every island in the Polynesian triangle.

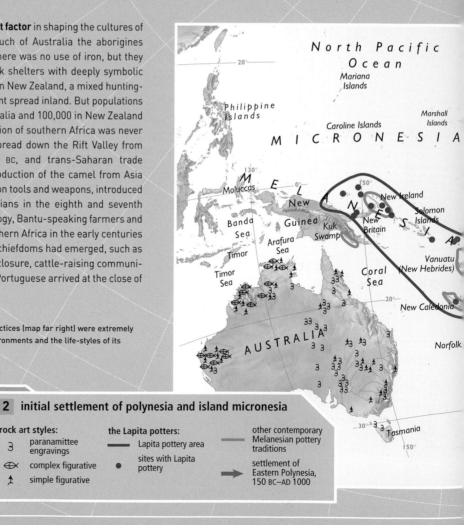

2 **initial settlement of polynesia and island micronesia**

rock art styles:

꒥ paranamittee engravings

⊕ complex figurative

⚔ simple figurative

the Lapita potters:

— Lapita pottery area

● sites with Lapita pottery

other contemporary Melanesian pottery traditions

➡ settlement of Eastern Polynesia, 150 BC–AD 1000

Mogador
Utica
Capeletti
Carthage
Atlas Mountains

Zemmour
S
Tichitt
iron
Adrar Tiouiyne
Meniet 6000-5000 BC
Uan Muhaggiag
Leptis (Homs)
Greek colonies from 700 BC Naucratis
Cyrene
Merimde 4200 BC
Saïs
Memphis
Fayum 4200 BC
EGYPT 4300 BC
Thebes

Adrar KINGDOM OF GHANA 1st millennium AD
iron
2000 BC
Immidir
Adrar Bous
Hoggar Massif
Tassili Massif
3000 BC
Arlit
Karkarchinkat
Air
Tibesti Massif
Jebel Uweinat
Ennedi
NUBIA
iron
Napata Nuri
KINGDOM OF MEROE 900 BC-AD 400
Napata Nuri
Meroe 500 BC
Adulis
Kadero
Shaheinab 400
Aksum
Jebel Moya 3200 BC
KINGDOM OF AKSUM AD 100-1000

Gao
Jenne-jeno proto-urban settlement by 1st century AD
Niger
Daima
Iron-working widespread north of equatorial forest by c. 500 BC
Sudanic Belt
Ethiopian Highlands

Ntereso 1400 BC
Kintampo
1500 BC
Taruga
Nok
500 BC
iron and cattle

Atwetwebooso
Ife
Igbo Ukwu shrines AD 800-900
Gulf of Guinea

possible spread of cultivation to lower Congo 1st millennium BC
Batalimo
Congo forests penetrated by pottery-using peoples late in 1st millennium BC
Funa River 270 BC
Congo
iron and cattle

Ileret
east African 'pastoral neolithic' sites
Urewe
Lake Victoria
Elmenteita
Manda & Shanga
Katuruka 5th century BC
Narosura
Crescent Is.
Kwale
Sandawe

late 1st millennium AD cemetery
Sanga
Kalambo
Lake Tanganyika
ports involved in overseas trade by AD 800
Kilwa

Lubusi
iron and cattle
Kamnama
iron and cattle
Lake Nyasa
Nkope
Salumano
Kapwirimbwe
AD 200
Zambezi
Kalundu
Ziwa
Gokomere
Great Zimbabwe
Mabveni
Malapati
AD 800

Namib Desert
Snake Rock
Falls Rock
Mirabib
Kalahari Desert
Broederstroom
AD 1100
Lydenburg
Silver Leaves
Phalaborwa
Blackburn
Madagascar
Austronesian settlement

Equus
Witkrans
Doornfontein
Blinkklipkop
Limerock
Dikbosch
domestic sheep herded by 1st century BC
Tortoise Cave
Eland's Bay
Diepkloof
Kasteelberg
Nelson Bay
Steenberg
Die Kelders
Hawston

ARABIA
Red Sea
Nile
KUSH

South Pacific Ocean inset:

Necker I.
Hawaiian Islands c. AD 400
Fanning Island
Line Islands
Marquesas Islands c. 150 BC

Tuvalu (Ellice Islands)
Tokelau Islands
Samoa
POLYNESIA
Fiji
Tonga
Tahiti
to Easter I. c. AD 400
Cook Islands
to Pitcairn I. c. AD 1000
Kermadec Is. c. AD 950
NEW ZEALAND
North Island
South Island
c. AD 750
South Pacific Ocean

1 africa: the stone age to the iron age

▲ fishing harpoon site

■ area of Saharan rock painting, c. 6000–1000 BC

▨ areas of rock painting in southern and eastern Africa

--- approximate extent of cattle herders, 6000–500 BC

● site of cattle domestication

▲ early agricultural site

▼ sites of southern African Stone Age herders

-- approximate extent of iron-using farmers, AD 200–1100

● important metal workers' sites

→ possible arrival of iron technology

Greek colonies

● Phoenician or Punic colonies

PART II | THE EARLIEST CIVILIZATIONS

peoples and cultures of the americas

America, like Australia (page 18), was colonized from Asia during the last Ice Age more than 10,000 years ago, and like Australia was later cut off from the Old World by the melting of the ice and the rise of the sea level which submerged the land bridge across the Bering Strait. Unlike the Australian aborigines, however, who never progressed beyond a Stone Age hunting and gathering culture, geographic isolation did not prevent the American Indians from developing independently a high level of civilization, based on agriculture (particularly the cultivation of maize), mining (particularly obsidian for tools and weapons), pottery manufacture and gold, silver and copper working. It was a civilization distinguished not only by magnificent art and remarkable mathematical and astronomical skills, but also by monumental building on a grand scale. In its prime, around AD 600, the city of Teotihuacán in the basin of Mexico covered 20 sq. km (8 sq. miles) and had a population of 125,000.

The first civilizations arose in the climatically favourable regions of Mesoamerica and the central Andes, where maize farming, permitting a rapid increase in population, became widespread from c.1500 BC. Between 800 and 500 BC the Olmecs on the Gulf of Mexico, the Zapotecs at Monte Albán and the inhabitants of Chavin in Peru had developed complex societies with populations numbering tens of thousands, possibly a professional priesthood, and several social ranks, including crafts-men and traders. Mesoamerica and the central Andes remained the main centres of civilization, but the diffusion of agriculture and growing commercial exchanges soon affected other regions. In North America the introduction of maize, beans and squashes from Mexico initiated a period of rapid development between 300 BC and AD 550. Its centre was the Hopewell territory in Illinois and Ohio, but trading contacts (mainly for precious metals) extended its influence as far as Florida and the Rockies. In South America a number of separate centres, each with its own distinctive artistic style, developed in the Andes, and were fused after AD 600 into the empires of Tiahuanaco and Huari. But this precarious unity broke down after AD 800 and it was not until the 15th century under the Incas that Peru was once again united.

In Mesoamerica, the early Olmec and Zapotec civilizations were complemented by new influences, including the Maya in Yucatán from the fourth century BC, then the Toltecs in the ninth century and finally the Aztecs in the 13th century. The classic period of Maya civilization falls between AD 300 and AD 900; but influences radiating from Teotihuacán were strong, and Maya civilization, like all the other civilizations of the classical period, was essentially a variant of a common Mesoamerican culture pattern. Internecine warfare appears to have weakened these civilizations and left them prey to invaders or local instability. Teotihuacán was destroyed c.750. Monte Albán was abandoned during the tenth century, and classic Maya civilization collapsed between AD 800 and 900.

For all their brilliant architectural and artistic achievements, the civilizations of Mesoamerica and the Andes account for only a small area of the Americas taken as a whole. Climatic variation alone dictated disparate ways of life. Particularly in the far north and far south, where conditions were too harsh for farming, the small nomadic populations depended on hunting and fishing. Climate was also a determining factor for the desert gatherers in the interior. The continent the Europeans encountered when they arrived in the 16th century was at widely different levels of development; but even the simpler societies had adapted themselves to the environment and its requirements.

2 By AD 250, Mesoamerica was dominated by Teotihuacán, the Maya and the Zapotecs . Three centuries later, new civilizations – the Totonacs, the Mixtecs and others – were emerging. From about AD 1000 another cycle began: the age of the Toltecs.

2 **the classic period in mesoamerica, AD 300–800**

- Teotihuacán civilisation
- classic Gulf coast civilisation
- Zapotec civilisation
- Maya civilisation
- ▲ city or ceremonial centre, AD 250–850

Pavón ▲

HUASTEC

Gu

pots and clay figures exported to west Mexico

obsidian mines of Pachuca

Teotihuacán ▲
VALLEY OF MEXICO
obsidian mines of Otumba ▲ Cacaxtla
Cholula ▲ *Maya-style murals resident Zapotecs occupy their own quarter of Teotihuacán*

OLM

Maya pott

Xochicalco ▲

Teotihuacán stone figurines and masks

Teotihuac

MIXTEC STATES

100°

Pacific Ocean

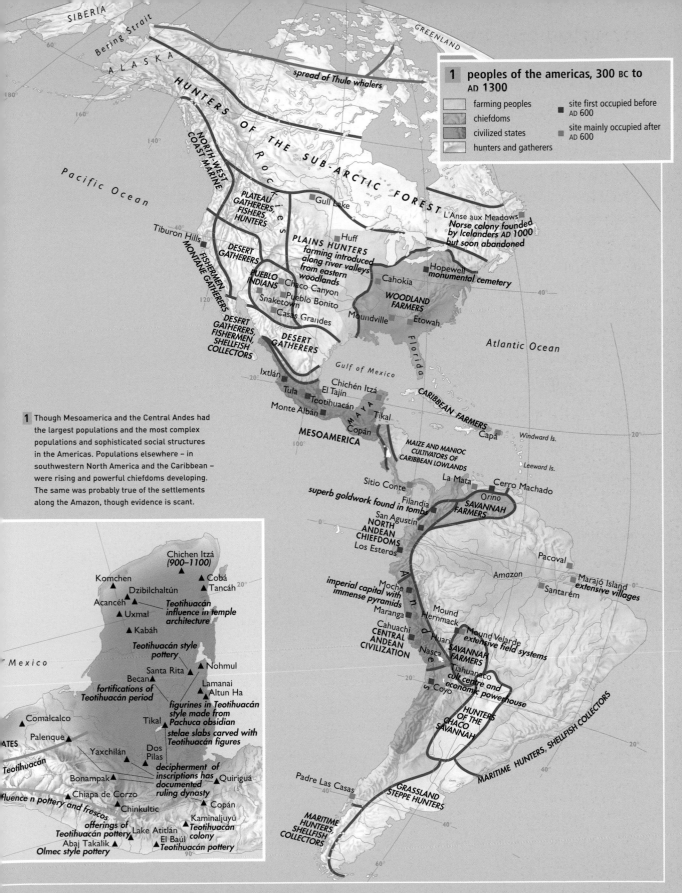

SIBERIA

Bering Strait

GREENLAND

ALASKA

spread of Thule whalers

HUNTERS OF THE SUB-ARCTIC FOREST

Pacific Ocean

NORTH-WEST COAST MARINE

PLATEAU GATHERERS, FISHERS, HUNTERS

Rockies

Gull Lake

L'Anse aux Meadows
Norse colony founded by Icelanders AD 1000 but soon abandoned

Tiburon Hills

FISHERMEN MONTANE GATHERERS

DESERT GATHERERS

Huff

PLAINS HUNTERS
farming introduced along river valleys from eastern woodlands

Hopewell monumental cemetery

PUEBLO INDIANS

Chaco Canyon
Pueblo Bonito

Cahokia

WOODLAND FARMERS

Snaketown
Casas Grandes

DESERT GATHERERS, FISHERMEN, SHELLFISH COLLECTORS

DESERT GATHERERS

Moundville

Etowah

Florida

Atlantic Ocean

Ixtlán

Gulf of Mexico

CARIBBEAN FARMERS

Tula
El Tajín

Chichén Itzá

Teotihuacán
Monte Albán

MAYA

Tikal

Copán

Capa

Windward Is.

MESOAMERICA

MAIZE AND MANIOC CULTIVATORS OF CARIBBEAN LOWLANDS

Leeward Is.

Sitio Conte

La Mata

Cerro Machado

superb goldwork found in tombs

Filandia

Orino

SAVANNAH FARMERS

San Agustín
NORTH ANDEAN CHIEFDOMS

Los Esteros

Pacoval

Amazon

Marajó Island
extensive villages

Santarém

Moche
imperial capital with immense pyramids

Maranga

Mound Hernmack

Cahuachi
CENTRAL ANDEAN CIVILIZATION

Huari

Mound Velarde
extensive field systems

Nasca

SAVANNAH FARMERS

Andes

Tiahuanaco
cult centre and economic powerhouse

Coyo

HUNTERS OF THE CHACO SAVANNAH

MARITIME HUNTERS, SHELLFISH COLLECTORS

Padre Las Casas

GRASSLAND STEPPE HUNTERS

MARITIME HUNTERS, SHELLFISH COLLECTORS

1 peoples of the americas, 300 BC to AD 1300

☐ farming peoples
▨ chiefdoms
▨ civilized states
☐ hunters and gatherers

■ site first occupied before AD 600
■ site mainly occupied after AD 600

1 Though Mesoamerica and the Central Andes had the largest populations and the most complex populations and sophisticated social structures in the Americas. Populations elsewhere – in southwestern North America and the Caribbean – were rising and powerful chiefdoms developing. The same was probably true of the settlements along the Amazon, though evidence is scant.

Chichen Itzá (900–1100)

Komchen

Cobá
Tancáh

Dzibilchaltún

Acanceh

Teotihuacán influence in temple architecture

Uxmal

Kabáh

Teotihuacán style pottery

Santa Rita

Nohmul

Becan

fortifications of Teotihuacán period

Lamanai
Altun Ha

figurines in Teotihuacán style made from Pachuca obsidian

Comalcalco

stelae slabs carved with Teotihuacán figures

Tikal

Palenque

Dos Pilas

Yaxchilán

decipherment of inscriptions has documented ruling dynasty

Bonampak

Quiriguá

Chiapa de Corzo

Copán

influence in pottery and frescos

Chinkultic

Kaminaljuyú
Teotihuacán colony

offerings of Teotihuacán pottery

Lake Atitlán
El Baúl
Teotihuacán pottery

Abaj Takalik

Olmec style pottery

Mexico

Teotihuacán

ATES

the **development** of **europe**

It was only after farming had been established in the Near East for several hundred years that it first spread westwards to Europe. The earliest European agriculturists settled in farming villages on the plains of Thessaly and Crete *c.* 6000 BC. The crops of wheat and barley which these communities grew were of Near Eastern type, and they relied heavily on the Near Eastern animal domesticates sheep and goat. As farming spread north and west into temperate Europe, however, major adjustments were necessary. New types of wheat and barley replaced those of Greece and the Near East, and cattle and pigs became the dominant species of livestock in forested parts of central, western and northern Europe in place of sheep and goat.

The new farming technology, including not only domesticated species of plants and animals but also pottery and polished stone tools, spread rapidly across Europe in the fifth and sixth millennia BC, reaching Britain and Denmark by 4000 BC.In the centuries of consolidation which followed, the early farmers of western and northern Europe built great burial mounds with megalithic chambers in which dozens if not hundreds of dead bodies were deposited. They also raised circles of standing stones.

By this time a new technology was spreading across Europe, supplementing the stone tools of the previous centuries: metallurgy. South-east Europe became an important centre of gold and copper-working as early as 4500 BC. By 2500 BC it had become common to alloy the copper with tin to produce bronze, an alloy of greater hardness, thus initiating the period known as the Bronze Age. The need to obtain access to the raw materials copper and tin led to the development of extensive trade networks along which other materials travelled, such as the Baltic amber which is found as far afield as Mycenae.

Around 1200 BC a more closely articulated political organization began to emerge, centred upon hillforts built to house and defend a warrior-aristocracy. The upper Rhine/upper Danube became an important core area where a distinctive Celtic culture emerged during the first millennium BC. Ironworking was introduced *c.* 1000–700 BC, which together with population growth fuelled a period of Celtic expansion in the La Tène period (from 480 BC). Contact with the Mediterranean world stimulated Celtic civilization, but it also prepared the way for Caesar's campaigns. Thus it was that by 50 BC most of the western Celtic world was under Roman control.

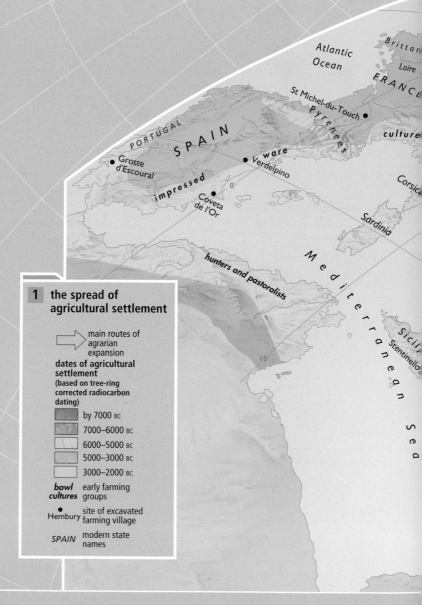

1 the spread of agricultural settlement

→ main routes of agrarian expansion

dates of agricultural settlement
(based on tree-ring corrected radiocarbon dating)

by 7000 BC
7000–6000 BC
6000–5000 BC
5000–3000 BC
3000–2000 BC

bowl cultures early farming groups

● Hembury site of excavated farming village

SPAIN modern state names

1 Early farmers spread from one side of Europe to the other by two main routes: the Vardar–Danube–Rhine corridor, and the Mediterranean littoral. The former was the more important. Nonetheless, for thousands of years the most 'developed' part of Europe was the southeast, which was the first to be settled.

70°

10°

North Sea

● Ballynagilly

IRELAND

cultures

BRITAIN

●embury

● Windmill Hill

S c a n d i n a v i a

h u n t e r s

bowl

● Cuiry-lès-Chaudardes

● Exloo

● Köln-Lindenthal

funnel

rim

60°

North European Plain

Rhine

Danubian linear incised

● Zwenkau

Elbe

pottery

cultures

Oder

Baltic Sea

20°

A   l   p   s

● Schussenried

pottery cultures

● Bylany

Vistula

● Arène-Candide

● Molino Casarotto

Apennine Mountains

● Ripabianca

Dinaric Alps

● Hódmezővásárhely

Carpathian Mountains

● Samborzec

B a l k a n s

H U N G A R Y

Balkan painted

● Coppa Nevigata

and impressed

Pripet

● Starčevo

Pindus Mountains

ware cultures

Vardar

Balkan Mountains

Danube

Dniester

30°

50°

● Argissa

early

● Karanovo

hunters and pastoralists

painted

● Varna

Aegean

Anatolia

Sea

ware

cultures

● Hacılar

B l a c k   S e a

● Crete

20°

● Knossos

40   30

egypt and mesopotamia

The rise of the great riverine civilizations in the fertile valleys of the Nile in Egypt, the Euphrates and Tigris in Mesopotamia, and the Indus valley in north-west India, was a decisive stage in the development of human society. Prosperous farming communities had grown up in the hill country around the foothills of the Fertile Crescent from 8000 BC, some of which, such as Jericho and Çatal Hüyük, were already small towns rather than mere villages. But the alluvial valleys of Egypt and Mesopotamia offered far greater potential, and it was here, around 3500 BC, that cities and city-states distinguished by size, planning, architecture and fortifications first appeared. It was here also that writing was first invented.

The early cities of Egypt and Mesopotamia were entirely dependent on the agricultural productivity of the alluvial plains. Water was the key to life in these semi-arid environments. In Egypt the annual flood of the Nile did most of the work, depositing rich alluvial silt to the farmlands of the valley and delta. In Mesopotamia, the rivers Tigris and Euphrates provided the water but to bring it to the fields an extensive network of irrigation canals was created.

Ancient tradition relates how King Menes of Upper (southern) Egypt conquered the delta kingdoms and founded a new capital at Memphis, which remained the administrative centre of Egypt for almost 2,000 years. Archaeological evidence, however, suggests Egypt emerged more gradually as a single state, possibly as a result of growing desertification and the consequent concentration of the population along the Nile valley, culminating in a single kingdom by around 3100 BC. During the Old Kingdom period (2685–2180 BC) Egyptian rulers built a series of massive pyramid-tombs along the desert edge opposite Memphis which emphasized their power and prestige and are among the greatest constructions of their age. Despite a period of setback in the political anarchy of the First Intermediate Period, the Egyptian state was sufficiently firmly established to recover and entered a second period of impressive cultural achievement under the able rulers of the Middle Kingdom (2040–1783 BC).

In Mesopotamia the basic political pattern until the second half of the 3rd millennium

1 mesopotamia in the later 3rd millennium BC

— Sumerian cultural area
— empire of Agade, c. 2296–2105 BC
— Ur III empire, 2047–1940 BC

principal traded commodities:

C	copper	▣	pearls
⁄	grain	T	tin
▭	lapis lazuli	▲	timber
◇	carnelian	⌂	ivory
⬗	obsidian	+	textiles

— main trade routes
— other trade routes

Map labels: Volga, Don, Caspian Sea, Caucasus Mountains, Black Sea, Malazgirt, Lake Van, Lake Urmia, Hattushash, ANATOLIA, Elazig, Ergani, Diyarbakir, Nusaybin, Rawandiz, Sulaymaniyah, Harhar, Ankara, Kayseri, Kanesh, Gürün, Malatya, Elbistan, Birecik, Chagar Bazar, Nineveh, Arbail, Arrapkha, Kermanshah, Gordium, Sariz, Carchemish, Harran, Ashur, MESOPOTAMIA, Eshnunna, Purushkhaddum, CILICIA, Tarsus, Aleppo, Euphrates, Mari, Tigris, Hit, Sippar, Der, Eskişehir, Afyon, Konya, Mersin, Alalakh, Ugarit, Ebla, SYRIA, Qatna, Palmyra, *ancient course of Euphrates*, Babylon, Agade, Inegöl, Karaman, Byblos, Damascus, Shuruppak, Uruk, Smyrna, Ephesus, Tyre, Hazor, Gaza, Mediterranean Sea, EGYPT, Kermanshah

BC remained one of city-states, with a shifting hegemony between them but no centralized control. The Sumerians who built these cities were also responsible for the invention of writing, at first pictographic but soon developing into the cuneiform script used on clay tablets and in inscriptions on stone. An important factor in Mesopotamian economic organization was the need to acquire scarce resources. Southern Mesopotamia lacked stone, metals and timber, which led the Sumerians to exploit the Zagros mountains and to develop trading relations with Iran and Asia Minor. Egypt was more self-sufficient, but here also the need for timber stimulated trade with Syria, and Syria served as a link between Egypt and Mesopotamia.

The first significant attempt at empire in Mesopotamia came when Sargon (2371–16 BC), of Akkadian immigrant descent, founded the city of Agade and made it his task to bring the old Sumerian city states under centralized control. From this base he and his successors, notably his grandson, Naram-Sin (2291–55 BC), undertook conquests from Elam in south-west Iran to Syria, including the city of Ebla, and possibly also into south-eastern Asia Minor. Motivated by trade, this expansion extended sea-links which reached as far east as the Indus valley.

Sargon's empire collapsed as a result of internal stresses and invasions from the central Zagros, and was followed by a revival of the Sumerian city-state system, in which Ur emerged as the dominant element. This was a highly bureaucratic empire, more stable than that of Agade; but it collapsed in turn (c.2000 BC) under the pressure of a new wave of Semitic invaders, the Amorites from the Syrian desert, who established control over the whole region from Syria to southern Mesopotamia, where they set up a number of small kingdoms, among which Assyria and Babylon eventually won pre-eminence. The former emerged under the Amorite Shamshi-Adad I (1813–1781 BC), who annexed the kingdom of Mari on the middle Euphrates and formed a powerful state extending from the Zagros mountains to the border of the Anatolian plateau. But the pre-eminence of Assyria was short-lived, and after Shamshi-Adad's death its place was taken by Babylon under Hammurabi (1792–50 BC). By the 17th century BC a new power centre was developing further north, in Anatolia, where the Hittites set up a kingdom with its capital at Hattushash. After 1650 BC they began to spread southwards and in 1595 they sacked Babylon. In the dislocation which ensued, the first Babylonian dynasty collapsed; but the ideal of a single south Mesopotamian kingdom with Babylon as its capital survived as Hammurabi's enduring legacy.

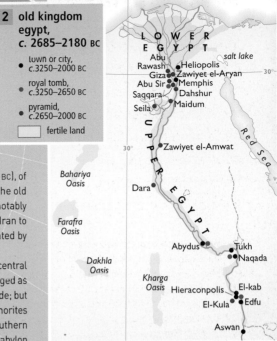

2 old kingdom egypt, c. 2685–2180 BC

● town or city, c.3250–2000 BC

royal tomb, c.3250–2650 BC

pyramid, c.2650–2000 BC

fertile land

1 The Greek historian Herodotus described Egypt as 'the gift of the river'. The kingdom of the pharaohs grew up at the fertile valley of the Nile below the first cataract at Elephantine. The kingdom was traditionally divided into 'two lands': Lower Egypt, the area of the Nile Delta, with its capital at Memphis; and Upper Egypt, with its capital at Thebes.

2 Mesopotamia in the later 3rd millennium. Mesopotamia occupies a key position on the lines of communication between central Asia and Europe and between the Persian Gulf and the Mediterranean. The need to ensure the supply of bronze and other goods, including timber, was an important stimulus to military campaigns and the growth of empires such as those of Agade and Ur.

the first **civilizations** of europe

The earliest civilizations in the western world arose in western Asia and the Nile valley in the fourth millennium BC, but within 2,000 years new civilizations, distinctively different in character, had appeared around the shores of the Aegean in Crete, Greece and western Asia Minor.

The first European civilization was that of Minoan Crete, based on elaborate palaces which were both the seats of rulers and the centres of a bureaucratic administration. The most famous of the Minoan palaces is that of Knossos in northern Crete, in later Greek legend the home of King Minos. Cretan civilization reached a level of considerable

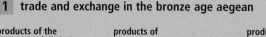

1 Bronze Age Greece and Crete were part of the wide eastern Mediterranean and Near East. The rulers of these developing civilizations needed raw materials such as copper and tin to make bronze, as well as luxury goods. In return, the Aegean supplied rare materials such as obsidian and fine works of craftsmanship. These goods often circulated as gifts or dowries rather than as items of trade.

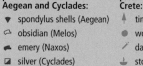

1 trade and exchange in the bronze age aegean

products of the Aegean and Cyclades:	products of Crete:	products of the Greek mainland:
▼ spondylus shells (Aegean)	▲ timber	▮ fine pottery (after 1600 BC)
⌒ obsidian (Melos)	● woven wool textiles	▼ metal vases (after 1600 BC)
⬬ emery (Naxos)	⚔ daggers (before 1600 BC)	
⬛ silver (Cyclades)	⬙ stone lamps and vases	⬜ Mycenaean world (1300 BC)
⚔ swords and daggers	⬙ fine pottery (before 1500 BC)	── trade routes
	▮ metal vases (before 1500 BC)	⟶ imports to the Aegean

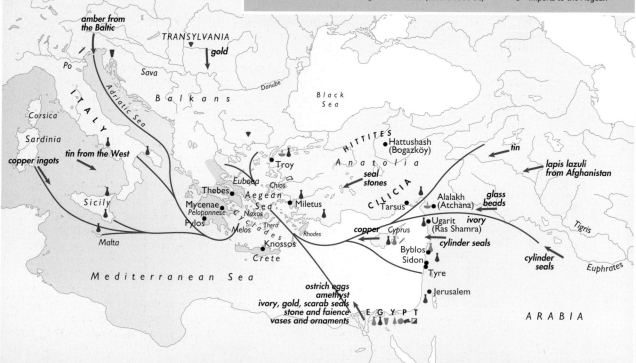

sophistication in the middle of the second millennium BC. The palaces were decorated with colourful frescos and equipped with elaborate sanitary and drainage systems. Cretan traders visited Egypt, and spread Minoan influence among the Aegean islands. Bureaucracy flourished with the adoption of writing in around 1600 BC, using the locally-invented Linear A script. With a powerful fleet giving security at sea, the development of Minoan civilization appears to have been interrupted only by the recurrent earthquakes of the region.

The development of civilization on the Greek mainland owed something to contact with Crete but was nonetheless a largely independent process. Soon after 1600 BC rich graves make their appearance at important centres such as Mycenae, with sumptuous offerings of gold

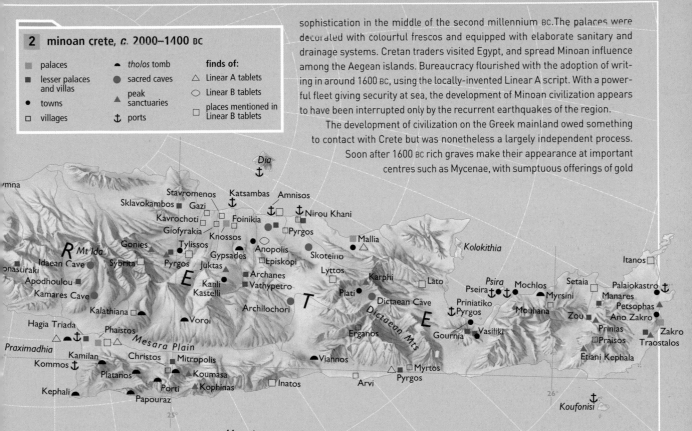

2 minoan crete, c. 2000–1400 BC

- ■ palaces
- ■ lesser palaces and villas
- ● towns
- □ villages
- ▲ tholos tomb
- ● sacred caves
- ▲ peak sanctuaries
- ⚓ ports

finds of:
- △ Linear A tablets
- ○ Linear B tablets
- □ places mentioned in Linear B tablets

2 Crete was urbanized at an early stage. Towns and villages clustered around regional centres usually called 'palaces', which had links in turn to smaller outlying 'villas'. Palaces usually contained religious shrines, and controlled other important religious sites in caves or on hill tops. After 1500 BC, Linear B tablets and tholos tombs are evidence of Mycenaean presence in Crete.

and jewellery, testifying to the rise of a wealthy and powerful aristocracy. These warlike rulers built themselves fortified palaces and drove to battle in horse-drawn chariots. The Mycenaeans were not only warriors, however, but also cultivated the arts and became successful traders whose products are found throughout the east and central Mediterranean.

In the 15th century BC the Mycenaeans conquered Minoan Crete and became the principal political and military power in the Aegean. They adapted the Minoan Linear A script and carried their modified version, Linear B, back to the mainland where it was used in the administration of their own kingdoms. Within 200 years their ambitions had stretched still further to the coast of Asia Minor. The legend of the Trojan war is generally thought to be a memory of a successful Mycenaean campaign of c.1250 BC against a rival power, the city of Troy, strategically situated at the mouth of the Dardenelles, controlling access to the Black Sea.

The Trojan war, if indeed it really happened, must have been the final fling of the Mycenaean warlords. By 1200 BC most of their palaces were in ruins, overthrown perhaps by civil strife, perhaps by piracy and a rebellious peasantry. With the demise of the Mycenaean kingdoms Greece entered a Dark Age which lasted some 400 years. It was only in the eighth century BC that trade and city life began to recover. The recovery was rapid, however, and two centuries later Greek colonies had been established all along the northern Mediterranean and Black Sea coasts. Writing was re-introduced, using an alphabetic script adapted from the Phoenician, and new styles of sculpture, architecture and vase-painting developed. Yet while sharing a common language and culture the Greek world of the eighth century BC was divided between hundreds of independent city-states and was to remain so throughout the Classical age of the fifth and fourth centuries BC until conquered and united by Philip of Macedon in 338 BC.

near eastern empires

Since the third millennium BC the rich lands of the Fertile Crescent had been subject to periodic invasion by warlike peoples from adjoining steppes and mountains, jealous of their civilization and greedy for their riches. Egypt alone was sheltered by the desert; but even Egypt fell prey about 1730 BC to an Asiatic people known as the Hyksos, who conquered the Delta and much of the Nile valley, and ruled there until 1567 BC. But the Hyksos occupation stimulated a great revival and, under the XVIIIth dynasty (1570–1320 BC), a policy of expansion was initiated. Egypt advanced through Palestine into Syria and created an empire which extended almost to the Euphrates for the next 400 years.

Egyptian control over Syria and Palestine may in part have been an attempt to shield the Nile valley from further invasions, but it in fact brought it directly into conflict with the Hittites of Asia Minor and the Mitannians of north-central Syria. In the 14th century BC the Hittites defeated Mitanni, which ceased to be a major actor in the struggle for the Levant. Egyptian power remained strong, however, and after the drawn battle of Kadesh in 1279 BC Hittites and Egyptians agreed to respect each other's sphere of influence. The Egyptian pharaohs channelled the profits of empire into vast building programmes, such as the massive rock-cut temple at Abu Simbel created by Ramesses II (1290–1224 BC). Memphis remained the administrative capital, but the power of Thebes as the religious centre of Egypt steadily grew.

The balance of power between Egyptians and Hittites in the Levant did not last long after Kadesh, since the Hittite empire collapsed around 1200 BC under internal pressure and attacks by their northern neighbours and by seaborne invaders – the so-called 'peoples of the sea'. Egypt successfully fought off similar attacks, but only with the loss of its Levantine possessions. Into the gap created by the decline of the Hittite and Egyptian empires new peoples entered; Phrygians in Asia Minor, Hebrews and Philistines in Palestine. The power vacuum enabled the Israelites under King David (c.1006–966 BC) to create a kingdom briefly controlling Palestine and Syria;

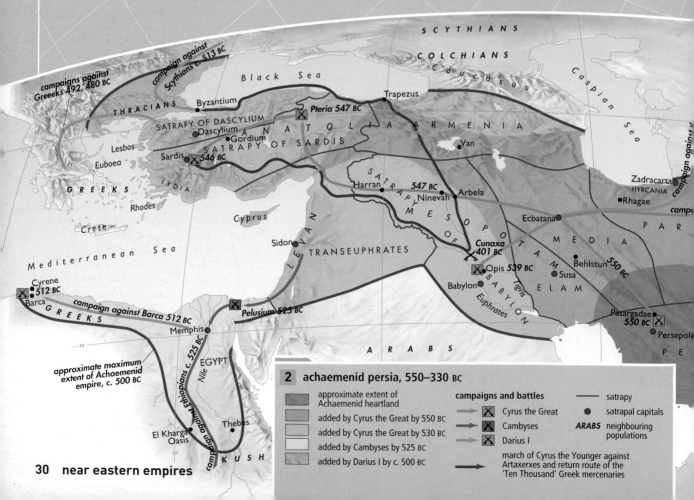

2 achaemenid persia, 550–330 BC

approximate extent of Achaemenid heartland	**campaigns and battles**	—— satrapy
added by Cyrus the Great by 550 BC	✕ Cyrus the Great	● satrapal capitals
added by Cyrus the Great by 530 BC	✕ Cambyses	*ARABS* neighbouring populations
added by Cambyses by 525 BC	✕ Darius I	
added by Darius I by c. 500 BC	march of Cyrus the Younger against Artaxerxes and return route of the 'Ten Thousand' Greek mercenaries	

approximate maximum extent of Achaemenid empire, c. 500 BC

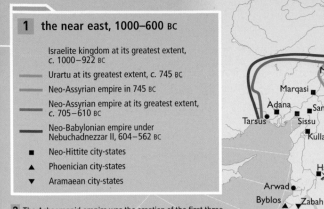

1 the near east, 1000–600 BC

- Israelite kingdom at its greatest extent, c. 1000–922 BC
- Urartu at its greatest extent, c. 745 BC
- Neo-Assyrian empire in 745 BC
- Neo-Assyrian empire at its greatest extent, c. 705–610 BC
- Neo-Babylonian empire under Nebuchadnezzar II, 604–562 BC
- ■ Neo-Hittite city-states
- ▲ Phoenician city-states
- ▼ Aramaean city-states

2 The Achaemenid empire was the creation of the first three Persian kings – Cyrus, Cambyses and Darius – who in less than 50 years united the very disparate inhabitants of the area from the Mediterranean to the Indus under a single administration (map below). According to the Greek historian Herodotus, there was a Persian saying that 'Cyrus was a father, Cambyses a tyrant and Darius a tradesman', and indeed it was under Darius that the empire was organized into satrapies, tribute-paying provinces usually ruled by Persian governors which nonetheless retained a variety of local forms of administration. The sheer size of the empire meant that its kings were sometimes slow to react to problems. The Greek mercenary and historian Xenophon described his involvement in an abortive attempt in 401 BC by the crown prince Cyrus to overthrow his brother Artaxerxes: Cyrus and his 'Ten Thousand' Greek mercenaries were able to march nearly half-way across the empire before they were stopped and Cyrus killed. Nonetheless, the empire remained a potent and united force until it was invaded by Alexander the Great in 334 BC.

1 The Near East that emerged from the upheavals of the late Bronze Age was characterized by new forms of political organization (map above). Along the Mediterranean coast city-states developed, sometimes united by powerful rulers into temporary kingdoms while to the north the new power of Urartu appeared. Meanwhile Assyria recovered to become the main power of the region, until its overthrow by the Babylonians and Medes.

671, 667 BC Assyrian campaigns against Egypt

605 BC (Carchemish)

605 BC (Hamath)

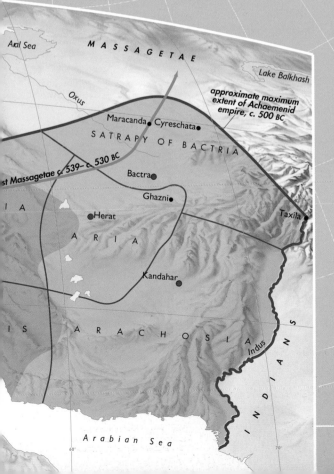

approximate maximum extent of Achaemenid empire, c. 500 BC

against Massagetae c. 539– c. 530 BC

but after Solomon (966–926 BC) the kingdom, inherently unstable because of its disparate tribal origins, quickly disintegrated. But change and fluidity had the effect of breaking down old geographical and cultural barriers and fusing the whole region into a single cosmopolitan society, over which, after 539 BC, Persia established hegemony.

The immediate beneficiary was Assyria. Already in the 13th century this city-state had joined the ranks of the great powers of the ancient Near East. Early in the ninth century, the Assyrian kings again began to flex their military muscle, embarking on a policy of conquest which soon brought them to the shores of the Mediterranean. The profits were ploughed back into the construction of the successive capitals of the Assyrian empire: Nimrud, Khorsabad and Nineveh. At its greatest extent, in the seventh century BC, the empire stretched from the Nile valley to the Persian Gulf and northwards into Armenia and eastern Turkey. But during the long reign of Ashurbanipal (668–627 BC) Assyria began to lose its military dominance and soon afterwards the assault of Medes and Scythians, combined with the secession of Babylonia, brought Assyrian power to ruin. The capital Nineveh was destroyed in 612 BC, and Assyria disappeared for ever in 605 BC. After an interlude in which Medes, Chaldeans and Egyptians divided the legacy, another conqueror, Cyrus the Persian, rebelled against the Median capital Ecbatana in 550 BC, and quickly overran most of the Middle East. When his son Cambyses (529–522 BC) conquered Egypt (525 BC), the Persian empire extended from the Nile to the Oxus. The ancient world was for the first time united under one administration. Persian attempts to extend their power to the west, however, met with resistance from the Greeks and defeat at Marathon (490 BC), Salamis (480 BC) and Plataea (479 BC), and the Persian empire entered a period of slow decline. The way was opened for the ultimate triumph of Hellenism and the conquest of Persia by Alexander the Great a century and a half later.

PART III THE CLASSICAL WORLD

497 to 185 BC

The fifth century BC was the great age of Greece – the age of Pericles and Socrates, of Sophocles and Euripides, of the Parthenon and the sculptures of Phidias. It was also the century when internal strains (the growing conflict between oligarchy and democracy) and internecine war undermined the stability of the Greek city states and their ability to withstand external pressures.

Colonization had already carried Greek civilization and Greek city life to Asia Minor. But here it came up against the Persian empire under Darius and Xerxes. Persian attempts to subdue Athens, which had been supporting the rebellious Ionians, were almost miraculously defeated at Marathon (490) and Salamis (480). But thereafter the alliance of cities which had united against Persia fell apart, and the Peloponnesian war between Athens and Sparta and their allies permanently weakened Greek resistance, and ensured the victory of Philip of Macedon (338). Under Philip's son, Alexander the Great, Macedonia became a world power, its dominion stretching from the Adriatic to India. Alexander's death in 323 BC at the age of 32 prevented the consolidation of his empire. In the succeeding struggles between his generals three major powers arose: Macedonia, shorn of its Asiatic conquests but still dominant in northern Greece; Egypt under the Ptolemies, with its capital at Alexander's newly founded city of Alexandria; and the Seleucid kingdom comprising the bulk of the Persian empire. To these were added in the east the Bactrian kingdom, extending over Afghanistan into northern India, and the Parthian empire, founded in 247 BC when a dissident provincial governor broke away from the Bactrian Greeks. This Parthian state eventually stretched from the Euphrates to the Indus and successfully withstood Roman expansion until it was displaced in AD 224 by a resurgent Persia under the Sasanian dynasty.

Although, politically, the empire of Alexander the Great proved ephemeral, in other respects its consequences were epoch-making. Alexander himself founded some 70 cities, not merely as military strongholds but as cultural centres – a policy continued by his Seleucid successors – and thus carried Greek civilization far to the east. Greek culture was now no longer the preserve of separate city-states but infused and Hellenized the whole civilized world (*oikoumene*) as far as India and China. Greek itself became the *lingua franca* of the whole region, though more subtly the Greek world itself was permeated by oriental influences as its contacts with the ancient civilizations of the Near East intensified. When Rome asserted control over the Hellenistic world after its defeat of Macedon at Cynoscephalae in 197 BC and of the Seleucids at Magnesia in 190 BC, this was its inheritance; and the longer the Roman empire existed, the greater was the part played by the Hellenic and oriental elements in its civilization.

1 The earliest Greek settlements overseas (map right) were from Chalcis and Eretria in Euboea, while Corinth was the first and most important Peloponnesian mother-city; in contrast Sparta and Athens had little involvement. It became usual to consult an oracle, especially at Delphi, before launching an expedition. Miletus, with its own oracle at Didyma, sent out many colonies to the Black Sea.

2 the peloponnesian war, 431–404 BC

- Athens and members of the Delian League
- ally of Athens
- Sparta and allies
- neutral states
- allies of Athens in Magna Graecia
- allies of Sparta in Magna Graecia
- → Athenian campaigns
- → Spartan campaigns
- ✕ Athenian victory
- ✕ Spartan victory

2 The whole Greek world became involved in the prolonged war between Athens and Sparta (map above). Sparta was stronger on land, but Athens kept firm control of the sea. After ten years an uneasy peace was made (421 BC), but when Athens lost almost its entire fleet in Sicily, the Spartans pressed home their advantage. Even so, it was only with considerable naval and financial support from the Persians that they were able to overcome the Athenian navy.

1 greek colonization in the mediterranean world, 750–550 BC

- Greek heartland in 750 BC
- ■ Greek parent community
- □ Greek oracular shrine
- Phoenician or Punic settlement
- Etruscan city
- ● 8th-century Greek colony
- ● 7th-century Greek colony
- ● 6th-century Greek colony
- Philistine city

3000 BC to AD 500

Trade is as old as the beginning of settled urban life. Though ordinary needs were met by local agriculture and local manufacture, even the earliest cities had requirements that could not be satisfied locally. Jericho imported stone for tools from Anatolia; the Sumerians, who lacked timber, stone and minerals, developed trading links with Asia Minor and with Dilmun on the Persian Gulf. But the formation of an intensive trading network throughout the Eurasian world only became possible after the rise of empires which provided peace and security and maintained roads and harbours.

The Achaemenids made a beginning in sixth-century Persia, where Darius's Royal Road ran 1,420 well-garrisoned miles (2,300 km) from Sardis to Susa. But the decisive step forward was the rise, after 202 BC, of the Roman empire in the west and the Han empire in China. By the close of the first century BC Rome's conquests from the Atlantic to Syria formed a single vast trading area, gathered round a Mediterranean axis, and the expansion of Han China under Wu-ti (140–87 BC) created an economic bloc of similar dimensions in the east. Both possessed an elaborate network of roads and a highly organized system of transport and marketing, which encouraged regional specialization and an unprecedented interchange of goods and manufactures. Nor did trade halt at the frontier. From around 600 BC the famous Silk Route came into operation. It started at Tun-huang on China's far western boundary, and skirted north or south of the Takla Makan Desert to Kashgar, before crossing the Pamirs and entering Bactria, Persia and the Mediterranean coastal belt. But the Silk Route, spectacular though it was, was less important in economic terms than the sea route to India and the Far East, traffic along which increased greatly after the discovery of the monsoon around 100 BC. Up to 120 Greek vessels a year plied direct to the Indian ports of Barbaricum, Barygaza and Muziris, where they picked up eastern cargoes from Go Oc Eo in southern Cambodia, and carried them to Berenice and other Red Sea ports for transport on to Alexandria and to all parts of the Roman empire.

Both the Roman and the Han empires were, however, self-sufficient in all essential commodities, and foreign trade was essentially a luxury trade, marginal to everyday needs. On the other hand, there is no doubt that foreign trade contributed directly to cultural interchange and to the spread of the great world religions. However, it also contributed to the spread of disease and pestilence. Earlier epidemics, like that which hit Athens in 430–29 BC may have been transmitted by armies; but their incidence after about 100 BC leaves little doubt that, both in east and west, they were carried by caravans or merchant shipping from India or tropical Africa. They seem to fall into two main groups, smallpox or measles, and bubonic plague. Their effects on vulnerable populations were devastating. 'One or two out of a hundred survived,' wrote the Chinese historian Ssu-ma Kuang of the epidemic of AD 317, and some later historians have attributed the failure both of China and of Rome to withstand the barbarian onslaughts of the fourth and fifth centuries to the sharp fall in manpower caused by imported pestilences.

1 The carrying of goods along the Silk Road to the Mediterranean began in the 6th century BC, and trade along this route flourished between c. 200 BC and AD 200 when stable empires controlled the territories through which the traders passed. The usual starting point was Tun-huang, from which the route continued west over the Pamirs, to Samarkand and Merv. At the same time traders began to take advantage of the monsoons for sea-borne trade with India and beyond.

2 Two factors made possible the spread of epidemic diseases: increased urban populations and long-distance trade. The earliest detailed account of a plague attack, in Athens in 429 BC, was written by the historian Thucydides. The population had been forced into unsanitary conditions within the city walls.

1 the commercial and cultural bonds of eurasia

- ● trading centre
- ——— trade route
- ═══ Silk Road

distribution of:

- ✎ Han mirrors
- ◠ Chinese silks
- ◆ treasures of the Shoso-in
- ▲ Graeco-Roman objects found in southeast Asia AD 1–300
- ■ sites known to the author of *A Voyage around the Red Sea*

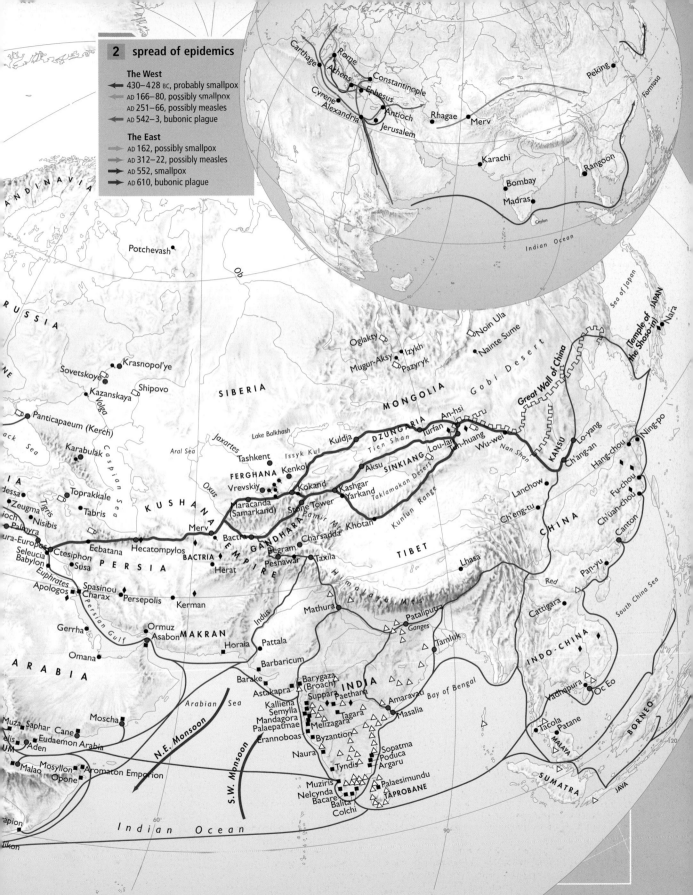

Carthage   Rome   Peking
Athens   Constantinople   Formosa
Cyrene   Ephesus
Alexandria   Antioch   Rhagae   Merv
Jerusalem
Karachi
Bombay   Rangoon
Madras
Ceylon
Indian Ocean

SCANDINAVIA
Potchevash
RUSSIA
Ob
Sovetskoye   Krasnopol'ye
Kazanskaya   Shipovo   SIBERIA   MONGOLIA   Gobi Desert   Great Wall of China   (Temple of JAPAN the Shoso-in)   Nara
Volga
Panticapaeum (Kerch)   Lake Balkhash   Oglakty   Noin Ula   An-hsi
Karabulak   Aral Sea   Mugur-Aksy   Izykh   Nainte Sume   DZUNGARIA   Turfan   KANSU   Lo-yang   Ning-po
Caspian Sea   Jaxartes   Pazyryk   Kuldja   Tien Shan   Lou-lan   Tun-huang   Ch'ang-an   Hang-chou
Black Sea   Tashkent   Issyk Kul   Aksu   SINKIANG   Wu-wei   Nan Shan   Fu-chou
Toprakkale   FERGHANA   Kenkol   Taklamakan Desert   Lanchow   CHINA   Ch'üan-chou
Odessa   Zeugma   Tigris   Tabris   KUSHANA   Vrevskiy   Kokand   Kashgar   Canton
Antioch   Palmyra   Oxus   Maracanda   Yarkand   Kunlun Range   Ch'eng-tu   Pan-yu
Dura-Europos   (Samarkand)   Stone Tower   Khotan   Cattigara
Seleucia   Ecbatana   Merv   Bactra   Pamir Mts   Charsadda   TIBET   Red   South China Sea
Babylon   Ctesiphon   Hecatompylos   EMPIRE   GANDHARA   Begram   Lhasa   INDO-CHINA
Euphrates   Susa   BACTRIA   Peshawar   Taxila
Spasinou   PERSIA   Herat   Himalaya Mts
Apologos   Charax   Persepolis   Kerman   Indus   Mathura   Pataliputra   Tamluk
Gerrha   Ormuz   MAKRAN   Ganges   Vadhapura   Oc Eo
Omana   Asabon   Horaia   Pattala   INDIA   Amaravati   Bay of Bengal
ARABIA   Barbaricum   Barygaza   BORNEO
Barake   (Broach)   Tacola
Muza   Saphar   Cane   Astakapra   Suppara   Paethana   Masalia   Patane   MALAYA
Moscha   Arabian Sea   Kalliena   Semylla   Tagara   SUMATRA
Eudaemon Arabia   Mandagora   Palaepatmae   Melizagara   Sopatma
Aden   N.E. Monsoon   Erannoboas   Byzantion   Poduca   JAVA
Malao   Mosyllon   Naura   Argaru
Opone   Aromaton Emporion   S.W. Monsoon   Tyndis   Palaesimundu
Muziris   TAPROBANE
Nelcynda   Bacare
Colchi   Balita
Indian Ocean

37

the **spread** of **world religions**

The period 550–500 BC saw the birth of great world religions in all the main centres of civilization. Their appearance perhaps reflected a need in the rising empires of the old world for more universal creeds than the local tribal deities could provide, and their diffusion – particularly the spread of the great missionary religions, Buddhism and Christianity – was an important factor in linking together the different areas of civilization. Their other major contribution – seen, for example, in the work of Anglo-Saxon missionaries in Germany or of Russian missionaries among the heathen tribes of the Urals – was to carry civilization to peoples outside the frontiers of the civilized world.

All the great religions shared, to one degree or another, a belief in a single spiritual reality. Not all were inspired by a missionary spirit. Hinduism, the oldest, was essentially the religion of the people of India, and Judaism, the religion of 'the chosen people of the Lord', was also exclusive. But Buddhism, originally a reformist movement within Hinduism, became perhaps the greatest of all missionary religions when it assumed its universalist, or Mahayana, form some 500 years after the death of its founder, Gautama (c. 563–483 BC). Judaism also spread as a result of the persecution of the Jews by more formidable neighbours, beginning with the Babylonian exile (586 BC). After the Roman destruction of the temple in Jerusalem in AD 70, the Jewish diaspora carried Judaism far and wide from its home in Palestine, until in time it became a worldwide religion. It also gave birth, directly or indirectly, to two of the world's great missionary religions, Christianity and Islam.

In the Far East the same period saw the rise of the ethical system of Kung Fu-tzu or Confucius (551–479 BC) and the mystical religion of the Tao, or 'the Way', associated with the shadowy figure of Lao-tzu. Later Buddhism spread eastward along the Silk Route through central Asia and with Taoism and Confucianism became one of the 'three religions' of traditional China. Buddhism also reached Japan in the sixth century AD, where it effectively displaced spirit-worship and traditional Shinto until the revival of the latter in the 19th century.

The other great religion of the period was Zoroastrianism, which originated in Persia and is associated with another shadowy figure, Zarathustra. Zoroastrianism, which sees life as a battle-ground between the forces of good and the forces of evil, spread rapidly through the Roman world in the form of Mithraism, with shrines as far afield as northern Britain. It was one of the many oriental cults that permeated the Roman empire when, after the beginning of the Christian era, belief in the Green pantheon and the household deities broke down. Until the end of the third century AD it was undecided which of the oriental mystery cults would prevail; but with the conversion of the emperor Constantine to Christianity and its recognition by the Edict of Milan (AD 313), still more after it became the official religion of the Roman empire under Theodosius (374–95), the die was cast. Pagan temples were uprooted; rival cults were condemned.

Christianity had begun as a Jewish splinter-movement; its founder, Jesus of Nazareth, was seen as the Messiah, or Saviour, sent to liberate the Jews from the Roman yoke. But when, after Jesus's condemnation and crucifixion (AD 29), Jewish orthodoxy rejected his message, his disciples, notably Paul of Tarsus, turned instead to the conversion of the 'gentiles', or people outside the law. Paul's journeys were a turning point. Thereafter Christianity spread rapidly, both in the Roman empire and also further east. Here the great Christian centres were Antioch and Edessa, the home of the Nestorian church which carried Christ's teaching to Persia and from there to China and India (page 40). This was the situation until the rise of Islam changed the scene.

1 Geography had a profound effect on the development of empires, (map right) and in turn the growth of empires had an effect on the development of religions. In general, in times of prosperity, imperial administrations tolerated and even encouraged local cult activity; the peace associated with successful imperial rule, and the communications and trade routes that allowed empires to function, encouraged the flow of religious ideas. When central control was threatened, greater emphasis was placed on religious orthodoxy, and persecution was more common. At the same time instability might itself have been a cause of religious change, with the enforced scattering of peoples, and the visible weakening of existing religious institutions making new cults and teachings more attractive.

india and china: the first empires

The fifth and sixth centuries BC were a period of consolidation in India and China. In India by the end of the fifth century the 16 political units in existence in 600 BC had been reduced to four. In China, by 400 BC, instead of the multiple feudal principalities of the Chou period, seven major states were contending for supremacy. In both countries iron tools increased both agricultural productivity and the resources of the rising states. In China the area of civilization had expanded from the Yellow River to the Yangtze valley and beyond. In India the deforestation of the north shifted the centre of power from the Indus, the seat of the earliest civilizations, to the fertile plain of the Ganges. Here the kingdom of Magadha emerged as the nucleus of the first Indian empire.

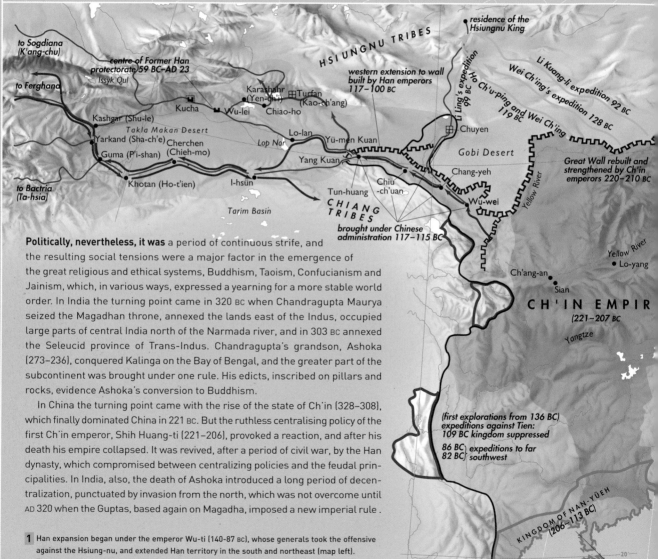

Politically, nevertheless, it was a period of continuous strife, and the resulting social tensions were a major factor in the emergence of the great religious and ethical systems, Buddhism, Taoism, Confucianism and Jainism, which, in various ways, expressed a yearning for a more stable world order. In India the turning point came in 320 BC when Chandragupta Maurya seized the Magadhan throne, annexed the lands east of the Indus, occupied large parts of central India north of the Narmada river, and in 303 BC annexed the Seleucid province of Trans-Indus. Chandragupta's grandson, Ashoka (273–236), conquered Kalinga on the Bay of Bengal, and the greater part of the subcontinent was brought under one rule. His edicts, inscribed on pillars and rocks, evidence Ashoka's conversion to Buddhism.

In China the turning point came with the rise of the state of Ch'in (328–308), which finally dominated China in 221 BC. But the ruthless centralising policy of the first Ch'in emperor, Shih Huang-ti (221–206), provoked a reaction, and after his death his empire collapsed. It was revived, after a period of civil war, by the Han dynasty, which compromised between centralizing policies and the feudal principalities. In India, also, the death of Ashoka introduced a long period of decentralization, punctuated by invasion from the north, which was not overcome until AD 320 when the Guptas, based again on Magadha, imposed a new imperial rule .

1 Han expansion began under the emperor Wu-ti (140-87 BC), whose generals took the offensive against the Hsiung-nu, and extended Han territory in the south and northeast (map left). Thanks to the pioneer exploration of Chang Chien, diplomatic initiatives were started to expand trade and forge alliances with some of the peoples of the northwest, and under his promptings the 'Silk Road' was established carrying Chinese trade to central Asia and beyond. To protect these routes, annexations and extensions to the Great Wall in the northwest followed. Chinese power was again briefly extended to the west under the later Han after AD 94.

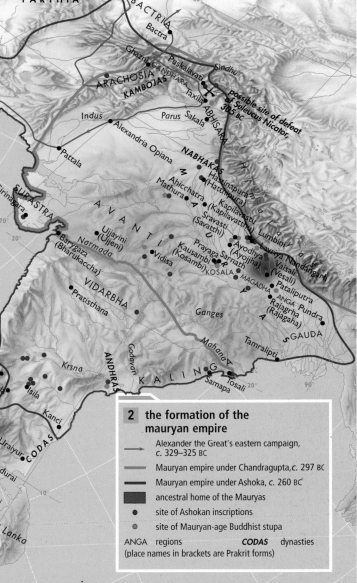

2 Chandragupta Maurya transformed the Magadhan kingdom into an empire, which was further extended and consolidated by his grandson Ashoka (map right). After the violent conquest of Kalinga, Ashoka converted to Buddhism and pursued a policy of conquest through moral teachings (dhamma). Many of his edicts are located near Buddhist places of worship. According to Buddhist legends, Ashoka built and embellished 84,000 stupas, and sent Buddhist missions to many regions, including the Hellenistic kingdoms to the west, south India and Sri Lanka.

2 the formation of the mauryan empire

→ Alexander the Great's eastern campaign, *c.* 329–325 BC

— Mauryan empire under Chandragupta, *c.* 297 BC

— Mauryan empire under Ashoka, *c.* 260 BC

■ ancestral home of the Mauryas

● site of Ashokan inscriptions

● site of Mauryan-age Buddhist stupa

ANGA regions   *CODAS* dynasties
(place names in brackets are Prakrit forms)

1 the expansion of han china

▨ China, 207 BC

☐ territory added under Former Han

— maximum extent of Former Han empire

☐ territory of Chinese protectorate of Western Regions, *c.* 59 BC

← journey of Chang Chien, envoy of Han emperor, 138–126 BC

— trade routes

⊞ administrative centre under Later Han from AD 126

▣ centre of Later Han protectorate, AD 73–126

— territory added under Later Han

← new route opened by General Pan Chao for Later Han

→ expeditions against Hsiungnu (Huns)

This classical age of Indian civilization survived beyond the collapse of the Gupta empire caused by the barbarian invasions of the fifth century.

The barbarian invasions were also a turning point in China. The Ch'in and the Han built and extended the Great Wall against the nomad Hsiung-nu in the north. Under the emperor Wu-ti (140–87) the Han extended their power to central Asia. With its efficient administration, a large export trade and an extensive network of roads and canals, Han China, with its capital at Ch'ang-an was extremely prosperous. But control over south China was tenuous, while in the north feudal magnates still exercised great power, which grew with the threat of war. Crisis came in AD 9, and although Han rule was restored, disintegration set in after *c.*160. When in 304 the Hsiungnu broke through the Great Wall, China remained divided until 589.

the **roman** empire

The rise of Rome from a collection of shepherds' huts on the hills overlooking the Tiber to a great world empire is a story of seven centuries of constant warfare. According to tradition, the city of Rome was founded in 753 BC by descendants of Aeneas, the egendary hero who had fled to Italy after the sack of Troy. Archaeology shows that it was only in the sixth century that it began to take on the trappings of a city.

In 510 BC the citizens of Rome expelled the last of the Etruscan kings and formed a republic. Over the next 300 years victories over Etruscans, Greeks and Celts gradually extended Roman control of the whole of Italy, but this expansion brought her into direct conflict with the imperialist ambitions of Carthage on the North African coast. Three fierce conflicts (the Punic Wars) were fought for supremacy between the two powers. In the second (218–201 BC), the Carthaginians under the brilliant generalship of Hannibal inflicted a series of crushing defeats on the Romans. But Roman resolve held, Hannibal was ultimately defeated, and some 50 years later Carthage itself was destroyed in the Third Punic War (146 BC).

The Punic Wars gave Rome control over Sicily (241 BC), Spain (206 BC) and North Africa (146 BC). At the same time, conflict with the Hellenistic kingdoms of the East Mediterranean resulted in the conquest of Macedon, Greece and western Asia Minor. In this way, almost by accident, Rome became an imperial power with far-flung possessions. In the first century BC the growing power of successful war-leaders led to fierce rivalries and civil wars, culminating in the struggle between Caesar and Pompey (49–45 BC), from which Caesar emerged victorious. His assassination in 44 BC, however, initiated a further 13 years of conflict, only ending with Augustus' victory over Antony and Cleopatra at Actium in 31 BC.

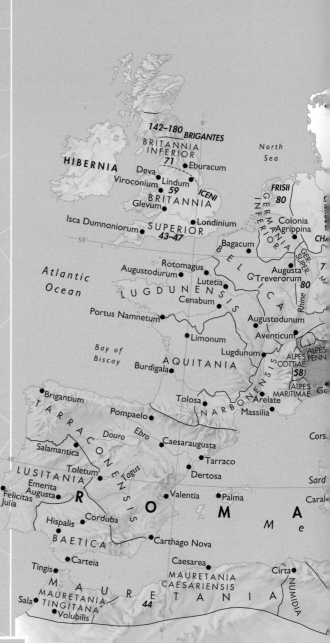

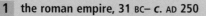

1 the roman empire, 31 BC– *c.* AD 250

- under administration of the Senate
- imperial provinces
- public provinces
- provinces added after AD 14, with date
- ------ later subdivisions of provinces, with dates

Augustus' rule initiated a period of two centuries of unprecedented peace and prosperity in the extensive lands of the Roman empire. Population increased, trade flourished and cities grew. Civic authorities and wealthy individuals embellished their cities with theatres, baths and temples, while roads, aqueducts and harbours brought in essential supplies from outside. This vast common market was further united by Roman law and by the use of Latin.

This peace was broken in the middle of the third century AD by Germanic invasions in the west and Persian victories in the east which brought the empire temporarily to its knees. Reform and reorganization under Diocletian (AD 284–305) and Constantine (306–337) ensured the continued survival of the eastern half of the empire, with its new capital at Constantinople (Byzantium), but the last western Emperor was deposed in 476 and Justinian's abortive efforts to recover the western provinces in the mid-sixth century showed clearly that the unified empire was a thing of the past. The ghost of the Roman empire lived on in the west, however, in the continued importance of Roman law and the continued use of Latin by the Christian church.

1 From 27 BC, the emperor himself was responsible for the administration of the imperial provinces (those in which legions were stationed). The others were governed by proconsuls appointed by the Senate. At the start of the imperial period some parts of the empire were ruled by friendly client kings; as they died their lands became Roman provinces. Emperors could gain great glory by extending the empire. Although campaigns in the first century AD in Germany had only limited success, the eastern Balkans, north Africa, Arabia and Britain were all added to Rome while in the following century Trajan added Dacia, Armenia, Assyria and Mesopotamia. Trajan's rule marked Rome's greatest territorial extent. Hadrian, his successor, abandoned Trajan's conquests other than Arabia and Dacia to consolidate more defensible frontiers.

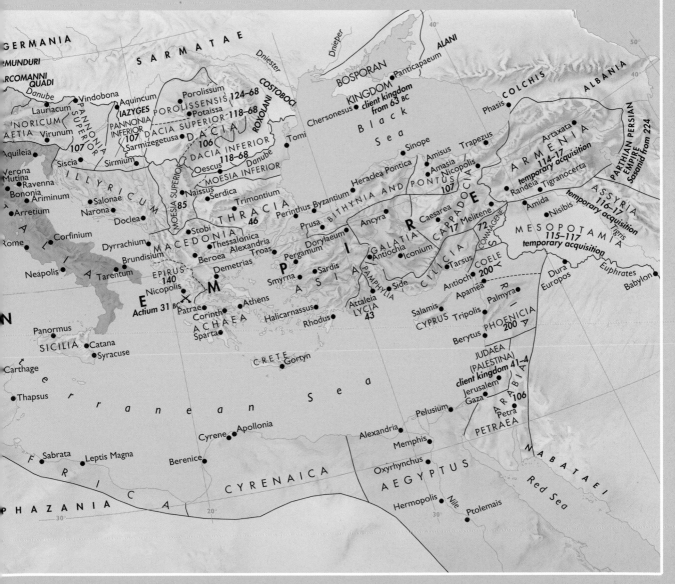

the **barbarian** invasions

In the fourth and fifth centuries AD the irruption of nomadic peoples from central Asia threw the civilized world into disarray. The invading nomads were under no form of central control though their movements radiated from a common centre. They were mostly Mongoloid and their languages mostly of the Turkish family; they were largely pastoralists with mobile encampments of tents and their success in war owed much to their mounted archers. All the established centres of civilization were affected by them: China, the Gupta empire in India, Sasanian Persia and the Roman empire in the west. In 304 the Great Wall of China was breached by the Hsiung-nu, forebears of the Huns; in 367, Picts and Scots broke through Hadrian's Wall into Britain. The setbacks were lasting. China remained disunited until 589, and western Europe (if we except the short-lived Carolingian revival) only began to recover from invasion around the middle of the 11th century.

The appearance of the Huns in Europe *c.* 370 immediately caused a great involuntary movement among the Germanic peoples who had long been settled in northern and central Europe beyond the confines of the Roman empire. The Visigoths defeated the Roman emperor at Adrianople in 378, sacked Rome in 410 and were settled in Aquitaine in 418. Behind the Visigoths followed other east and west Germanic peoples: Alans, Vandals, Sueves, Alemans, Franks, and finally the Ostrogoths who, having earlier been forced into subjection, liberated themselves after the defeat of the Huns in 451, and descended into Italy, where they were in control by 493. Only the Anglo–Saxon invasion of Britain, beginning *c.* 440, followed a different course. Here scattered bands of warriors and settlers, moving by ship up the estuaries of the Humber, Thames and the Wash, met with stubborn resistance. It was to be almost two centuries before the invaders, following their victories at Deorham (577) and Chester (616) established control of Britain. Here continuity with the Roman past was at a modest level at best.

In continental Europe continuity was more evident. Political control passed from Roman officials to German kings; but, except for the Anglo–Saxons and Franks, who could draw manpower from their homeland, the invaders were too few in number to change decisively the character of Roman society. This in part explains the success of the counter-offensive which Justinian launched in 533. But Justinian's wars, and the havoc they wrought, left the way open for another wave of invasion from Asia, this time the Avars, and it was their onslaught, beginning *c.*560, that drove the Lombards into Italy (568). But they were unable to occupy the whole peninsula, and Italy remained divided between the Lombards, the Byzantine emperor and the Papacy. When the Lombard ruler Aistulf advanced south, seeking to establish his authority over the Lombard dukes of Spoleto and Benevento, occupied Ravenna in 751 and drove out the Byzantine exarch, the Pope, fearing for his independence, called on the Franks for aid. Thus was sealed the momentous alliance of the Carolingians and the Papacy, which resulted in Charles the Great's invasion, conquest and annexation of the Lombard kingdom in 774.

The appearance of the Avars also unsettled the Slav peoples who had greatly extended their settlement in eastern Europe following the Germanic migration westwards. Beginning *c.* 600 Slav warbands descended into Greece and the Balkans, while the Bulgars took control of the western shore of the Black Sea. The arrival of the Slavs, cutting the landbridge between Byzantium and the west, was a cardinal fact in European history. The rise of the Bulgarian Empire and the gradual consolidation of Serbia and Croatia left a permanent imprint on the demography and historical geography of Europe.

CALEDONIA

PICTS

Hadrian's Wall

SCOTS

Eburacu

ANGLES

ANGLES

Glevum

BRITONS

CELTIC PEOPLES

Londinium

SAXONS JUTES

Atlantic Ocean

Rotomagus

FRANKS Lute

Catalaunic

BRITONS Fields 451

Portus Namnetum

VANDALS ALANS SUEVES 406–9

Burdigala AQUITANIA Vouillé

KINGDOM OF THE VISIGOTHS

Tolosa (Toulouse)

Lucus Augusti

SUEVES (SUEBI) 411–585

Pompaelo

WESTE

KINGDOM OF THE SUEVES

VISIGOTHS 507–711

Tarra

Toletum overrun by Moors 711

Palm

Valentia

Felicitas Julia

Corduba

VANDALS ALANS 409–429

Gades

Carthago Nov

Caesa

Tingis

BERBER

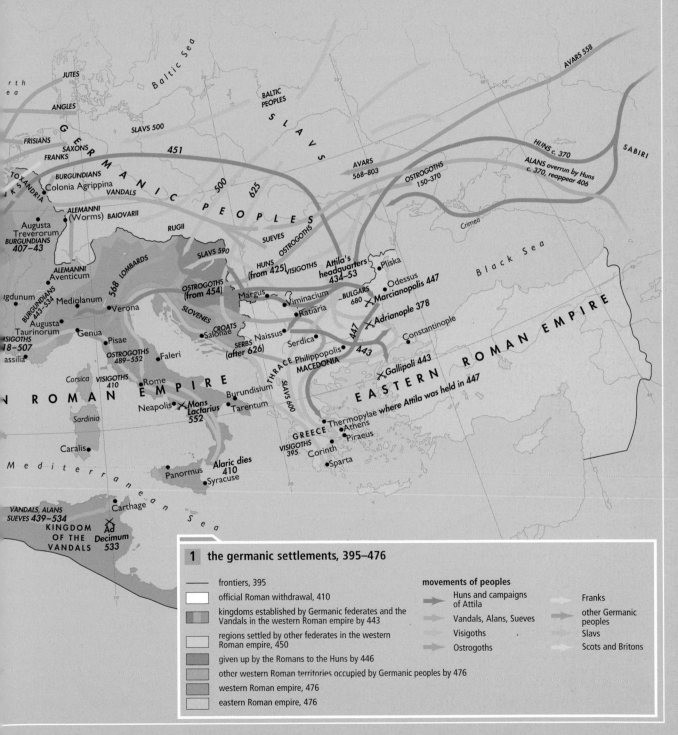

1 In the frontier regions of the Roman empire, there was much interchange with, as well as raids by, neighbouring peoples (map above). On occasion entire peoples were settled as 'federates' associated with the army for defence purposes. Other 'barbarians' served in the ranks and in the top military posts of the imperial armies. The Huns created a major disruption and pushed groups such as the Goths and Vandals from the frontier regions of the empire. By the early sixth century, especially in the west, a number of successor states of mixed population had emerged on its former territory.

1 the germanic settlements, 395–476

— frontiers, 395

official Roman withdrawal, 410

kingdoms established by Germanic federates and the Vandals in the western Roman empire by 443

regions settled by other federates in the western Roman empire, 450

given up by the Romans to the Huns by 446

other western Roman territories occupied by Germanic peoples by 476

western Roman empire, 476

eastern Roman empire, 476

movements of peoples

→ Huns and campaigns of Attila

→ Vandals, Alans, Sueves

→ Visigoths

→ Ostrogoths

→ Franks

→ other Germanic peoples

→ Slavs

→ Scots and Britons

Map labels:

Baltic Sea · North Sea · Black Sea · Mediterranean Sea · Crimea

JUTES · ANGLES · FRISIANS · SAXONS · FRANKS · TOXANDRIA · Colonia Agrippina · BURGUNDIANS · VANDALS · ALEMANNI (Worms) · BAIOVARII · RUGII · SUEVES · OSTROGOTHS · HUNS (from 425) · VISIGOTHS · Attila's headquarters 434–53 · Pliska · Odessus · Marcianopolis 447 · BULGARS 680 · Adrianople 378 · Constantinople

GERMANIC PEOPLES · SLAVS · BALTIC PEOPLES · SLAVS 500 · AVARS 568–803 · OSTROGOTHS 150–370 · HUNS c. 370 · SABIRI · ALANS overrun by Huns c. 370, reappear 406 · AVARS 558

451 · 500 · 625

Augusta Treverorum · BURGUNDIANS 407–43 · ALEMANNI · Aventicum · SLAVS 590 · OSTROGOTHS (from 454) · SLOVENES · CROATS · Salonae · SERBS (after 626) · Naissus · Serdica · Philippopolis · THRACE · MACEDONIA · 447 · 443 · Gallipoli 443

Lugdunum · BURGUNDIANS 443–534 · Mediolanum · Verona · 568 LOMBARDS · Margus · Viminacium · Ratiaria

Augusta Taurinorum · VISIGOTHS 418–507 · Genua · Pisae · OSTROGOTHS 489–552 · Faleri · Massilia

Corsica · VISIGOTHS 410 · Rome · WESTERN ROMAN EMPIRE · Brundisium · SLAVS 600 · EASTERN ROMAN EMPIRE

Neapolis · Mons Lactarius 552 · Tarentum · Thermopylae where Attila was held in 447 · GREECE · Athens · Piraeus

Sardinia · VISIGOTHS 395 · Corinth · Sparta

Caralis · Alaric dies 410 · Panormus · Syracuse

VANDALS, ALANS SUEVES 439–534 · Carthage · KINGDOM OF THE VANDALS · Ad Decimum 533

47

germanic kingdoms of western europe

Within a century of the Germanic invasions there were settled kingdoms in western Europe, except in Britain where invaders still met resistance. Among these the Ostrogothic kingdom of Theodoric the Great (493–526) was outstanding. In Spain, the kingdom of the Visigoths was to endure from the late fifth century until the Arab conquest in 711. But monarchical institutions were still weak and religious differences divided the Arian rulers from their Catholic subjects. Justinian's attack on the Ostrogothic kingdom destroyed equilibrium in the west and opened the way for the advance of the Franks.

The Franks also had appeared on the scene as scattered warbands, but Clovis (486–511) ruthlessly eliminated his rivals, made himself sole king, and reconciled the Gallo–Roman population by embracing the Catholic faith (497). He then turned against the neighbouring peoples, the Alemanni and Burgundians, defeated the Visigoths at Vouillé (507), near Poitiers, and forced them to withdraw to Spain and Septimania. But Theodoric's support for the other Germanic kingdoms checked further advance, and only after his death was a new phase of Frankish expansion possible. Deprived of Ostrogothic support, the Thuringians (531), Burgundians (532–4), and the Alemanni (535) succumbed, and in 537 the Franks seized Provence.

Once the initial wave of conquest was present, however, decline set in. Division of the royal patrimony, dynastic quarrels and alienation of the royal estates to buy aristocratic and ecclesiastical support, seemed after the death of Dagobert I (629–39) to presage the break-up of the kingdom. In Britain, on the other hand, the seventh century saw the emergence and consolidation of the kingdoms known as the Heptarchy. It seems that the kingdoms of the south-east (Sussex, Kent, Essex, East Anglia) were prevented from expanding by geographical obstacles,

2 the empire of charlemagne

- ▢ Frankish realm 714
- ▢ added to Frankish empire by 814
- ▨ Frankish dependencies (with date of formation)
- ⚜ Frankish royal residences
- ☉ archbishoprics
- ⊕ important monasteries
- **GASCONY** province with date of acquisition
  769

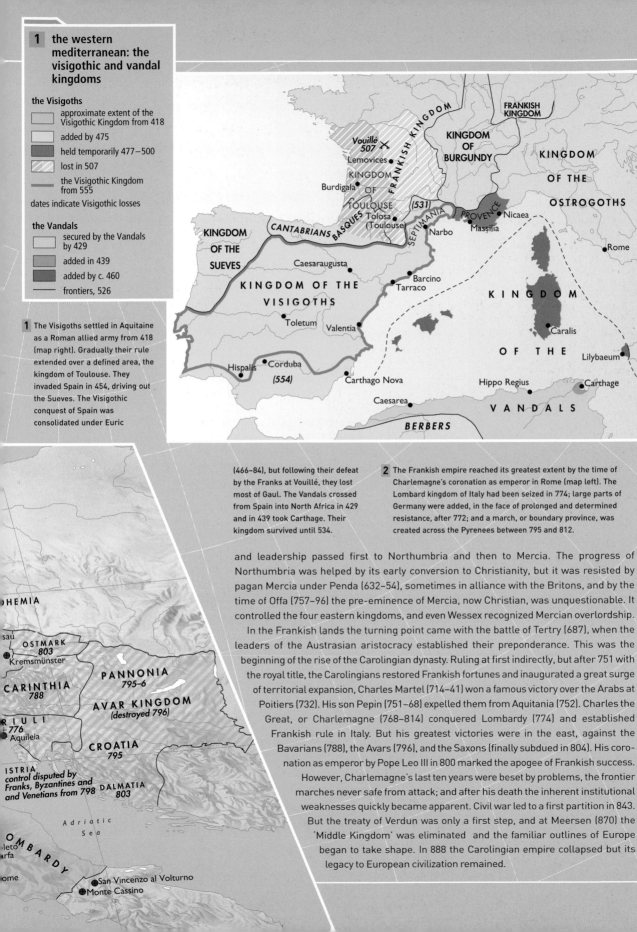

1 the western mediterranean: the visigothic and vandal kingdoms

the Visigoths

- approximate extent of the Visigothic Kingdom from 418
- added by 475
- held temporarily 477–500
- lost in 507
- the Visigothic Kingdom from 555

dates indicate Visigothic losses

the Vandals

- secured by the Vandals by 429
- added in 439
- added by c. 460
- frontiers, 526

1 The Visigoths settled in Aquitaine as a Roman allied army from 418 (map right). Gradually their rule extended over a defined area, the kingdom of Toulouse. They invaded Spain in 454, driving out the Sueves. The Visigothic conquest of Spain was consolidated under Euric

Map labels: FRANKISH KINGDOM · KINGDOM OF BURGUNDY · KINGDOM OF THE OSTROGOTHS · Vouillé 507 · Lemovices · KINGDOM OF TOULOUSE · Burdigala · Tolosa (Toulouse) · SEPTIMANIA · (531) · PROVENCE · Nicaea · Narbo · Massilia · Rome · CANTABRIANS · BASQUES · KINGDOM OF THE SUEVES · Caesaraugusta · Barcino · Tarraco · KINGDOM OF THE VISIGOTHS · Toletum · Valentia · Caralis · KINGDOM OF THE VANDALS · Lilybaeum · Hispalis · Corduba · (554) · Carthago Nova · Hippo Regius · Carthage · Caesarea · BERBERS

(466–84), but following their defeat by the Franks at Vouillé, they lost most of Gaul. The Vandals crossed from Spain into North Africa in 429 and in 439 took Carthage. Their kingdom survived until 534.

2 The Frankish empire reached its greatest extent by the time of Charlemagne's coronation as emperor in Rome (map left). The Lombard kingdom of Italy had been seized in 774; large parts of Germany were added, in the face of prolonged and determined resistance, after 772; and a march, or boundary province, was created across the Pyrenees between 795 and 812.

and leadership passed first to Northumbria and then to Mercia. The progress of Northumbria was helped by its early conversion to Christianity, but it was resisted by pagan Mercia under Penda (632–54), sometimes in alliance with the Britons, and by the time of Offa (757–96) the pre-eminence of Mercia, now Christian, was unquestionable. It controlled the four eastern kingdoms, and even Wessex recognized Mercian overlordship.

In the Frankish lands the turning point came with the battle of Tertry (687), when the leaders of the Austrasian aristocracy established their preponderance. This was the beginning of the rise of the Carolingian dynasty. Ruling at first indirectly, but after 751 with the royal title, the Carolingians restored Frankish fortunes and inaugurated a great surge of territorial expansion, Charles Martel (714–41) won a famous victory over the Arabs at Poitiers (732). His son Pepin (751–68) expelled them from Aquitania (752). Charles the Great, or Charlemagne (768–814) conquered Lombardy (774) and established Frankish rule in Italy. But his greatest victories were in the east, against the Bavarians (788), the Avars (796), and the Saxons (finally subdued in 804). His coronation as emperor by Pope Leo III in 800 marked the apogee of Frankish success. However, Charlemagne's last ten years were beset by problems, the frontier marches never safe from attack; and after his death the inherent institutional weaknesses quickly became apparent. Civil war led to a first partition in 843. But the treaty of Verdun was only a first step, and at Meersen (870) the 'Middle Kingdom' was eliminated and the familiar outlines of Europe began to take shape. In 888 the Carolingian empire collapsed but its legacy to European civilization remained.

Map labels (lower left): BOHEMIA · OSTMARK 803 · Kremsmünster · sau · PANNONIA 795–6 · CARINTHIA 788 · RIULI 776 · Aquileia · AVAR KINGDOM (destroyed 796) · CROATIA 795 · ISTRIA control disputed by Franks, Byzantines and and Venetians from 798 · DALMATIA 803 · Adriatic Sea · LOMBARDY · leto · arfa · ome · San Vincenzo al Volturno · Monte Cassino

The relative stability of western Europe under Charles the Great (Charlemagne) and of England under Offa of Mercia was shattered in the ninth century by attacks by Saracens in the south, Magyars in the east and Norwegians and Danes in the north and west. The Saracens pillaged Rome in 846 and after establishing a base at Fraxinetum in 890 raided deep into southern Gaul. Northern Italy and Germany were a prey to the Magyars who had moved into the Hungarian plain after Charlemagne's destruction of Avar power. The Vikings of Norway and Denmark also began as raiders; but in their case an initial phase of plunder was followed by settlement and colonization, first in Orkney and Shetland, then in Ireland where Dublin was founded c. 841, later (c. 870) in Iceland and in England, where the Danish armies occupied the countryside round the Five Boroughs of the Midlands after 876. In France the West Frankish king conferred the lands at the mouth of the Seine – the later duchy of Normandy – on the Danish leader Rollo in 911.

The invasions were accompanied by widespread devastation and depopulation. Inevitably recovery was slow. In Germany Otto I's defeat of the Magyars at the river Lech (955) was a turning point. In England only determined resistance by Alfred the Great of Wessex (871–99) held the Danes at bay. After 909 his

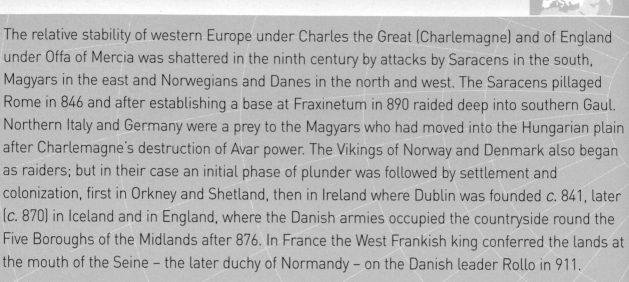

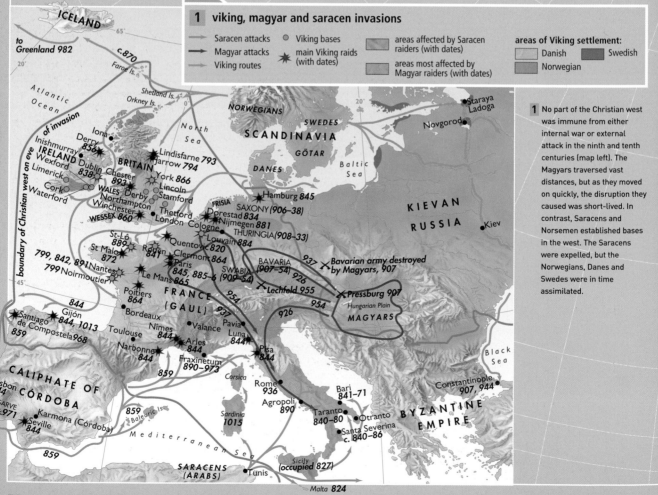

1 viking, magyar and saracen invasions

→ Saracen attacks
→ Magyar attacks
→ Viking routes
○ Viking bases
✳ main Viking raids (with dates)

▨ areas affected by Saracen raiders (with dates)
▨ areas most affected by Magyar raiders (with dates)

areas of Viking settlement:
☐ Danish
☐ Norwegian
■ Swedish

1 No part of the Christian west was immune from either internal war or external attack in the ninth and tenth centuries (map left). The Magyars traversed vast distances, but as they moved on quickly, the disruption they caused was short-lived. In contrast, Saracens and Norsemen established bases in the west. The Saracens were expelled, but the Norwegians, Danes and Swedes were in time assimilated.

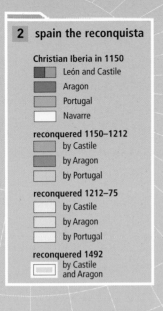

Christian Iberia in 1150

- León and Castile
- Aragon
- Portugal
- Navarre

reconquered 1150–1212

- by Castile
- by Aragon
- by Portugal

reconquered 1212–75

- by Castile
- by Aragon
- by Portugal

reconquered 1492

- by Castile and Aragon

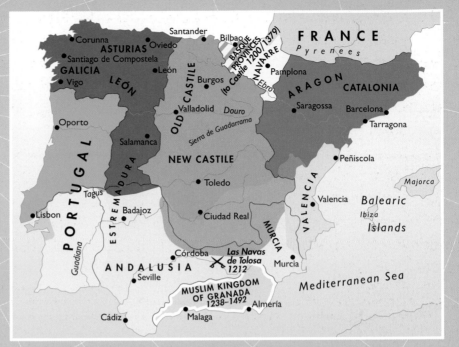

2 From around 1150 the balance of power in Spain began to favour the Christian states. In the 1140s Alfonso VII of Léon expanded his power to the Tagus and in 1147 the Portuguese took Lisbon, aided by a fleet on its way to the Second Crusade. The Reconquista gathered pace in the 13th century (map above). In 1212 Alfonso VIII of Castile heavily defeated Caliph al-Nasir at Las Navas de Tolosa. The subsequent collapse of the Almohad empire helped the Christians overrun most of southern Spain by 1275, including Córdoba in 1235 and Seville in 1248.

successors went over to the offensive and by 939 Scandinavian England had been subjugated. But after the death of Edgar (959–75) a second wave of Danish invasion began.

In southern Europe, the Mediterranean was by 950 virtually a 'Muslim lake'. But the collapse of Arab unity after 936 facilitated a Christian revival. After the fall of Fraxinetum in 972 the fleets of Pisa and Genoa went over to the offensive, attacking the Muslim bases in North Africa, while Venice cleared the Adriatic. After the First Crusade (1096–99) and the great Venetian naval victory off Ascalon in 1123, the Italian cities dominated Mediterranean trade. The period of the First Crusade also saw the beginning of the Christian reconquest of Spain under Alfonso VI (1065–1109), king of León and Castile, who actually advanced as far as Toledo in 1084. But the first wave of reconquest was halted by the great Islamic revival under the Almoravid and Almohad dynasties. The Christian advance only resumed in the 13th century after the decisive victory at Las Navas de Tolosa (1212) which led to the conquest of Córdoba (1236), Valencia (1238), Murcia (1243), Seville (1248) and Cádiz (1262).

The ninth- and tenth-century invasions also disrupted royal authority and created political fragmentation. In Gaul the Frankish rulers virtually capitulated to the Norse invaders, leaving defence to the local magnates. The result was a great upsurge of feudalism. Peasant freemen virtually disappeared and society was polarized between nobles and serfs. In Germany power devolved into the hands of dukes and margraves who defended the frontiers, and in Italy only the walled cities could withstand the Magyar onslaught. The kingdom of Wessex was the exception, unique in 10th-century Europe beyond the borders of Muslim Spain and Byzantium. Here the monarchy took control, creating during the reconquest of the Danelaw a system of shires and hundreds administered by sheriffs who were officials, not feudatories. But this royal government could not withstand the renewal of Danish attacks during the reign of Aethelred II (978–1016). By the beginning of the 11th century England seemed destined to pass into a Scandinavian orbit. The Norman Conquest decisively halted this development. William the Conqueror quickly established control in the south; but in the north, where Danish and Scottish intervention underpinned resistance, he only made his authority secure by systematic devastation (1069). Danish reconquest was still a threat until 1085; but after 1066 England was permanently aligned with the Christian and feudal civilization of western Europe. The period of invasions had irrevocably changed the structure of Western society.

the **expansion** of christianity

By the time of Pope Leo I (440–461) an organized Christian church existed with a hierarchy of bishops and a full-scale framework of patriarchates, provinces and dioceses. But the attempt to enforce orthodoxy, particularly at the Council of Chalcedon (451), caused serious internal conflict. The Monophysite or Coptic Christians of Egypt were alienated, the Nestorians driven into exile in Persia. Here they carried on great missionary work (map 1), only halted centuries later by the advance of Islam. In the west, however, where Christianity was the official religion of the Roman empire, the church suffered from the setbacks inflicted by the Germanic invasions of the western provinces, and subsequent rivalry between Rome and Constantinople resulted after 1054 in schism between Catholicism and Orthodoxy. A period of stagnation had set in, only ended by the Irish and later Anglo–Saxon missionaries, who converted the heathen tribes of Germany, reformed the Frankish church and inaugurated a great missionary drive to Scandinavia and eastern Europe. In addition a counter-offensive against Islam was launched in a series of Crusades beginning in 1096.

The resurgence of Christianity, particularly marked after the pontificate of Leo IX (1048–54) was a disaster for the Jewish communities which had spread throughout Europe before and after the suppression of the Jewish revolts in Palestine by the Romans in AD 66 and 132. The Jews suffered no restrictions in the Roman empire and, with their widespread international connections, were welcomed as traders by the Carolingians and other early medieval kings. But the Crusades inaugurated a wave of intolerance, and the third and fourth Lateran Councils (1179, 1215) passed discriminatory legislation. The rise of a native merchant class also made Jews less indispensable to Christian rulers, and later they became the scapegoats for the economic setbacks of the 14th century. The result was the series of expulsions, beginning in England in 1290. In 1492 the Sephardic Jews were expelled from Spain, in 1497 from Portugal. The Ashkenazi in the German lands took refuge in Poland and Lithuania, where they formed tight communities in what later was called 'the Pale'. Only the 18th-century Enlightenment brought a beginning of reconciliation, but the Nazi experience was to show that it was far from complete.

1 The medieval expansion of Christianity into central and east Asia was largely the work of Nestorian and Monophysite Christians, who had been separated from the rest of the church since the fifth century. Their work along the trade routes of China, central Asia and the Persian Gulf was tolerated by non-Christian rulers until the 14th century. Nestorianism and Manichaeism in China eventually died out, but Nestorianism survives in modern Iraq and Monophysitism remains the indigenous form of Christianity in Egypt (the Coptic church), Ethiopia and India (the Syrian Orthodox or St Thomas Christians), where distinctive traditions of worship and theology are preserved.

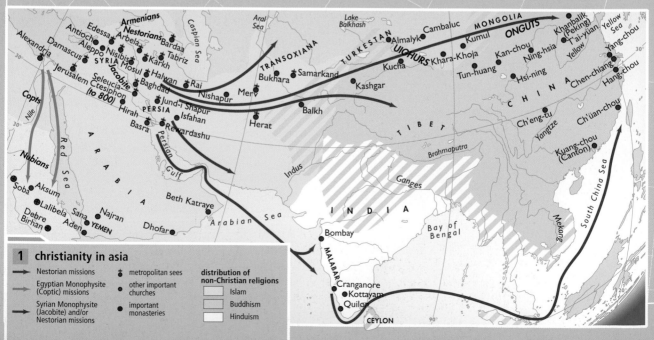

1 christianity in asia

→ Nestorian missions

→ Egyptian Monophysite (Coptic) missions

→ Syrian Monophysite (Jacobite) and/or Nestorian missions

✝ metropolitan sees

● other important churches

● important monasteries

distribution of non-Christian religions

Islam

Buddhism

Hinduism

2 From about 700, Christianity began to expand into Germany and, from the ninth century, into central Europe, where the Roman and Byzantine churches competed for the allegiance of newly converted rulers. The conversion of Scandinavia began in the mid-10th century, that of Russia in 988. Most of Spain was overrun by Islam in 711 but slowly reconquered by Christian rulers during the rest of the Middle Ages. From 1096, crusader armies from western Europe campaigned to recover the Holy Land from Islam: Christian rule was established in Jerusalem and Antioch, but these territories were lost by 1291. With the conversion of Prussia and Lithuania in the 14th century most of Europe had become at least nominally Christian, though the Church had been permanently divided between Catholic west and Byzantine east.

2 the irish and anglo–saxon missions

➜ Irish missions
➜ Anglo-Saxon missions
⊕ monastery
● important missionary bishopric

3 Irish missionaries such as Columba (c. 521–97) and Aidan (d. 651) were instrumental in converting Scotland and northern England to Christianity; Columbanus (d. 615) founded monasteries in the Frankish kingdom. The Anglo–Saxon kingdoms also sent missionaries (with Roman and Frankish support) to western Germany. The most important were Willibrord (658–739) and Boniface (c. 675–754), bishops of Utrecht and Mainz.

3 christianity in europe

☐ Roman-rite Christians, c. 1400
☐ Byzantine-rite Christians, c. 1400
☐ Monophysite Christians
☐ Islam

─── extent of Catholic (Frankish) Christianity, c. 700
----- maximum extent of crusader states in the east in the 12th century
● important bishoprics
(743) date of foundation of a bishopric or of conversion of a region to Christianity

the **jewish** diaspora

For over 2,000 years the history of the Jews has combined external dispersal with internal cohesion. The decisive dispersal of the Jewish people took place under Rome. Although the Jewish revolts of AD 66–73 and 132–5 and their vigorous suppression by the Romans, as well as Hadrian's measures to de-Judaize Jerusalem, caused rapid deterioration in the position of the Jews in Judaea, elsewhere in the Roman world their legal and economic status and the viability of their communities remained unaffected. This stimulated a constant flow of migration from Palestine, Mesopotamia and Alexandria to the western and northern shores of the Mediterranean. Consequently, widely scattered but internally cohesive Jewish communities developed all over the west and north of the Roman empire: in Italy, in Spain and as far north as Cologne.

The resilience of Judaism can be chiefly ascribed to the evolution of the Jewish religion following the destruction of the First Temple in Jerusalem in 586 BC, and the gradual emergence of a faith based on synagogue and communal prayer. New local leaders of Jewish life, the men of learning, or rabbis, emerged. Jewish religious and civil law was gradually codified in the Mishnah (AD 200) and the commentary and discussions systematized as the Talmud (AD 500).

During the High Middle Ages Jews from the Near East and north Africa settled in southern Italy, Spain, France and southern Germany. They flourished in Spain under the first Umayyad caliph of Córdoba, 'Abd ar-Rahman III (912–61). Despite the massacres which attended the First Crusade in the 1090s, the 11th and 12th centuries constituted the golden age of medieval German Jewry.

A series of expulsions from western Europe, beginning in England in 1290, led to a steady eastwards migration of German Jews (Ashkenazim) to Prague (from the 11th century) and Vienna. Jewish communities arose in Cracow, Kalisz, and other towns in western and southern Poland in the 13th century and, further east, at Lvov, Brest–Litovsk, and Grodno in the 14th. The period of heaviest immigration from the west into Poland-Lithuania came in the late 15th and 16th centuries. Most of the expelled Spanish and Portuguese Jews (Sephardim) settled in the Ottoman empire and north Africa.

After the disruption of the Thirty Years' War (1618–48), Jews from central and eastern Europe, as well as the Near East, were once again able to settle, usually in ghettos, in northern Italy, Germany, Holland and, from the 1650s, in England and the English

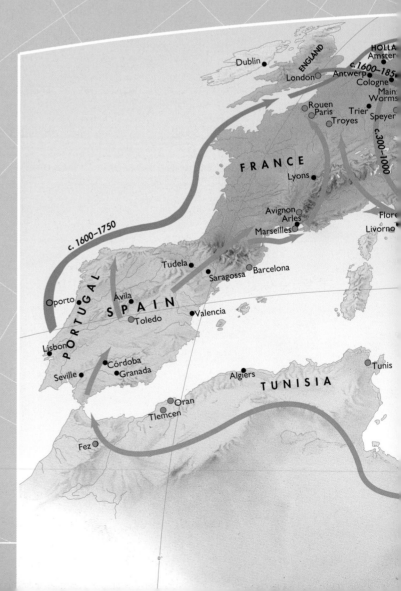

colonies in the New World. In the central European cities of Vienna, Berlin, Hamburg and Budapest, Jewish communities grew considerably during the 18th and 19th centuries and made major contributions to the development of their countries, in particular engaging in financial enterprises forbidden to Christians. During the 17th and 18th centuries, some of the largest and wealthiest, as well as culturally most sophisticated, communities in the Jewish world lived in Amsterdam, Hamburg, Frankfurt, Livorno, Venice, Rome, Berlin and London. Amsterdam's Jews were especially important in the areas of commerce, finance, printing and book production.

Nevertheless until the 1940s by far the greater proportion of world Jewry continued to live in eastern Europe. The small Jewish populations in Hungary and Romania in 1700 increased in the 18th and 19th centuries through immigration from Poland and the Czech lands. Under the tsars, the bulk of the Jewish population in the Russian empire was confined by law to western areas (the 'Pale of Settlement'). The demographic preponderance of eastern Europe in world Jewry ended with the Nazis: Jewish life in Poland, Czechoslovakia and the old Pale of Settlement was largely destroyed though significant Jewish populations survived in the USSR, Romania, Bulgaria and Hungary. Large-scale emigration from the USSR (and its successor states) to Israel in the 1980s and 1990s dramatically reduced the community's size there.

1 The Jews in medieval Europe were tolerated by the authorities for economic reasons, but were subjected to restrictions and frequent persecution. They formed two major sub-groups (map right): Sephardim from the Hebrew word Sepharad (for Spain) who lived in Spain until 1492; and Ashkenazim (from the Hebrew word *Ashkenaz*, for the Germanic lands) who originally lived in the Rhineland until, as a result of migration and expulsion, by the late 15th century they flourished primarily in Poland and Lithuania. By 1500 much of Europe, including England, France, Spain and Portugal was closed to Jews.

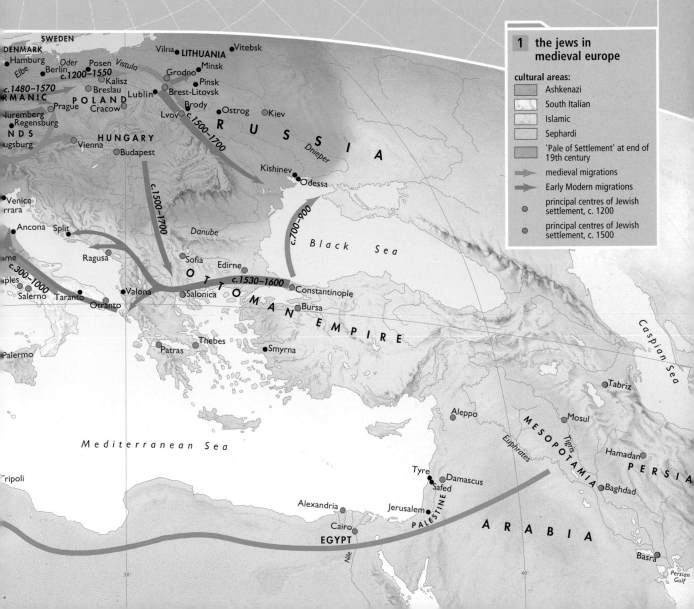

1 the jews in medieval europe

cultural areas:

- Ashkenazi
- South Italian
- Islamic
- Sephardi
- 'Pale of Settlement' at end of 19th century
- → medieval migrations
- → Early Modern migrations
- ● principal centres of Jewish settlement, c. 1200
- ● principal centres of Jewish settlement, c. 1500

the **islamic** world

The rise and expansion of Islam was one of the most significant and far-reaching events in modern history. 'Islam' means 'submission to the will of God'; God's message has been conveyed to mankind through a series of prophets, culminating in Mohammed. The Koran is the Word of God. Mohammed is the Seal of the Prophets, and no others will come after him. Mohammed was born in Mecca about AD 570, and received his first revelations in 610. As his followers grew in number they aroused the hostility of the merchant aristocracy of Mecca, and the group was eventually obliged to withdraw to Medina, some 280 miles north-east of Mecca. This migration, *hijra* in Arabic, marks the beginning of the Islamic era and of the Muslim calendar. Mohammed eventually returned to Mecca in triumph in 630. He died in 632, but Islam expanded rapidly; over the next century Arab armies brought the new religion as far west as Spain and the Mediterranean islands and as far east as northern India.

In 661 the political control of the Arab–Islamic empire passed to the Umayyads, a dynasty originating from the pre-Islamic Meccan aristocracy, whose power was now centred on Damascus. In 750 the Umayyads were replaced by the Abbasids, a family claiming direct descent from Mohammed. The capital now shifted from Syria to Baghdad, and power began to pass from the Arab minority to the non-Arab Muslims, who had always formed the numerical majority in the Muslim empire. The Abbasid period was a time of great prosperity and cultural and intellectual achievement, although the Muslim world gradually lost its political unity and split into a number of local dynastic entities. Among these were the Umayyads and Almoravids of Spain and North Africa, the Fatimids of Egypt and the Chamavids of north India.

1 The spread of Islam outside the Arabian peninsula began almost immediately after the Prophet's death in 632 (map right). By 711, Arab armies were simultaneously attacking Sind in north-east India and preparing for the conquest of the Iberian peninsula. In general, the conquests in the east exceeded those in the west in both size and importance. By 750, when the Abbasids ousted the Umayyad dynasty, the empire to which they succeeded was the largest civilization west of China.

In 945, the centre of the empire itself was captured by the Buyids, who ruled in the Abbasids' name for over a century. These were displaced in their turn by the Seljuks, Turks from central Asia, who gradually expanded into Anatolia. Their defeat of the Byzantine army at Manzikert in 1071 caused the Byzantines to seek the aid of Western Christendom which was to materialize in the form of the Crusades, principally in the late 11th and 12th centuries. The Crusades had little impact upon Arab society, but the Norman conquest of southern Italy and the southward expansion of the Christian states of northern Spain combined to push the Muslims out of Europe by the end of the 15th century, and to move the centre of gravity of the Muslim world permanently further east.

In the 12th and 13th centuries the Islamic world was disrupted by a new wave of invaders, the Mongols, who founded states in Iran, central Asia and south Russia. The Mongols defeated the Seljuk Turks in 1243 and sacked Baghdad in 1258, bringing about the end of the Abbasid Empire, but their defeat by the Mamelukes of Egypt at Ain Jalut in Palestine in 1260 marked their furthest westward advance. The Mongols' retreat created a vacuum which was filled by the rise of a number of Turcoman dynasties, one of which, the Ottomans, had risen to pre-eminence by the beginning of the 14th century. Islam continued to expand in India, Indonesia and in sub-Saharan Africa; today there are about 400 million Muslims, forming about one-seventh of the population of the world.

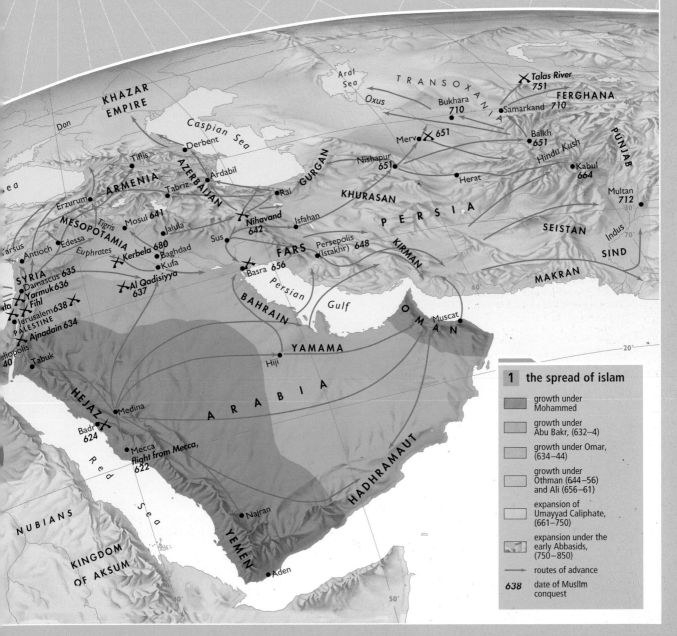

1 **the spread of islam**

- growth under Mohammed
- growth under Abu Bakr, (632–4)
- growth under Omar, (634–44)
- growth under Othman (644–56) and Ali (656–61)
- expansion of Umayyad Caliphate, (661–750)
- expansion under the early Abbasids, (750–850)
- → routes of advance
- **638** date of Muslim conquest

the **byzantine** world

The history of the Roman empire was marked almost from the outset by a shift of focus to the east. The original cause was the lure of the wealth of the older oriental civilizations and the economic strength of the great commercial centres of Egypt and western Asia. Later, the loss of the western provinces to Germanic invaders hastened the trend. Simultaneously the great Persian revival under the Sasanians forced Rome to concentrate its efforts on defence of its eastern frontier. After Justinian, the west was neglected, the Roman empire became an eastern, Greek-speaking dominion. The change is conventionally placed in the reign of Heraclius (610–641). From this time it is customary to speak of a Byzantine rather than a Roman empire.

Heraclius brought the long contest with Persia to a victorious close at Nineveh (628), but almost immediately was confronted by an even more redoubtable foe: Islam. The struggle with Islam and with the Slavs, pressing against the European frontier in the Balkans, now became the dominant fact in Byzantine history. What is remarkable is Byzantine resilience. To meet the Arab threat, Asia Minor was reorganized into military districts, or 'themes', manned by a peasant militia. After two long Arab sieges of Constantinople had been repelled (674–8, 717–8), the new Macedonian dynasty (867–1056) launched a vigorous counter-offensive. By the death of Basil II (976–1025) the frontiers had been pushed back almost to their earlier limits. The Arabs were driven back to Jerusalem (976), and Bulgaria was finally reduced to a group of Christian provinces. Even later Manuel I (1143–80) still planned to recover the former Byzantine territories in Italy. But constant war imposed heavy financial strains, as well as profound and debilitating social change, and in spite of phases of aggressive counter-offensive and expansion, the frontiers steadily shrank.

After Basil I, the decisive fact was the appearance of a new foe, the Seljuk Turks. The crushing Seljuk victory at Manzikert (1071) induced Alexios I (1081–1118) to call on the west for help, thus initiating the sequence of events that led to the First Crusade. In

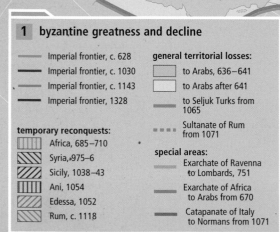

1 byzantine greatness and decline

——	Imperial frontier, c. 628
——	Imperial frontier, c. 1030
——	Imperial frontier, c. 1143
——	Imperial frontier, 1328

temporary reconquests:

- Africa, 685–710
- Syria, 975–6
- Sicily, 1038–43
- Ani, 1054
- Edessa, 1052
- Rum, c. 1118

general territorial losses:

- to Arabs, 636–641
- to Arabs after 641
- to Seljuk Turks from 1065
- Sultanate of Rum from 1071

special areas:

- Exarchate of Ravenna to Lombards, 751
- Exarchate of Africa to Arabs from 670
- Catapanate of Italy to Normans from 1071

1 In 641 the old Roman frontiers which Heraclius had largely inherited were everywhere under attack. They retreated, almost without interruption, until the mid-9th century (map right), but then re-expanded, reaching their greatest extent around 1030. The final boundary shows them in 1328, at the accession of the emperor Andronicus III.

retrospect, it was a disastrous move. The Franks were less concerned to aid Byzantium than to set up their own principalities in Palestine and Asia Minor. The Normans, by now in control of Sicily and Byzantine Italy, were greedy for Byzantine territory in the Morea (Peloponnese) and further east. The Italian cities, Venice to the fore, were striving to engross the oriental trade. The outcome, after a century of vicissitudes, was the Fourth Crusade (1202–4), the conquest and pillage of Constantinople, the partition of the Byzantine empire, and the establishment in its place of a Latin empire. But the Latin empire proved short-lived. The Greek-speaking population resented it, and a new dynasty, the Palaeologi, restored the Greek empire in 1261.

It was, nevertheless, only a shadow of the former Byzantine empire; and when a new Turkish people, the Ottomans, established itself in Anatolia, and then, outflanking Constantinople, advanced into Byzantium's European territories, its fate was sealed . The rest of the story is an epilogue, ending with the fall of Constantinople in 1453. Nevertheless the story of Byzantium is not without greatness and lasting achievements. For centuries it was ahead of the west in government and in the arts of civilization. It also passed on its culture and its religion to the Balkan peoples and to Russia. 'Two Romes have fallen,' a Russian monk wrote shortly after 1453, 'but the third is standing, and there shall be no fourth.' He was speaking of Moscow. Russia, gradually consolidated under its Varangian rulers and their Muscovite successors, now emerged as heir to the Byzantine inheritance. This was to be a fact of lasting importance in world history.

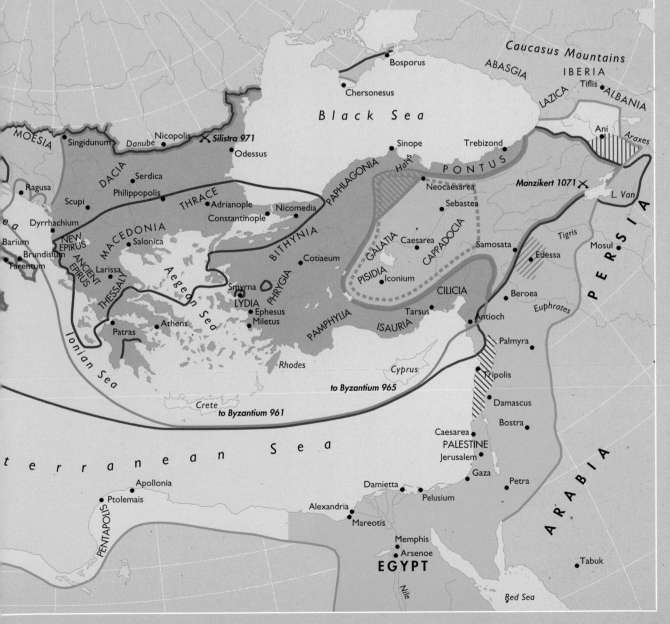

early **russia**

Three factors shaped the early history of Russia: the movement eastward of Slav tribal settlers; the impact of the Vikings or Varangians, seafaring raiders and traders from Sweden who entered northern Russia *c.* 850 and imposed tribute on the neighbouring Slavs and Finns and the basic geography of the region, particularly the division between the forests of central and northern Russia and the treeless steppes of the south through which successive waves of invaders from Asia poured into Europe. Fierce Pechenegs controlled the fertile steppelands. To avoid them Slav colonists moved into central Russia, where they settled in the river basins, clearing the forests and living by agriculture, hunting, trapping and by the fur trade.

2 varangian russia, 862–1054

	Varangian territory, c.980
Ulichi	East Slav tribes
KHAZARS	Finno-Ugrian and Asiatic people
→	Varangian (Viking) trade routes
--->	Varangian raids on Constantinople, 907, 944
→	Svyatoslav's campaigns, 964-71
→	Pecheneg raids

At first the Slavs resisted the Varangians. But in 862 they called in 'Rurik the Viking' to restore order and protect them from Pecheneg raiders. Rurik occupied Novgorod, but the Varangians immediately pushed south to Smolensk and then along the Dnieper to Kiev (882). They thus controlled the trade route from the Baltic to the Black Sea. At the same time they imposed their rule over the Slav tribes on both sides of the river. It was nevertheless only a loose tributary overlordship, and it was not until the time of Vladimir I of Kiev (980–1015) that the tribal regions were welded together into a single state.

The reign of Vladimir's son, Yaroslav I (1019–54) was the high point of Kievan Russia. Converted to Christianity under Vladimir and in close contact with Constantinople, Kiev ranked high among European cities. But the new state had grown too quickly and after 1054 its decline was rapid. Dynastic conflict was incessant, and the administration ineffective. At the same time the destruction of the Khazar empire by Svyatoslav (965) opened the way for a new wave of Asiatic nomads, the Polovtsy, who broke through the defences erected by Vladimir I and sacked Kiev in 1093. The result was a great exodus of peasants northwards to the region between the Oka and the Volga, where many new towns were founded including Vladimir, Suzdal, Rostov, Moscow and Tver. Novgorod-Seversk, and in the west, Galich and Vladimir-Volynsk broke away from Kiev. After 1125 the axis of Russian life shifted north and the state broke up into warring principalities, among which Vladimir-Suzdal was outstanding.

The final blow to the old order was the Mongol invasions, which fell upon the Volga region before turning south against Kiev which was sacked in 1240, while Novgorod was exposed simultaneously to German and Swedish attack. Mongol control was only indirect, but its results were far-reaching. Kievan Russia, already debilitated, disappeared for ever, and the way was open for the rise of Moscow.

Map labels

Ilmen Slavs · Novgorod · *Krivichi* · Volga · MUROMA · Bolgar 966 × · VOLGA BULGARS · Dvina · Oka · MORDVA · Radimichi · Smolensk · Don · Vyatichi · Ural · Dregovichi · *Severyane* · Elbe · Drevlyane · Chernigov · KHAZARS · Pripet · Polyane · Pecheneg siege 968 · Volga · Kiev · Pereyaslavl · Itil · Volynyane · Ulichi · Dnieper · Sarkel 965 × · Danube · Tivertsy · PECHENEGS · Caspian Sea · Prut · Dniester · Sea of Azov · MAGYARS · HUNGARY · Tmutarakan · 966-7 · Pereslavets · Dristov 971 × · Black Sea · Danube · BULGARIA · 970 · Constantinople

1 In 1054 there was still a unified Russian state, but by the early 13th century it had disintegrated. Southern centres, such as Kiev, were weakened by nomadic attack, while northern towns, such as Novgorod, Vladimir and Moscow, exploited their positions on river trade routes in the security of the forest. Novgorod established a vast fur-trading empire stretching to the Arctic and the Urals.

2 The first Russian state was established by the Vikings with the Dnieper as its axis (map above). It lay athwart the northern forest and the southern steppe. Kiev was a natural capital.

1 kievan russia, 964–1242

——	Kievan Russia, 1054	→	campaigns of Svyatoslav, 964–71
Yatvagi	tribes of the East Slavs	- - -	waterway trade routes
MARI	other peoples	⌇⌇⌇	defensive works built against nomads
→	movements of steppe nomads in the 11th century	♔	Russian principalities, c.1200

White Sea

SAMOYED

Pechora

PERM

YUGRA

NOVGOROD EMPIRE

CHUD

Mezen

Pinega

Northern Dvina

Onega

Vychegda

VYATKA TERRITORY

KARELA

L. Onega

Sukhona

MARI

Beloozero

Ves

Galich

Kama

Baltic Sea

Gulf of Finland

Staroyn

Ladoga

Neva

Volkhov

Vod

Ilmen

L. Ladoga

Yaroslavl

Rostov

Kostroma

Nizhniy Novgorod

ESTS

L. Peipus

Yuriev

Novgorod

L. Ilmen

VLADIMIR

-SUZDAL

Merya

Bolgar

966

Bilyar

Gulf of Riga

Riga

KURS

Pskov

Izborsk

Slavs

Torzhok

Tver

Pereyaslavl

Dmitrov

Suzdal

Vladimir

Klyazma

Suvar

LIVONIAN ORDER

Western Dvina

Kukeynoys

Gertsike

Polochanye

Toropets

Lovat

Moscow

Murom

Muroma

VOLGA BULGARIA

ZHMUD

TEUTONIC ORDER

LITVA

Polotsk

Vitebsk

SMOLENSK

Krivichi

Golyad

Kolomna

Ryazan

Mordva

POLOTSK

Orsha

Smolensk

Oka

Meshchera

Gorodno

Minsk

Kopys

Koselsk

Vyatichi

MUROM

-RYAZAN

Yatvagi

Nesvizh

Klechesk

TUROV

-PINSK

Radimichi

Bryansk

Novosil

Berestye

Drogochin

Rechitsa

Desna

Karachev

Pinsk

Turov

1024 ✕

NOVGOROD

-SEVERSK

Drevlyane

Listem

Lyubech

Novgorod-Severskiy

Kursk

Vruchy

Korosten

Chernigov

Rylsk

VLADIMIR-VOLYNSK

Volynyane

Kholm

Vladimir

Cherven

Belz

1036 ✕

Gorodets

Severyane

Kiev

Kiev

PEREYASLAV

Rodiya

Pereyaslavl

Donets

KIEV

Polyane

Poltava

Ros

Don

GALICH

Kamenets

Tiversy

Kolomyya

PECHENEGS

Bug

Dnieper

Y

P O L O V T S

Donets

TORKI

POLOVTSY

(in 1054)

965 ✕

965

Volga

966

Peremyshl

Terebovl

Galich

Belgorod

Oleshe

KHAZARS

Sarkel

SAKSINY

Te Khorvaty

Peresechen

Prut

KURS

Itil

HUNGARIAN KINGDOM

Carpathian Mts

Pereslavets

Dniester

Sea of Azov

966-7

Kuma

Caspian Sea

Dorostol

✕ 971

Sugdeya

Khersónes (Korsun)

Tmutarakan

Kuban

YASI

Dube

BULGARIA

70

971

Black Sea

KASOGI

61

the **mongol** empire

The Mongols, a primitive nomadic people from the depths of Asia, had tremendous influence of the course of world history. Few in number, but augmented by Turcoman auxiliaries, they threw themselves against the old centres of civilization in east and west. After overrunning the Ch'in empire in north China between 1211 and 1234, they defeated the Sung army and ruled over the whole of China from 1280 to 1367. They even launched seaborne expeditions against Java and Japan, though neither was successful. In the west the first victim was the Muslim empire of Khwarizm (1220), after which they turned against the Abbasid caliphate, sacking Baghdad in 1258. But the decisive Mameluke victory at Ain Jalut (1260) halted their advance in this direction. Meanwhile, they had thrown themselves against Christian Europe, overrunning the northern Russian principalities in 1237–38 and sacking Kiev in 1240, before advancing into Hungary and Poland and destroying a German–Polish army at Legnica in 1241.

The architect of these amazing victories was a certain Temujin, known to history as Genghis Khan, son of a Mongol chief, who united the different Mongol tribes under his leadership (1206) and subdued other neighbouring, mainly Turcoman, tribes, before turning against China in 1211. Genghis died in 1227, but his wars of conquest were continued by his sons and grandsons, among whom Ogedei, elected Great Khan in 1229, and Möngke, who succeeded in 1251, were outstanding. But the vast empire lacked coherence and stability, and the Mongols failed to develop appropriate institutions. Genghis himself divided his empire among his four sons, like earlier Frankish rulers in the west, and with similar results. Already on the death of Ogedei (1241), Genghis' grandson Batu, commander-in-chief in the west, withdrew his army from Poland to the base on the lower Volga, in order to take part in the choice of a successor. It never returned and western Europe was spared, though Russia remained a Mongol tributary for over two centuries. Finally, on the death of Möngke (1259), the brittle unity dissolved. Kublai (d. 1294) was elected Great Khan, but instead of a general overlordship, his authority was confined to the east, and the western khanates (Chagatai, Il-Khan and the Golden Horde) went their own way. By the 16th century only the eastern khanate survived: in Persia the Ilkhanids were displaced by a local Turcoman dynasty in 1353, and later the successors of the Golden Horde, which had broken up into a number of smaller khanates at the time of Tamerlane the Great, were mopped up by a resurgent Russia.

1 the mongol empire

- the Mongol empire by 1259
- campaigns under Genghis Khan
- campaigns of his successors
- Mongol incursions and limited Mongol control
- *OIROTS* Mongol tribes around 1220
- empire of Kublai Khan, 1260–94
- *CUMANS* other peoples

1 The Mongol empire was the greatest land empire in world history (map below). It was secured by the ruthless and brilliant cavalry armies of Genghis Khan. It stretched from Korea in the east to Poland in the west, from the Arctic in the north to Turkey and Persia in the south. Their field intelligence and signals enabled them to mount bewildering flank attacks and encirclements. Byzantium and Europe were saved by the death of Ogedei in 1241 and Japan by the storms (or kamikaze, sacred wind) that destroyed Kublai Khan's navy.

It was, paradoxically, Timur, or Tamerlane (1336–1405), traditionally the last great Mongol conqueror (though he was in fact a Turcoman from Transoxiana), whose victorious career initiated the decline. Timur's vast empire fell apart rapidly after his death while leading an expedition against China; but in the course of his conquests he destroyed the Chagatai khanate, which ceased to exist in 1405, and dislocated the Golden Horde. Henceforward the Mongols were under attack from all sides, increasingly at a disadvantage as the introduction of firearms weighed the balance on their adversaries' side. In the west, Russia absorbed the former territories of the Golden Horde. In the east, the Mongols threw back a major Chinese assault in 1449 and resumed their offensive under Altan Khan (1507–82); but in the end Mongolia itself was brought under Chinese dominion in 1696 by the new Ch'ing dynasty. Nevertheless the Mongol impact had lasting results. All the older civilizations were affected; faced by the Mongol challenge, their history took a new course.

unsuccessful expedition to Java 1292–3

1301 to 1639

The revival of Islam after 1300, and the great wave of Muslim expansion that followed, dominated the next four centuries, far more so than European expansion, which had only marginal effects before 1700. After 1354 the Christian west stood on the defensive, while the Turks conquered the whole of Europe east of the Adriatic and south of the Danube. The progress of Islam in the east was equally remarkable. By 1500 northern India was under Muslim rule, and most of the south after 1565 when the last surviving Hindu state, Vijayanagar, succumbed. It prevailed also in the oases of central Asia, in the outlying provinces of Ming China and was making rapid headway in Java.

This amazing revival was the more remarkable because in 1258, when the Mongols sacked Baghdad and overthrew the caliphate, the Muslim world was in disarray. The Seljuk sultanate had broken up after half a century, and only the Mamelukes of Egypt and Syria maintained any sort of political stability. Two factors transformed the situation. One was the revitalization of Islam itself under the impact of Sufi mysticism. The other was the infiltration, with or in the wake of the Mongols, of Turkic peoples from central Asia, who, after conversion and assimilation, became the spearhead of Muslim advance. It was they who, in 1206, set up the Delhi Sultanate, the leading Indian state until the appearance in 1526 of Babur, another warrior from inner Asia. In the west Turkish warriors settled around 1265 in north-west Anatolia, and here in 1301 their leader, Osman, founded a state which became the core of the future Ottoman empire. By 1354 the Turks had crossed the Dardanelles to Gallipoli, and their victory at Kosovo (1389) and repulse of a Christian counter-offensive at Nicopolis (1396) left them masters of the Balkans. Only the invasion of Timur and his destruction of the Turkish army at Ankara (1402) gave hard-pressed Byzantium respite. But the renewal of expansion under Murad II (1421–51) and Mehemmed II (1451–81) sealed its fate. In 1453 Constantinople fell, and Mehemmed went on to extend control over Moldavia, the Crimea and Trebizond, turning the Black Sea into an Ottoman lake.

By the time that Suleiman the Magnificent (1520–66) succeeded to the throne, the Ottoman empire was one of the world's leading powers, comparable with Ming China or Charles V's empire in the west. But now two other empires arose to share pre-eminence in the Muslim world. One was the Mughal empire, founded by Babur in 1526, but only consolidated by his grandson, Akbar (1556–1605). The other was Persia, which had been in a state of chaos ever since it was overrun by Timur. Here, in 1500, the leader of a Shi'a sect, Ismail Safavi, seized Tabriz, crowned himself shah as Ismail I (1500–24), and quickly reunited the country. Safavid Persia reached its peak under Abbas I (1587–1629), by which time the three Muslim empires controlled a wide belt of territory from the frontiers of Austria and Morocco to the borders of China, the foothills of the Himalayas and the Bay of Bengal. But their divisions and rivalries, particularly the clash between Sunni Turkey and Shi'a Persia, drove a wedge into the Muslim world, comparable to the conflict between Catholics and Protestants in western Europe. Shi'ism had originated centuries earlier over the question of the true succession to the Prophet Mohammed; but wider issues, religious and political, were involved. In Persia a resurgent nationalism certainly played a part. The Safavids were the first native Persian dynasty since Sasanian times, and Ismail I's decision to make Shi'ism the Persian state religion was a challenge to the Sunni Turkish sultan. The Ottoman reaction was swift. In 1514 Ismail's armies were defeated at Çaldiran, and in 1516–17 the Ottomans captured Syria and Egypt from the Mamelukes. These successes enabled Suleiman to resume the Ottoman advance in Europe. After the battle of Mohács (1526) Hungary was overrun and Vienna was besieged (1529). But Persia remained a thorn in the Ottoman side. The long wars against the Safavids (1534–35, 1554–55, 1577–90, 1603–19) were not the only reason for the Muslim decline which became apparent after 1560, but they certainly hastened it. This was a great age of Islamic art and architecture, particularly in Persia and India. But in a changing world Islam remained static. All three Muslim empires were essentially land-based; but now hegemony was passing to the sea, and to the peoples on the fringe – the Dutch, the French, the English – who knew how to master and exploit it.

1 the rise of the ottoman empire

	probable extent of Ottoman state, c. 1300
-----	conquests of Osman, c. 1300–26
———	conquests of Orkhan, 1326–62
———	conquests of Murad I, 1362–89
TEKE *1390*	absorbed Emirates with date of first absorption
———	conquests of Bayezid, 1389–1402
✕	major battles
1398	dates of Ottoman control
	Venetian territories, 1510
◉	successive centres of Ottoman state, with dates of conquest
———	reduced frontiers of Ottoman state after Tamerlane's invasion and civil war of 1403–13
●	Emirates restored by Tamerlane, 1402
1427	final reincorporation into Ottoman empire
———	boundary of Ottoman state at the accession of Mehmed II, 1451
	vassal states, 1512
	Ottoman empire, 1512
———	western frontiers of Safavid state, c. 1512 including tributary states
———	Ottoman sphere of influence, c. 1520

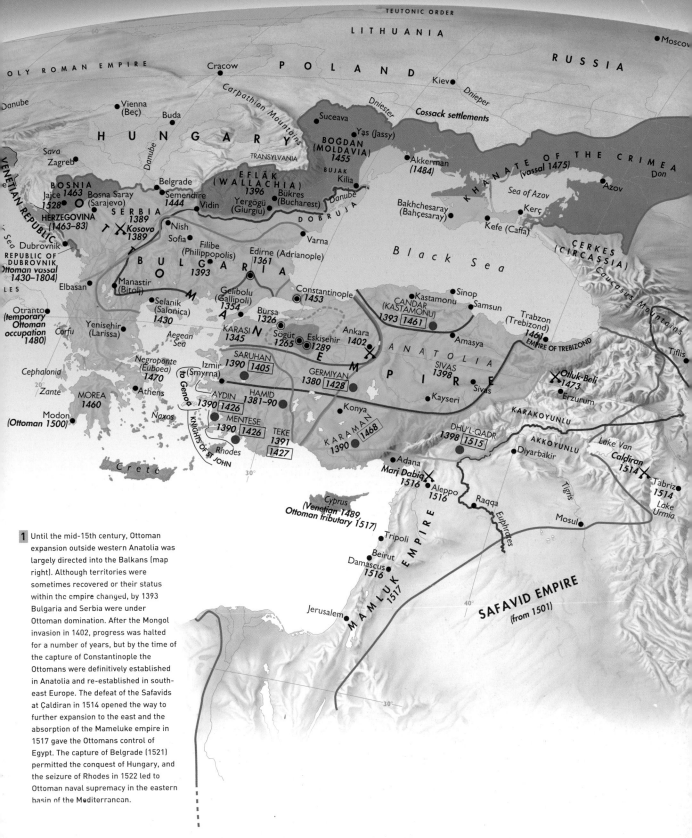

1 Until the mid-15th century, Ottoman expansion outside western Anatolia was largely directed into the Balkans (map right). Although territories were sometimes recovered or their status within the empire changed, by 1393 Bulgaria and Serbia were under Ottoman domination. After the Mongol invasion in 1402, progress was halted for a number of years, but by the time of the capture of Constantinople the Ottomans were definitively established in Anatolia and re-established in south-east Europe. The defeat of the Safavids at Çaldiran in 1514 opened the way to further expansion to the east and the absorption of the Mameluke empire in 1517 gave the Ottomans control of Egypt. The capture of Belgrade (1521) permitted the conquest of Hungary, and the seizure of Rhodes in 1522 led to Ottoman naval supremacy in the eastern basin of the Mediterranean.

china and its neighbours

The recovery of China from the barbarian invasions of the fourth and fifth centuries was the work of the Sui dynasty (581–617). But it was the T'ang (618–907) who ushered in one of the great ages of Chinese history. Under the T'ang and their successors, the Sung (960–1279), China attained a level of prosperity, social stability and civilization far ahead of contemporary Europe; and it was only another wave of invasion from inner-Asia, this time the Mongols, that brought this era of well-being to a temporary halt. During the period of Mongol domination (1280–1368) much of the land was devastated, particularly in the north, and the population, which in 1280 probably topped 100 million, was reduced, by 1393, to 60 million. The Ming dynasty (1368–1644) reversed these setbacks and put China back on the course charted by its T'ang predecessors.

1 The Ming period began with the new regime consolidating its control in China and in the south-west, which the Mongols had incorporated into China for the first time (map right). The first half of the 15th century was one of rapid expansion – great sea voyages and invasions of Mongolia and of Annam. Thereafter China went on to the defensive, protected by vast armies along the rebuilt Great Wall. In the following century the Ming were beset by attacks from resurgent Mongols and Japanese-based pirates.

T'ang China was a centralized empire with a uniform administrative organization of prefectures, in which the old ruling aristocracy was replaced by officials recruited by an examination system which lasted into the 20th century. A massive movement of population into the fertile Yangtze valley and southern China produced large agricultural surpluses which stimulated trade and urban development. The T'ang also embarked on an ambitious programme of external expansion which carried them in the north-west to the Tarim Basin before they were halted by the Arabs at the Talas river in 751. By 649, the end of the reign of T'ai-tsung, 88 Asiatic peoples recognized Chinese overlordship. But the widespread military expeditions over-extended the empire's resources, many of the gains proved only temporary, and after 1127 even north China was lost and only recovered after the fall of the Mongol dynasty in 1386. Their successors, the Ming, also engaged in an active foreign policy, particularly against the Mongols in the north, but these ventures proved too costly and sparked off a series of rebellions which, coupled with external pressures from the Manchus in Liaotung and Japanese raiders, toppled the dynasty.

Military and political reverses did not impede the expansion of Chinese culture and political institutions to all her neighbouring states. Those most directly affected were Korea, under Chinese rule from 668 to 676 and a vassal state after 1392, Japan and South-East Asia, though in the latter region, where they came into contact with Indian and (from about AD 1300) Islamic influences, they were largely confined to north Vietnam. In South-East Asia the small temple states of the ninth to 12th centuries (Prambanan, Angkor, Pagan), established under Hindu and Buddhist influence, gave way after the 13th century to new political centres (Ava, Pegu, Phnom Penh), while in Vietnam, where Chinese attempts at reconquest failed, a new kingdom of Dai Viet arose. But behind the fluctuating political fortunes the outstanding fact was the formative influence of Hinduism, Buddhism and Confucianism; their assimilation defined the distinctive character of South-East Asian civilization.

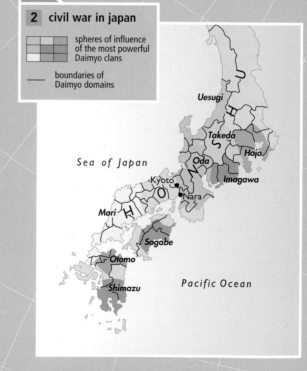

2 civil war in japan

spheres of influence of the most powerful Daimyo clans

— boundaries of Daimyo domains

Sea of Japan

Uesugi
Takeda
Hojo
Oda
Kyoto
Nara
Imagawa
Mori
Sogabe
Otomo
Shimazu

Pacific Ocean

2 In 1336, the second shogunate was established by Ashikaga Takauji after a brief return to direct imperial rule under Go-Daigo. His regime was forced to devolve ever more power to its own regional representatives, the shugo, a process which culminated in the Onin Wars, in which shugo factions led by the Yamana and Hosokawa families vied for control of the capital (map above). The factions soon proved unable to control the forces they had unleashed. The fighting led to the complete political disintegration of Japan.

In Japan Chinese influence was more direct. As early as AD 645 the whole administration had been remodelled on the pattern of T'ang China. The two capitals, Nara (710) and Kyoto (794), were copied from the T'ang capital of Changan, and Buddhism was introduced from China. But after 1192 the bureaucratic state was displaced by a feudalized society, until finally, between 1467 and 1590, the country broke up into a series of warring Daimyo clans. It was the work of Oda Nobunaga (1534–82) and Hideyoshi Toyotomi (1535–98) to bring the anarchy under control, and prepare the way for the Tokugawa shogunate which gave Japan 250 years of internal peace and prosperity until, in the middle of the 19th century the western powers forced Japan into the modern world.

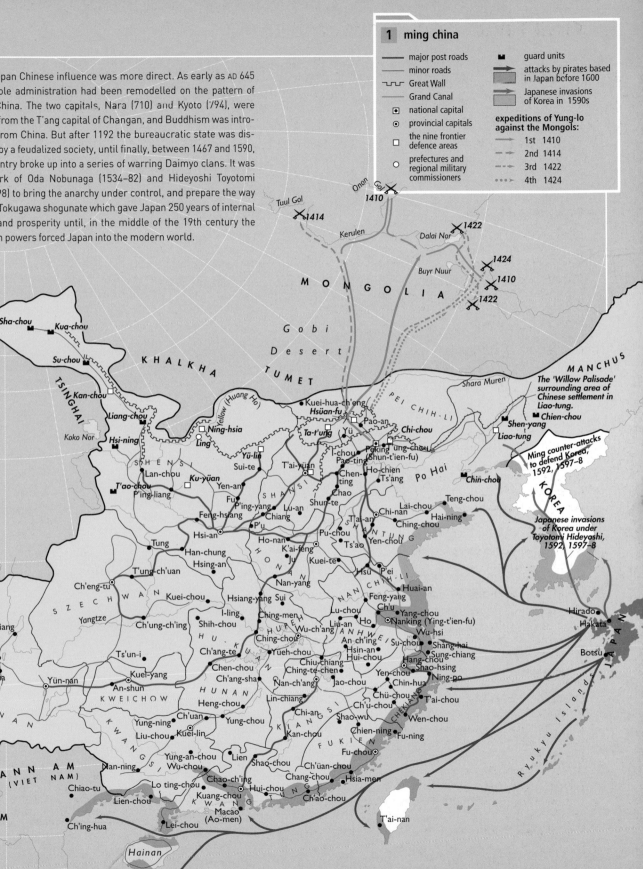

major post roads
minor roads
Great Wall
Grand Canal
national capital
provincial capitals
the nine frontier defence areas
prefectures and regional military commissioners

guard units
attacks by pirates based in Japan before 1600
Japanese invasions of Korea in 1590s

expeditions of Yung-lo against the Mongols:
1st 1410
2nd 1414
3rd 1422
4th 1424

Two features characterized the period following the Viking and Magyar invasions in northern and western Europe; the emergence of settled states and the spread of Christianity. The two went hand in hand.

Both in Scandinavia and in the Slavonic east the Christian church, introduced in Denmark by Harold Bluetooth in 965, in Norway by Olaf Tryggveson (995–1000), in Bohemia by Boleslaw II (967–99), and in Poland by Miesko I (960–92), contributed substantially to political cohesion. The rise of powerful kingdoms in Poland and Denmark was also in part a response to German pressure. In Poland the Piást dynasty united the tribes of Great (or northern) Poland, Boleslaw Chrobry (992–1025) not only added Little Poland, Silesia and Lausitz but also temporarily Bohemia and Moravia. In Denmark Harold Bluetooth (940–86) defended Slesvig from German attack, strengthening and extending the fortified Danevirke. In Norway and Sweden development was hampered by formidable geographical obstacles. Under Sweyn I, who also became king of England in 1013, both countries were under Danish control; and Sweyn's son Canute the Great (1014–35) ruled a great but short-lived Anglo–Scandinavian empire. Following an interlude under Edward the Confessor (1042–66) England passed under Norman rule. Norway achieved independence and was united under Magnus the Good (1033–47). Sweden (except for the southern provinces which remained under Danish rule) was welded together by the kings of Uppland, and Denmark itself settled down within its frontiers after the death of Sweyn II (1047–74).

Nevertheless, all countries were plagued by dynastic conflict and aristocratic resistance. In Poland Boleslaw Chrobry's ambitious foreign policy provoked a sharp reaction after his death. In England William the Conqueror was faced by baronial unrest as early as 1074. But it was France that suffered most from feudal disruption. The Capetian kings, who displaced the Carolingians in 987, were confined to the Ile de France, and even here royal authority was insecure until the reign of Louis VI (1108–37). Even then the Capetians lagged behind the feudal princes. The continental possessions of Henry II of England (the so-called Angevin Empire) far outmatched the French royal domain. When Philip Augustus (1180–1223) conquered Normandy (1204) and the Angevin Empire collapsed, English rule was confined to Gascony, and the Capetians embarked on a policy of expansion which carried them to the Mediterranean by 1229.

In England expansion had begun on the morrow of the Conquest when Norman barons invaded Wales and set up extensive marcher lordships. A century later they moved on to Ireland. By 1250, two-thirds of the country had been occupied, but Ireland remained divided and rebellious. So also did Wales which had seen a remarkable national resurgence under Llewellyn the Great (1197–1240). But Edward I (1272–1307) would not brook Welsh independence. After a first campaign (1276), followed by systematic castle building to enforce English control, a second campaign in 1283 placed the principality directly under royal administration in 1284. Edward's attempt in 1296 to repeat the process in Scotland was a costly failure, culminating in the English defeat at Bannockburn in 1314. Like his French contemporary, Philip the Fair (1285–1314), defeated by the Flemings in 1302, Edward had over-reached himself. The great baronial families, still firmly ensconced, forced him in 1297 to confirm the charters wrested from King John in 1215. It was a prelude to the aristocratic reaction and the setbacks of the 14th century.

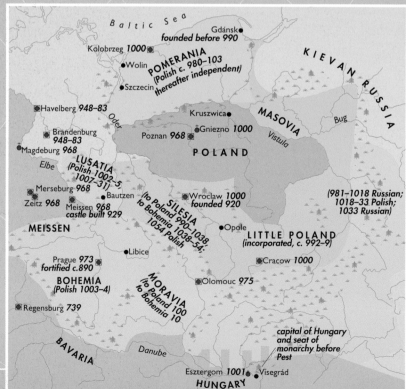

2 poland under boleslaw chrobry

	Polish territory from 960
	lands added by Bolesław Chrobry, 992–1025
	lands temporarily under Polish occupation
	Hungarian territory
	German territory
⊙	bishopric
⊙	archbishopric
1000	date of foundation of bishopric
	wasteland (forest and swamp)

1 the growth of the french and english monarchies

England, Scotland, Wales and Ireland
- ▬▬ boundary of England and Scotland, 1157
- land claimed by Scotland, 1139–57
- English Marcher lordships in Wales
- Principality of Wales, 1284
- Norman conquests in Ireland, 1171–1215
- Norman conquests in Ireland, 1215–1307
- Irish lands, 1307

France
- French royal domain in 987
- French royal domain at death of Louis VII in 1180
- areas dependent on French monarchy in 1180
- English possessions in France in 1259
- additions to French royal domain before death of Louis IX in 1270
- additions before death of Philip IV in 1314
- additions before death of Charles IV in 1328

1 The institutional strength of monarchy, developing in the 12th century, expanded rapidly in the 13th century. In France the kings extended the extent of their control from a tiny 10th-century royal domain around Paris and Orléans. By 1300 western kings, like their early medieval predecessors, were acknowledged executors of effective public authority.

2 After the unification of the tribes of Great (northern) Poland under Mieszko I, his son Boleslaw Chrobry ('the Brave') attempted to carve out a larger kingdom. Most of the gains were temporary and involved long debilitating wars on all frontiers; but Little Poland, centred on Cracow, was permanently acquired, and became the royal residence under Casimir I (1038–58).

69

the medieval **german** empire

Germany, or the eastern half of the Frankish empire, was the first country in Europe to recover from the setbacks of the ninth-century invasions. This fact assured its predominance for upward of three centuries. German rulers never sought to assert control over the West Frankish lands, but, as heirs to the Carolingians, they claimed the imperial title and the right to rule over Italy and the lands of the former 'Middle Kingdom'. Germany's control of the Alpine passes between Lombardy and the Rhinelands assured not only its political preponderance but also gave it a leading place in the cultural exchange between Mediterranean and northern Europe.

There was, at first, no sense of a common German, or East Frankish, identity, and the effective control of the first German ruler, Henry I of Saxony (919–936), scarcely extended beyond Saxony and Franconia. But his son, Otto I (936–973), brought the other German duchies under royal control. Also, by defeating the Magyars at the battle of Lechfeld (955), he freed Germany from external threats and was able, in 951 and 961, to intervene effectively in Italy. His coronation as emperor (962) sealed the historic connection between Germany and Italy. As heir to the Carolingian tradition, he also inaugurated a Christian drive against the pagan Slavs on the eastern frontier. But the great Slav revolt of 983 halted this advance until the 12th century, and German efforts were concentrated instead on the south and south-west. The result, in 1034, was the addition of Burgundy to the imperial domains.

In spite of these successes, aristocratic resistance to royal centralization was never overcome, and an opportunity to renew it came in 1075, when the outbreak of conflict between the emperor Henry IV (1056–1106) and the papacy, which saw imperial power in Italy as a threat to its independence, played into the German princes' hands. The ensuing civil war (1076–1122) was a turning point in German history. Although the monarchy emerged successful, its position was permanently weakened. German power was apparently restored during the reign of Frederick I (1152–1190), but it depended increasingly on the riches of Italy, and this embroiled Frederick not only with the papacy but also with the Italian cities. The marriage of his son,

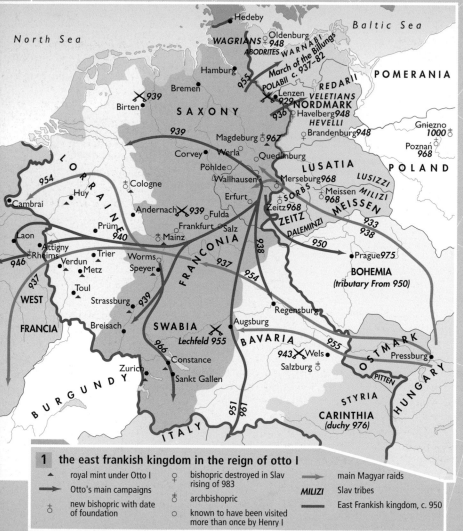

1 Otto I established a firm grip on the East Frankish lands (map left). After the ducal revolts of 938–9 he was able to exercise power even in the more prosperous south and west. Magyar raids were halted. The drive eastward against the Slavs was normally left to the Margraves, while Otto himself ranged more widely.

2 At the height of their power, the Emperors held sway over territories stretching from the Baltic to Sicily (map right). Within these extended frontiers they faced the German princes, the growing wealth and independence of the north Italian towns of the Lombard League and the papacy at its most aggressive.

1 the east frankish kingdom in the reign of otto I

- ▲ royal mint under Otto I
- → Otto's main campaigns
- ⚲ new bishopric with date of foundation
- ⚲ bishopric destroyed in Slav rising of 983
- ☦ archbishopric
- ○ known to have been visited more than once by Henry I
- → main Magyar raids
- *MILIZI* Slav tribes
- ━━ East Frankish kingdom, c. 950

North Sea

Baltic Sea

HOLSTEIN

✕ Bornhöved 1227

Hamburg · Lübeck · Schwerin · Stettin · Cammin · Gdańsk (Danzig)

Bremen · Lüneburg · POMERANIA · Gniezno · Poznań

SAXONY · ALTMARK DUCHY OF BRUNSWICK (after 1235) · Havelberg · Brandenburg · LUSATIA

Utrecht · Münster · DUCHY OF WESTPHALIA (after 1180) · Paderborn · Magdeburg · Goslar · Meissen · SILESIA · Wrocław (Breslau)

LOWER LORRAINE · Tiel · Nymwegen · Dortmund · THURINGIA · ANHALT · MEISSEN · Naumburg · Freiberg

uges · Ghent · Brussels · Aachen · Cologne · Hersfeld · DUCHY OF BRUNSWICK (after 1235) · Erfurt · Attenburg

BRABANT · Liège · KINGDOM · Fulda · Eger · Prague · KINGDOM OF BOHEMIA

✕ Bouvines 1214

HAINAUT · Cambrai · Stavelot · Mainz · Frankfurt · Bamberg · Würzburg · MORAVIA

Verdun · Trier · FRANCONIA · Gelnhausen · Nuremberg · Regensburg · AUSTRIA

Metz · Kaiserslautern · Worms · Speyer · OF · Vienna

Toul · Hagenau · Strassburg · Hohenstaufen · Ulm · Augsburg · BAVARIA · Munich · Salzburg · STYRIA · Semmering

UPPER LORRAINE · ALSACE · SWABIA · GERMANY

Besançon · Basel · Constance · Zurich · Brenner · TYROL · Brixen · CARINTHIA · Pontebba

BURGUNDY · Septimer · Bozen

Fribourg · St Gotthard · Trient · FRIULI · Aquileia · CARNIOLA

Lyons · St Bernard · Como · Bergamo · VERONA · Vicenza · Treviso

KINGDOM · Mont Cenis · Novara · Milan · Brescia · Padua · Venice · VENETIAN TERRITORIES

Turin · Vercelli · Lodi · Crema · Verona · Mantua

OF · SAVOY · Asti · Pavia · Piacenza · Cremona · Ferrara

Alessandria · Tortona · Parma · Reggio · Modena · Ravenna

ARLES · LOMBARDY · Canossa · Bologna · Rimini · expansion of Papal States under Innocent III

Avignon · Genoa · Imola · Faenza

Arles · KINGDOM · Pistoia · Lucca · Pisa · Florence · Arezzo · Ancona

PROVENCE · OF · ITALY · Siena · TUSCANY · Perugia · Assisi · Spoleto

Marseilles · Orvieto · Viterbo · Rieti · ✕ Tagliacozzo 1268

PAPAL PATRIMONY · Tivoli · Tusculum · 1190 · Apricena · Lucera

Rome · Anagni · San Germano 1193 · Foggia · Troia · Barletta

Ostia · 1191–3 · Benevento 1266 · Bari

Gaeta · Capua · 1194 · Melfi

Naples · Salerno · Amalfi · KINGDOM · Brindisi · Taranto · Lecce

Cosenza

OF

Monreale · Palermo · Messina · Reggio

Trapani · Cefalù · Catania

SICILY · Syracuse

2 the german empire to 1250

- eastward spread of German peasant settlement, 12th century
- German settlement, 1200–1250
- • city with over 10,000 inhabitants
- ⊙ member of Lombard Leagues of 1167 and 1226
- ◗ member of 1167 League only
- ◖ member of 1226 League only
- — main royal routes
- → German invasions, 1190–94
- ⇢ Henry VI's Genoese and Pisan fleet, 1194
- ⌂ main Hohenstaufen palaces and castles
- ▲ monasteries

Henry VI, with Constance, the heiress of Sicily (1186), held out new possibilities. But the prospect of the union of Sicily and the empire alarmed the papacy, which saw itself being encircled and led to the final struggle between Frederick II (1212–1250) and Pope Innocent IV (1243–1254).

Meanwhile Germany was being overtaken by the western monarchies. The empire under Frederick II was still the most imposing political body in Europe, but by 1200 Paris was the intellectual and cultural centre of Europe, and by comparison with England and Sicily Germany's financial organization was antiquated. Eastward expansion had begun again after 1138. It added two-thirds to the German territories and shifted the seat of power from Rhine to Elbe. But the beneficiaries were the princes on the eastern frontier, not the monarchy. Later, the Teutonic Knights conquered pagan Prussia, but within the empire the tendency was to fragmentation rather than expansion, and gains in the east were offset by loss of control over Italy which now went its own way. In default of royal authority local leagues were formed to resist princely encroachments and to preserve the peace. The most famous and enduring was the Swiss Confederation, formed in 1291. The Golden Bull of 1356, formally recognizing the autonomy of the princes, marked the beginning of a new era in German history; but the age of German preponderance in Europe had already ended a century earlier.

After the rise and consolidation of national monarchies in Spain, France and England in the 13th century, the 14th century was a period of setbacks on all fronts in western Europe. In part, this may be attributed to a sudden climatic deterioration (the onset of the 'little ice age') which brought to an end the agricultural boom that had been virtually continuous since 1150.

Already in 1315–17 Europe had experienced a 'great famine', and the weakening of human powers of resistance induced by inadequate nourishment may have been one factor accounting for the rapid spread of the Black Death, or bubonic plague, which first appeared in the Crimea in 1346 and spread from there first by ship to Italy and then to the west. But there were also other factors. All the western monarchies had over-extended themselves financially, and the economic setback accentuated their difficulties. Philip IV's unsuccessful attempts to subdue Flanders played after his death (1314) into the hands of the aristocracy; so also did the involvement of Catalonia in Italy after the death of James II (1285–1327); and in England the attempt to subdue Scotland proved to be a running sore. Ireland also virtually went its own way until Tudor times, and Wales, conquered but not subdued by Edward I, had a great national revival under Owain Glyndwr (1400–1409). Germany broke apart into rival principalities after the extermination of the Hohenstaufen dynasty, and Italy went the same way once Hohenstaufen rule was removed, breaking up into a number of local lordships or *signorie*. In the end, even the Catholic church was affected by the economic and fiscal stringency. From 1378 to 1417 it was divided by schism, which undermined its authority, while its financial extortions gave impetus to the anti-papal, reformatory movements of Hus in Bohemia and Wyclif in England.

Eastern Europe, on the other hand, was in process of recovery from the Mongol incursions of the 13th century, Bohemia under Charles IV (1333–78) Poland under Casimir III (1339–70) and Hungary under Louis the Great

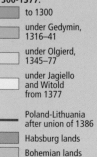

1 famine, plague and popular unrest

1346	end 1349	
1347	1350	
mid-1348	c. 1351	
end 1348	c. 1353	
mid-1349	little or no plague mortality	

social unrest

areas of disturbance during Peasants' Revolt in England, 1381

● centre of urban revolt

rural uprisings

⊗ defeat of lower orders in battle

religious unrest

spread of Lollardy in England to death of Richard II, 1399

area of Hussite influence

■ Hussite centre

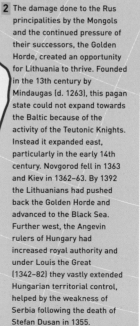

2 The damage done to the Rus principalities by the Mongols and the continued pressure of their successors, the Golden Horde, created an opportunity for Lithuania to thrive. Founded in the 13th century by Mindaugas (d. 1263), this pagan state could not expand towards the Baltic because of the activity of the Teutonic Knights. Instead it expanded east, particularly in the early 14th century. Novgorod fell in 1363 and Kiev in 1362–63. By 1392 the Lithuanians had pushed back the Golden Horde and advanced to the Black Sea. Further west, the Angevin rulers of Hungary had increased royal authority and under Louis the Great (1342–82) they vastly extended Hungarian territorial control, helped by the weakness of Serbia following the death of Stefan Dusan in 1355.

2 eastern europe 1278–1389

growth of Lithuania, 1300-1377:

to 1300

under Gedymin, 1316–41

under Olgierd, 1345–77

under Jagiello and Witold from 1377

━━ Poland-Lithuania after union of 1386

Habsburg lands

Bohemian lands

1 Inadequately financed and weakened by war and internal dissension, western Europe underwent severe strains in the 14th century (map above). Recession, compounded by famine and pestilence, led to conflicts in almost all countries between the autocracy and the urban oligarchies on the one hand and the peasants and urban workers on the other. The effect of the Black Death was particularly severe. After 1346, a plague of Asiatic origin spread from the south east across virtually all of Europe, wiping out between a quarter and a half of the population. As well as economic and social turmoil, Europe saw religious dissent, too, with the Lollard movement in England and the Hussites in Bohemia.

(1342–82); all made rapid strides, helped perhaps by the fact that the impact of the Black Death was less severe in the east than in the west, and also by exploitation of their natural resources, such as the silver mines of Kutna Hora. In the west, on the other hand, the set-back was lasting. Two English kings, Edward II (1327) and Richard II (1399) were murdered. The Hundred Years' War between England and France resulted in widespread devastation. Overall, the Black Death reduced the population of Europe by roughly one-third. Further, the misery caused by economic recession and military ravages sparked off a series of popular risings, the Jacquerie in France and the Peasants' Revolt in England being best known, although urban discontent – the weavers' rising in Flanders under Artevelde, or the Ciompi in Florence – was no less significant in the long run. It was not until after c.1450 that recovery began; but even then undercurrents of popular resentment persisted, which found their outlet in the Peasants' War of 1524–25 and the Messianic movements of the Reformation.

c. 1000 to 1500

Trading connections had been remarkably widespread during late antiquity, and they had brought with them important cultural interchanges. The barbarian invasions, beginning *c.* 300 AD and lasting some 200 years, had disastrous results. The Silk Route from Rome to China was cut, and even within the Roman empire communications broke down. There was a short-lived recrudescence in Carolingian times, involving trade in the North Sea, centred on Dorestad and Quentovic; but it was only after *c.* 1000, with the restoration of relatively stable conditions, that trade picked up. In particular, the Italian cities, already in contact with the Near East, established connections with north-west Europe, where the fairs of Champagne were becoming clearing-houses for trade between Italy and the rising industrial centres of Flanders.

1 Before AD 1000 perhaps four-fifths of Europe north of the Alps and Pyrenees was covered by dense forest (map below). Over the next 200 years much of this was cleared to make land available for human settlement and agriculture. Even in the Rhineland the highlands bounding the river were still largely uninhabited. Forests such as the Ardennes and the Eifel constituted an almost impenetrable barrier to communications. Certain areas – Flanders, Lombardy and the Rhine valley – became centres of commerce from 1100. But it was only after 1150 that Italian merchants regularly attended the Champagne fairs (Troyes, Provins, Lagny), buying Flemish cloths in exchange for Oriental goods.

The consolidation of the German empire under the Saxon and Salian dynasties gave impetus to trade from west to east, along a line running from the Low Countries via Cologne to Magdeburg, and along the Main valley to Bamberg and Prague. German control of the Alpine passes, particularly after the opening of the Septimer and St. Gotthard passes during the Hohenstaufen period, stimulated trade with Italy, which contributed to the growing wealth of the south German cities, among them Augsburg, which later became a major commercial and financial centre after the rise of the Fugger merchant family in the 15th century. In the north the most important city was Lübeck (founded 1158), the key point controlling trade between the North Sea and the Baltic, and the seat of the Hanseatic League, an association of German merchants which took shape in 1259 and was formally constituted in 1358. With its far-flung network of associated cities, and with branches in London, Bruges and Bergen, the Hansa dominated the trade of northern Europe in the 14th and 15th centuries. It also had connections with Venice and Genoa, the cities which dominated Mediterranean and Levantine commerce.

Levantine trade fell into two broad categories: the spice trade, in which Venice predominated, and the silk trade, largely in the hands of Genoa and its merchant colonies in Constantinople and at Kaffa, Tana and Trebizond. The latter profited greatly from the restoration of order and settled government in central Asia by the Mongols, which allowed a resumption of overland trade, and for a time

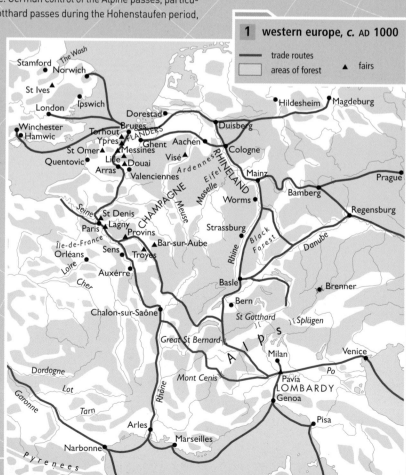

1 western europe, c. AD 1000

— trade routes
▢ areas of forest
▲ fairs

there was extensive east–west traffic, exemplified by the famous journeys of Marco Polo between 1271 and 1295. But the roads opened by the rise of the Mongol empire in the 13th century were closed by its decline in the mid-14th century. The important spice trade from Ormuz to the Black Sea was also badly affected; but the trade via the Red Sea and Alexandria to Venice continued without interruption until the Ottoman conquest of Egypt in 1517.

Spices were indispensable, easy to handle and highly profitable, and they were the staple of inter-continental trade in this period. Both Europe and China were dependent for supplies on the spice-producing regions of Asia, particularly the Moluccas and the Malay archipelago, and the resultant transactions, largely in the hands of Arab and Indian middlemen, created a complicated network of sea routes, hinging on Malacca, which stretched from the Red Sea and the Persian Gulf to the South China Sea. In the early 15th century, between 1405 and 1433, the Chinese sent seven expeditions through the Strait of Malacca to the Indian Ocean and beyond; but this enterprise ceased abruptly after 1440. Meanwhile, Portugal was probing down the west coast of Africa in search of gold; but later, when Genoa, which had lost its eastern markets after the fall of Constantinople in 1453, provided financial backing for the Portuguese ventures, the main objective became the search for an alternative route to the east, to cut out Genoa's rival, Venice. When the Portuguese reached India in 1498, and Columbus, despatched by Portugal's rival, Spain, reached America, a new era had begun. The 1,000-year-old pattern, centred on the Mediterranean, gave way to an Atlantic economy, and the whole economic and political balance in Europe shifted dramatically.

2 the economies of the world

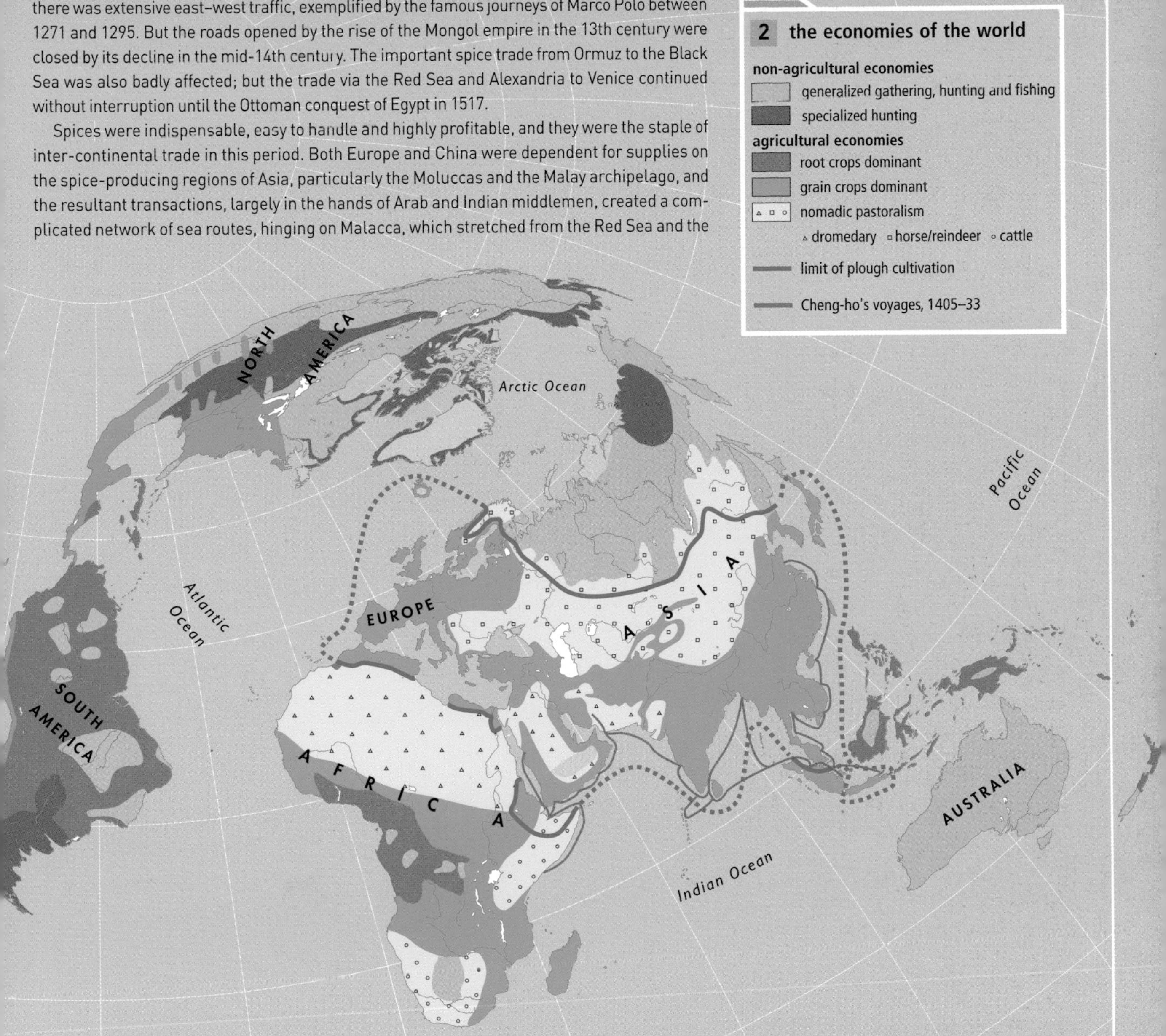

non-agricultural economies
generalized gathering, hunting and fishing
specialized hunting
agricultural economies
root crops dominant
grain crops dominant
nomadic pastoralism
dromedary
horse/reindeer
cattle
limit of plough cultivation
Cheng-ho's voyages, 1405–33
NORTH AMERICA
Arctic Ocean
Pacific Ocean
Atlantic Ocean
EUROPE
ASIA
SOUTH AMERICA
AFRICA
Indian Ocean
AUSTRALIA

2 In the 15th century, the bulk of the world's population was primarily concerned with the provision of food: gathering wild plants, herding domesticated animals or cultivation with hoe or plough. The map shows these divisions, and also the dominant civilizations, of which the richest and most populous by far was China, as they stood in the 16th century.

By the end of the first millennium AD great changes had taken place in Africa. The rise of a culture based on iron-working led to a large-scale displacement of Khoisan-speaking Bushmen and Hottentots by settled Bantu-speaking agriculturists and to the appearance of extensive states and empires based on trade.

In the south, Zimbabwe, with its monumental stone buildings, exported gold and copper to the Orient via the port of Sofala, and the impressive Kongo state on the west coast had an important trade in ivory. Further north, the Arab conquest of the Maghreb and the rise of the Almoravid and Almohad empires marked a watershed. The Arabs, great traders, developed and extended the trans-Saharan caravan routes, and there is no doubt that trade was an important factor in the development of the great empires that arose in the sub-Saharan savannah. The early history of Ghana (some 500 miles north-west of the modern state with the same name) precedes the Islamic era; but its successors, Mali and Songhay, owed much of their wealth and civilization, described in glowing terms by Arab travellers, to the Islamic impact. So also did the Kanem-Borne empire around Lake Chad, and after the 15th century, the city states of Hausaland . Arab merchant colonies also spread far down the east coast from Mogadishu to Kilwa. The staples of trade in all cases were gold, ivory and slaves. According to a conservative estimate, the trans-Saharan slave trade before the coming of the Europeans amounted to almost 5 million.

From the late 15th century large political units multiplied in Africa. In 1464 Sunni Ali became ruler of the Songhay people around Gao in the eastern Niger bend. Under Askia the Great (1493–1528), Songhay became a great empire, incorporating a number of important commercial cities, including Timbuktu and Jenne, which developed into centres of learning and Muslim piety. In the savannah and forest country to the south, trading communities gave rise to similar poilities. Well before 1500, Oyo and Benin had emerged in the woodlands to the west of the Niger delta, producing superb terracottas and bronzes.

The arrival of the Portuguese on the African coast and the building in 1448 of a first European fort and warehouse at Arguin, followed (1482) by a second at Elmina on the Gold Coast, had at first little impact on Africa. The immediate objective was to share directly in the gold trade, hitherto dominated by Muslim middlemen, and the slave trade was a secondary by-product. But with the development of sugar plantations in Brazil and later in the West Indies, the slave trade became a major source of profit, particularly after Dutch and British traders ousted the Portuguese. Along the length of the Gold and Slave Coasts, from Axim to the Niger Delta, fortified trading stations (or 'factories') were set up as bases for this trade, and the Portuguese continued to export slaves further south in Angola. Of some 15 million Africans shipped abroad between 1450 and 1870, some 90 per cent went to South America and the Caribbean, most of them between 1700 and 1800. The effects on Africa of this appalling trade in human beings are not easy to quantify. Furthermore, the loss of population was not evenly divided and some areas suffered disproportionately. Others profited from the trade. After the invasion and destruction of the great Songhay empire by Morocco in 1591, the forest states of Asante, Dahomey and Benin, having direct access to the Atlantic and to European trade, increased in importance and political power. The Europeans remained largely ignorant of the African interior, and their influence was limited. In the far south the Dutch were established in the Cape Colony; but, in a continental perspective, its extent was still minimal. In the north-east Islam was spreading; but the Christian kingdom of Ethiopia, despite a serious setback in the 1520s, still held its own. By 1800, with the exception of the Ottomans in the north (and even their power was more nominal than real), Africa remained independent of foreign control. Nevertheless, there is little sign that it was ready to meet the European challenge that developed in the 19th century. It was a world unto itself, but in no position to compete with the technological dynamism of the West.

1 Africa has few natural harbours south of the Sahara, so internal lines of communication for the passage of commerce and ideas proved more important than sea routes, with the exception of the Red Sea and parts of the coast of east Africa. In this respect the medieval history of Africa differed profoundly from that of Europe; the great empires of Africa which arose and flourished between 1000 and 1500 (map right) were mostly interior states often lying deep in the heart of the continent. Africa, unlike Europe, tended to develop inwards.

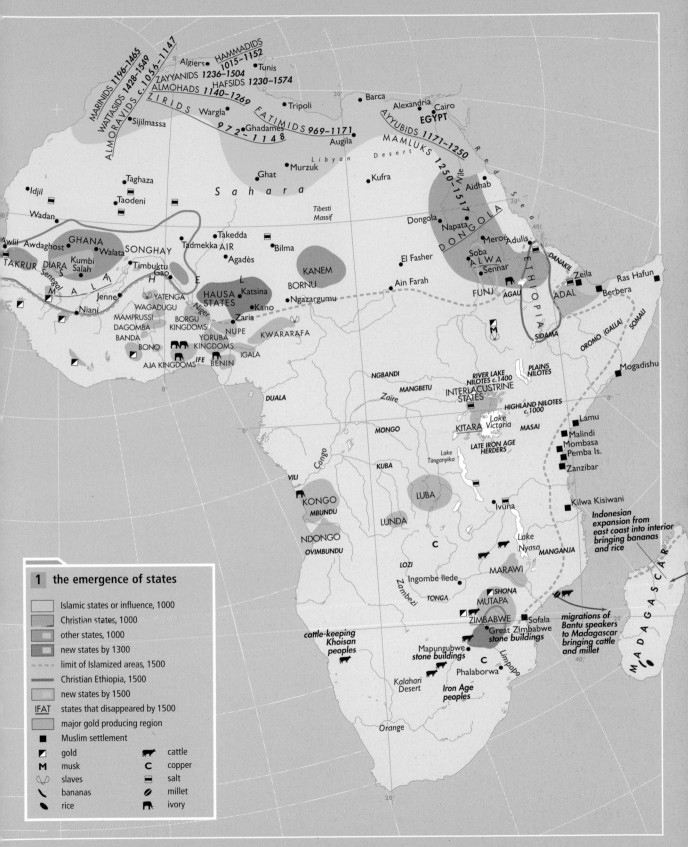

the emergence of states

- Islamic states or influence, 1000
- Christian states, 1000
- other states, 1000
- new states by 1300
- limit of Islamized areas, 1500
- Christian Ethiopia, 1500
- new states by 1500
- IFAT states that disappeared by 1500
- major gold producing region
- ■ Muslim settlement
- gold
- M musk
- slaves
- bananas
- rice
- cattle
- C copper
- salt
- millet
- ivory

MARINIDS 1196–1465
WATTASIDS 1428–1549
ALMORAVIDS c.1056–1147
HAMMADIDS 1015–1152
ZAYYANIDS 1236–1504
HAFSIDS 1230–1574
ALMOHADS 1140–1269
ZIRIDS 972–1148
FATIMIDS 969–1171
AYYUBIDS 1171–1250
MAMLUKS 1250–1517

Algiers
Tunis
Tripoli
Barca
Alexandria
Cairo
EGYPT
Wargla
Ghadames
Augila
Sijilmassa

Libyan Desert

Red Sea

Murzuk
Ghat
Kufra
Aidhab
Nile

S a h a r a

Idjil
Taghaza
Taodeni
Tibesti Massif
Dongola
Napata
Meroë Adulis

Wadan
Awlil Awdaghost
GHANA
Walata
SONGHAY
Takedda
AIR
Bilma
El Fasher
Soba
ALWA
Sennar
DANAKIL
Zeila

TAKRUR DIARA
Kumbi Salah
Senegal
Niger
Timbuktu
Gao
Tadmekka
Agadès
KANEM
BORNU
Ain Farah
FUNJ
AGAU
ETHIOPIA
ADAL
Berbera
Ras Hafun

MALI
Jenne
Niani
YATENGA
WAGADUGU
HAUSA STATES
Katsina
Kano
Zaria
Ngazargumu
SIDAMA
OROMO (GALLA)
SOMALI

MAMPRUSSI
DAGOMBA
BANDA
BONO
BORGU KINGDOMS
NUPE
IGALA
KWARARAFA
YORUBA KINGDOMS
AJA KINGDOMS IFE BENIN

Mogadishu

NGBANDI
MANGBETU
Zaire
DUALA
RIVER LAKE NILOTES c.1400
PLAINS NILOTES
INTERLACUSTRINE STATES
HIGHLAND NILOTES c.1000
Lamu
Malindi
Mombasa
Pemba Is.
Zanzibar

MONGO
KITARA
Lake Victoria
MASAI
LATE IRON AGE HERDERS

Congo
VILI
KUBA
Lake Tanganyika
LUBA
Ivuna
Kilwa Kisiwani

KONGO
MBUNDU
LUNDA
NDONGO
OVIMBUNDU

Indonesian expansion from east coast into interior bringing bananas and rice

LOZI
C
Lake Nyasa
MANGANJA
migrations of Bantu speakers to Madagascar bringing cattle and millet

Ingombe Ilede
Zambezi
TONGA
MARAWI
SHONA
MUTAPA
ZIMBABWE
Sofala
Great Zimbabwe stone buildings

cattle-keeping Khoisan peoples
Mapungubwe stone buildings
C
Phalaborwa
Limpopo

Kalahari Desert
Iron Age peoples

MADAGASCAR

Orange

77

america on the eve of european conquest

Two great and wealthy civilizations confronted the Spaniards when they arrived in America at the beginning of the 16th century: the Aztec empire in Mexico and the Inca empire in Peru. The former had a population of 10–12 million, the latter 6 million or possibly considerably more.

A few other centres of civilization existed, such as the Chibcha state in modern Colombia; but the remainder of the continent was sparsely inhabited (perhaps one million north of the Rio Grande and one million in the rest of South America) and divided among more than a thousand small tribal societies, with distinct, often unrelated languages. Few regions, particularly in the north, had reached the stage of settled agriculture.

The Aztec and Inca empires were different in character, and there is no evidence of any contact between them. The Aztecs, like the Toltecs who controlled much of Mexico in the 11th and 12th centuries, were raw warriors from the north who entered Mexico during the 13th century and settled on islands in Lake Texcoco, where c. 1325 they founded the town of Tenochtitlán, which was to become their capital. The Inca empire was created by one of the numerous tribes of Quechua stock inhabiting the central Andes, which established itself in the Cuzco valley in the 12th century. The expansion of both came late and only reached its full extent on the eve of the Spanish conquest. In the case of the Aztecs, the first step was to ally with the neighbouring tribes in Texcoco and Tlacopán against their overlords in Azcapotzalco, and then to turn against their allies. This aggressive policy began c. 1427 under Itzcoatl and was continued by Montezuma I. It reached its peak under Montezuma II (1502–20), when the Aztecs, in control of the greater part of Mexico, were beginning to enter Maya territory in Yucatán. Inca expansion began under the eighth emperor, Viracocha, and his son Pachacuti (1438–63), whose son Topa subdued the coastal civilization of Chimú (1470), and then, after his accession as emperor (1471), pushed south into Chile and northern Argentina, Huayna Capac (1493–1525) advanced north into modern Ecuador, where he founded a second capital at Quito. By now the Inca empire was some 200 miles wide and 2,500 miles long, held together by an impressive system of highways and post-stations, with relays of runners who conveyed imperial orders to all parts of the empire.

1 The Aztecs entered central Mexico from the north. In the course of the 15th century they built a large, tribute-based empire (map right) controlled from Tenochtitlán, their capital city, which was founded in the early 14th century. The gargantuan appetite of the Aztec empire for food, gold and sacrificial victims was the source alike of its strength and weakness, explaining both its tentacular reach and its unsustainable consumption. The descendants of the 'Classic Maya' civilization still controlled the Yucatán peninsula in 1535, although the 16 separate provinces were constantly at odds with each other over land rights.

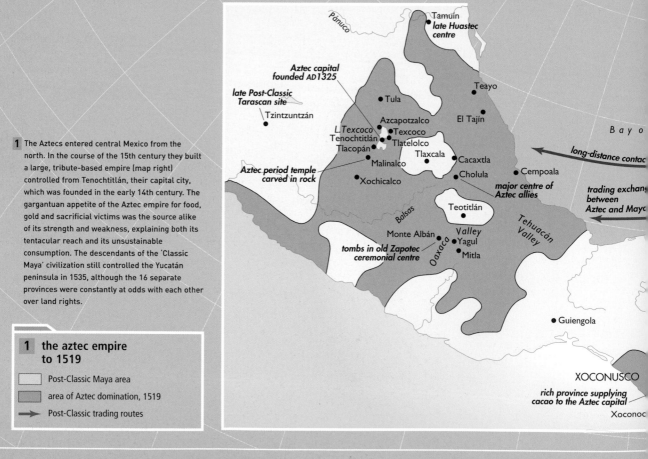

1 the aztec empire to 1519

Post-Classic Maya area

area of Aztec domination, 1519

→ Post-Classic trading routes

The Incas created a genuine imperial system, with an hereditary dynasty, a Quechua aristocracy and a highly trained bureaucracy. All land was state-owned, and there was a complex system of irrigation. The ordinary Indian spent nine months of the year working for the state, but in return was protected from famine by large state-owned food repositories and provided for in sickness and old age. The Aztec empire, on the other hand, rather like that of the Mongols in Europe, was essentially a harsh military dominion over vassal peoples, left to rule themselves on condition that they paid heavy tribute to Tenochtitlán in food, textiles, pottery and other goods, but increasingly in human beings for sacrifice to the Aztec gods. The number of sacrificial victims rose from 10,000 a year to 50,000 a year at the time of the Spanish conquest. This was certainly one reason why the Totonacs and Tlaxcalans welcomed the Spanish invaders of Mexico, and resentment against Inca oppression probably played a similar role in Peru. Neither empire was as stable as it seemed. Nevertheless, their collapse at the hands of small bands of adventurers (Cortés had only 600 men, a few small cannon, 13 muskets and 16 horses when he invaded Mexico in 1519, and Pizarro had only 180 men, 27 horses and two cannon, when he attacked the Inca empire in 1531) is not easily explained.

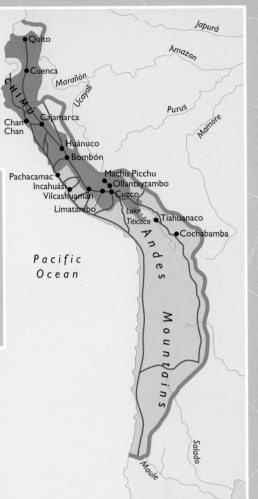

2 the inca empire, 1438–1525

■ under Pachacuti, 1438–63

■ added under Pachacuti and Topa Inca, 1463–71

□ added under Topa Inca, 1471–93

— territory under Huayna Capac, 1493–1525

— imperial roads

2 The Inca empire expanded rapidly in the 15th century (map above). From Cuzco, the Inca emperor exerted rigid control over this extensive territory by means of a highly trained bureaucracy, a state religion, a powerful army and an advanced communications network. The final expansion under Huayna Capac put the Inca world under great strain, however, and by the arrival of the Spanish conqueror Pizarro, in 1531, civil war had split the empire in two.

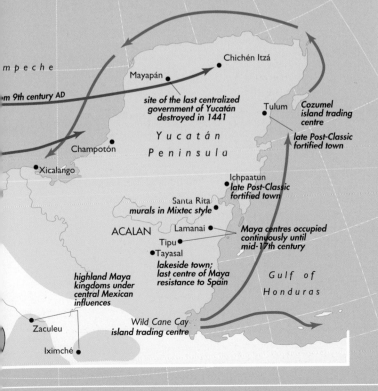

site of the last centralized government of Yucatán destroyed in 1441

Cozumel island trading centre

late Post-Classic fortified town

Yucatán Peninsula

late Post-Classic fortified town

murals in Mixtec style

Maya centres occupied continuously until mid-17th century

ACALAN

lakeside town; last centre of Maya resistance to Spain

highland Maya kingdoms under central Mexican influences

Gulf of Honduras

Wild Cane Cay island trading centre

european voyages of discovery

The European voyages of discovery opened a new era in world history. They began early in the 15th century when Portuguese navigators advanced southward, round the coast of Africa, in search of gold, slaves and spices, until in 1487 Dias and de Covilhã brought them into the Indian Ocean. Thenceforth voyages of exploration multiplied, particularly after the resurgence of Islam made the old route to the east via Alexandria and the Red Sea precarious.

While the Portuguese explored the eastern route to Asia, the Spaniards sailed west. Once in the Indian Ocean the former quickly reached their goal: Malabar (1498), Malacca (1511) and the Moluccas (1512). The Spanish search for a western route to the Spice Islands was less successful. Its unintended but momentous result was Columbus' discovery of the New world in 1492, followed by the Spanish conquest of America. But it was not until after 1524, when Verrazzano traced the coastline of North America as far north as Nova Scotia, that the existence of a new continent was generally accepted, and meanwhile the search for a western route to Asia continued, leading to extensive exploration of the Caribbean. Finally, in 1521, Magellan rounded South America, entered the Pacific, and reached the Philippines, but the route was too long and hazardous for commercial purposes. In 1557 the Portuguese occupied Macao, and after 1571 Spanish galleons traded between Manila and Acapulco in Mexico; but otherwise the exploration of the Pacific was delayed until the 18th century. This was the work of British, Dutch and Russians seeking a navigable passage via the Arctic, between the Atlantic and the Pacific, and hoping also to locate a hypothetical southern continent. Both proved illusory; but the result was the charting of New Zealand and the eastern coast of Australia, both, in a few years, opened to European colonization.

Meanwhile, England and France, unwilling to recognize the monopoly claimed by Spain and Portugal in the Treaty of Tordesillas (1494), had embarked on a series of voyages intended to reach Asia by a northern route. All of these proved abortive and were abandoned after 1632, but they resulted in the opening of North America to European settlement. The English, French and Dutch were also unwilling to abandon the profitable trade with South and South-East Asia to the Portuguese and Spaniards, and the later years of the 16th and first half of the 17th centuries saw a determined and ultimately successful effort to breach their privileged position. After 1500, direct sea contact was established between continents and regions which hitherto had gone their own way in isolation. It was necessarily a slow process, and for long the European footholds in Asia and Africa remained tenuous and precarious. But by the time of the death of the last great explorer, James Cook, in 1779, the worldwide network of relationships had been formed which characterizes the modern era and differentiates it from all preceding times.

VOYAGES INTENDED FOR ASIA BY NORTHWEST AND NORTHEAST ROUTE

19/Cabot 1497 (outward) re-discovered Newfoundland, first sighted by Norsemen 11th C.

20/Corte-Real 1500 re-discovered Greenland.

21/Verrazzano 1524 traced e. coast of N. America from (probably) 34°N to 47°N; revealed continental character of N. America.

22/Cartier 1534 and 1535 explored Strait of Belle Isle and St Lawrence as far as Montreal.

23/Willoughby and Chancellor 1553 rounded North Cape and reached Archangel.

24/Frobisher 1576 reached Frobisher Bay in Baffin Island, which he took for a 'strait'.

25/Davis 1587 explored w. coast of Greenland to the edge of the ice in 72°N.

26/Barents 1596–7 discovered Bear Island and Spitsbergen; wintered in Novaya Zemlya.

27/Hudson 1610 sailed through Hudson Strait to the s. extremity of Hudson Bay.

28/Button 1612 explored w. coast of Hudson Bay, concluded Bay landlocked on the w.

29/Baffin and Bylot 1616 explored whole coast of Baffin Bay; concluded no navigable nw. passage existed in that area.

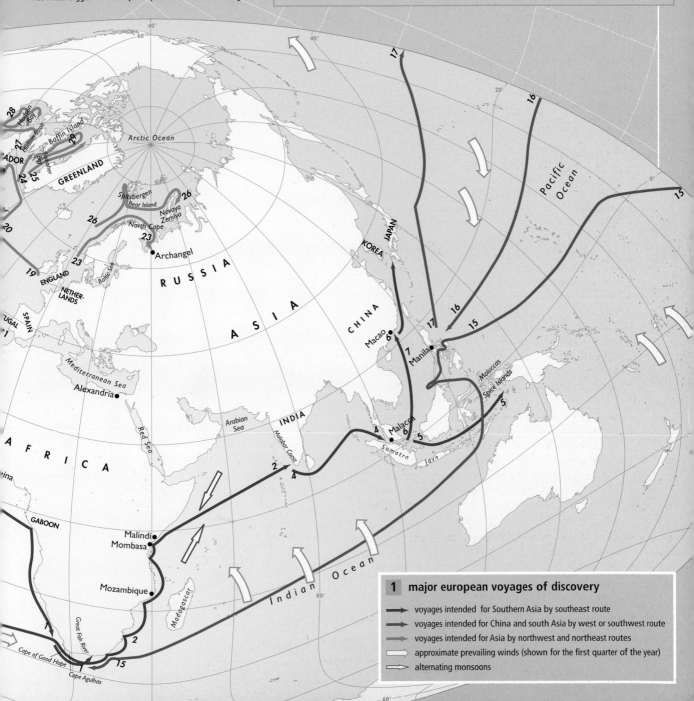

VOYAGES INTENDED FOR SOUTH ASIA BY SOUTHEAST ROUTE

1/Dias 1487–8 (outward) discovered open waters of Cape Agulhas; entered Indian Ocean; reached Great Fish River.

2/Vasco da Gama 1497–8 (outward) made best use of Atlantic winds on way to Cape of Good Hope; reached India, guided by local pilot.

3/Cabral 1500 (outward) second Portuguese voyage to India; landed Brazil, probably accidentally.

4/First Portuguese voyage to Malacca, 1509.

5/Abreu 1512–3 visited Moluccas.

6/First Portuguese visits to Macao, 1516.

VOYAGES INTENDED FOR CHINA AND SOUTH ASIA BY WEST OR SOUTHWEST ROUTE

7/Da Mota, Zeimoto and Peixoto 1542–3 Portuguese discovery of Japan.

8/Columbus 1492–3 (outward and homeward) discovered Bahama group, explored n. coasts of Cuba and Hispaniola; found best return route.

9/Columbus 1493–4 (outward) explored s. coast of Cuba; reported it as peninsula of mainland China.

10/Columbus 1498 (outward) discovered Trinidad and Venezuela; recognized coast as mainland.

11/Columbus 1502–4 explored coast of Honduras, Nicaragua and the Isthmus.

12/Ojeda and Vespucci 1499–1500 (outward) reached Guiana coast, failed to round Cape São Roque, followed coast w. to Cape de la Vela.

13/Coelho and Vespucci 1501 (outward) followed coast s. from Cape São Agostinho to 35°S.

14/Solis 1515 entered River Plate estuary and investigated n. bank.

15/Magellan and Elcano 1519–22 discovered Strait of Magellan, crossed Pacific, reached Moluccas via Philippines; first circumnavigation.

16/Saavedra 1527 discovered route from Mexico across Pacific to Moluccas.

17/Urdaneta 1565 found feasible return route Philippines to Mexico in 42°N, using w. winds.

18/Schouten and Le Maire 1616 discovered route into Pacific via Le Maire Strait and Cape Horn.

1 Explorers seeking sea routes to Asia found, in addition, a continent hitherto unknown to Europe – America – and an ocean of unsuspected extent – the Pacific (map below). They proved that all the oceans were connected, and that the world was much bigger than many accepted authorities had taught.

1 major european voyages of discovery

— voyages intended for Southern Asia by southeast route

— voyages intended for China and south Asia by west or southwest route

— voyages intended for Asia by northwest and northeast routes

⇨ approximate prevailing winds (shown for the first quarter of the year)

⇨ alternating monsoons

european expansion overseas

The Portuguese were the first to exploit the European voyages of discovery. Theirs was essentially a trading empire, and by the middle of the 16th century they had more than 50 forts and factories reaching from Sofala on the Zambezi to Nagasaki in Japan. In 1557 they occupied Macao on the Chinese mainland. The Spaniards, on the other hand, set out on a deliberate policy of conquest and settlement, first in Hispaniola and, a decade or so later, in Mexico and Peru. The result was the foundation of the great Spanish colonial empire. But the Iberian preponderance did not go unchallenged. Particularly after the foundation of the English and Dutch East India Companies, in 1600 and 1602 respectively, Portuguese trade came under attack. With the acquisition of Batavia (1619) as an eastern headquarters and of the Cape of Good Hope (1652) as a station on the route to the east, Dutch commercial pre-eminence in Asian waters was assured.

While there was no direct attack on Spain's mainland empire, the islands of the Caribbean, coveted as a prime source of sugar for the European market, became an object of intense rivalry and competition, in which all the leading powers engaged. Furthermore, whatever Spanish pretensions may have been it was unable to make its presence felt much north of the

2 Columbus's first landfall in 1492 was in the West Indies (map below). On his second visit, in 1493, he encountered the Carib Indians who would subsequently give their name to this region of tropical islands. The Spanish settlement of Hispaniola began in the same year, with the settlers hoping to find gold and to use the island as a launch-pad for trade with China, which they erroneously thought nearby. Hispaniola became the Spanish base for the settlement of Central America, Cuba for that of Mexico. In the 17th century, the British, French and Dutch began to challenge the supremacy Spain had established over the Caribbean. Over the course of time, the West Indies would become famous for their sugar crop (sugar was the most profitable of all the exotic products imported into Europe in Early Modern times). From the middle of the 17th century until after the end of the 18th, sugar-producing islands in the West Indies were frequently regarded by the British, French and Dutch governments as the most valuable of all their colonial possessions. They were often subjects of dispute between the governments.

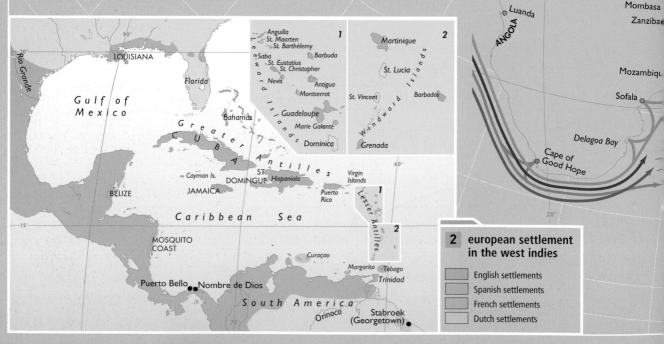

2 european settlement in the west indies

- English settlements
- Spanish settlements
- French settlements
- Dutch settlements

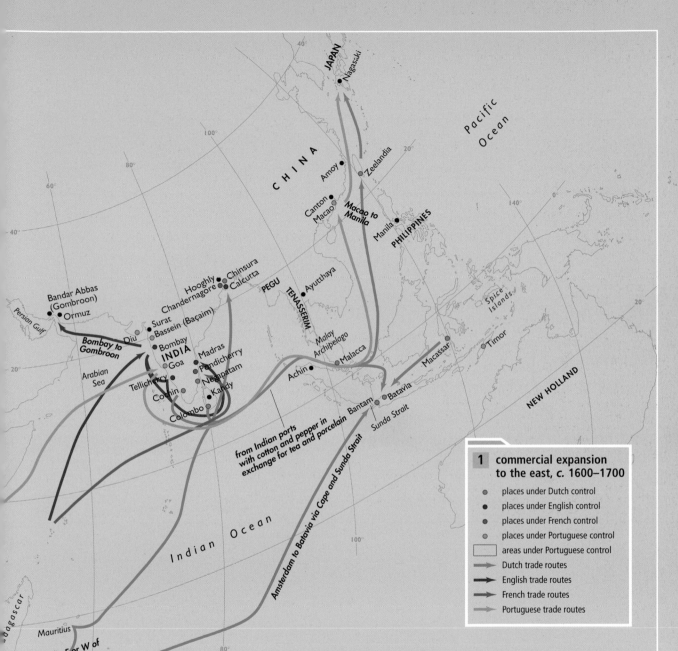

JAPAN
Nagasaki

Pacific Ocean

C H I N A

Amoy
Zeelandia

Canton
Macao
Macao to Manila
Manila
PHILIPPINES

Spice Islands

Hooghly Chinsura
Chandernagore Calcutta
PEGU
Bandar Abbas (Gombroon)
Ormuz
Persian Gulf
TENASSERIM
Ayutthaya

Surat
Bassein (Baçaim)
Diu
Bombay to Gombroon
Bombay
INDIA
Goa
Madras
Pondicherry
Malay Archipelago
Malacca
Timor

Arabian Sea
Tellicherry
Negapatam
Achin
Macassar
NEW HOLLAND

Cochin
Kandy
Bantam
Batavia

Colombo
Sunda Strait
Sunda Strait

from Indian ports with cotton and pepper in exchange for tea and porcelain

1 commercial expansion to the east, c. 1600–1700

- places under Dutch control
- places under English control
- places under French control
- places under Portuguese control
- ☐ areas under Portuguese control
- → Dutch trade routes
- → English trade routes
- → French trade routes
- → Portuguese trade routes

Indian Ocean

Amsterdam to Batavia via Cape and Sunda Strait

Madagascar
Mauritius
to ports in India E or W of Madagascar according to the time of year

1 The Portuguese empire in the East consisted of fortified bases and trading posts, few of them bigger than a single city and its immediate hinterland (map above). Some of them were mere warehouse compounds. Nonetheless, by 1600 there were more than 50 such establishments. In the next century, the Dutch, English and French established their own trading stations and gradually supplanted the Portuguese. But as their trading posts in the East were eliminated, the Portuguese reinforced their position in South America. By 1600, coastal Brazil had become the foremost sugar-producing territory in the western hemisphere.

Rio Grande. There was a slow advance in the west into California; but on the east coast Spanish power was limited to a tenuous foothold in Florida. Here the states of northern Europe, led by England and France, took the lead. France, in particular, advancing down the St. Lawrence estuary, penetrated deep into the interior, exploring the whole Mississippi valley (1682) and establishing fortified posts all the way to the Gulf of Mexico. The English, on the other hand, established a series of settlements along the eastern coast, beginning with Virginia in 1607. The clash of commercial and colonial interests which ensued ushered in the first age of imperial rivalry and conflict. Its prelude was the Anglo–Dutch wars of 1652–73 which resulted in the British seizure (1664) of the Dutch settlement of New Amsterdam, subsequently renamed New York. It marked the decline of the Netherlands and the rise of England and France to the paramount position in the overseas world.

colonial **america**

The conquest of Mexico by Hernán Cortés in 1519–20, and of Peru by Francisco Pizarro in 1531–33, laid the foundations of the Spanish colonial empire in America. With the help of rebellious tribes, oppressed by their Aztec and Inca conquerors, both were amazingly successful. By 1535, when vice-regal government was set up in Mexico and Lima was founded as the capital of Peru, the first dramatic phase of conquest was over. By 1550 all the chief centres of settled population were in Spanish hands, though the task of pushing forward frontiers into unexplored territory continued until the end of the colonial period. New vice-royalties were set up in New Granada (1739) and Rio de la Plata (1776), and new military governments in Texas (1718) and California (1767). But none of the later, sparsely inhabited conquests compared with Mexico and Peru in wealth and importance. Potosí in Upper Peru and Zacatecas in Mexico became the biggest sources of silver in the world, and by 1560 silver was the chief export from the American colonies to Spain.

Elsewhere on the American mainland colonization was slower to take effect. The Portuguese, on the eastern coast of South America, were only goaded into action by fear of the French. But in 1549 they founded Bahía as an administrative capital, and sugar plantations and mills, worked by slaves from Africa, were introduced. Between 1575 and 1600 coastal Brazil became the foremost sugar-producing territory in the western world, and attracted many land-hungry immigrants from Portugal and the Azores. But the vast Brazilian interior remained largely unexplored and in the hands of native Indian tribes. The same was true of the whole of North America at this date, beyond the frontier of New Spain. With its harsh climate and poor soil, the eastern seaboard of North America was uninviting territory, and for the first century after its discovery the great Newfoundland fisheries were its main attraction. There was also a fur trade with the natives, and by 1535 French explorers had penetrated far up the St. Lawrence river in the quest of skins and furs. When, after 1670, the English also built up a fur-trading empire, based on Hudson Bay, the result was a rivalry which erupted in the colonial wars of the 18th century. Nevertheless, fish and furs were the original staple of North America, and settlement, strongly opposed by fishing interests, only began in the seventeenth century, with the foundation of Acadia, or Nova Scotia, by the French in 1604, of Virginia (1607) and Massachusetts Bay (1629) by the English, and of New Netherland, later New York, by the Dutch in 1623. Even so, progress was slow. As late as the 17th century, the total population of the 12 English colonies was a mere 250,000.

The pattern of settlement was also different in the north. The English colonists wanted land for farms and plantations, expelling or exterminating the native population. The history of the

1 In the 16th century, Spaniards colonized much of South and Central America (map right). Much of their power and wealth arose from the conquest of the Aztec and Inca empires. In the 17th century, both Spain and Portugal were placed on the defensive by the colonial ambitions of France, Holland and Britain. By the last third of the 18th century, Britain, with her 13 colonies and Canadian possessions, dominated North America. Yet in 1776 the 13 colonies rebelled and emerged as a new country, the United States. From around 1810, the Spanish and Portuguese colonies, too, began to assert their independence.

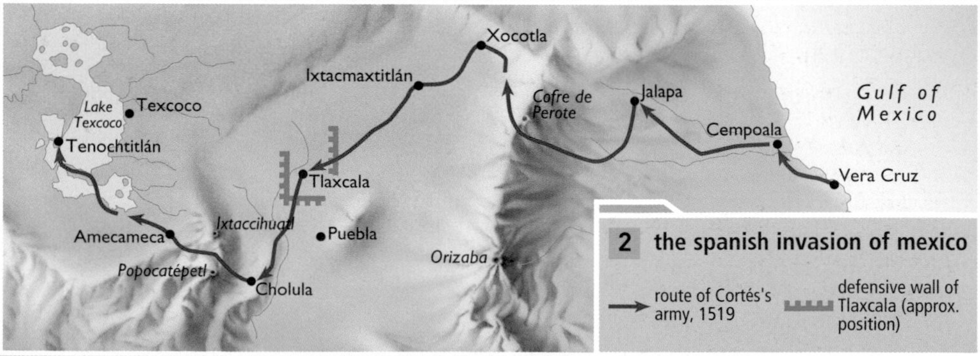
Xocotla
Ixtacmaxtitlán
Lake Texcoco
Texcoco
Tenochtitlán
Cofre de Perote
Jalapa
Gulf of Mexico
Cempoala
Vera Cruz
Tlaxcala
Ixtaccihuatl
Puebla
Amecameca
Popocatépetl
Cholula
Orizaba
2 the spanish invasion of mexico
route of Cortés's army, 1519
defensive wall of Tlaxcala (approx. position)

2 The Spanish invasion of Mexico (map left) showing old Vera Cruz, the first Spanish city; Cempoala, whose ruler was encouraged by Cortés in revolt against the Aztecs; Tlaxcala, home of Cortés's principal allies; and Tenochtitlán, capital of the Aztecs, on its island in Lake Texcoco. The conquest was not easy: Cortés's small force only just escaped destruction in the first stages of the conflict.

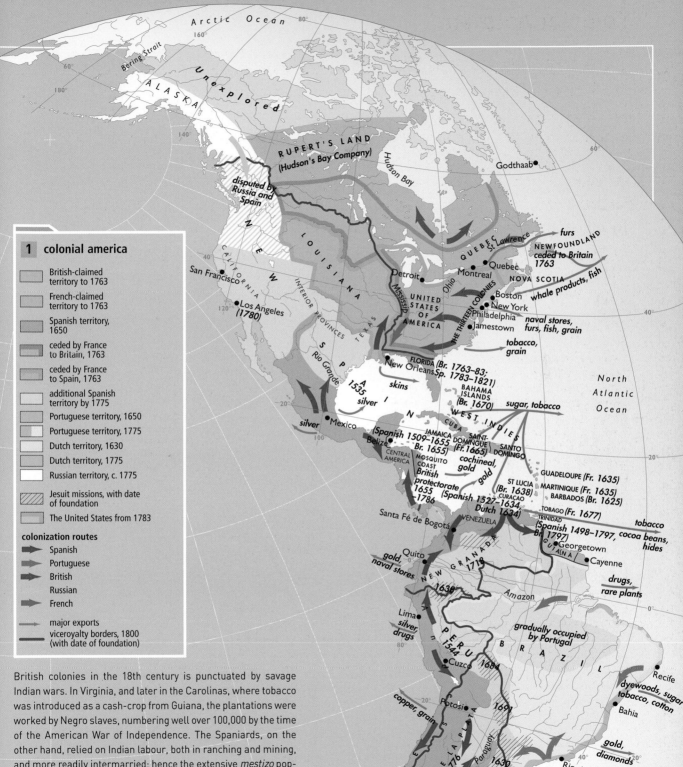

1 colonial america

- British-claimed territory to 1763
- French-claimed territory to 1763
- Spanish territory, 1650
- ceded by France to Britain, 1763
- ceded by France to Spain, 1763
- additional Spanish territory by 1775
- Portuguese territory, 1650
- Portuguese territory, 1775
- Dutch territory, 1630
- Dutch territory, 1775
- Russian territory, c. 1775
- Jesuit missions, with date of foundation
- The United States from 1783

colonization routes

- Spanish
- Portuguese
- British
- Russian
- French
- major exports
- viceroyalty borders, 1800 (with date of foundation)

Arctic Ocean

Bering Strait

ALASKA

Unexplored

RUPERT'S LAND
(Hudson's Bay Company)

Hudson Bay

Godthaab

disputed by Russia and Spain

NEW

CALIFORNIA

San Francisco

Los Angeles (1780)

LOUISIANA

INTERIOR PROVINCES

Detroit

Mississippi

Ohio

QUEBEC

St. Lawrence

Quebec

Montreal

NOVA SCOTIA

NEWFOUNDLAND ceded to Britain 1763

furs

whale products, fish

UNITED STATES OF AMERICA

THE THIRTEEN COLONIES

Boston

New York

Philadelphia

Jamestown

naval stores, furs, fish, grain

tobacco, grain

TEXAS

Rio Grande

SPAIN 1535 silver

skins silver

New Orleans

FLORIDA (Br. 1763-83; Sp. 1783-1821)

BAHAMA ISLANDS (Br. 1670)

North Atlantic Ocean

silver

Mexico

Spanish 1509-1655 Br. 1655

Belize

CENTRAL AMERICA

MOSQUITO COAST British protectorate 1655-1786

CUBA

JAMAICA

SAINT-DOMINGUE (Fr. 1665)

SANTO DOMINGO

WEST INDIES

sugar, tobacco

cochineal, gold

gold

Spanish 1527-1634

GUADELOUPE (Fr. 1635)

ST LUCIA (Br. 1638)

MARTINIQUE (Fr. 1635)

BARBADOS (Br. 1625)

CURAÇAO Dutch 1634

TOBAGO (Fr. 1677)

TRINIDAD (Spanish 1498-1797, Br. 1797)

GUIANA

Georgetown

Cayenne

tobacco, cocoa beans, hides

drugs, rare plants

Santa Fé de Bogotá

VENEZUELA

NEW GRANADA 1718

gold, naval stores

Quito

1638

Amazon

gradually occupied by Portugal

Recife

dyewoods, sugar tobacco, cotton

Bahia

Lima

silver drugs

PERU 1544

Cuzco 1684

ANDES

BRAZIL

copper, grain

Potosí

1661

gold, diamonds

Rio de Janiero

CHILE

RIO DE LA PLATA

1776

Paraguay

1630

beef

Indian frontier

hides, silver

Buenos Aires

British colonies in the 18th century is punctuated by savage Indian wars. In Virginia, and later in the Carolinas, where tobacco was introduced as a cash-crop from Guiana, the plantations were worked by Negro slaves, numbering well over 100,000 by the time of the American War of Independence. The Spaniards, on the other hand, relied on Indian labour, both in ranching and mining, and more readily intermarried; hence the extensive *mestizo* population, particularly in Mexico and Peru. At the same time, all the colonies were firmly administered in the interests of the mother country. This inevitably provoked resentment on the part of the colonial élites, and lay behind the demand for independence which erupted in the north in 1775 and in Latin America in 1808.

south-east **asia**

When European traders and adventurers broke through into the Indian Ocean at the close of the 15th century, the great prize, drawing them forward, was the spices of South-East Asia. Here was untold wealth to be tapped. But here also, at one of the world's main crossroads, where cultural influences from China and India intermingled, they found themselves in a region of great complexity, divided in religion between Buddhism, Hinduism and Islam, and politically fragmented and unstable. On the mainland, rival peoples and dynasties competed for hegemony. In the Malayan archipelago the empires of Srivijaya and Majapahit had disappeared, leaving behind scores of petty states, with little cohesion. This was the situation when Albuquerque conquered the great international emporium of Malacca for the king of Portugal in 1511.

The Portuguese presence changed little at first. Albuquerque and his successors were there to dominate the spice trade through a chain of fortified trading-stations, linked by naval power. Provided this was accepted, they had no wish to interfere with the native potentates. Far more important, after the arrival on the scene of the Dutch and English, was the challenge to their trading monopoly by their European rivals. For most of the 17th century this rivalry was the dominant factor. The Dutch, in particular, began a systematic conquest of the Portuguese settlements, capturing Malacca in 1641, and then turned against the British. But in doing so, they were inevitably drawn into local politics. After establishing a base at Batavia in 1619, they interfered in succession disputes among the neighbouring sultans, to ensure their own position, and in this way gradually extended control over Java, expelling the British from Bantam in 1682. Already earlier they had driven them out of the Spice Islands by the 'massacre of Amboina' (1623) and the seizure of Macassar (1667), in this way forcing the English East India Company to turn instead to the China trade. With this in view the British acquired Penang on the west coast of Malaya in 1786, the first step in a process which was ultimately to make them masters of the Malay peninsula.

But this was still exceptional. European activities encroached on the outlying islands, but had little impact on the mainland monarchies, which had no direct interest in European trade and were mainly concerned with extending their power at the expense of their neighbours. This is a complicated story, because all the main centres were also under pressure from the hill peoples of the interior, always waiting to assert their independence; but the main lines of development are indicated on map 1. They include the advance of Annam at the expense of Cambodia, the rise of a new Burmese empire under Alaungpaya (1735–60), after a Mon rebellion in 1740, and successful Siamese resistance to Burmese encroachment, in spite of Burmese conquest in 1767. These events occurred for the most part without European involvement, but

2 Under the Treaty of London of 1824 the Dutch were to withdraw from the Malay peninsula (map right). The British settlements there – Penang, Singapore and Malacca – were bound by the doctrine of non-intervention laid down in Pitt's India Act. The immediate danger to the independence of the Malay states in 1826 lay in Siamese expansionism; the Burney Treaty in that year halted Siam's pressure upon them, though only after two incidents in which the Penang government safeguarded Perak's independence.

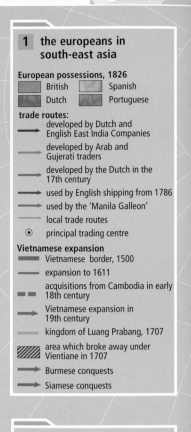

1 the europeans in south-east asia

European possessions, 1826
- British
- Spanish
- Dutch
- Portuguese

trade routes:
- developed by Dutch and English East India Companies
- developed by Arab and Gujerati traders
- developed by the Dutch in the 17th century
- used by English shipping from 1786
- used by the 'Manila Galleon'
- local trade routes
- ⊙ principal trading centre

Vietnamese expansion
- Vietnamese border, 1500
- expansion to 1611
- acquisitions from Cambodia in early 18th century
- Vietnamese expansion in 19th century
- kingdom of Luang Prabang, 1707
- area which broke away under Vientiane in 1707
- Burmese conquests
- Siamese conquests

2 the malay states in 1826

- Malay states tributary to Siam in 1826
- British possessions

SIAM

PERLIS

KEDAH

PENANG

PERAK

KELANTAN

TRENGGANU

South China Sea

Straits of Malacca

SELANGOR

PAHANG

NEGRI SEMBILAN

MALACCA

JOHORE

SUMATRA

SINGAPORE

1 European contact with south-east Asia though driven initially by demand in Europe for spices, paved the way for the foundation of substantial European empires across the region. The Spanish had ruled the Philippines since the 16th century and, though other European contacts had little impact on mainland societies, by the early 19th century the British had put in place the basis of their subsequent colonial rule in Malaya, while Dutch control of the East Indies was also firmly established.

FORMOSA Spanish colonies in north Taiwan, 1626–37; Dutch in southwest Taiwan, 1624–61

during the struggle for empire between England and France in the 18th century some states were implicated. Already, under Louis XIV, France had intervened in Siam against the Dutch. During the Anglo–French war in India after 1746 it supported the Mon rebellion in Burma, and in reply the English East India Company seized the island of Negrais at the mouth of the Bassein river. Later, when the Burmese, foiled in their attempt to conquer Siam, switched their efforts to the north, the British, fearing for the security of Bengal, again intervened. The result was the first Anglo–Burmese war (1824–26) and the British annexation of Assam, Arakan and Tenasserim.

In Malaya there was similar encroachment on the independent rulers when the British, after acquiring Penang in 1786, established Singapore in 1819 as a free trade port after its acquisition by Raffles. This led to a conflict of interests with Holland which was only settled by the Anglo–Dutch treaty of 1824 when the British withdrew from Sumatra in return for Dutch withdrawal from Malacca. The future Dutch and British colonial empires in South-East Asia were taking shape. But their control was still loose and indirect. Only after the Industrial Revolution in Europe, and the expanding demand for raw materials and markets, were the lives and fortunes of the peoples of the region seriously affected.

new **monarchy** in **europe**

In Europe revival after the setbacks of the 14th century began around 1450. The whole continent was affected. In the east Ivan III (1462–1505) profited from the decline of the Mongol khanates to inaugurate a rapid expansion of the territory of Muscovy and to attack the independence of Tver, Novgorod and the land-owning aristocracy. In the west endemic civil war in Spain was ended after the union of Castile and Aragon in 1479. The ending of the Hundred Years' War between England and France (1453) and the expulsion of the English from French territory saw a rapid extension of the area controlled by the French monarchy, while in England Edward IV (1461–83) began a restoration of royal power which was carried further by the new Tudor dynasty after 1485. Only in Ireland did Tudor attempts at integration fail and English power was effectively limited to the Pale around Dublin.

Not all attempts at state-building were a success. The efforts of the dukes of Burgundy to erect an independent state in the rich lands between France and the Empire collapsed when the ambitious Charles the Bold was killed at Nancy in 1477. The empire of Matthias Corvinus of Hungary (1458–90) also proved ephemeral. Italy remained divided,

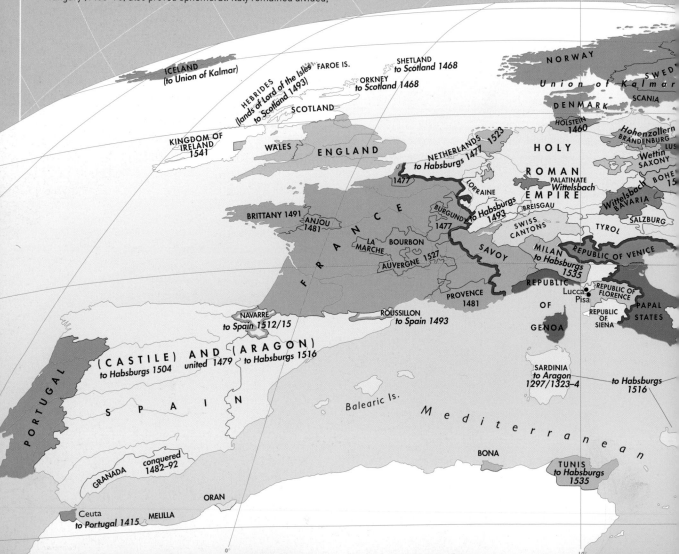

in spite of a marked strengthening of government under rulers such as Lorenzo de' Medici (1469–92) at Florence and Ludovico Sforza (1460–99) at Milan, and after the French invasion of 1494 internal divisions left Italy a prey to foreign intervention. The main beneficiary in all instances was the house of Habsburg, which succeeded to the Spanish possessions in 1516 and emerged, under Charles V (1519–56), as the preponderant power in western Europe. But the diversified Habsburg empire lacked cohesion, and when the Ottoman advance, halted on the middle Danube since 1456, was resumed after 1520, and at the same time the emperor was involved in the religious wars in Germany, the strain was too great. In 1556 Charles V abdicated and the empire was divided between the Austrian and Spanish Habsburgs. Only ten years later the Dutch revolt began.

The Dutch revolt, although the most formidable uprising, was not exceptional. In England, from Henry VII to Elizabeth I, the Tudors were faced by repeated rebellions, and elsewhere, even in Russia, resistance to centralization became a powerful force after 1550. The rise of the new monarchies was less a new beginning than the culmination of the long struggle of aristocracy and monarchy. Their financial and administrative machinery was not enough to raise a modern system of government in place of the feudal order, and the decisive change from the old to the new was not made until after another century of strife and turmoil.

1 In the early 16th century, more consolidated state structures began to emerge (map below). In the east, Muscovy challenged Poland–Lithuania for the inheritance of Kievan Rus, while in the 1520s the Ottomans destroyed the composite monarchy of Hungary and Bohemia which had reached its zenith under Matthias Corvinus in 1485. The collapse of the Scandinavian Union in 1523 was the exception to the rule. Elsewhere, though Italy and the Holy Roman Empire remained fragmented, unions were formed or strengthened: in the Iberian peninsula (between Castile and Aragon in 1479 and Spain and Portugal in 1580); Poland–Lithuania (1569); and Britain (1603).

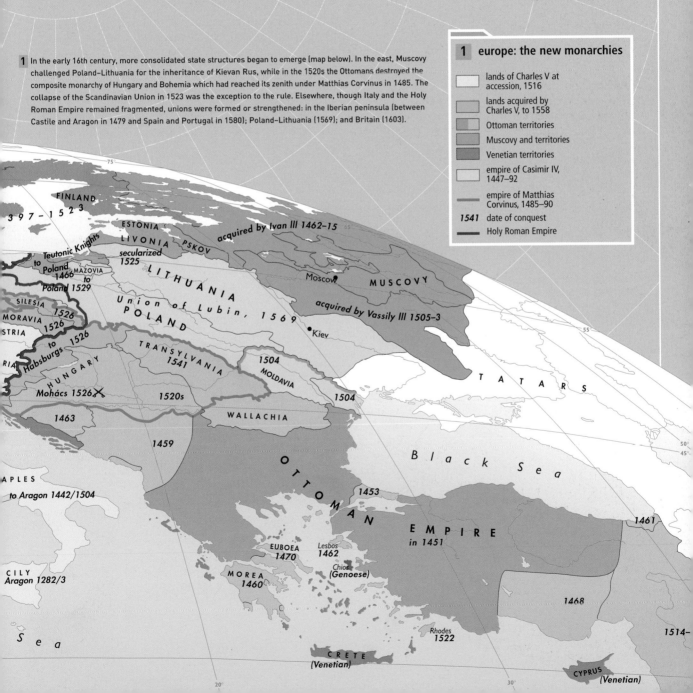

1 europe: the new monarchies

- lands of Charles V at accession, 1516
- lands acquired by Charles V, to 1558
- Ottoman territories
- Muscovy and territories
- Venetian territories
- empire of Casimir IV, 1447–92
- empire of Matthias Corvinus, 1485–90
- *1541* date of conquest
- Holy Roman Empire

the **reformation** in **europe**

The closing years of the 15th century saw a great revival of popular religion in Europe, but the established church, which never fully recovered from the effects of the schism of 1378–1417, was ill equipped to satisfy its needs. Except in Bohemia and Moravia, where the Hussites comprised over half the population, and in England, where small groups of Lollards survived, heresy was virtually dead by 1500; but the materialism of the Renaissance popes and the self-seeking of the higher clergy discredited the hierarchy in the eyes of many laymen.

Particularly in Germany and German-speaking Switzerland, financial and other abuses fired revolt. In 1517 Martin Luther (1483–1546) posted his 95 theses on the church door at Wittenberg. In 1520, under the impulse of Huldreich Zwingli (1484–1531), Zurich renounced allegiance to Rome. Their denunciations of the clergy and the supremacy of the pope, and their demand for a return to the standards of early Christianity, exercised a vast appeal. By 1560 seven in 10 of the Emperor's subjects were Protestants, and the reformed faith prevailed in Scandinavia, Baltic Europe and England. Further impetus came from the teaching of John Calvin (1509–64). In France there were around 700 Calvinist churches by 1562, and Calvinism also made rapid progress in Poland, Hungary and Scotland, where it became the official religion in 1560. In addition, a number of more radical sects sprang up, Anabaptists, Mennonites and others, which rejected theology, ritual and clerical order in favour of Biblical simplicity, combining evangelism with social protest.

However, the Reformation was soon entangled in politics. Princes and kings, including Henry VIII of England, saw an opportunity to despoil the church of its wealth. Some German princes espoused Protestantism out of fear of imperial power. Luther himself, dependent on princely support, turned against the more radical sectaries and condemned the peasants' revolt of 1525. Foreign policy also played a part. The Valois kings of France, though combating the protestant Huguenots at home, supported the German Protestant princes against the Habsburg emperor. Although the French Huguenots won toleration by the Edict of Nantes (1598), their numbers were severely reduced during the religious wars between 1562 and 1598, and elsewhere in Europe the second half of the 16th century saw a great Catholic revival, led by the Jesuit Order, founded in 1534 by St. Ignatius Loyola (1491–1556), and inspired by the reforms of the Council of Trent between 1545 and 1563. Using the Jesuits as their spearhead, Catholic rulers went over to the offensive. Protestants were expelled from Bavaria (1579) and Styria (1600), and in Poland the number of Protestant churches decreased from 560 in 1572 to 240 in 1650.

The decisive phase of the struggle between Protestants and Catholics, the Thirty Years War, took place in the Holy Roman Empire. It began in 1618–21 when the emperor Ferdinand II defeated the Bohemian Protestants at the battle of the White Mountain (1620) and won back Bohemia and Moravia for Catholicism. England and the Dutch intervened on the Protestant side, but the imperial forces were initially successful and in 1629 an Edict of Restitution was promulgated which reclaimed large areas of church lands held by Protestant princes. Only the intervention of Gustavus Adolphus of Sweden saved the Protestant cause from collapse. But the Swedish victories at Breitenfeld (1631) and Lützen (1632) brought in Spain on the imperial side, while France allied with Sweden and declared war on Spain (1635). The war was now a struggle in which it seemed that neither side could hope for outright victory, until in 1648 the Peace of Westphalia brought a compromise solution. Lutherans and Calvinists retained the lands they held in 1624, and the wars of religion were over. But Germany, the scene of battle, suffered a lasting setback.

1 In 1570, Catholicism appeared to be in retreat on virtually every front (map right). Yet Protestantism, despite its introduction as the official religion in England, Scotland, Denmark, Sweden and much of north Germany, and its rapid spread in France, Poland and Hungary, was not yet firmly rooted anywhere. It took time for people to be educated in the new faith, especially where rulers had not turned Protestant and church land had not been secularized.

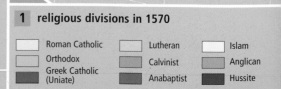

1 religious divisions in 1570

Roman Catholic	Lutheran	Islam
Orthodox	Calvinist	Anglican
Greek Catholic (Uniate)	Anabaptist	Hussite

The second half of the 16th and the first half of the 17th centuries were a time of turbulence throughout Europe. In Russia the 'time of troubles' after the death of Ivan the Terrible (1584) lasted until 1613. Northern Europe was embroiled in almost continuous war from 1561 to 1658, as Sweden, independent since the time of Gustavus Vasa (1523–60), struggled with Denmark, Russia, Poland and Brandenburg for control of the Baltic and its important trade. The rise of the Swedish empire, leading to Gustavus Adolphus' intervention in the Thirty Years War and the Swedish acquisition of western Pomerania, Wismar and the bishopics of Bremen and Verden at the Peace of Westphalia, vitally affected the balance of power in Europe and was one of the most significant developments of the period. In western Europe developments were more confused. The new monarchies of the preceding period had over-reached themselves, and from around 1530 reaction set in, particularly when rising prices, recession and widespread unemployment reinforced existing discontents. The Elizabethan Poor Law and other legislation of 1563 was no remedy; indeed, the reign of Elizabeth I (1558–1603) was less auspicious than often painted, and Elizabeth, whose relations with parliament deteriorated sharply at the end of her reign, left her Stuart successors on the English throne a legacy of unsolved problems with which they failed to cope.

From around 1530, sometimes earlier, the history of France and England was punctuated by revolts. As in Germany, they reflected a combination of religious, social and political grievances. In England the northern risings of 1536 and 1569 were Catholic protests against the suppression of the old faith, but they also embodied the resistance of the northern gentry to centralization and control from London. On the other wing the unrest of radical dissenters combined dissatisfaction with Henry VIII's and Elizabeth's conservative church settlements with resistance to the enclosure of common lands for the benefit of grasping landlords. A similar mixture of motives permeated the frequent uprisings, 500 in all, in France. These were largely revolts of the common people, driven to extremes by economic hardship; but in the end the most influential factor, visible in France in the revolt of the judges and nobility which drove the king from Paris in 1649, was resistance to autocracy, centralization and taxation. The Dutch revolt, which began in the North Netherlands in 1572 and ended in 1648, was inspired by fear that the central government, controlled from Spain, intended to override the traditional liberties of the Netherlands. Similar motives underlay the Catalan and Portuguese revolts against Castile (1640).

In the British Isles, united from 1603 under a single monarch, the efforts of Charles I (1625–49) to change the traditional religious and political structure resulted in rebellions in Scotland (1638) and Ireland (1641). The king's innovations were no more popular with many of England's political leaders, called to parliament to vote the taxes required to restore royal control in the other two kingdoms: their refusal provoked a civil war in England (1642). In a complex sequence of political and military moves, a small parliamentary faction not only contrived the defeat and execution of the king (1649), creating an English Republic under the Lord Protector Oliver Cromwell, but went on to establish London's direct control over the entire British Isles (1649–51). Even though the Monarchy was restored in 1660, power was now shared between the crown and parliament (in constant existence from 1689).

In France, the failure of the Fronde broke the power of the aristocracy and cleared the way for the absolutism of Louis XIV. A more sensitive government, combined with a rapidly expanding standing army after 1661, ensured that France remained largely free of unrest until the Revolutionary outburst of 1789. Only in Germany was the disarray caused by a century of religious and political conflict enduring. Here the devastation of the Thirty Years War resulted in a decline of population from some 21 million in 1618 to around 13 million in 1648, and though some regions were spared, the setback was undeniable. The outcome was a major shift in the European balance. The Habsburgs, who had dominated the previous period, were in retreat, and the future in the west was in the hands of a resurgent France and its rivals, the maritime powers.

1 The states of north-west Europe were plagued by rebellion between 1500 and 1688. More than a dozen major rebellions broke out in England. Spain faced a continuous revolt in the Netherlands from 1572 onwards as well as having to face revolts in Portugal and Catalonia in 1640. In France, over 500 popular uprisings culminated in the Fronde of 1648. After 1660, however, the rise of standing armies coupled with greater attention to the interests of landed élites meant that revolts were increasingly rare. But as internal tensions subsided, the three governments took to fighting each other, above all for control of the seas. England emerged the stronger from the Anglo–Dutch Wars, and, as the Dutch republic was drawn into war with France, the English established their naval prowess not just in Europe but in the wider world.

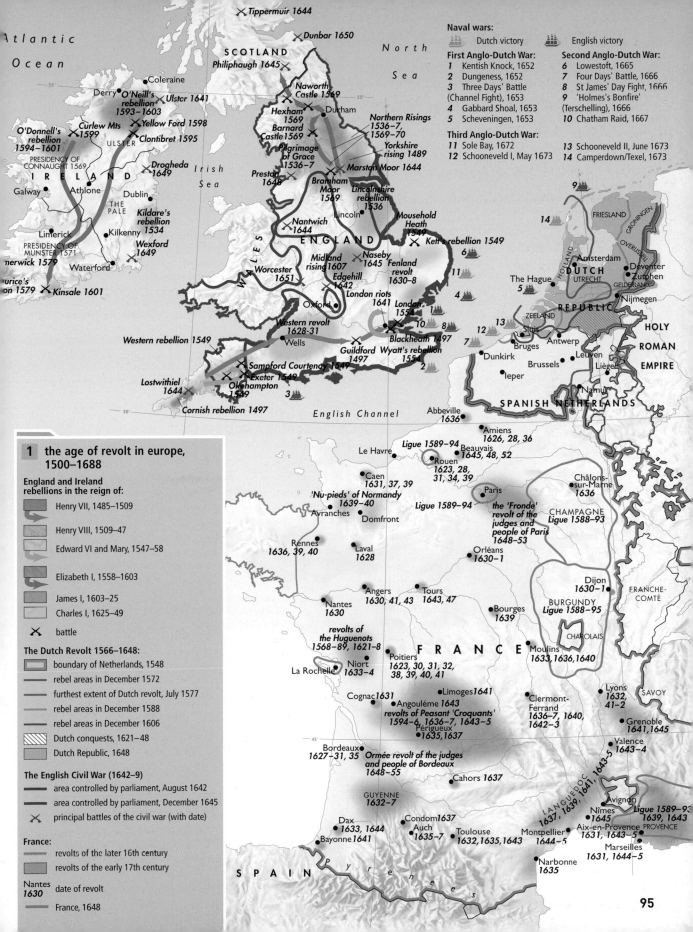

1 the age of revolt in europe, 1500–1688

England and Ireland rebellions in the reign of:

- Henry VII, 1485–1509
- Henry VIII, 1509–47
- Edward VI and Mary, 1547–58
- Elizabeth I, 1558–1603
- James I, 1603–25
- Charles I, 1625–49
- ✕ battle

The Dutch Revolt 1566–1648:

- boundary of Netherlands, 1548
- rebel areas in December 1572
- furthest extent of Dutch revolt, July 1577
- rebel areas in December 1588
- rebel areas in December 1606
- Dutch conquests, 1621–48
- Dutch Republic, 1648

The English Civil War (1642–9):

- area controlled by parliament, August 1642
- area controlled by parliament, December 1645
- ✕ principal battles of the civil war (with date)

France:

- revolts of the later 16th century
- revolts of the early 17th century
- Nantes 1630 date of revolt
- France, 1648

Naval wars:
🚢 Dutch victory   🚢 English victory

First Anglo-Dutch War:
1 Kentish Knock, 1652
2 Dungeness, 1652
3 Three Days' Battle (Channel Fight), 1653
4 Gabbard Shoal, 1653
5 Scheveningen, 1653

Second Anglo-Dutch War:
6 Lowestoft, 1665
7 Four Days' Battle, 1666
8 St James' Day Fight, 1666
9 'Holmes's Bonfire' (Terschelling), 1666
10 Chatham Raid, 1667

Third Anglo-Dutch War:
11 Sole Bay, 1672
12 Schooneveld I, May 1673
13 Schooneveld II, June 1673
14 Camperdown/Texel, 1673

germany and its neighbours

The Peace of Westphalia (1648), besides bringing to a close the wars of religion, was a milestone in German history. The failure of the emperor to impose his will on the Protestant princes confirmed the political fragmentation which had gathered pace since the 14th century. After 1648 Germany was a patchwork of some 300 small, petty states and free cities. In addition, the independence of Holland and Switzerland was formally recognized. Theoretically the rights of the princes were limited by the rights of the Holy Roman Empire, but in practice every prince was emperor in his own lands, with full sovereign powers including the laws to make foreign alliances.

Political disruption was also compounded by a sharp economic setback, due partly to the devastation and depopulation resulting from the Thirty Years' War, but also to a long-term shift in the European economy. The great south German banking houses of Welser and Fugger went bankrupt in 1614 and 1627 respectively. The Hanseatic League, in disarray since the closing years of the 16th century, was dissolved in 1669. Everywhere the towns were in decline, particularly in Austria, Prussia and Bavaria, but even worse was the plight of the peasantry. In Bohemia and Moravia their legal rights were abolished; in the north and north-east they were ejected from their holdings to permit the consolidation of Junker estates, and reduced to serfdom. Impoverishment and stagnation were the result. A modest economic recovery occurred after 1750; but with its resources dissipated on ostentatious building and the upkeep of princely households, Germany was an economic and social backwater. It was also a pawn in great power politics. Divided among themselves and fearful of Habsburg ambitions, the princes were clients of foreign powers, including Britain and Sweden, but

1 the growth of the habsburg empire

- hereditary Habsburg lands, 1525
- acquisitions, 1526
- acquisitions, 1648–99
- acquisitions, 1699–1772
- acquisitions, 1772–1805
- boundary of the Holy Roman Empire, 1789
- military frontier

North Sea · Baltic Sea

Flensburg · Schleswig · Kiel · Lübeck · Wismar · Rostock · Stralsund · Hamburg · Lüneburg · Bremen

Tauroggen · Tilsit · Königsberg · EAST PRUSSIA 1618 · Allenstein

EASTERN POMERANIA 1648 · WEST PRUSSIA 1772 · Danzig · Neustettin · Marienwerder

W. POMERANIA 1720 · Kolberg 1761 · Kammin · Stettin

Thorn · Vistula · P O L A N D

BRANDENBURG · Brandenburg · Berlin · Potsdam · Frankfurt · Zorndorf 1758 · Schwiebus · Posen · Warsaw

MAGDEBURG 1648 · Magdeburg · Kunersdorf 1759 · Kalisch · Lodz

Cleves · Tecklenburg · Minden · Hanover · Brunswick · RAVENSBERG · Münster · Nijmegen · Wesel · Dortmund · Geldern · E. FRISIA 1744 · Ems · Weser

Goslar · Dessau · SAXONY · Halle · Cottbus · SILESIA 1742 · Breslau · Oder

Göttingen · Kassel · Mansfeld · Leipzig · Hochkirch 1758 · Liegnitz 1760 · Görlitz · Leuthen 1757

Cologne · Weimar · Jena · Dresden · Chemnitz · Pirna 1756 · Hohenfriedberg 1745 · Mollwitz 1741

Rhine · Frankfurt · Schweinfurt · Lobositz 1756 · HABSBURG EMPIRE · Elbe · Kolin 1757

Mainz · Worms · Bamberg · Prague 1757 · Tarnów

Mannheim · Main · Nuremberg

2 the rise of prussia, 1648–1795

- Brandenburg in 1648
- Prussian acquisitions, 1648–1707
- acquisitions, 1715, 1720
- acquisitions, 1742, 1744, 1772
- acquisitions, 1793
- acquisitions, 1795
- ✗ battles between Austria and Prussia
- ✗ battles between Saxony and Prussia
- ✗ battles between Russia and Prussia
- ✗ battles between Austria with Russia and Prussia

2 The electors of Brandenburg acquired a series of scattered territories in the 17th century (map above). Frederick William (the Great Elector) gained recognition of his full sovereignty from Poland in 1657; his son Frederick I was crowned king in Prussia in 1701. Frederick II (the Great) seized Silesia from the Habsburgs. Prussia's participation in the Partitions of Poland sealed its position as a Great Power. In three Partitions (1772, 1793, 1795), Russia, Austria and Prussia divided up the whole of Poland. Austria gained 4,150,000 inhabitants, Russia 5,500,000 inhabitants and Prussia 2,600,000 inhabitants.

1 The Austrian branch of the Habsburg dynasty was founded by Charles V's brother Ferdinand, elected king of Bohemia and Hungary in 1526. For 200 years, the Habsburgs disputed possession of Hungarian territory with the Ottomans (map left). After the Turkish defeat at the siege of Vienna (1683), the Habsburgs extended control rapidly down the Danube, consolidating their gains at the treaties of Carlowitz (1699) and Passarowitz (1718), though some territory was lost at the Peace of Belgrade (1739). Austria lost Silesia to Prussia in the War of the Austrian Succession (1740–48) and failed to recover it in the Seven Years War (1756–63); compensation came in the shape of the land won in the First and Third Partitions of Poland, though Austrian possession of West Galicia was short-lived.

particularly of France, which used its position to make inroads on German territories in the west, annexing the Franche-Comté of Burgundy (1678), Strassburg (1681), most of Alsace (1697) and Bar and Lorraine (1766).

After 1648, apart from Austria, only Saxony, Bavaria and Brandenburg could claim even the status of second-rate powers. Saxony, with the mineral resources of the Erzgebirge and its varied industries, was the most advanced, while Bavaria was falling behind; but Brandenburg-Prussia was beginning, under the Great Elector (1640–88), the long climb which made it by 1786 the second German power and the rival of Austria. The rise of Prussia is a story of single-minded devotion to building a strong military and administrative apparatus to weld together the scattered territories stretching from the Vistula to the Rhine. The Hohenzollern domains lacked internal and external cohesion. Prussia itself was until 1657 a Polish fief; and it was only in 1772, after the first partition of Poland, that Frederick the Great (1740–86) succeeded in creating a continuous Prussian territory from Memel to Magdeburg. More impressive was the recovery of Austria after its setbacks in the Thirty Years War and the creation of a vast new Austrian empire. This was largely the work of the great field marshal, Prince Eugene of Savoy (1663–1736). As late as 1683 Vienna itself was besieged by Turkish armies. Eugene turned the tide and by 1699 they had been thrown back and the whole of Hungary brought under Habsburg rule. Austria was now a major power in eastern Europe, while in the west the peace settlement of 1714 brought it the Spanish Netherlands and the Spanish inheritance in Italy. Serbia and Belgrade, acquired in 1718, were lost again in 1739, Lombardy and southern Italy in 1734–35. When, on the death of Charles VI (1711–40) and the accession of Maria Theresa (1740–80), Frederick II of Prussia seized Silesia, Austria's inherent weaknesses were exposed. Although the struggle went on until 1763, it proved impossible to dislodge the Prussians. Later both Prussia and Austria took advantage of the disarray of Poland to enlarge their territories in the east. But in the three partitions they had to share the spoils with Russia, and their mutual suspicions and rivalry left the west exposed to France. When the French revolutionary armies marched into Germany in 1793 the old order was doomed, and in 1806 the Holy Roman Empire passed unmourned from the map of Europe.

france and europe

Under Louis XIV who succeeded to the throne in 1643, France became the leading country of Europe. His long minority, during Cardinal Mazarin's rule, saw the last major revolts of the aristocracy in defence of its prescriptive right. When in 1661 Louis became effective ruler, the ground had been prepared for a new regime of centralization and absolutism. This was the work of Mazarin, who had broken the aristocratic revolts and who turned the *intendants* into permanent representatives of the royal will in the provinces; of Louvois, who reformed the army; and particularly of Colbert's programme of financial reform. At the same time Vauban encircled France with a chain of defensive fortresses. All this was accompanied by great public works, including the Languedoc canal, connecting the Atlantic and the Mediterranean, the palace of Versailles, and much building in Paris which became the centre of the cosmopolitan civilization of Europe.

Louis XIV's wars, inspired by an almost neurotic fear of the revival of the empire of Charles V and the encirclement of France by Habsburg power, seriously damaged this solid achievement. Beginning with his attack on the Spanish Netherlands in 1667, they imposed a growing burden of taxation and gradually united Europe against him. England and Holland, maritime and colonial rivals since 1652, settled

1 the war of the spanish succession, 1701–14

✗ Allied victory
✗ Bourbon (French) victory
✗ inconclusive

principal territorial changes

to Spanish House of Bourbon
to Great Britain
to Austria
to Savoy
to France
to Prussia

their differences by the Treaty of Breda (1667) and in alliance with Sweden compelled Louis to make peace at Aix-la-Chapelle in 1668. Thereupon Louis detached England from the anti-French alliance by the Secret Treaty of Dover (1670), won over Sweden, and turned against Holland in 1672; but he was halted by an alliance between Austria, Spain and Brandenburg (which defeated his Swedish allies at Fehrbellin in 1675), and at the Peace of Nijmegen (1678) Holland emerged unscathed.

These inconclusive results convinced Louis that there was little hope of major territorial acquisitions by direct conquest, and after 1679 he turned to a policy of indirect aggression, nibbling away at German territory in the east, particularly in Alsace, the object being to absorb the remainder of the Burgundian territories which had been partitioned between France and Austria after the death of Charles the Bold in 1477. Strasbourg was annexed in 1681, the Palatinate burnt and ravaged in 1689. But these provocative and often brutal actions united German opinion against him, and the revocation of the Edict of Nantes (1685) and the persecution of the French Huguenots incensed the Protestant powers. The result was the formation of the Grand Alliance (1689), led by William of Orange, who had succeeded to the English throne after the revolution of 1688 and the deposition of James II. Louis' attempts to foment rebellion in Ireland failed after the defeat of the French navy at La Hogue (1692), but fighting continued inconclusively on the continent until 1697, when the Peace of Ryswick registered Louis' first serious setback.

A new phase opened with the death without heirs of Charles II of Spain in 1700. This event had long been anticipated, but plans to divide the Spanish dominions in such a way as to maintain the balance of power were thwarted not only by the rivalry of France and Austria, but also by the maritime powers (England and Holland), which feared French ascendancy in overseas trade if it acquired the Spanish overseas empire. The result was the long War of the Spanish Succession, ended, in spite of the victories of Prince Eugene of Savoy and the Duke of Marlborough, by the compromise Peace of Utrecht in 1713. The French candidate retained the Spanish throne as Philip V, and France kept most of its gains on its eastern frontier. But the ruinous expense of Louis' wars left France in a desperate situation, with a legacy of financial disorder and internal discontent from which his successors never fully recovered.

2 With Paris and later Versailles vulnerable to invasion from the north-east, Louis was anxious to expand into the Spanish Netherlands and to fortify the frontier defences (map below). This can be partly explained by Louis's fear that at the death of Carlos II of Spain, Spanish possessions on Louis's north-east frontier would be left to the Austrian Habsburgs, raising the spectre of a resurrection of the empire of Charles V. For the same reason, he conquered Franche-Comté, widened his hold on Alsace, occupied Lorraine and in 1681 annexed Strasbourg.

1 Carlos II, ruler of Spain, Spanish America, the south Netherlands and half of Italy, died childless in 1700, bequeathing his empire to Philip, grandson of Louis XIV. This concentration of territory in Bourbon hands overturned the balance of power in Europe, provoking war with Britain, the Dutch Republic, the Holy Roman Empire, Portugal and Savoy. Bourbon victories were followed by a string of defeats. By the peaces of Utrecht (1713) and Rastatt (1714), Philip kept Spain and Spanish America; Savoy and the Austrian Habsburgs partitioned the rest.

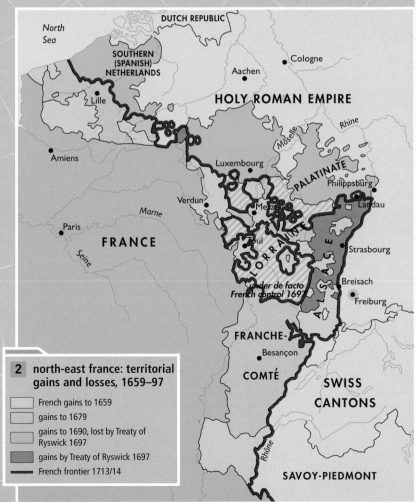

2 north-east france: territorial gains and losses, 1659–97

- French gains to 1659
- gains to 1679
- gains to 1690, lost by Treaty of Ryswick 1697
- gains by Treaty of Ryswick 1697
- French frontier 1713/14

the european **economy**

Recovery from the economic setbacks of the 14th century began around 1450, and Europe's population expanded rapidly, though the fast growth of the 16th century was interrupted by war, rebellion, famine and plague in the 17th century and not resumed until the middle of the 18th century.

Overall it increased from an estimated 69 million in 1500 to 188 million in 1800, but the increase was uneven and most marked in Britain and the Netherlands, by 1700 the greatest textile producers of Europe, the most active traders, with the largest merchant fleets and rapidly growing ship-building and metalware industries. The result was a shift in the economic axis. In 1500 industry was concentrated in the narrow corridor running north–south from Antwerp and Bruges through Ulm and Augsburg to Milan and Florence. By 1700 the axis ran west–east from England and Holland through the metal and woollen districts of the lower Rhine to the industrial concentrations of Saxony, Bohemia and Silesia, and thence to Russia, now beginning to build up an industrial base. The great expansion of overseas trade, particularly after 1700, also favoured the maritime powers. A consequence was the decline of the great trading cities of northern Italy, dominant two centuries earlier. In 1500 only four cities – Paris, Milan, Naples and Venice – had more than 100,000 inhabitants. By 1700 this number had trebled, and the majority of the rising urban centres lay west of the Rhine; London and Paris had already passed the half-million mark.

Significant as these developments were, agriculture was still Europe's most important industry. As late as 1815 three-quarters of its population were employed on the land, though here again there were sharp regional differences. In most of Europe farmers were subsistence peasants, whose smallholdings of two to ten hectares produced only about 20 per cent more than their immediate needs. But in the west the need to feed growing urban populations led, first in Holland and then in Britain, to an agricultural revolution. The Dutch poured capital into land reclamation, recovering some 180,000 hectares between 1540 and 1715, and developed intensive cultivation, eliminating the need to leave land fallow by means of a rotation of crops, which was later taken over in England. The growing population was also sus-tained by the introduction of new, more productive crops, mainly from America, including maize, which gave a far higher yield than the old regional cereals of southern Europe, and the potato, introduced in c.1565, which spread slowly until it became a key field crop after 1700. Urban demand also stimulated specialization (Holland was exporting 90 per cent of its cheese by 1700), and generated a massive demand in western Europe for wheat and rye from Pomerania, Prussia, Poland and Russia, greatly to the profit of Holland which vir-tually monopolized the Baltic carrying trade in the 16th and 17th centuries.

The profitable grain-export trade of eastern Europe adversely affected the position of the peasant population which had enjoyed rela-tive freedom before 1500 but now was reduced to a state of abject serfdom on large commer-cial estates. Only on the frontiers (e.g. in Hungary and on the

1 By 1812, the peasants of Britain, Scandinavia and the Netherlands had long been free. Those of Denmark and Austria were encouraged in their efforts by the French Revolution, which had revived emancipation movements in Poland and Germany, the latter scene of the most famous peasant revolt (1525). Only Russia, Spain, Portugal and Italy remained fully under the landlords' yoke.

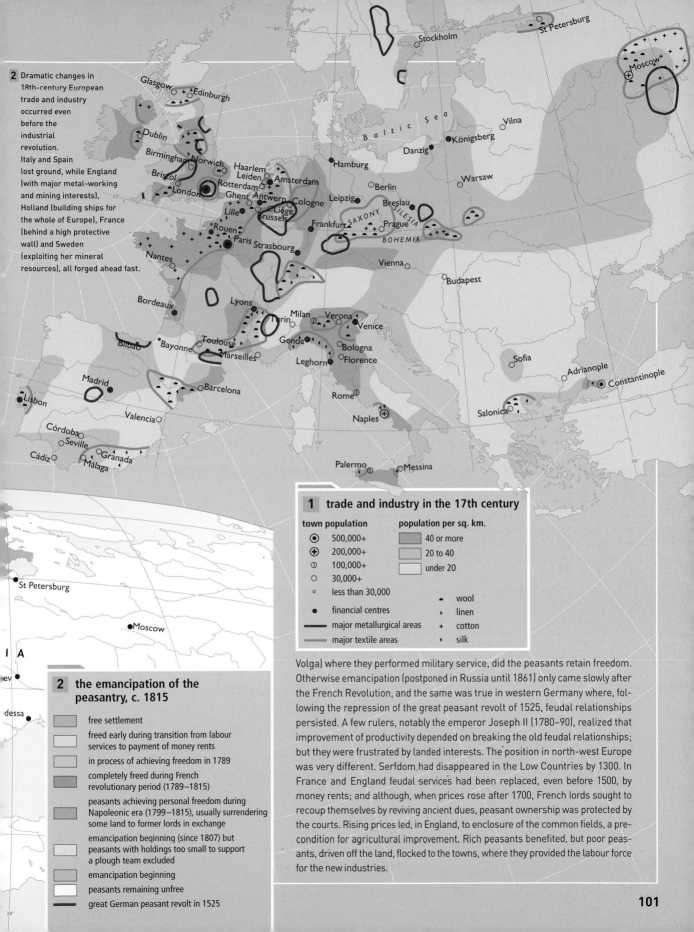

2 Dramatic changes in 18th-century European trade and industry occurred even before the industrial revolution. Italy and Spain lost ground, while England (with major metal-working and mining interests), Holland (building ships for the whole of Europe), France (behind a high protective wall) and Sweden (exploiting her mineral resources), all forged ahead fast.

1 trade and industry in the 17th century

town population

- ⊙ 500,000+
- ⊕ 200,000+
- ⊖ 100,000+
- ○ 30,000+
- ∘ less than 30,000
- ● financial centres
- ▬ major metallurgical areas
- ▬ major textile areas

population per sq. km.

- 40 or more
- 20 to 40
- under 20

- ◣ wool
- › linen
- + cotton
- ‹ silk

2 the emancipation of the peasantry, c. 1815

- free settlement
- freed early during transition from labour services to payment of money rents
- in process of achieving freedom in 1789
- completely freed during French revolutionary period (1789–1815)
- peasants achieving personal freedom during Napoleonic era (1799–1815), usually surrendering some land to former lords in exchange
- emancipation beginning (since 1807) but peasants with holdings too small to support a plough team excluded
- emancipation beginning
- peasants remaining unfree
- ▬ great German peasant revolt in 1525

Volga) where they performed military service, did the peasants retain freedom. Otherwise emancipation (postponed in Russia until 1861) only came slowly after the French Revolution, and the same was true in western Germany where, following the repression of the great peasant revolt of 1525, feudal relationships persisted. A few rulers, notably the emperor Joseph II (1780–90), realized that improvement of productivity depended on breaking the old feudal relationships; but they were frustrated by landed interests. The position in north-west Europe was very different. Serfdom had disappeared in the Low Countries by 1300. In France and England feudal services had been replaced, even before 1500, by money rents; and although, when prices rose after 1700, French lords sought to recoup themselves by reviving ancient dues, peasant ownership was protected by the courts. Rising prices led, in England, to enclosure of the common fields, a precondition for agricultural improvement. Rich peasants benefited, but poor peasants, driven off the land, flocked to the towns, where they provided the labour force for the new industries.

the **expansion** of russia

The rise of modern Russia dates from the reign of Ivan III (1462–1505). During the preceding century the principality of Moscow had expanded at the expense of its immediate neighbours; but it was still a tributary of the Mongols, and in the west it was hemmed in by the great Polish–Lithuanian state, which extended deep into the Ukraine. Ivan III threw off the Mongol overlordship (1480), and in the west his conquest of the ancient republic of Novgorod (1478) opened the way to Livonia and the White Sea.

Under his son Vassily (1505–33) and his grandson Ivan IV (1533–84) the advance continued. The subjection of the Khanate of Kazan (1552) opened the way across the Urals into Siberia; the conquest of the Khanate of Astrakhan (1556) gave Moscow control of the Volga to the Caspian Sea. But in the west Lithuania and Poland, joined after 1560 by Sweden, fought back vigorously, and during the 'time of troubles' following the death of Ivan IV made substantial gains at Russian expense. This, on the other hand, was the time of the great Russian thrust across Siberia, which, beginning in 1582, reached the Sea of Okhotsk by 1639.

Siberia, where the population in 1720 was only about 400,000, still counted for little. The axis of Russian expansion was in the west, its thrust symbolized by Peter the Great's foundation of the new capital, St. Petersburg (1703). His long Swedish wars, concluded by the Peace of Nystad (1721), brought him Estonia, Livonia and part of Karelia. Russia now had free access to the Baltic. Under Catherine II (1762–96) it won control of the northern shore of the Black Sea, where Odessa (founded 1794) became a main outlet for Russian exports. But the question of secure access from the Black Sea to the Mediterranean remained unsolved. It was to be a central concern of Russian policy in the 19th century, and when it was thwarted by the other European powers in 1856 and again in 1878 Russia turned from Europe to Asia, securing control of the Caucasus (1857–64) and then of the Khanates of Tashkent (1865), Samarkand (1868), Bukhara (1868), Khiva (1873) and Kokand (1876), while in the Far East it conquered the Amur and Ussuri regions at the expense of China. But defeat in the Crimean War (1854–56) convinced Russia of its backwardness, and in 1861, as a first step to modernization, the serfs were liberated. Some went to Siberia, far more to the towns, where they provided a working force for industrialization which began in the 1870s and was especially rapid in 1893–1904 and 1909–13, when it exceeded the American growth rate. A metallurgical industry was developed in the Ukraine producing mainly rails for the expanding railways. But the achievement was unstable. Russian ambitions in the Far East excited British and Japanese fears, and the result was the Anglo–Japanese alliance (1902) and the Russo–Japanese war of 1904–05, which halted Russian expansion until 1945. At home the consequences were even more ominous. An urban proletariat had been formed which became the mainstay of the revolution of 1905 and more fatefully still in 1917.

1 From a small base in the late 13th century, Muscovy expanded first through cooperation with the Mongols, then in opposition to them (map right). By the early 16th century it had absorbed the republics of Novgorod and Pskov, before expanding east and south-east into the nomadic steppelands of Asia. The developed states of Poland–Lithuania and the Ottoman empire offered more of a barrier. Expansion to the west and south only became possible after 1648 and reached its peak after 1750.

2 Though the Russian population of Siberia was only 200,000 by the mid-17th century, the speed of Russia's expansion was nonetheless prodigious (map below). Other than the Amur basin, annexed from China but returned by the 1689 Treaty of Nerchinsk, most of this vast area was acquired from indigenous peoples.

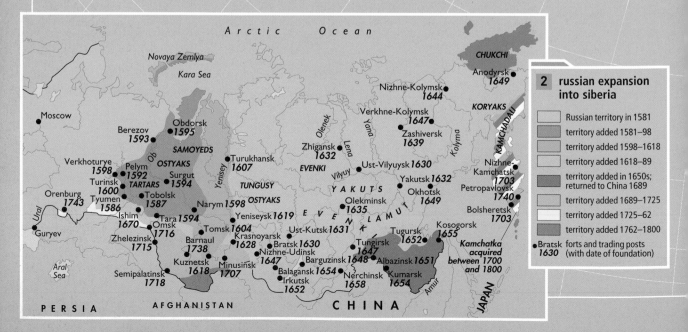

2 russian expansion into siberia

Russian territory in 1581
territory added 1581–98
territory added 1598–1618
territory added 1618–89
territory added in 1650s; returned to China 1689
territory added 1689–1725
territory added 1725–62
territory added 1762–1800
Bratsk 1630 forts and trading posts (with date of foundation)

BARENTS SEA

Kola Peninsula

White Sea

PECHORA

Pechora

Obdorsk 1595

Berezov 1593

1501

YUGRA

1478

Archangel 1584

Kholmogory

Kama 1472

Solvychegodsk

Ustyug

1393-1425

Solikamsk

NOVGOROD TERRITORY

SWEDEN

FINLAND 1809

1743

Åbo

Åland Islands

Stockholm

Helsingfors

1721

Gulf of Finland

Vyborg

Kronstadt 1704

Revel

1721

Narva 1703

St. Petersburg

ESTONIA

LIVONIA 1510

Pskov

1478

1772

Riga

COURLAND

Memel

LITHUANIA

Königsberg

Danzig

Kovno

Vilna

Polotsk

Vitebsk

Smolensk

1514

Grodno

Bialystok

1807

1795

Minsk

Mogilev

1772

Warsaw

Vistula

Kalisz 1815

POLAND

1793

Brest-Litovsk

Lublin

Lwów

AUSTRO-HUNGARIAN EMPIRE

Debrecen

Kolozsvár

TRANSYLVANI

Brassó

MOLDAVIA

WALLACHIA

Bucharest

Danube

Ruschuk

OTTOMAN EMPIRE

Sofia

Varna

BALTIC SEA

Lake Ladoga

Lake Onega

Kargopol

Novgorod

1478

1389-1425

1364

Yaroslavl

1503

Velikiye Luki

1514-21

1389-1425

1494

Vyazma

1353-59

1634

1494

Bryansk

Orel 1564

Gomel

1503

Chernigov

1503 1586

1634

Kiev

UKRAINE

1667

Kharkov 1654

Vinnitsa

1793

Kamenets Bratslav

Kishinev

1791

BESSARABIA

Jassy

Dniester

Akkerman

1794

Odessa

1812

Nikolaev

Kherson 1774

Yekaterinoslav (Kodak)

1786

ZAPOROZH'YE

1789

KHANATE OF CRIMEA

Yevpatoriya

Sebastopol

1783

Simferopol (Ak-Mechet)

1784

BLACK SEA

Kerch

1362-89

Vologda

1364

Soligalich

Kostroma

1364

Tver

1451

1302

1364

Vladimir

Murom

Moscow

1301

Kolomna

1364

Arzamas

1425-62

Tula

1521

Yelets

1586

Tambov 1636

Voronezh 1586

Belgorod 1593

Kursk 1586

Poltava

1709

Don

Donets

DON COSSACKS

Taganrog

1783

Azov

1783

Cherkassk

KUBAN COSSACKS

Yekaterinodar

1792

Stavropol

Pyatigorsk

Sukhum-Kale

1810

Poti

Kutaisi

1804

Sukhum-Kale

Vladikavkaz

1784

Terek

1806

Tiflis

GEORGIA

1806

Erivan

AZERBAIJAN

1805

Kura

Baku 1806

1813

Derbent

DAGHESTAN

Caucasus

Kuma

KALMYKS

Astrakhan

KHANATE OF ASTRAKHAN

1556

Guryev 1645

NOGAI TATARS

Kamyshin

Tsaritsyn

1589

Saratov

1590

Samara

1586

Syzran

1683

Simbirsk

1648

Penza

1650

MORDVA

1393

MESHCHERA

Nizhniy Novgorod

1393-45

MARI

CHUVASHI

1552

KHANATE OF KAZAN

Kazan 1552

Volga

1489

Vyatka

Ufa 1586

UDMURTY

Perm 1724

Kungur

Nizhniy Tagil 1724

Yekaterinburg 1725

SIBERIA

Orenburg 1743

Ural

CASPIAN SEA

PERSIA

ceded temporarily by Persia, 1723-32

1478

Nizhniy Novgorod

1478

---

1 from muscovy to russia

— boundary of all Russian territories in 1462

— Lithuania, 1462

1783 date of foundation of new town

KALMYKS native peoples

the expansion of Muscovy:

Moscow territory at end of 13th century

1478 date of acquisition by Muscovy

acquisitions to 1462

acquisitions under Ivan III, 1462-1505

acquisitions during 16th century

acquisitions during 17th century

acquisitions during 18th century

acquisitions, 1801-15

territory ceded to Sweden 1617 and Poland-Lithuania, 1618

acquired from Poland-Lithuania, 1634

acquired from Poland-Lithuania, 1667

103

the **struggle** for empire

The Treaty of Utrecht (1713), which ended the War of Spanish Succession, sought to establish stability in Europe and overseas on the basis of a balance of power. But owing to commercial disputes and colonial rivalries, particularly in America, peace remained precarious.

In 1739 war broke out between England and Spain; in 1740 Frederick II of Prussia, supported by France, seized Silesia; and when France, supported by Spain, declared war on England in 1744, the European and overseas wars were fused into a single global conflict. It also quickly turned into a duel between England and France, particularly when, after the inconclusive Treaty of Aix-la-Chapelle (1748), fighting again broke out in North America in 1754. Here the French, with their strategically situated forts, were initially successful. But the whole situation changed when William Pitt the Elder, later Earl of Chatham, became British prime minister in 1756. By allying with and subsidizing Prussia, struggling to retain Silesia against an overwhelming French–Austrian–Russian coalition, Pitt compelled France to concentrate on the continental war. Naval victories at Quiberon Bay and Lagos in 1759 assured British control of the Atlantic and prevented reinforcements reaching Canada. The result was the loss of the French and, when Spain entered the war on the French side in 1761, of the Spanish colonial empires in North America. At the Peace of Paris (1763) the French and Spanish possessions in the West Indies were restored, but England retained the North American mainland east of the Mississippi, including Florida which was ceded by Spain.

2 the franco–british struggle for india

- under British control by 1783
- under British control by 1815
- Indian states in subsidiary alliance with Britain by 1818
- main area of Anglo-French naval conflict 1759–63 and 1781–83
- gained by British from Dutch 1815
- Portuguese territory
- ● gained by British 1815
- ◉ gained by British from French 1815
- ● French towns and territories
- ○ Portuguese towns
- → French attacks with date
- ⟶ British attacks with date
- ✕ French victory
- ✕ British victory
- ✕ Afghan victory over Marathas

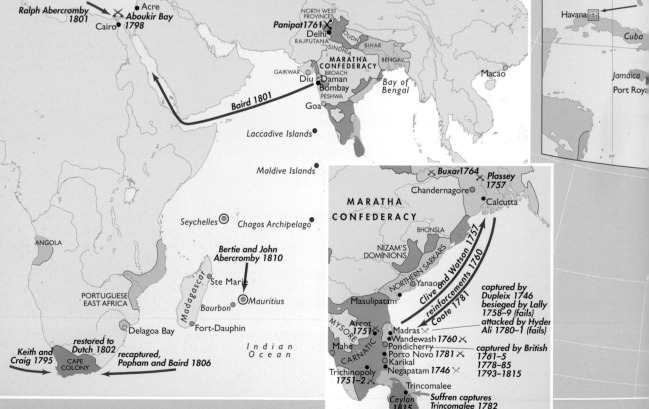

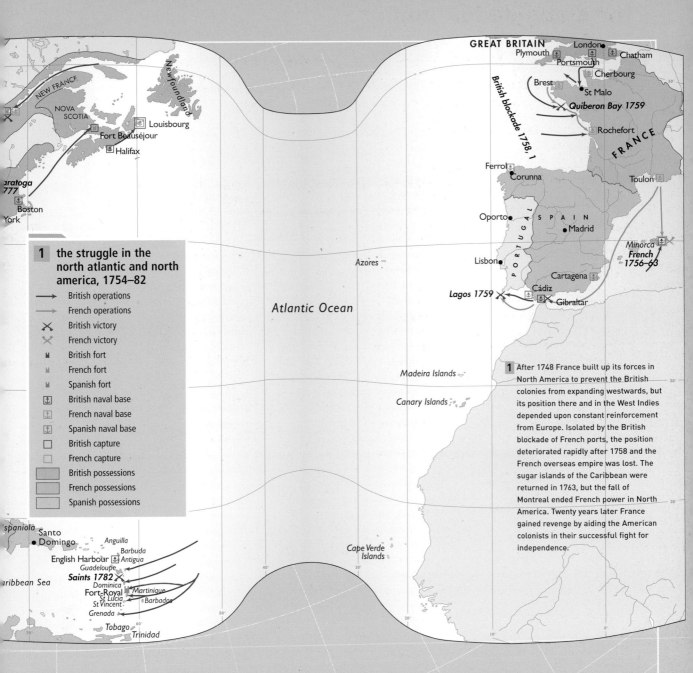

1 the struggle in the north atlantic and north america, 1754–82

→ British operations
→ French operations
✕ British victory
✕ French victory
Ⓜ British fort
Ⓜ French fort
Ⓜ Spanish fort
⬆ British naval base
⬆ French naval base
⬆ Spanish naval base
☐ British capture
☐ French capture
▅ British possessions
▅ French possessions
▅ Spanish possessions

Map labels:
GREAT BRITAIN · London · Plymouth · Portsmouth · Chatham · Cherbourg · Brest · St Malo · *Quiberon Bay 1759* · Rochefort · FRANCE · British blockade 1758, 1 · Ferrol · Corunna · Toulon · Oporto · SPAIN · Madrid · PORTUGAL · Lisbon · Minorca · *French 1756–63* · Cartagena · *Lagos 1759* · Cádiz · Gibraltar

NEW FRANCE · Newfoundland · NOVA SCOTIA · Louisbourg · Fort Beauséjour · Halifax · Saratoga 1777 · Boston · York

Atlantic Ocean · Azores · Madeira Islands · Canary Islands · Cape Verde Islands

Hispaniola · Santo Domingo · Anguilla · Barbuda · Antigua · English Harbour · Guadeloupe · *Saints 1782* · Dominica · Fort-Royal · Martinique · St Lucia · St Vincent · Barbados · Grenada · Tobago · Trinidad · Caribbean Sea

1 After 1748 France built up its forces in North America to prevent the British colonies from expanding westwards, but its position there and in the West Indies depended upon constant reinforcement from Europe. Isolated by the British blockade of French ports, the position deteriorated rapidly after 1758 and the French overseas empire was lost. The sugar islands of the Caribbean were returned in 1763, but the fall of Montreal ended French power in North America. Twenty years later France gained revenge by aiding the American colonists in their successful fight for independence.

2 The capture of Madras by the French under Dupleix in 1746 began the struggle for India (map left). As in America, British sea power proved decisive. Dupleix was checked at Trichinopoly in 1752, and after the capture of Bengal in 1757 the British could reinforce the Carnatic at will. The capture of Pondicherry in 1761 destroyed French power, and with control of the sea the British were able to hold off all subsequent challenges.

The British triumph was nevertheless short-lived. When the 13 colonies rebelled in 1776, France, which had rebuilt its navy, supported the rebels and by naval action compelled Great Britain to recognize American independence in the Treaty of Versailles (1783). In India, on the other hand, Britain built an empire which lasted until 1947. Here again, sea-power was decisive, enabling the English East India Company to checkmate the ambitions of the able French governor, Joseph Dupleix, to expand French influence in south India. By 1763 France was eliminated as a rival in India. An important determinant of the pace of British expansion was the decline of the Mughal Empire after the death of Aurangzeb in 1707. Some states, the Marathas and the Sikh Punjab for example, asserted their independence, while former Mughal provinces, such as Oudh, Bengal and Hyderabad, achieved virtual autonomy. The British both feared and profited from these developments. By the end of the governor-generalship of Richard Wellesley (1797–1805) British supremacy was an acknowledged fact. Revolutionary France attempted a comeback, and Napoleon planned an invasion of India. But once again sea-power was decisive, and in 1815 Great Britain occupied an unrivalled position in the colonial world.

the **age** of **revolution**

The second half of the 18th century was a time of revolutionary ferment throughout the western hemisphere, from the Volga, where a great peasant insurrection under Pugachev in 1773 took Kazan and threatened Moscow, to Haiti, where the black population rose in rebellion in 1791 under Toussaint l'Ouverture and won control of the island by 1801. The character of the many rebellions of the period (map 1) was varied, but all derived, directly or indirectly, from the Enlightenment, with its assertion of the rights of man, its rationalism and rejection of traditional authority.

Provinces like the Austrian Netherlands (1787) and Hungary (1790) rose in rebellion against the centralizing policies and reforming edicts of progressive rulers; colonial peoples resisted dictation by the home government and demanded autonomy or at least no taxation without consent, as in North America in 1775 and in South America after 1808. The demand for independence was the commonest motive for revolt, and lay behind the risings in Ireland (1798), Corsica (1755, 1793), Sardinia (1793), Spain (1808), Serbia (1804) and the Tyrol (1809). Sometimes they were underpinned by social unrest; but this was exceptional: peasants had more to hope for from reforming monarchs than from nobles who were their oppressors. Hence their failure to support the gentry in the Polish revolts of 1791 and 1794. Revolts against patrician oligarchies occurred in Geneva (1768) and the Netherlands (1784–87); but usually it was only when concerted aristocratic opposition to the monarchy opened the flood-gates that the peasants and the labouring class took a hand. This was what happened in France after 1787.

The immediate cause of the French Revolution was the financial crisis arising from the American war. By 1786, the government was faced with bankruptcy and Louis XVI was forced by a rebellious aristocracy to summon the Estates-General which had not met since 1614. When the Estates-General turned itself into a National Assembly on June 17, 1789, the revolution had begun, but it was still a middle-class revolution, and the constitution drawn up in 1791 showed their distrust of the masses by limiting the right to vote. But in 1792 a republic was proclaimed; in 1793 Louis XVI was executed and a Committee of Public Safety set up, first under Danton and then under Robespierre, which instituted a reign of terror against enemies at home, while Carnot mobilized an army of 770,000 men against enemies abroad.

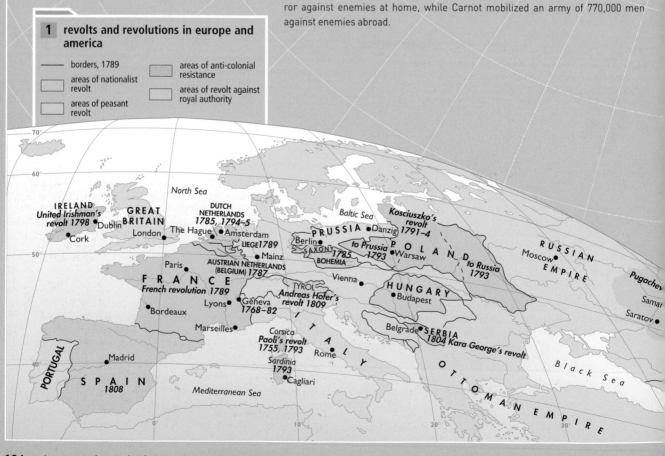

1 revolts and revolutions in europe and america

— borders, 1789

areas of nationalist revolt

areas of peasant revolt

areas of anti-colonial resistance

areas of revolt against royal authority

By 1795 the French armies were victorious and the revolution had spent itself. French troops held Belgium and the left bank of the Rhine, while William V of Holland was deposed and his country turned into a Batavian republic, closely bound to France, forerunner of other similar republics from Naples to Switzerland. French influence was spreading far and wide, a victory not simply for French arms but for the ideas and achievements of the revolution, equality before the law, the abolition of feudalism, and the 'rights of man' as defined in the famous declaration of October 2, 1789. Except among the conservative peasantry, who fought the revolution in France itself from 1793 to 1802, the principles of the French revolution had immense appeal; and though their appeal was later dimmed, they lighted a torch which was never extinguished, even during the reaction which set in after 1815.

1755, 1793 Corsica Local clans led by Paoli rebelled against Genoese rule. A second attempt by Paoli to secure independence from (revolutionary) France in 1793, led to a brief British occupation; the rise of Bonaparte put an end to the separatist movement.

1768 Geneva Middle-class citizens of the city-state rebelled against domination by a few patrician families.

1773 South-east Russia Cossacks, peasants and Asiatic tribes rebelled in the Volga and Ural regions under Pugachev, a Don Cossack.

1775 America Prolonged resistance by the Thirteen Colonies to Britain's financial policies resulted in open warfare and the Declaration of Independence, 1776. The defeat of Britain led to the formation of the United States in 1783. Numerous slave revolts from 1790s.

1785, 1794–45 Dutch Netherlands Three-cornered struggle for power between the 'Stadholder', patrician families who controlled the Estates-General and the middle-class Patriot party which aimed to democratize the government.

1787 Austrian Netherlands (Belgium) A revolt against the centralizing policy of Emperor Joseph II led to the proclamation of the Republic of the United Belgian Provinces in 1790.

1789 France In 1789 Louis XVI called the Estates-General to try to solve the financial crisis, but the gathering turned into a national assembly and with army support royal authority was overturned. In 1791 a constitution was introduced loosely based on the 'rights of man', and in 1793 the king was executed and a republic declared.

1789 Liège Middle-class citizens, workers and peasants expelled the prince-bishop.

1790 Hungary Magyar nobles rejected edicts of Austrian emperor and demanded greater independence for Hungary within Habsburg empire.

1791 Poland The king adopted a constitution to modernize government. Russia invaded Poland to restore the old system and divided large areas with Prussia. In 1794 a popular revolt led by Kosciuszko was brutally crushed by Russian armies and Poland was partitioned between Russia, Prussia and Austria.

1791 Haiti A slave rising in the western (French) part of the island (Saint-Domingue) resulted in the rise of a black leader, Toussaint l'Ouverture; by 1801 he had conquered the rest of the island from the Spaniards and secured virtual independence.

1793 Sardinia Islanders demanded autonomy within combined kingdom of Piedmont-Sardinia.

1798 Ireland The rebellion of United Irishmen under Wolfe Tone.

1804 Serbia Revolt against Ottoman atrocities led to demands for autonomy within the Ottoman empire and later for independence.

1808 Spain A national rising against the French provided an opening for an expeditionary force under Wellington.

1809 Tyrol Peasant revolt led by Andreas Hofer against Bavarian and French occupation.

1810 Spanish America Discontent increased after 1808 when the colonists were faced with the prospect of new imperialist policies from either Napoleon or Spanish liberals; beginning of the revolutionary movement which secured independence by 1826.

napoleonic europe

In 1799 the 31-year-old general Napoleon Bonaparte seized power in France and was to rule until 1814, first as First Consul and then, after 1804, as emperor. His reign was a watershed in the history not only of France but of the whole of Europe.

1 napoleon and the reshaping of europe

French territories ruled from Paris, c. 1812	☒ battles of the Italian campaign
states ruled by members of Napoleon's family, c. 1812	⊠ battles of the War of the Second Coalition
	⬛ battles of the War of the Third Coalition
other dependent states, c. 1812	⬛ battles in the Austrian War, 1809
	☒ battles in the Peninsular War
☒ French victory	⬛ battles of the Russian campaign
☒ French defeat	⬛ battles of the War of Liberation from French rule
	☒ battles in the defence of France
	☒ battles in the War of the 100 Days

Napoleon had won his reputation by his spectacular victories over Sardinia and Austria in the Italian campaign of 1796; but after 1799, particularly during the Consulate, he proved as brilliant a states-man and administrator as a general. In 1799 Frenchmen, particularly the urban and rural middle classes, wanted peace and security. Napoleon gave them both. The wars were ended by the treaties of Lunéville (1801) and Amiens (1802); for the first time in 10 years there was general peace in Europe. At home he gave the citizens who had supported the 'Thermidorian reaction' of 1794 the stability which the Directory (1795–99) had failed to provide. But he was no reactionary. He made it his task to mould the essential achievements of the revolution into permanent institutions. In 1800 the 83 *départements* into which France had been divided in 1789 were reorganized under prefects responsible to the First Consul. The new civil code of 1804 confirmed the property rights created by the revolution and won him the lasting support of the peasant proprietors who were the backbone of the country. At the same time a career open to talents was provided for men of ability rising through the system of state schools and universities established in 1802.

These achievements outlived Napoleon himself, but peace proved elusive. A durable settlement might have been reached with the continental powers, Prussia and Austria; but the issues between France and England were too deep-seated for compromise, and in 1803 Great Britain declared war on France. Thereafter war continued almost without interruption until 1815. In essence it was a continuation of the Anglo–French conflict of the 18th century, complicated by the traditional British fear, ever since the French occupation of the Austrian Netherlands in 1792, of a hostile great power on the Scheldt. From that time Great Britain was the moving spirit behind the anti-French coalitions which it kept going, as in the Seven Years War, by subsidies. France, on the other hand, had not abandoned the hope of recovering the overseas empire lost in 1763. Napoleon's expedition to Egypt (1798–99) was intended to open the back door to India, and there were other plans for recuperating France's position in the Caribbean and on the American mainland. They were foiled by British control of the sea. Nelson's destruction of the French fleet at Aboukir sealed the fate of the Egyptian expedition, and elsewhere the French navy was no match for the British, which thwarted French attempts to intervene in Ireland (1797–98) and a projected invasion of England in 1804. After Nelson's victory at Trafalgar (1805), British control of the seas was assured, and Napoleon had no alternative except to turn against Britain's continental allies, hoping in this way to seal off Europe and bring Britain to heel by economic pressure.

Napoleon's campaigns against Austria, Prussia and Russia in 1806 and 1807 were brilliantly successful, and 1810 saw him at the peak of his power, directly controlling the whole of western Europe from Catalonia to Lübeck as well as Italy west of the Apennines, with satellite kingdoms and duchies in Spain, the remainder of Italy and Westphalia. But so long as Britain held out, Napoleon's position was insecure. Control of the sea enabled the British to land an expeditionary force under the future Duke of Wellington in Spain (1808). His attempt to close the continent to British trade led to his breach with Russia. The invasion of Russia (1812) was a gamble which failed, and after the retreat from Moscow and the battle of Leipzig (1813) Napoleon's fate was sealed. In the reaction which followed much, but not all, of his system perished. In Germany, in particular, the Napoleonic settlements of 1797–98 and 1803 reduced the 234

1 By 1812 Napoleon dominated most of Europe west of Russia. In western Europe (map above) French administrators and local notables tried to modernize law and government. The persistent hostility of Britain undermined the empire.
The British supported a series of shifting coalitions against Napoleon. Spain rebelled in 1809 and Russia refused to collaborate in 1812. The failure to conquer Russia weakened France and led to Napoleon's fall in 1814–15. The Congress of Vienna in 1815 tore up the Napoleonic empire.

territories of the old empire to 40, and after 1815 there was no going back. Equally important were the institutional changes introduced on the French model. A society based on wealth and merit rather than prescription and privilege was introduced in the Netherlands, the Rhinelands and north-east Italy, and even countries like Prussia reformed to meet the French challenge. The political geography of Europe was rationalized and the modern national state was born, fragile at first but destined to command the future.

the **united states**

The disputes and difficulties leading to the American War of Independence and the foundation of the United States began almost immediately after the English victory over France and the acquisition of Canada at the Peace of Paris in 1763.

When the British government reorganized its vastly expanded North American possessions, establishing a huge Indian reserve west of the Alleghenies (1763) and extending the boundaries of Quebec to the Mississippi and Ohio rivers (1774), its measures were bitterly resented by the colonists in New England, Virginia and Pennsylvania as a check to westward expansion. This resentment, combined with resistance to English tax demands and trade controls, was one of the factors behind the revolt of the American colonies. The War of Independence began at Lexington and Concord in Massachusetts in April 1775 and was ended, after the British surrender at Yorktown (October 1781), by the Treaty of Versailles (1783), which extended the frontiers of the newly independent United States to the Great Lakes in the north and the Mississippi in the west.

Once independence was achieved, expansion proceeded rapidly. In 1783 the new republic comprised some 800,000 square miles of territory. The purchase of Louisiana from France (1803) more than doubled its extent. Thereafter expansion in the south and west was largely by conquest at the expense of Mexico, though the Oregon question, finally settled in 1846, looked for a moment as though it might bring war with Great Britain. In the north settlers moved into the 'back country' in increasing numbers after 1800, but it was the arrival of a new wave of European immigrants, predominantly German and Irish, which populated the Midwest. By 1850 the frontier of settlement had reached the 100th meridian, the dividing line between sparse and adequate rainfall.

This vast territorial expansion, which raised the population from approximately 3,000,000 in 1783 to 31,000,000 on the eve of the Civil War, had important political consequences. By 1860 the original 13 states had increased to 34. The result was a deterioration in the relative position of the Southern states with their plantation economy and black slave population, as a result of which the plantation aristocracy saw itself being swamped by the industrializing North and the growing Midwest. This, rather than the simple issue of slavery, was the underlying cause of the American Civil War, but the issues were in fact inseparable because, with over 90 per cent of the black population living in the South, the moral

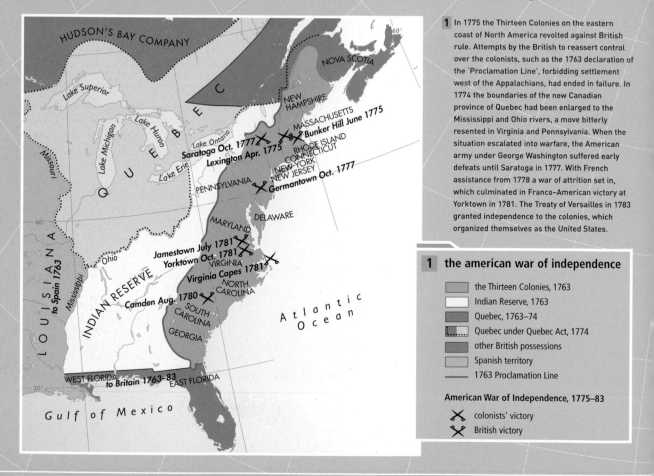

1 In 1775 the Thirteen Colonies on the eastern coast of North America revolted against British rule. Attempts by the British to reassert control over the colonists, such as the 1763 declaration of the 'Proclamation Line', forbidding settlement west of the Appalachians, had ended in failure. In 1774 the boundaries of the new Canadian province of Quebec had been enlarged to the Mississippi and Ohio rivers, a move bitterly resented in Virginia and Pennsylvania. When the situation escalated into warfare, the American army under George Washington suffered early defeats until Saratoga in 1777. With French assistance from 1778 a war of attrition set in, which culminated in Franco–American victory at Yorktown in 1781. The Treaty of Versailles in 1783 granted independence to the colonies, which organized themselves as the United States.

1 the american war of independence

- the Thirteen Colonies, 1763
- Indian Reserve, 1763
- Quebec, 1763–74
- Quebec under Quebec Act, 1774
- other British possessions
- Spanish territory
- 1763 Proclamation Line

American War of Independence, 1775–83

- ✕ colonists' victory
- ✕ British victory

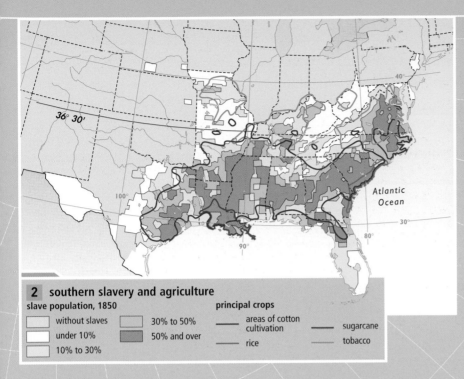

2 southern slavery and agriculture

slave population, 1850

☐	without slaves
☐	under 10%
☐	10% to 30%
☐	30% to 50%
■	50% and over

principal crops

—	areas of cotton cultivation
—	rice
—	sugarcane
—	tobacco

question was also a regional question. Abraham Lincoln, elected President in 1860 by a Northern vote, was right when he said that the nation could not permanently remain 'half-slave and half-free'.

The North fought at first to preserve the Union; but, significantly, it was over the question of whether slavery should be permitted in Kansas and Nebraska that the conflict came to a head. Soon after Lincoln's election South Carolina seceded from the Union and was quickly joined by 10 other states which came together as the Confederate States of America with their capital at Richmond, Virginia. The war opened with an attack on Fort Sumter in April 1861. Northern strategy was to deny the South vital resources by a naval blockade, to gain control of key river routes and forts in the west and to capture the Confederate capital of Richmond. In spite of the preponderance of the North in manpower and resources, the South held out for four years, a fact which heightened the bitterness and resentment during the subsequent period of Reconstruction. The outcome has been called 'the Second American Revolution'; by crippling the Southern ruling class and liberating its labour force, it determined that the thrusting, urban, industrialized North, with its creed of competitive capitalism, would stamp its pattern – for good or ill – on the entire post-bellum United States.

3 Some states, though they had slaves, declined to join the Confederacy (map right). At the start of the Civil War, West Virginia split from Virginia in order to stay with the Union. Once the war was over, 'Reconstruction' governments were established in the South, backed by northern Republicans. The last of these survived until 1877.

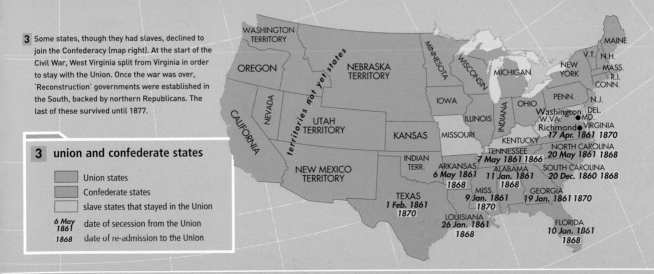

3 union and confederate states

■	Union states
■	Confederate states
☐	slave states that stayed in the Union
6 May 1861	date of secession from the Union
1868	date of re-admission to the Union

the **expansion** of the **united states**

The dominant fact in the history of the United States during the 19th century was the opening of the continent. In 1783 the effective frontier of the new Republic was the Allegheny Mountains. The Louisiana Purchase (1803) opened vast new areas for explorers, led by the famous expedition of Lewis and Clark (1804–08), and for settlers who quickly followed in their wake. After the Mexican wars (1846–48) and the discovery of gold in California (1848) prospectors, miners, speculators and settlers pushed west across the mountain chains from Salt Lake City and Santa Fe or by the Overland Trail from San Antonio. The great westward movement, bolstered by a confident belief in America's 'manifest destiny', could not, however, proceed without brutal disregard for the native population.

The destruction of the North American Indians had begun much earlier in New England in the Pequot war of 1636, and the Delaware Indians were uprooted and driven west before the end of the 18th century; but it was in the 1830s, when the land-hunger of the white planters and settlers became insatiable, that the expulsion of whole tribes, Cherokee, Chocktaw, Creek and Chickasaw, and their deportation to the Midwest (and later to Indian reservations) got under way. By 1850 the frontier had reached the 100th meridian, and it was here, in the Midwest and West, that the great battles of the 1860s and 1870s took place, which reduced the Indian population to scarcely more than 200,000 by the end of the 19th century.

In their place, and usurping their lands, poured in a flood of immigrants, mainly from Europe, which reached its peak in the last decade of the century. In the later phases most of the immigrants (from southern and eastern Europe) remained in the cities on the eastern seaboard, where they swelled the industrial proletariat; but by mid-century Germans and Scandinavians had formed a preponderant element on the farming frontier of Wisconsin, Iowa and Minnesota, and in the last quarter of the century British and Irish settlers, as well as native Americans, played an important part in the development of cattle ranching and stock raising in Texas, Wyoming and New Mexico. British capital and British land companies also contributed. But the most important area of European investment before 1914 was the financing of American railways, particularly the trans-continental lines. Railroads in operation in 1840 were confined to a few industrial regions in the east. British

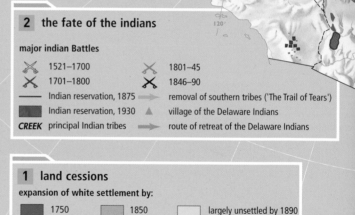

2 the fate of the indians

major indian Battles

⚔	1521–1700	⚔	1801–45
✕	1701–1800	✕	1846–90

—— Indian reservation, 1875   → removal of southern tribes ('The Trail of Tears')

▨ Indian reservation, 1930   ▲ village of the Delaware Indians

CREEK principal Indian tribes   → route of retreat of the Delaware Indians

1 land cessions

expansion of white settlement by:

▨ 1750	▨ 1850	☐ largely unsettled by 1890
▨ 1790	☐ 1890	

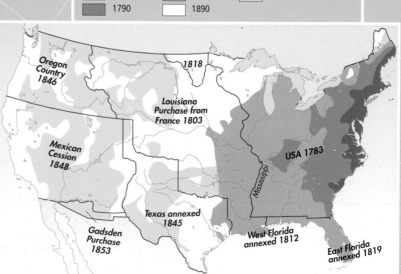

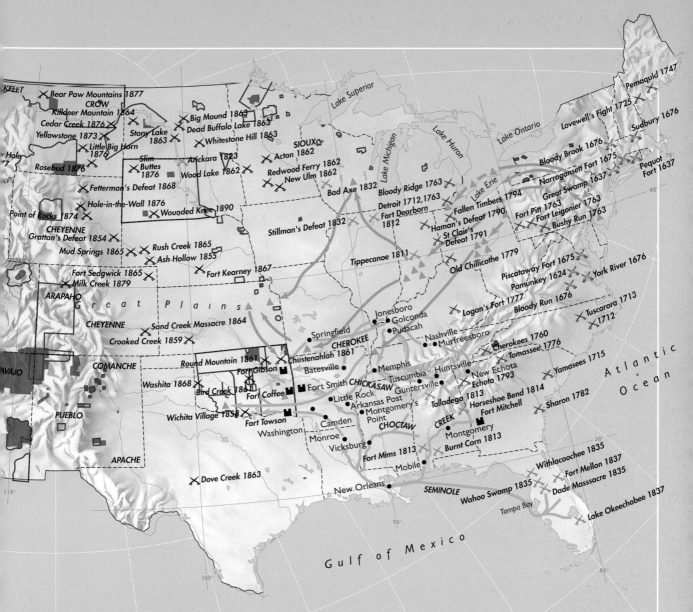

Map labels:

KEET

Bear Paw Mountains 1877
CROW
Killdeer Mountain 1864
Cedar Creek 1876
Yellowstone 1873
Little Big Horn 1876
Hole 7
Rosebud 1876
Slim Buttes 1876
Stony Lake 1863
Arickara 1823
Wood Lake 1862
Big Mound 1863
Dead Buffalo Lake 1863
Whitestone Hill 1863
Fetterman's Defeat 1868
Hole-in-the-Wall 1876
Point of Rocks 1874
Wounded Knee 1890
CHEYENNE
Grattan's Defeat 1854
Mud Springs 1865
Rush Creek 1865
Ash Hollow 1855
Fort Sedgwick 1865
Milk Creek 1879
ARAPAHO
CHEYENNE
Sand Creek Massacre 1864
Crooked Creek 1859
Fort Kearney 1867
G r e a t   P l a i n s
Round Mountain 1861
Fort Gibson
Washita 1868
Bird Creek 186
Fort Coffee
COMANCHE
Wichita Village 1858
Fort Towson
PUEBLO
Washington
APACHE
Dove Creek 1863
NAVAJO

SIOUX
Acton 1862
Redwood Ferry 1862
New Ulm 1862
Bad Axe 1832
Bloody Ridge 1763
Stillman's Defeat 1832
Detroit 1712, 1763
Fort Dearborn 1812
Tippecanoe 1811
Chustenahlah 1861
Batesville
Fort Smith
CHICKASAW
Little Rock
Arkansas Post
Montgomery's Point
Camden
Monroe
Vicksburg
Fort Mims 1813
Mobile
New Orleans
Springfield
Jonesboro
Golconda
Pudacah
CHEROKEE
Memphis
Tuscumbia
Guntersville
CHOCTAW
SEMINOLE
Wahoo Swamp 1835
Tampa Bay

Lake Superior
Lake Michigan
Lake Huron
Lake Ontario
Lake Erie
Fallen Timbers 1794
Haman's Defeat 1790
St Clair's Defeat 1791
Old Chillicothe 1779
Logan's Fort 1777
Nashville
Murfreesboro
Cherokees 1760
Tomassee 1776
Huntsville
New Echota
Echota 1793
Talladega 1813
Horseshoe Bend 1814
Fort Mitchell
CREEK
Montgomery
Burnt Corn 1813
Withlacoochee 1835
Fort Mellon 1837
Dade Massacre 1835
Lake Okeechobee 1837

Pemaquid 1747
Lovewell's Fight 1725
Sudbury 1676
Bloody Brook 1676
Narragansett Fort 1675
Great Swamp 1675
Pequot Fort 1637
Fort Pitt 1763
Fort Leigonier 1763
Bushy Run 1763
Piscataway Fort 1675
Pamunkey 1624
York River 1676
Bloody Run 1676
Tuscarora 1713 1712
Yamasees 1715
Sharon 1782
A t l a n t i c   O c e a n

G u l f   o f   M e x i c o

---

2 The main victims of the western movement by whites were Indians (map above). In the Great Plains and Far West, there were perhaps a quarter of a million Indians. As settlers moved into Indian areas there were a series of wars. The Indians had some temporary successes – for example, the defeat of General Custer's force at the Little Big Horn by Sioux and Cheyenne in 1876. But by 1890 Indian resistance had effectively been brought to an end and the Indians themselves were largely confined to their reservations.

1 In 1783 the new nation extended from the Atlantic coast to the Mississippi river. Its territory was enlarged in just two great spates of expansion (map left). During the first (1803–19), three Virginian presidents acquired Louisiana and the Floridas. During the second, the heyday of 'manifest destiny' (1845–53), Texas, Oregon, California and the remainder of the south-west were added, thereby completing the area occupied by the 48 contiguous states of today.

capital provided the finance to double the mileage between 1866 and 1873 and to carry it west, and this westward shift of transport and population was accompanied by a similar shift of agricultural production. The effects were dramatic. By 1890, when the rail network was larger than that of the whole of Europe, including the British Isles and Russia, a population moving on to virgin lands, with improved mechanization, such as the steel plough, new strains of cotton, wheat and maize, and the ubiquitous barbed wire fence, had made the United States the world's leading agricultural producer.

By 1890 the frontier was closed, the prospect of indefinite opportunities within the boundaries of the United States becoming a thing of the past. West of the 100th meridian population was still sparse, and urban and industrial development negligible; the great upsurge in the colonization and development of California and the Pacific seaboard was still to come. Nevertheless 1890 marked a turning point, registered in 1898 when the United States, denying its own past refusal to involve itself in other continents, turned from the American continent to the wider world of Asia. In 1898 American history merged into world history, with incalculable consequences for the future.

independent **latin america**

Napoleon's invasion of Spain and Portugal in 1808 enabled their colonies to assert their independence. The revolt began in Argentina in 1810 and Venezuela in 1811, and was later helped by Great Britain and the United States, which prevented intervention by the Iberian powers. After the fall of Lima (1821) and Bolivar's victory at Ayacucho (1824) Spain's fate in South America was sealed. In the north, early revolts in Mexico were suppressed, but in 1823 a republic was proclaimed, and a last Spanish attempt at reconquest in 1829 was defeated by Santa Ana. Only Brazil made the transition to nationhood peacefully. Here Portugal agreed to a constitution, and in 1822 the Portuguese king's eldest son became ruler of an independent Brazilian empire, as Pedro I. Only in 1889 when, following the abolition of slavery (1888), disgruntled plantation-owners rose in revolt, was the empire replaced by a federal republic.

Independence essentially was a political movement in the hands of the colonial aristocracy, who wanted a transfer of authority but a minimum of social upheaval. After 1826 the old colonial division between a privileged minority, monopolizing land and office, and a barely subsisting mass of peasants, grew sharper. Though the period was rarely without civil strife, the *caudillos*, or military dictators, who dominated the scene during the 50 years following independence, ruled in the interests of the privileged classes, and there was only marginal reform before the Indian, Benito Juárez, took over in Mexico in 1861. There were also repeated territorial disputes between the different republics, the fiercest being the War of the Pacific for control of the Atacama Desert nitrate deposits to say nothing of the wars with the United States which deprived Mexico of 40 per cent of its territory. Bolivar had plans for an all-encompassing South American Union, but they came to nothing at the Congress of Panama (1826). Instead, such federations as existed (e.g. Great Colombia, 1819–30) quickly fell apart into their constituent elements, usually representing former Spanish administrative units.

For most of the century there was virtually a subsistence economy in most republics. Brazil, with its coffee plantations based on slave labour, was an exception. Elsewhere the *hacendados* treated their estates more or less as self-supporting and self-sufficient, and had little interest in production for the market. Change only came after about 1880 when foreign investment, hitherto modest, increased rapidly. Even so, it was highly selective, concentrated mainly in Argentina, Brazil, Mexico and Chile. Except in Mexico, where the United States predominated, Britain had the lion's share, much of it in railways. The stimulus was undoubted, but it also shifted the economy sharply to the export of primary products. Argentina's 'revolution on the pampas' made it a main supplier of grain and meat; Chile

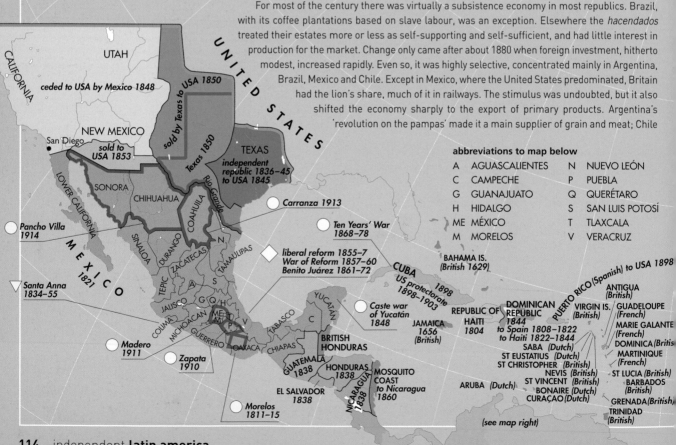

abbreviations to map below

A	AGUASCALIENTES	N	NUEVO LEÓN
C	CAMPECHE	P	PUEBLA
G	GUANAJUATO	Q	QUERÉTARO
H	HIDALGO	S	SAN LUIS POTOSÍ
ME	MÉXICO	T	TLAXCALA
M	MORELOS	V	VERACRUZ

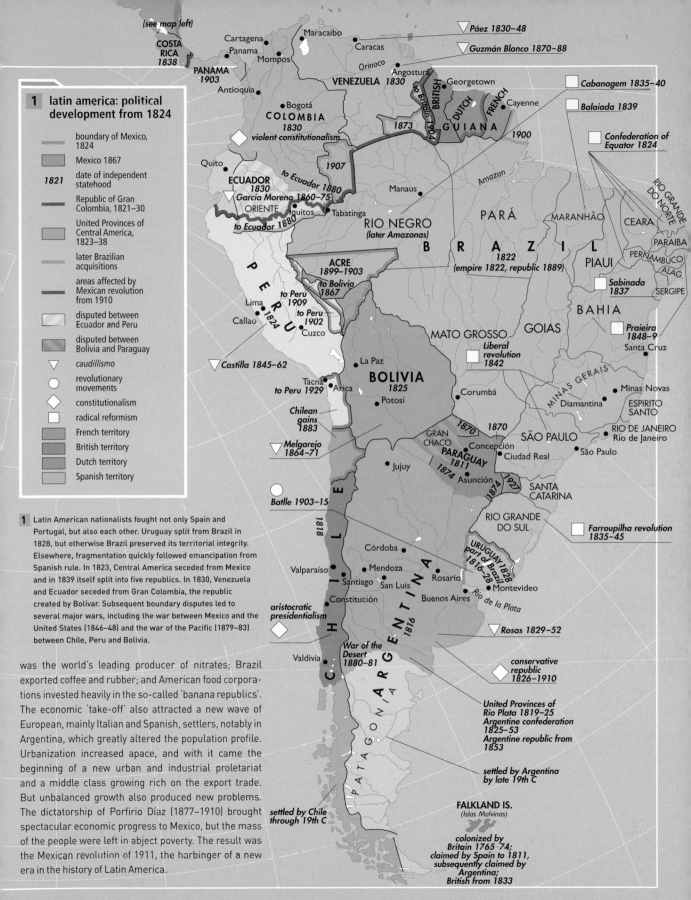

1 latin america: political development from 1824

Legend:
- boundary of Mexico, 1824
- Mexico 1867
- *1821* date of independent statehood
- Republic of Gran Colombia, 1821–30
- United Provinces of Central America, 1823–38
- later Brazilian acquisitions
- areas affected by Mexican revolution from 1910
- disputed between Ecuador and Peru
- disputed between Bolivia and Paraguay
- ▽ *caudillismo*
- ○ revolutionary movements
- ◇ constitutionalism
- ☐ radical reformism
- French territory
- British territory
- Dutch territory
- Spanish territory

1 Latin American nationalists fought not only Spain and Portugal, but also each other. Uruguay split from Brazil in 1828, but otherwise Brazil preserved its territorial integrity. Elsewhere, fragmentation quickly followed emancipation from Spanish rule. In 1823, Central America seceded from Mexico and in 1839 itself split into five republics. In 1830, Venezuela and Ecuador seceded from Gran Colombia, the republic created by Bolívar. Subsequent boundary disputes led to several major wars, including the war between Mexico and the United States (1846–48) and the war of the Pacific (1879–83) between Chile, Peru and Bolivia.

was the world's leading producer of nitrates; Brazil exported coffee and rubber; and American food corporations invested heavily in the so-called 'banana republics'. The economic 'take-off' also attracted a new wave of European, mainly Italian and Spanish, settlers, notably in Argentina, which greatly altered the population profile. Urbanization increased apace, and with it came the beginning of a new urban and industrial proletariat and a middle class growing rich on the export trade. But unbalanced growth also produced new problems. The dictatorship of Porfirio Díaz (1877–1910) brought spectacular economic progress to Mexico, but the mass of the people were left in abject poverty. The result was the Mexican revolution of 1911, the harbinger of a new era in the history of Latin America.

Map labels:

(see map left)

COSTA RICA 1838

PANAMA 1903

Cartagena · Panama · Mompos · Antioquia · Maracaibo · Caracas · Orinoco · Angostura

Páez 1830–48
Guzmán Blanco 1870–88

VENEZUELA 1830

BRITISH · DUTCH · FRENCH · GUIANA

Georgetown · Cayenne

1873 · 1900 · 1904

COLOMBIA 1830
violent constitutionalism

Bogotá

Cabanagem 1835–40
Balaiada 1839
Confederation of Equator 1824

Quito

ECUADOR 1830
García Moreno 1860–75
ORIENTE

1907 · to Ecuador 1880 · 1867 · to Ecuador 1880

Manaus · Tabatinga · Iquitos

Amazon

RIO GRANDE DO NORTE · CEARÁ · PARAIBA · PERNAMBUCO · ALAG. · SERGIPE

RIO NEGRO (later Amazonas)

PARÁ · MARANHÃO · PIAUI

BRAZIL 1822 (empire 1822, republic 1889)

ACRE 1899–1903
to Bolivia 1867

PERU

to Peru 1909 · to Peru 1902

Lima · 1824 · Callao · Cuzco

MATO GROSSO · GOIAS

Sabinada 1837
Santa Cruz

BAHIA

Praieira 1848–9

Liberal revolution 1842

Minas Novas · Diamantina · ESPIRITO SANTO

MINAS GERAIS

Castilla 1845–62

Tacna · Arica · to Peru 1929 · Potosí · La Paz

BOLIVIA 1825

Corumbá

Chilean gains 1883

Melgarejo 1864–71

GRAN CHACO

1870 · 1870

SÃO PAULO

RIO DE JANEIRO
Rio de Janeiro
São Paulo

Concepción · Ciudad Real

PARAGUAY 1811 · Asunción

1874 · 1874 · 1921

SANTA CATARINA

RIO GRANDE DO SUL

Farroupilha revolution 1835–45

Battle 1903–15

CHILE · 1818

Jujuy

Córdoba

URUGUAY 1828 part of Brazil 1816–28

aristocratic presidentialism

Valparaíso · Mendoza · San Luis · Rosario · Montevideo

Santiago · Constitución · Buenos Aires · Rio de la Plata

ARGENTINA 1816

Rosas 1829–52

War of the Desert 1880–81

Valdivia

conservative republic 1826–1910

United Provinces of Rio Plata 1819–25
Argentine confederation 1825–53
Argentine republic from 1853

settled by Argentina by late 19th C

PATAGONIA

settled by Chile through 19th C

FALKLAND IS. (Islas Malvinas)

colonized by Britain 1765–74; claimed by Spain to 1811, subsequently claimed by Argentina; British from 1833

115

the **industrial revolution** in europe

The Industrial Revolution, which began in England in the reign of George III (1760–1820), was the catalyst of the modern world. Nevertheless the speed of change should not be exaggerated. Even in continental Europe its impact was limited before 1850 to a few industrial enclaves, and it was not until the last quarter of the 19th century – in the case of France, Italy and Russia only after 1890 – that the great surge forward occurred.

Outside Europe, with the sole exception of the United States, its impact was delayed for much longer. Even in Germany 35 per cent of the population was engaged in agriculture in 1895, and most of eastern Europe (Poland, Romania, Bulgaria) and much of southern Europe (Spain, Greece, southern Italy) was virtually untouched by industry. Until 1900, when it began to be challenged by Germany and the United States, the United Kingdom was the workshop of the world, and its industrial strength, which enabled it to dominate world markets, accounts for its pre-eminence in the age of imperialism.

Many factors account for the precedence of Great Britain. It was not only that it was well endowed with coal, iron and other basic materials: so were many other countries. It was also spared the ravaging effects of warfare on its own soil, unlike most of continental Europe during the revolutionary and Napoleonic wars. Unlike France and Germany, where markets and trade were limited by a multiplicity of customs barriers and internal and external frontiers, Great Britain after the union of England and Scotland in 1707 was a single economic unit, where men and goods moved freely. It also enjoyed an advantageous position in Atlantic trade, from which capital flowed into industry. In an age of sailing ships, ports like Liverpool, Glasgow and Bristol had obvious advantages over Hamburg and Bremen. The English social structure was also favourable. In contrast to continental Europe, where most peasants were still tied to the soil, the early disappearance of serfdom in England meant that the surplus labour released by the enclosure of common land during the 18th century could move, without legal obstacles, to the growing industrial centres. Finally, England had a unique network of navigable rivers and canals, which was of inestimable importance before the railway age for moving both raw materials and finished goods.

In its earliest phase English manufacturers had relied on water power; hence the location of the early cotton and woollen mills on the slopes of the Pennines. But essentially the Industrial Revolution, in the century to 1870, was a revolution of coal and iron. Its basis was the application of steam power to machinery, and a series of technical innovations – Watt's rotative engine (1782) and Cartwright's power loom (1792) among others – quickly demonstrated the superiority of steam-power driven machines. In continental Europe, apart from Belgium, where industrialization proceeded rapidly after 1820, the use of steam power came more slowly. The famous German steel firm of Krupp, later to be a giant of German industry, was founded in 1810 in green fields outside Essen, where a stream provided water power; it had only seven employees in 1826 and 122 in 1846. Here, and elsewhere, large-scale industry was held back by political fragmentation, lack of capital and, above all, by poor communications, which severely limited markets. What changed this, primarily, was railway development, beginning in the 1830s. By 1860 the railway networks of Britain, Belgium and Germany were virtually complete, although in Austria–Hungary and Russia large-scale construction was only beginning. With their demand for rails, sleepers, engines and carriages, railways also provided immense impetus to heavy industry. A second factor was the dismantling of obstructions to trade. In France internal tariffs had been demolished in 1790 as part of the revolutionary reorganization. In 1818 Prussia followed suit, setting up free trade between its provinces, followed by a Prussian Customs Union (1828) including other smaller German territories, and finally (1834) the German Customs Union, or *Zollverein*, comprising 17 states and some 26 million people. Here was a solid basis for the development of German industry.

A new period, sometimes called the Second Industrial Revolution, opened after 1870. The new German Empire, founded in 1871, was in the forefront. Coal and iron were still basic, and here Germany forged ahead, increasing its cost output from 18 million tons in 1871 to 279 million tons in 1913 and its iron output from 1.5 million tons to 15 million tons. But it was in the new branches of industry – steel, electricity and chemicals – that Germany outpaced all other nations. German steel production leapt from 1.5 million tons in 1880 to over 13 million tons in 1910, by which time Krupps was employing 70,000 men. Steel, electricity and chemicals were the index of the new industrial society, and at a time of growing international tension Germany's headstart was bound to produce a defensive reaction among its rivals. The intensive industrialization which occurred in France after 1895 and in northern Italy after 1905 represented a deliberate national effort not to be left behind. The same was true of the great upsurge of Russian industry after 1890, particularly the massive development of the iron and steel industry of the Donets basin. By now much of heavy industry was keyed to armaments. Industrialization had changed the face of Europe by 1914; but it had also made it more dangerous and more explosive.

1 Industrial development proceeded slowly in Europe until the coming of the railways in the 1840s and 1850s and the emergence of a more sophisticated banking system (map below). The strong traditions of craft and luxury production survived, but on the coal- and ironfields close to navigable rivers or canals there grew up iron, steel and machinery production. Much manufacturing – textiles, metal goods, leatherwork – was still carried out in 'industrial villages'. Urbanization on any scale occurred only in Britain.

1 the industrialization of Europe, 1870–1914

 areas of industrial concentration 1870–1914
+ centres of textile industry
o coalfields
⊞ centres of engineering, armaments and metal industries
△ iron ore fields
⊙ lignite fields
⊖ potash fields
⌐ centres of petroleum industry
—— railway network, 1870

european **imperialism**

Between 1815 and 1914 the character of European imperialism changed. Earlier the motivating force had been the search for the riches of the Orient, and the European stake in Asia and Africa was confined to trading stations and the strategic outposts necessary to protect the trade. In 1815, with the important exception of India, this was still the situation.

But in the 19th century two new factors came into play. The first was the enforced opening of the world – Turkey and Egypt (1838), Persia (1841), China (1842), even Japan (1858) – to European, particularly British, commerce; in short, the breaking down of barriers to European penetration. The second, setting in around 1880, when a new phase of the Industrial Revolution got under way, was the search for the raw materials without which industry, in its new form, could not exist. Tin and rubber from Malaya, nickel from Canada, copper from Australia and South America were now the sinews of European industry. Between 1880 and 1914 Europe added over 8½ million square miles, or one-fifth of the land area of the globe, to its overseas colonial possessions.

Nevertheless no clear line divides the period before and the period after 1880. Criticism of imperialism was certainly strong in the first half of the century. Free traders of the so-called 'Manchester school' argued cogently that empire was unnecessary, even detrimental, to commerce, and the burgeoning trade with the ex-colonial countries of North and South America seemed to prove their point. Nevertheless imperial expansion was continuous after 1815. Both Great Britain and France – particularly France, which had lost its first empire in 1815 and was determined to constitute a new empire – steadily

1 colonial penetration, 1818–70 (see key right)

The key to Europe's imperial prowess (map below) was industrial and technological power. Large areas of the world had little resistance to European technology, enabling Europe to press home its technical advantages. As shipping routes and railway lines were consolidated, so raw materials began to flood into Europe and America, where they were turned into expensive manufactured goods to be sold back at a profit to the territories from which they had originated.

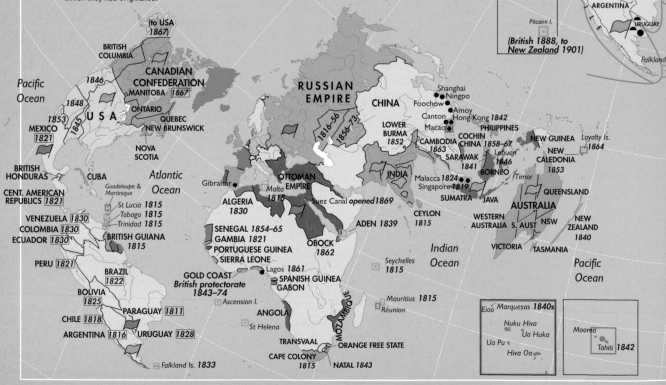

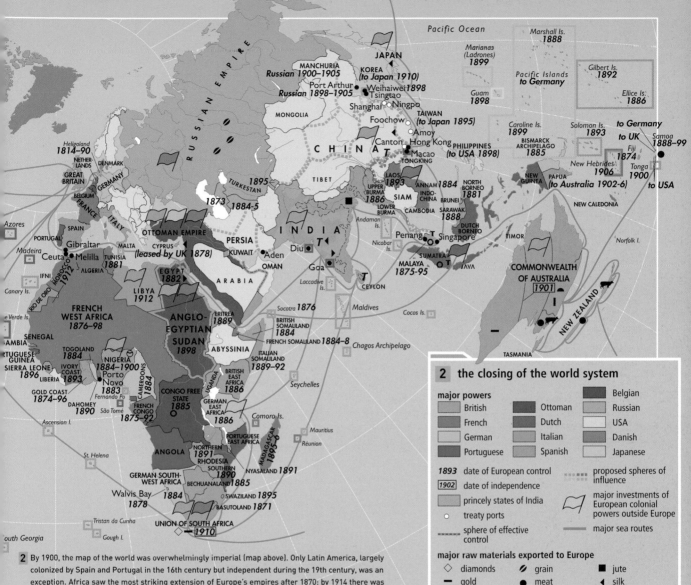

2 the closing of the world system

major powers

British	Ottoman	Belgian
French	Dutch	Russian
German	Italian	USA
Portuguese	Spanish	Danish
		Japanese

1893 date of European control
[1902] date of independence
princely states of India
○ treaty ports
------ sphere of effective control

proposed spheres of influence
major investments of European colonial powers outside Europe
—— major sea routes

major raw materials exported to Europe

◇ diamonds	∅ grain	■ jute
– gold	● meat	◄ silk
S silver	T tea	O rubber
T tin	⊞ cane sugar	⊖ veg oil
I copper	dairy produce	● copra
► cotton		⌒ wool

2 By 1900, the map of the world was overwhelmingly imperial (map above). Only Latin America, largely colonized by Spain and Portugal in the 16th century but independent during the 19th century, was an exception. Africa saw the most striking extension of Europe's empires after 1870: by 1914 there was scarcely a flagpole on the continent from which a European flag did not fly. Empire had become a mark of national virility, sometimes justified by ideas of mission (most notably against slavery), more usually assumed to be the reward for innate superiority.

advanced. The French conquered Algeria in the 1830s, annexed Tahiti and the Marquesas in the 1840s, expanded their colony in Senegal in the 1850s, and began the conquest of Indo–China in 1859. Great Britain, which had retained the Cape of Good Hope, the maritime provinces of Ceylon and other strategically important footholds (Malta, Mauritius, the Seychelles) in 1815, also continued to expand. Fearing a French challenge, it claimed sovereignty over Australia and New Zealand. It built up its power in India, acquired Singapore (1819), Malacca (1824), Hong Kong (1842), Natal (1843), Lower Burma (1852) and Lagos (1861). Many of these acquisitions were defensive reactions against France; most were intended to secure its position in India which, with its army of 150–200,000, made Britain the strongest territorial power in the east. Even so, except for India, imperialism still only touched the outer fringes of Asia and Africa. Even the Russian empire, which by 1886 was to engross much of central Asia, still only affected the periphery.

After 1880 a fundamental change came about. Its causes were partly economic, but still more important were the rivalries of the European powers, each of which feared that its competitors would steal a march on it. Even as late as 1870 colonial penetration was marginal. By 1914 the European powers had engrossed nine-tenths of Africa and a large part of Asia. Between 1871 and 1914 the French empire grew by nearly 1 million square miles and 47 million people. New claimants such as Italy and Germany came in to challenge the established colonial powers. By 1914 almost the whole of Africa had been divided up among competing European nations.

19th-century **africa**

Although European exploration began in the 18th century, its impact on Africa was limited until after 1870, except in the far south where Dutch settlers, or Boers, in Cape Colony, who had been brought under British rule in 1806, moved north in the Great Trek (1835) in search of land and freedom, and founded settlements which eventually became the republics of the Orange Free State and Transvaal. The only other area of European settlement was Algeria, conquered by France between 1830 and 1847 after fierce resistance under Abd al Kadir.

Nevertheless this was a period of great change and instability in Africa. In the north-east Mohammed Ali conquered northern Sudan in 1820, founded Khartoum as its capital in 1830 and inaugurated the attempt to build a great Egyptian empire reaching the length of the Nile and east to the Horn of Africa. In the north-west a great Muslim religious revival, beginning around 1804 under Uthman dan Fodio, carried the Fulani south into Hausaland, where they founded the Sultanate of Sokoto. Later, another empire was carved out further west, between the Ivory Coast and the Upper Niger, by a Mandingo Muslim leader, Samory. In the south, the outstanding event was the rise of the Zulus, which resulted in a great political and demographic revolution (the so-called *Mfecane* or 'time of troubles').

This was the situation when the European 'scramble for Africa' got under way after 1882, and the countries named above were leaders of African resistance. The Zulus held out fiercely until the war of 1879–81, when their country was annexed. Resistance elsewhere was equally strong. Samory was only defeated by the French in 1898; Sokoto only fell to the British in 1903. In the north the British established a *de facto* protectorate over a bankrupt Egypt after 1882 (turned into a full-scale protectorate in 1914); but they were only able to secure control of the Sudan in 1898 after the slaughter of some 20,000 Sudanese. Nowhere was occupation unchallenged, as the great Herero and Maji-Maji revolts of 1904–06 against German colonization showed. But the only lasting success was the Ethiopian defeat of Italy at Adowa in 1896. Morocco kept a precarious independence until 1912 before being divided between France and Spain, and Libya and Cyrenaica were occupied by Italy in the same year. By 1914 the European powers were in full control. Apart from Ethiopia, only Liberia could claim independence.

The position of the Boer republics in the south was different. Transvaal also had been annexed by Great Britain in 1877 and then restored to independence in 1881. But the discovery of diamonds at Kimberley and of gold on the Witwatersrand (1886) sealed their fate. The entry of foreign speculators (*Uitlanders*) sparked Boer hostility, and when an attempt by Cecil Rhodes (Prime Minister of Cape Colony, 1890–96) to stage a take-over failed dismally (Jameson Raid, 1895), the outcome was the Boer War (1899–1902), in which, after initial Boer successes, ruthless British suppression forced the Boers to capitulate. Nevertheless the Afrikaners secured favourable terms after the Peace of Vereeniging (May 31, 1902), including the use of their own language and the exclusion of blacks from the franchise, and this compromise made possible the formation (1910) of the Union of South Africa as a dominion of the British Commonwealth. It was nevertheless a betrayal of black Africans by Britain which led step by step to the policy of *Apartheid* (1948) and to the radical conflicts which bedevilled South Africa after the rest of the continent had won its independence.

1 alien rule in africa

French	Anglo-Egyptian condominium
British	independent
German	1882–95 date of determination of colonial boundary
Portuguese	frontiers, 1914
Belgian	
Spanish	
Italian	

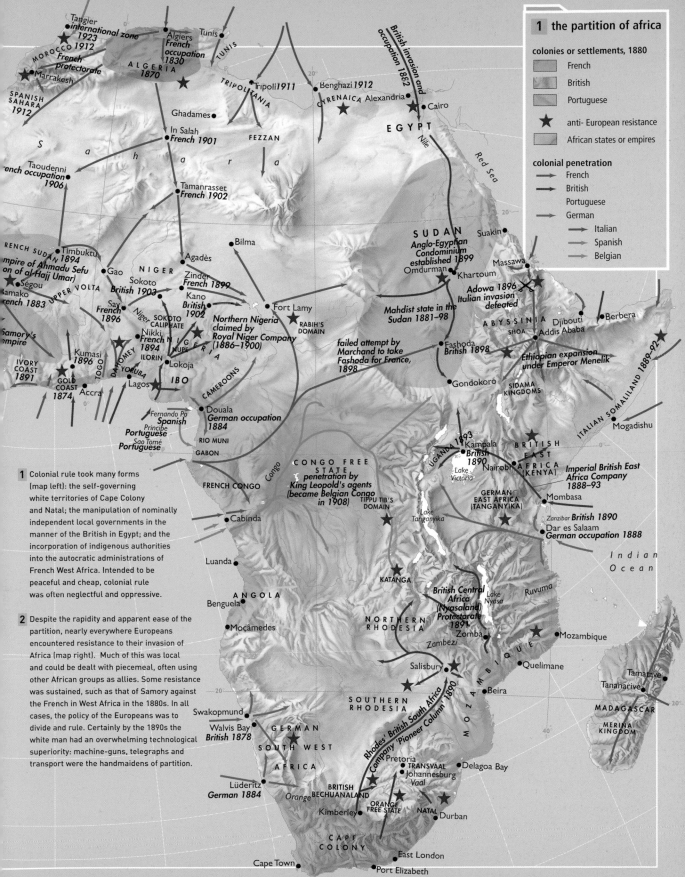

colonies or settlements, 1880
French
British
Portuguese
★ anti- European resistance
African states or empires

colonial penetration
→ French
→ British
→ Portuguese
→ German
→ Italian
→ Spanish
→ Belgian

Tangier
**international zone
1923**
Tunis
Algiers **French
occupation
1830**
TUNIS
MOROCCO 1912
**French
protectorate**
Marrakesh
ALGERIA
1870
TRIPOLITANIA
Tripoli 1911
Benghazi 1912
CYRENAICA
Alexandria

British invasion and
occupation 1882

SPANISH
SAHARA
1912
S   a   h   a   r   a
Ghadames
In Salah
French 1901
FEZZAN
EGYPT
Cairo
Red Sea
Nile

Taoudenni
rench occupation
1906
Tamanrasset
French 1902
Bilma
Agadès
SUDAN
**Anglo-Egyptian
Condominium
established 1899**
Suakin
Massawa

RENCH SUDAN
Timbuktu
1894
mpire of Ahmadu Sefu
on of al-Hajj Umar)
Gao
NIGER
Zinder
French 1899
Omdurman
Khartoum
Adowa 1896
Italian invasion
defeated
ABYSSINIA
Berbera
Djibouti
SHOA
Addis Ababa

Segou
UPPER VOLTA
Sokoto
British 1903
Kano
**British
1902**
Fort Lamy
RABIH'S
DOMAIN
**Mahdist state in the
Sudan 1881–98**
Bamako
rench 1883
Say
**French
1896**
Niger
SOKOTO
CALIPHATE
**Northern Nigeria
claimed by
Royal Niger Company
(1886–1900)**
**failed attempt by
Marchand to take
Fashoda for France,
1898**
Fashoda
British 1898
ITALIAN SOMALILAND 1889–92

Samory's
empire
Nikki
**French
1894**
NUPE
ILORIN
NIGERIA
Lokoja
Gondokoro
SIDAMA
KINGDOMS
**Ethiopian expansion
under Emperor Menelik**

IVORY
COAST
1891
Kumasi
1896
DAHOMEY
TOGO
YORUBA
IBO
CAMEROONS
Mogadishu

GOLD
COAST
1874
Accra
Lagos
Fernando Po
Spanish
Principe
Portuguese
Sao Tomé
Portuguese
Douala
**German occupation
1884**
RIO MUNI
GABON
UGANDA 1893
**British
1890**
Kampala
BRITISH
EAST
AFRICA
(KENYA)
**Imperial British East
Africa Company
1888–93**
Nairobi
Lake
Victoria

1 Colonial rule took many forms
(map left): the self-governing
white territories of Cape Colony
and Natal; the manipulation of nominally
independent local governments in the
manner of the British in Egypt; and the
incorporation of indigenous authorities
into the autocratic administrations of
French West Africa. Intended to be
peaceful and cheap, colonial rule
was often neglectful and oppressive.

FRENCH CONGO
Congo
CONGO FREE
STATE
**penetration by
King Leopold's agents
(became Belgian Congo
in 1908)**
TIPPU TIB'S
DOMAIN
GERMAN
EAST AFRICA
(TANGANYIKA)
Mombasa
Zanzibar **British 1890**
Dar es Salaam
German occupation 1888

Cabinda
Lake
Tanganyika
Indian
Ocean

Luanda
ANGOLA
Benguela
Moçâmedes
KATANGA
NORTHERN
RHODESIA
**British Central
Africa
(Nyasaland)
Protectorate
1891**
Lake
Nyasa
Ruvuma
Mozambique
Zomba

2 Despite the rapidity and apparent ease of the
partition, nearly everywhere Europeans
encountered resistance to their invasion of
Africa (map right). Much of this was local
and could be dealt with piecemeal, often using
other African groups as allies. Some resistance
was sustained, such as that of Samory against
the French in West Africa in the 1880s. In all
cases, the policy of the Europeans was to
divide and rule. Certainly by the 1890s the
white man had an overwhelming technological
superiority: machine-guns, telegraphs and
transport were the handmaidens of partition.

Zambezi
Salisbury
Beira
SOUTHERN
RHODESIA
MOZAMBIQUE
Quelimane
Tamatave
Tananarive
MADAGASCAR
MERINA
KINGDOM

Swakopmund
**Rhodes' British South Africa
Company 'Pioneer Column' 1890**
Walvis Bay
British 1878
GERMAN
SOUTH WEST
AFRICA
Lüderitz
German 1884
Orange
BRITISH
BECHUANALAND
Pretoria
TRANSVAAL
Johannesburg
Vaal
Delagoa Bay

Kimberley
ORANGE
FREE
STATE
NATAL
Durban

CAPE
COLONY
East London
Cape Town
Port Elizabeth

india under british rule

By 1805 the hegemony of the English East India Company in the Indian sub-continent was an established fact. With the conquest of Sind (1843) and the Sikh kingdom of the Punjab (1849) its domination became co-terminous with the country's natural frontier in the north-west, while in the north a war with Nepal (1814–16) extended it to the Himalayan foothills. To the east the British clashed with the Burmese empire and in 1826 and 1852 annexed most of its territories, including Assam. Upper Burma itself was brought under British rule in 1886. Within India Dalhousie's Doctrine of Lapse led to the absorption of several small kingdoms in central India, and in 1856 the kingdom of Oudh was annexed following charges of 'misgovernment'.

Not surprisingly, this policy provoked disaffection which found a violent outlet in the rebellion of 1857. Beginning as a mutiny of the Company's Indian sepoys, the revolt soon involved princes, landlords and peasants throughout northern India, but the loyalty of the Sikhs and the passivity of southern India enabled the British to crush it after 14 months of bitter fighting.

The mutiny was a watershed in the history of British India. It discredited the Company and in 1858 the British government assumed direct control, though the autonomy of the Indian princes was respected. The impetus to economic development was immediate. First-class roads were built, totalling 57,000 miles by 1927, but it was the railways which made possible the exploitation of raw materials and the profitable introduction of export crops, such as tea. Between 1869 and 1929 India's foreign trade increased sevenfold. How far this benefited the rural masses is a moot question; but modern industries brought into existence an Indian entrepreneurial class. After 1919, when protective tariffs were introduced, industrial expansion made further progress.

1 The Indian Mutiny (map right) began at Meerut on 10 May 1857 and spread swiftly to other parts of northern India. Hindus and Muslims alike rose against their British overlords. Sikh loyalty in the Punjab, coupled with passivity in the Deccan and the south, turned the tide in favour of the British after an orgy of bloodletting.

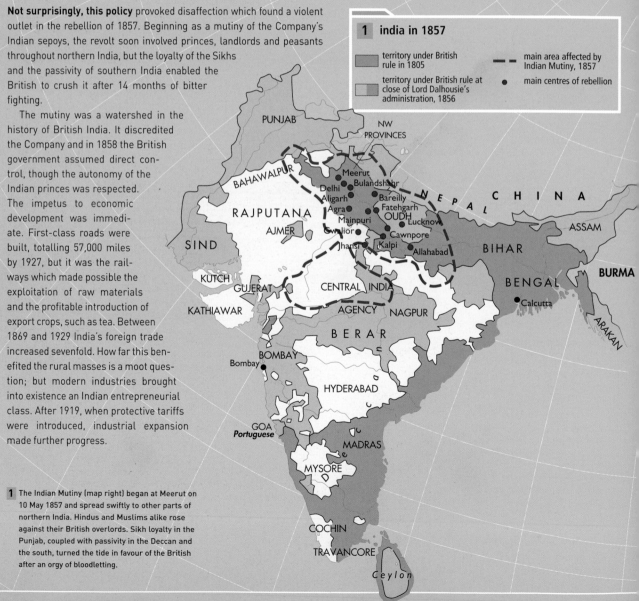

1 india in 1857

- territory under British rule in 1805
- territory under British rule at close of Lord Dalhousie's administration, 1856
- — — — main area affected by Indian Mutiny, 1857
- • main centres of rebellion

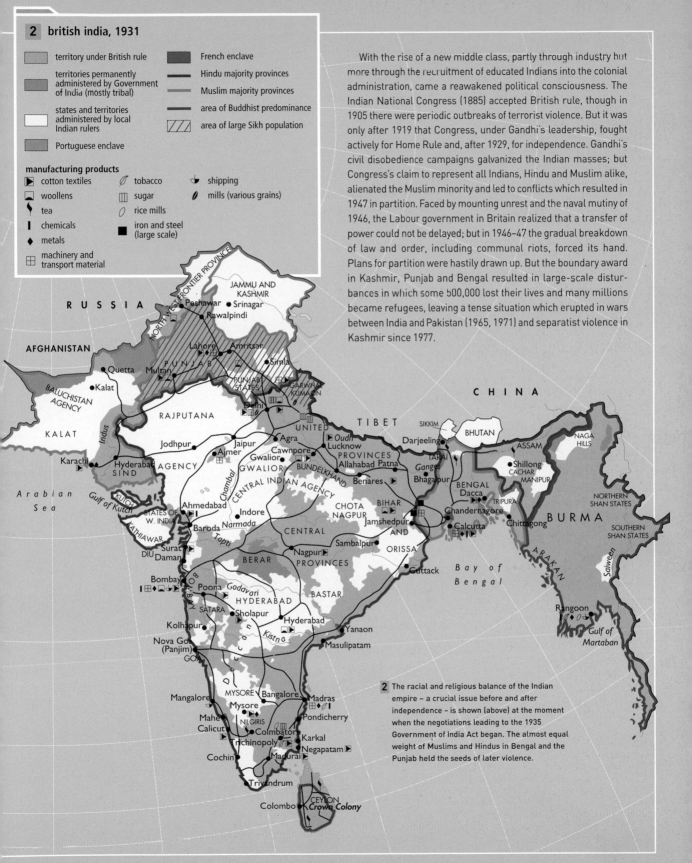

2 british india, 1931

manufacturing products

- ▶ cotton textiles
- ▱ woollens
- ♦ tea
- ▮ chemicals
- ♦ metals
- ⊞ machinery and transport material
- ∅ tobacco
- ▥ sugar
- ∅ rice mills
- ⊐ shipping
- ∅ mills (various grains)
- ■ iron and steel (large scale)

Legend:
- territory under British rule
- territories permanently administered by Government of India (mostly tribal)
- states and territories administered by local Indian rulers
- Portuguese enclave
- French enclave
- Hindu majority provinces
- Muslim majority provinces
- area of Buddhist predominance
- area of large Sikh population

With the rise of a new middle class, partly through industry but more through the recruitment of educated Indians into the colonial administration, came a reawakened political consciousness. The Indian National Congress (1885) accepted British rule, though in 1905 there were periodic outbreaks of terrorist violence. But it was only after 1919 that Congress, under Gandhi's leadership, fought actively for Home Rule and, after 1929, for independence. Gandhi's civil disobedience campaigns galvanized the Indian masses; but Congress's claim to represent all Indians, Hindu and Muslim alike, alienated the Muslim minority and led to conflicts which resulted in 1947 in partition. Faced by mounting unrest and the naval mutiny of 1946, the Labour government in Britain realized that a transfer of power could not be delayed; but in 1946–47 the gradual breakdown of law and order, including communal riots, forced its hand. Plans for partition were hastily drawn up. But the boundary award in Kashmir, Punjab and Bengal resulted in large-scale disturbances in which some 500,000 lost their lives and many millions became refugees, leaving a tense situation which erupted in wars between India and Pakistan (1965, 1971) and separatist violence in Kashmir since 1977.

2 The racial and religious balance of the Indian empire – a crucial issue before and after independence – is shown (above) at the moment when the negotiations leading to the 1935 Government of India Act began. The almost equal weight of Muslims and Hindus in Bengal and the Punjab held the seeds of later violence.

china under the ch'ing dynasty

A new era in Chinese history opened in 1644 when the Ming dynasty, beset for a century by Mongol invasions, Japanese raids and civil war, was displaced by a line of foreign, Manchurian, emperors which ruled China until 1911. The Ch'ing, or Manchu, dynasty was resisted in south China for half a century but it quickly established good relations with the dominant Chinese gentry (*shen-chin*) and with its support began a successful policy of territorial expansion which went on until late in the 18th century.

At the same time there was a great economic upsurge and a huge increase in population, from 100 million in 1650 to 300 million in 1820 and 420 million in 1850. There was also a considerable export trade in tea, silk and porcelain with the West from Canton and with Russia from Kyakhta. But the financial strain of the wars of expansion and the pressure of the growing population on the land imposed hardships which led to recurrent unrest and revolts, not only among the minority peoples who were harshly exploited by Chinese and Manchus alike, but also in the heart of China itself. Of these the most serious was the White Lotus rebellion between 1795 and 1804. Meanwhile the export surplus was converted after 1825 into a net outflow as a result of the opium trade. Manchu China was still the world's largest and most populous empire. But its growing economic difficulties, coupled with the failure to expand the administration to match the rapid growth of population, and the pressures of the western powers, seeking to open the China market for their manufactures, resulted in a crisis which came to a head after Chinese attempts to halt the illicit opium trade were decisively defeated by the British in the Opium War of 1839–42.

The Opium War had two major consequences. First, it resulted in the cession of Hong Kong to the British and in the opening of the first five Treaty Ports (their number was thereafter steadily increased) in which foreigners enjoyed extra-territorial rights. Secondly, it weakened imperial authority and led to the great Taiping rebellion (1850–64) the most serious but only one of many rebellions which shook Manchu power to its foundations. The Taiping and Nien rebellions alone left 25 million dead and vast areas, including the wealthy region around Nanking, were devastated. They also convinced the western powers that Ch'ing China was on the point of collapse and inaugurated a scramble for concessions.

The response of the Manchu court and bureaucracy was hesitant and half-hearted, more intent on maintaining traditional institutions and Confucian values than on modernization. Foreign powers had taken advantage of the situation: the British and French occupied Peking in 1856 and forced open more treaty ports, the Russians occupied the Amur region in 1858 and the Maritime Province in 1860, and China was defeated by France in a war over Indo-China in 1884–85. But it was the overwhelming success of Japan in the war of 1894–95 that convinced a section of the Chinese intelligentsia that only a break with the past could save China, and they secured the support of the young emperor Kuang-su. But the reform movement of 1898 was defeated by the dowager empress Tzu-hsi whose reaction was to turn the popular discontent against the foreigners. The result was the Boxer Rising of 1900, an outburst of xenophobia savagely suppressed by the western powers, who imposed a heavy indemnity and wrung still further concessions from China. By now even the imperial government realized that modernization was imperative; but, in spite of a number of reforms, its attitude was still essentially conservative. Convinced that the imperial government was the main obstacle to change, revolutionary groups sprang up everywhere after 1901, and when in 1911 a small-scale army mutiny broke out in Wuchang, disaffection spread throughout the whole country. The imperial government fell, almost without fighting; but China had still to undergo more than 40 years of tribulation before it finally made the transition to the modern world.

1 the dismemberment of the ch'ing empire, 1860–1929

- boundary of Ch'ing empire in 1850

colonial possessions:

spheres of influence:
- Russian
- British
- Japanese
- French
- German

- states formerly tributary to China

railways:
- Russian
- British
- Japanese
- French
- German
- Chinese

1 During the 19th century China was forced to cede Hong Kong to Great Britain and to open to foreign trade ever more regions in which foreigners enjoyed extra-territorial rights (map above). It also lost extensive territories in the north and north-east to the expansionist Russian empire, and was challenged in peripheral states which had been her vassals. With the collapse of the Ch'ing empire in 1911 China also lost control of Tibet and Mongolia.

EMPIRE

TANNU TUVA
Russian protectorate 1912

MONGOLIA
*tributary territory;
autonomous 1912*

*Yellow River
(Huang Ho)*

Manchouli

*occupied by Russia 1897–1905
Japanese influence after 1905*

Aigun

to Russia 1860

Harbin

Suifenho

MARITIME
PROVINCE

Changchun

Hunchun

Mukden

Vladivostok

Kalgan

Newchwang

Peking

Antung

Tientsin

Dairen

Taiyüan

Port Arthur

*to Russia 1898
to Japan 1905*

Sea of Japan

Chefoo

KOREA

Weihaiwei
to Britain 1898

*to Japan
1910*

Tsinan

Tsingtao
to Germany 1898

CHINA

Nanking

Chinkiang

Soochow

Wusung

Wuhu

Shanghai

Ichang

Yangtze

Hangchow

Kiukiang

Ningpo

Chungking

Yochow

Changsha

ASSAM
to Britain 1826

Wenchow

Ryukyu Is.

Santuao

to Japan 1872

Foochow

Kunming

Tamsui

Tengyueh

Amoy

*Taiwan
to Japan 1895*

Mengtze

*New Territories
to Britain 1898*

Canton

Manhao

Nanning

Macao
*to Portugal
1557*

Kowloon *to Britain 1898*

BURMA

Lungchow

to Britain 1886

TONGKING

Pakhoi

Hong Kong *to Britain 1842*

Haiphong

Kwangchowwan
to France 1898

LAOS
*to France
1893*

Kiungchow

FRENCH
INDO
CHINA
1884

SIAM

Hainan

Treaty ports and towns:
◖ 1842 Treaty of Nanking
⊗ 1858 Treaty of Tientsin
◉ 1860 Peking Convention
◑ 1876 Chefoo Convention

▲ 1897 Sino-French
Trade Convention
○ additional ports
opened by 1911
● other towns and cities

the world **economy**

After the middle of the 19th century the Industrial Revolution, which had radiated from Great Britain to north-west Europe and the eastern seaboard of the United States, spread to the rest of the world. The result, by 1914, was the formation of a single interdependent world economy. But the impact was extremely varied. Though the United States after 1890 was becoming an important subsidiary centre, the focus throughout was on Europe, and most of the development was keyed to the needs of European industry for raw materials and fed by European capital. In 1914 Great Britain was the largest source of foreign investment, with overseas assets totalling nearly $4,000 million, while the United States, like Russia, was still a net borrower; but in world trade it was losing the predominance it had enjoyed in 1860 to Germany and the United States.

One factor behind these developments was the vast, unprecedented flow of population, mainly from Europe to the New World, but also from China and India to South-East Asia and East Africa. Between 1850 and 1920 over 40 million Europeans emigrated overseas or to Siberia, carrying with them European institutions and skills which they had used to exploit the vast overseas territories. Much foreign investment went into building the infrastructure of railways, ports and shipping and creating the network of communications upon which the functioning of the world economy depended. Outside Europe and the United States there were only 9,100 miles of railroad track in 1870. By 1911 it had increased to 175,000 miles. Equally important was the expansion of world shipping and the replacement of sailing ships by ocean-going steamships of large capacity. The opening of the Suez Canal (1869) and the Panama Canal (1914) gave a great fillip to world trade. Traffic via Suez rose from 437,000 tons in 1870 to over 20 million tons in 1913, and foreign trade increased threefold in volume during the same period.

Nevertheless the effects of industrialization were distinctly one-sided. The main shipping routes were between the advanced countries and the white dominions, or between them and the producers of raw materials. Even as late as 1929 the world was still a white man's world. A few countries such as India and China had begun to develop their own industries; but, with the exception of Japan, they were small enclaves in a vast rural population. In 1914 there were still only 900,000 factory workers in the whole of India, and 69 per cent of cotton operatives in 1919 were in Bombay province. Nowhere outside the United States and Europe was the income produced by manufacturing substantial in 1930 and in most cases it accrued to foreign investors. This was true of Malaya, which by 1900 was producing nearly half the world's tin and by 1910 was a major exporter of rubber, and of Katanga, where copper production rose from nothing in 1900 to 305,000 tons (including Northern Rhodesia) in 1930. Here, as elsewhere, the bulk of the population benefited only marginally, and per capita income in most countries seems actually to have declined. This was the situation which led, a generation later, to the conflict of rich nations and poor nations and the demand for a New International Economic Order.

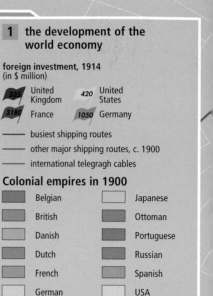

1 the development of the world economy

foreign investment, 1914
(in $ million)

3930	United Kingdom	420	United States
3180	France	1050	Germany

—— busiest shipping routes
—— other major shipping routes, c. 1900
—— international telegragh cables

Colonial empires in 1900

Belgian	Japanese
British	Ottoman
Danish	Portuguese
Dutch	Russian
French	Spanish
German	USA
Italian	other countries

Panama canal,

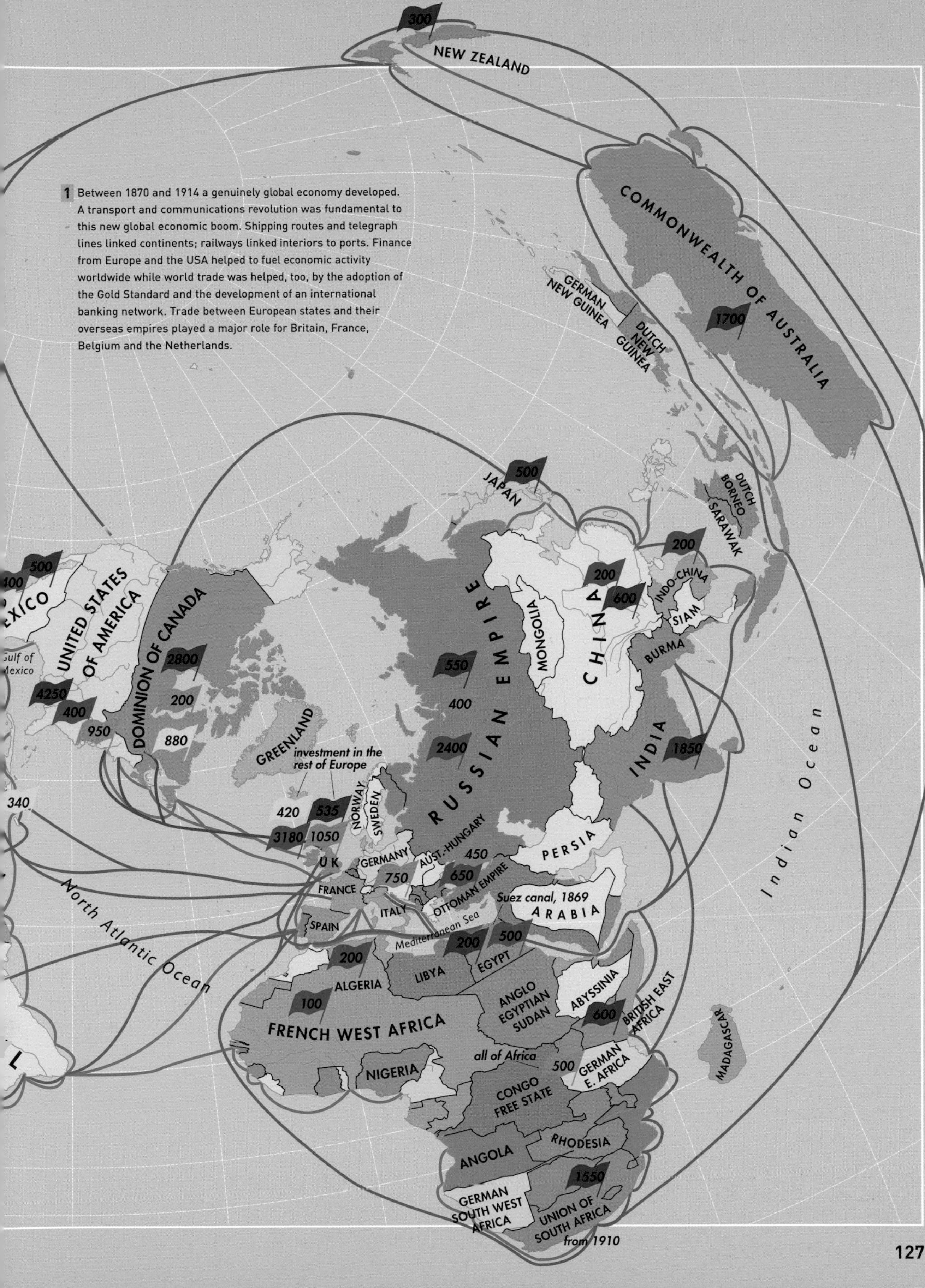

1 Between 1870 and 1914 a genuinely global economy developed. A transport and communications revolution was fundamental to this new global economic boom. Shipping routes and telegraph lines linked continents; railways linked interiors to ports. Finance from Europe and the USA helped to fuel economic activity worldwide while world trade was helped, too, by the adoption of the Gold Standard and the development of an international banking network. Trade between European states and their overseas empires played a major role for Britain, France, Belgium and the Netherlands.

300
NEW ZEALAND

COMMONWEALTH OF AUSTRALIA
1700

GERMAN NEW GUINEA
DUTCH NEW GUINEA

DUTCH BORNEO
SARAWAK

JAPAN 500

200
600
CHINA
MONGOLIA

INDO-CHINA 200
SIAM
BURMA

INDIA 1850

500
400 MEXICO
400
4250
950

UNITED STATES OF AMERICA

DOMINION OF CANADA
2800
200
880

GREENLAND
investment in the rest of Europe

RUSSIAN EMPIRE
550
400
2400

420 535
3180 1050
NORWAY
SWEDEN
UK
GERMANY
FRANCE 750
ITALY
SPAIN
AUST.-HUNGARY
450
650
OTTOMAN EMPIRE

PERSIA

340

North Atlantic Ocean

Indian Ocean

Mediterranean Sea
Suez canal, 1869
ARABIA

200
ALGERIA
LIBYA
200 EGYPT 500
100
FRENCH WEST AFRICA
ANGLO EGYPTIAN SUDAN
ABYSSINIA
BRITISH EAST AFRICA
600

all of Africa
NIGERIA
CONGO FREE STATE
500 GERMAN E. AFRICA
MADAGASCAR

L

ANGOLA
RHODESIA
GERMAN SOUTH WEST AFRICA
UNION OF SOUTH AFRICA
1550
from 1910

Gulf of Mexico

The rise of the modern United States dates effectively from the Civil War, but development was very uneven. For the defeated South the period of Reconstruction (1865–77) was a bitter experience. South Carolina had ranked third in the nation in per capita wealth in 1860; 10 years later it was 40th, and Mississippi, Alabama and Georgia fared no better. Worst of all was the position of the four million liberated slaves, who found themselves (as the black leader Frederick Douglass said) without money, property or friends. The great upsurge in population, from 31 million in 1860 to 92 million in 1910, bypassed the South and concentrated wealth and power in the north-east where, with the exploitation of the rich ore reserves of the Mesabi Range in Minnesota and the vast coal reserves of the Appalachians, industry spread rapidly from the original manufacturing belt between Boston and New Jersey to Pittsburgh, Detroit and Chicago. Only around 1920 did cheap labour attract the textile industry from New England to the South.

The Civil War itself had stimulated Northern industry. After 1865 it forged ahead. But the most striking achievement of the immediate post-war period was the opening of the Great Plains, made possible by the railroad boom after 1870. In 1860 some 30,000 miles of railway were in operation, but few lines extended beyond the Great Lakes. By 1870 the mileage had reached 53,000, by 1880 93,000 and by 1890 163,000 miles. Land grants of more than 132 million acres encouraged railway promoters, and homestead grants of 285 million acres attracted settlers. The number of farms rose from two million in 1860 to six million in 1910, and grain exports, which the rail network made possible, were an important source of capital for industrial development. The population west of the Mississippi rose from six million in 1870 to 26 million in

1 By 1914, rapid industrialization meant that the United States was the world's largest industrial producer, combining its vast natural resources with a large population swollen by mass immigration from Europe and a tradition of technical and scientific innovation. The United States' new-found industrial strength enabled it to join the club of great powers.

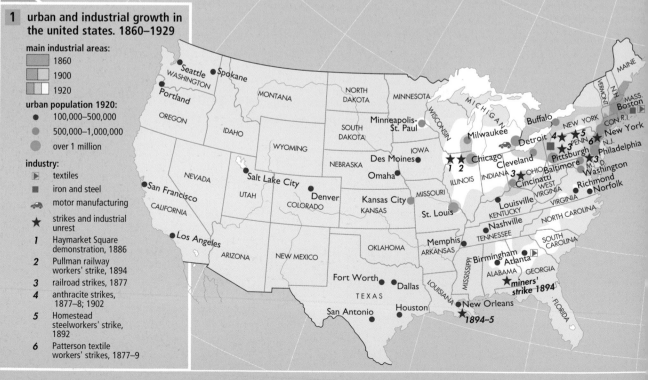

1 urban and industrial growth in the united states. 1860–1929

main industrial areas:
- 1860
- 1900
- 1920

urban population 1920:
- 100,000–500,000
- 500,000–1,000,000
- over 1 million

industry:
- ▷ textiles
- ■ iron and steel
- motor manufacturing
- ★ strikes and industrial unrest

1 Haymarket Square demonstration, 1886
2 Pullman railway workers' strike, 1894
3 railroad strikes, 1877
4 anthracite strikes, 1877–8; 1902
5 Homestead steelworkers' strike, 1892
6 Patterson textile workers' strikes, 1877–9

2 Canada in 1915 (map right). By 1915, Canada had experienced a quarter of a century of rapid economic development. An influx of people and capital followed hard on the heels of expanding exports of wheat and timber after 1890. Mining was well under way by 1914 and manufacturing grew mainly after that date.

2 canada, 1867–1929

land occupied;
- prior to 1851
- 1851–1871
- 1871–1901
- 1901–1921

population of towns, 1871;
- 25,000-100,000 people
- over 100,000 people

population of towns, 1911;
- 25,000-100,000 people
- over 100,000 people

railways 1916:
- Canadian Pacific Railway
- Canadian Northern (Main Line)
- National Trans-continental Railway
- main industrial regions

ALBERTA date of accession to
1905 Dominion of Canada

1910. Nevertheless the bulk of the population was concentrated in the north-east, and most of the 23 million immigrants between 1870 and 1914 remained there, providing cheap labour for American industry. Their miserable conditions, and those of the southern blacks, lay behind the unrest which erupted in the 1890s.

In Canada railway development was even more important than in the United States. Hitherto the 'small and unimportant' eastern colonies (as Lord Durham described them in his famous Report of 1839) had gone their separate ways, more closely linked to the United States, which made no secret of its hope to absorb them, than with each other. After the acquisition of Alaska from Russia, United States' pressure grew, and to meet it the Canadian Federation was formed in 1867 and completed by the adhesion of Manitoba (1870) and British Columbia (1871). The great transcontinental railways – the Great Western and Canadian Pacific (completed 1885), followed by the Canadian Northern and Grand Trunk Pacific – were the lifeblood of the new Dominion and changed the axis of Canadian life. Railway development opened Manitoba and Saskatchewan, and made Canada into one of the world's leading wheat producers. It also led to the discovery of rich mineral deposits, particularly copper and nickel (1883). The other major industry in 1914 was lumber and the manufacture of paper and newsprint. In general, however, industrialization was only beginning, though the value of Canada's industrial output increased from $190 million in 1890 to over $500 million in 1914.

In the United States, on the other hand, the 1880s and 1890s saw an astounding industrial upsurge. Output of coal and iron increased 20-fold between 1870 and 1913, by which date steel production exceeded that of Britain and Germany combined. But the 'Gilded Age' was also a time of gross inequalities, and speculation and over-production caused serious economic setbacks, particularly in 1873 and 1893, which led not only to industrial unrest but also to a search for new markets, particularly in eastern Asia. Already in 1867 the United States had annexed Midway Island as a Pacific base; in 1887 it secured Pearl Harbor. The other area of advance was the Caribbean and Latin America, where by the Hay-Pauncefote agreement of 1901, Great Britain gave the United States a free hand. But the turning point came with the Spanish–American war of 1898, which made Cuba into an American protectorate and brought the Philippines – 'a stepping-stone to China' – under American rule. By 1914, when the Panama Canal was opened, the United States was the world's greatest industrial power. It was also, without fully realizing it, involved in world politics. The way was prepared for the United States' entry into the First World War.

australia and new zealand

Although Australia and New Zealand were discovered by the Dutch explorer Tasman in 1642, colonization only began after Cook hoisted the British flag at Botany Bay in 1770. New South Wales served as a penal colony from 1788 to 1839, Van Diemen's Land (later Tasmania) from 1804 to 1853, and in 1829 the British government, fearing to be forestalled by the French, claimed the whole Australian continent. Fear of France also led to the annexation of New Zealand in 1840.

But in both lands geographical obstacles, lack of exportable products, and, in the case of New Zealand, the bitter Maori wars between 1860 and 1871, made the early years of colonization difficult. New South Wales was hemmed in by the Blue Mountains. Beyond the Great Dividing Range the country soon became arid and inhospitable. Coastal settlements at Perth (1829), Melbourne (1835) and Adelaide (1836) established bridgeheads for exploration in the west, but as late as 1850 the total white population was only around 350,000, while in New Zealand it was still below 100,000 in 1860. Inducements to settle were few. Neither country was self-supporting, and early trade (chiefly seal products and sandalwood) was insufficient to pay for imports, and was further hampered by the East India Company's monopoly in the area.

The discovery of gold in New South Wales and Victoria in 1851 and in Otago (South Island, New Zealand) in 1861 initiated a new phase. Even more important was the rapid growth of sheep farming. In 1860 Australia sent 39 million lb of wool to Great Britain. By 1879 the quantity had increased to 100 million lb. In New Zealand, where wool was largely a South Island product, exports rose from £67,000 in value in 1853 to £2,700,000 20 years later. The development of the North Island, held back by the Maori wars, came

The Maoris, of east Polynesian extraction, inhabited New Zealand from c. AD 750 until the 18th century, when they numbered 150,000. British sovereignty was proclaimed in 1840 on the basis of equal rights for both Maoris and Europeans, but race inequality soon grew. The colonists' demand for land led to war – MAP **2** – and to confiscation of Maori lands. In the last decade of the 20th century, large tracts of land have been transferred back to the Maoris. New Zealand was granted a constitution in 1852. The colony's early progress was based on wool and gold. Its economy strengthened from 1900 due to a wide range of refrigerated primary products – MAP **3**. Long dependent on British trade, New Zealand's major trading partner is now Australia.

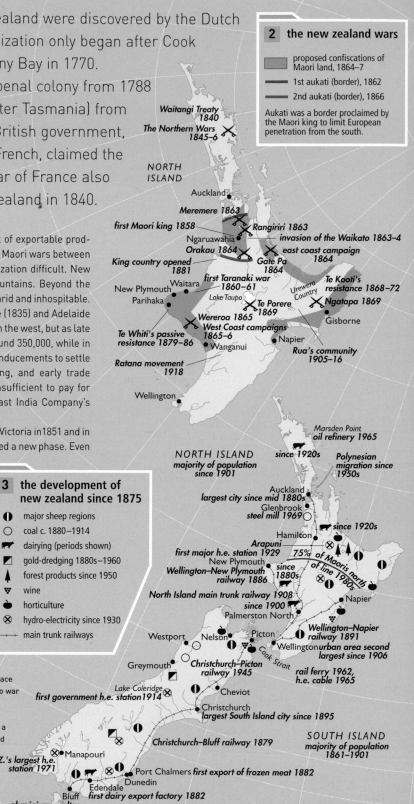

2 the new zealand wars

- proposed confiscations of Maori land, 1864–7
- 1st aukati (border), 1862
- 2nd aukati (border), 1866

Aukati was a border proclaimed by the Maori king to limit European penetration from the south.

NORTH ISLAND

Waitangi Treaty 1840
The Northern Wars 1845–6
Auckland
Meremere 1863
first Maori king 1858
Rangiriri 1863
Ngaruawahia
invasion of the Waikato 1863–4
Orakau 1864
east coast campaign 1864
King country opened 1881
Gate Pa 1864
first Taranaki war 1860–61
New Plymouth Waitara
Te Kooti's resistance 1868–72
Parihaka
Lake Taupo
Urewera Country
Te Porere 1869
Ngatapa 1869
Wereroa 1865
Gisborne
West Coast campaigns 1865–6
Te Whiti's passive resistance 1879–86
Napier
Wanganui
Rua's community 1905–16
Ratana movement 1918
Wellington

3 the development of new zealand since 1875

- major sheep regions
- coal c. 1880–1914
- dairying (periods shown)
- gold-dredging 1880s–1960
- forest products since 1950
- wine
- horticulture
- hydro-electricity since 1930
- main trunk railways

NORTH ISLAND majority of population since 1901
since 1920s
Marsden Point oil refinery 1965
Polynesian migration since 1950s
Auckland largest city since mid 1880s
Glenbrook steel mill 1969
Hamilton
since 1920s
Arapuni first major h.e. station 1929
New Plymouth
Wellington–New Plymouth railway 1886
75% of Maoris north of line 1980s
since 1880s
North Island main trunk railway 1908
since 1900
Palmerston North
Napier
Wellington–Napier railway 1891
Westport
Nelson
Picton
Wellington urban area second largest since 1906
Greymouth
Christchurch–Picton railway 1945
Cook Strait
rail ferry 1962, h.e. cable 1965
Lake Coleridge
first government h.e. station 1914
Cheviot
Christchurch largest South Island city since 1895
SOUTH ISLAND majority of population 1861–1901
Christchurch–Bluff railway 1879
N.Z.'s largest h.e. station 1971
Manapouri
Port Chalmers first export of frozen meat 1882
Edendale first dairy export factory 1882
Dunedin
Bluff
aluminium smelter 1971

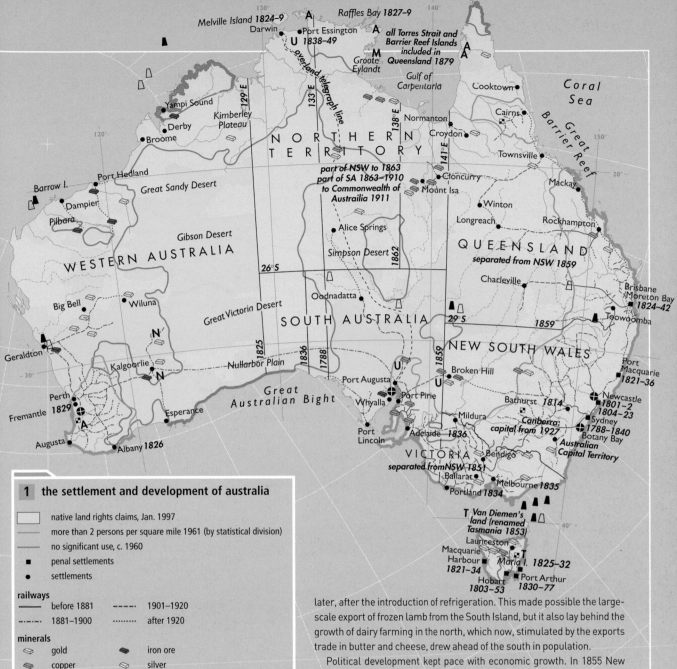

1 the settlement and development of australia

native land rights claims, Jan. 1997

more than 2 persons per square mile 1961 (by statistical division)

no significant use, c. 1960

■ penal settlements

● settlements

railways

—— before 1881	- - - - 1901–1920
—·—·— 1881–1900	········ after 1920

minerals

▱	gold	◈	iron ore
◈	copper	◇	silver
▱	lead	◈	zinc
⬠	natural gas	◣	oil
T	tungsten	N	nickel
▣	tin	A	alumina/bauxite
U	uranium	M	manganese
⊕	blast furnace		

1 After 1820 settlement spread inland from scattered coastal towns, but vast arid areas remained sparsely populated even in 1961 (map above). Extensive mineral discoveries have contributed to a high standard of living, but many of these are on lands subject to aboriginal land claims.

later, after the introduction of refrigeration. This made possible the large-scale export of frozen lamb from the South Island, but it also lay behind the growth of dairy farming in the north, which now, stimulated by the exports trade in butter and cheese, drew ahead of the south in population.

Political development kept pace with economic growth. In 1855 New South Wales, Victoria, South Australia and Tasmania became self-governing colonies followed by Queensland in 1859, and in 1901 joined together to form the Commonwealth of Australia. New Zealand, which had been divided in 1852 into six provinces, each with an elected council, became a united Dominion in 1876, after measures had been taken to safeguard the rights of the Maori population. Both dominions remained heavily dependent on primary exports. For long they enjoyed preferential treatment in the British market; but developments after 1945, particularly the British retreat from Asia, brought important changes. In 1952 both dominions joined for security with the United States in the ANZUS Pact, and when Great Britain entered the European Common Market (1973) and dismantled imperial preference, they were forced to diversify their economies and seek new markets. The process of reorientation is still continuing.

european **nationalism**

The flame of nationalism was kindled in Europe by the French Revolution. In France itself the revolution forged a sense of national unity, and elsewhere, notably in Spain and Prussia, the humiliation of defeat and French occupation after 1807 produced a short-lived national reaction. For the most part, however, nationalism was confined to a narrow segment of the middle class. It was anathema to the ruling classes, and rarely touched working people.

Polish peasants held aloof from the insurrections of 1831, 1846 and 1863; in Ireland only acute agrarian distress after 1877 lined them up behind the nationalists. Down to 1848, liberal and constitutional reform was the main demand, and it was against this, rather than nationalism, that the victorious powers set their faces after the fall of Napoleon at the Congress of Vienna in 1815. Their other main objective was to erect a barrier against a resurgence of revolutionary France. Hence their decision to transfer the Austrian Netherlands (later Belgium) to Holland, to install Prussia in Westphalia and most of the Rhineland, and to hand over the ancient republic of Genoa to Sardinia–Piedmont. As compensation for the loss of the Netherlands, Austria received the Venetian republic and the duchy of Milan, as well as indirect control of Parma, Modena and Tuscany. Sweden, which had to surrender Finland to Russia, was compensated with Norway.

After 1815 the great powers sought above all to uphold the Vienna settlement and to combat the threat of liberalism and nationalism, but by 1830, when a new wave of liberal and nationalist agitation broke out, the eastern and western powers were drawing apart. This divergence of interests enabled Greece and Belgium to obtain independence. In Norway the forced union with Sweden aroused resentment similar to that felt in Belgium towards Holland. There was friction, but little active resistance, and eventually a Norwegian declaration of independence was accepted by Sweden. The course of events in Poland (1831, 1846) and in Italy, Germany and Hungary in 1848–49 was more eventful. Here nationalist agitation erupted in full-scale war; but the solidarity of the conservative powers and divisions among the nationalists themselves brought all to nothing.

What changed this situation was the rise of a new generation of statesmen. Louis Napoleon, emperor of France since 1852, Cavour, who became prime minister of Sardinia–Piedmont in the same year, and Bismarck,

2 In 1815 the German Confederation (map below) was a patchwork of city-states and principalities dominated by Prussia and Austria. From the 1850s relations between the two powers deteriorated, and after 1864 they squabbled over the administration of the annexed territory of Schleswig–Holstein. In 1866 Austria led the Confederation in a war against Prussia. After victory at Sadowa, Prussia absorbed Hanover, Hesse–Nassau and Frankfurt. In 1867 the North German Confederation was established, and following war with France in 1870, the southern states joined the Prussian-dominated federation in a new German empire.

2 the unification of germany

Prussia in 1815	free city
acquired by Prussia, 1815–66	German Empire, 1871
German Confederation, 1815	Austro-Prussian forces attack on Denmark, 1864
North German Confederation, 1867	Prussian armies in the war with Austria, 1866
Imperial territory of Alsace-Lorraine, 1871	German armies in the Franco-Prussian war, 1870–71

the unification of italy

1 the unification of italy

French from 1768, formerly Genoese
Kingdom of Sardinia in 1815
territory annexed 1859
territory annexed March 1860
territory annexed November 1860
territory lost to France 1860
territory annexed 1866
territory annexed 1870
Austrian empire, 1815
Italian border, 1914

SWITZERLAND

AUSTRO-HUNGARIAN EMPIRE

TYROL

VENETIA

Udine
Görz (Gorizia)
Trieste

Trent (Trento)

SAVOY
PIEDMONT
Aosta
Como
Bergamo
Monza
Brescia
LOMBARDY
Milan
Magenta 1859
Novara 1849
Solferino 1859
Verona
Venice
Padua
Fiume
Pola

Susa
Turin
KINGDOM OF SARDINIA
Alessandria
Genoa
Pontremoli
La Spezia
Parma
PARMA
Guastalla
Ferrara
Modena
MODENA
ROMAGNA
Bologna
Rimini
SAN MARINO
Pesaro
Zara

Custoza 1848, 1866
Mantua

FRANCE
NICE
LIGURIA
Monaco
Nice

CORSICA

Lucca
Pisa
Arno
Florence
Livorno (Leghorn)
Arezzo
Siena
Elba
TUSCANY
UMBRIA
Spoleto
Urbino
Ancona
Castelfidardo
MARCHES
Lissa 1866
Dalmatia

OTTOMAN EMPIRE

PAPAL STATES
Rieti
Tiber
Civitavecchia
Mentana
Rome
Terracina
Gaeta
Pontecorvo

Adriatic Sea

1 Italy was unified by war and revolution. In 1848 Charles Albert of Piedmont-Sardinia tried to expel Austria from northern Italy but was defeated at Custoza and Novara. Ten years later, with Napoleon III's France as an ally, Piedmontese forces together with nationalist volunteers defeated Austria at Magenta and Solferino. In return, Napoleon obtained Nice and Savoy, but Lombardy was joined to Piedmont, followed swiftly by the smaller central Italian duchies. When Sicily rose in revolt against the Kingdom of Naples in 1860, Garibaldi led a nationalist army southwards which defeated the Bourbon king. The northern states then joined with the liberated south to form a Kingdom of Italy ruled by the Piedmontese king, Victor Emmanuel.

KINGDOM OF SARDINIA
Sassari
Cagliari

Volturno 1860
Benevento
Naples
Castellammare
Salerno
Potenza

KINGDOM
OF
THE
TWO
SICILIES

NAPLES
Bari
Taranto
Cosenza

Lipari Is.
Aspromonte 1862
Messina
Reggio
Palermo
Marsala
Catania
Syracuse

minister-president of Prussia after 1862, all toyed with nationalism, confident of their ability to use it for their own ends. These were not the ends of the liberals who had led the nationalist movements of 1848–49. Cavour's purpose was to ensure that Italian unification was carried out by and in the interests of Sardinia; hence his opposition to the famous Sicilian expedition of the patriot Garibaldi (1807–82) in 1860. Bismarck was determined to ensure that Germany was merged in Prussia, not Prussia in Germany. Both also realized that their objectives could only be achieved by war and diplomacy. Hence Cavour's alliance with France against Austria (1858) and Bismarck's wars of 1864, 1866 and 1870. The result was the unification of Italy (except for Venetia and the Papal State) in 1861 and the unification of Germany in 1871. Both were retrospectively endorsed by liberal nationalists, but neither satisfied the nationalism they aroused. Italy still laid claim to the Alto Adige, Fiume and Trieste. Bismarck's 'small German' solution, excluding Austria, disappointed those who hankered after a Greater Germany. Indeed, it was after 1870, when the problems of the multi-nationalist claims became loudest. The confusion of peoples and languages in eastern Europe defied easy solutions and exacerbated the conflicts which led, step by step, to war in 1914.

1878 to 1914

After the unification of Germany and of Italy, it seemed for a time as though the major questions which had disturbed the peace of Europe since 1848 had been resolved. Bismarck, the architect of German unification, concentrated his efforts after 1871 upon building a system of alliances which would ensure the future of the new German Reich. The 'wild Junker' had become a conservative, anxious only to preserve what had been won; and his alliances were defensive. But the history of the next 40 years is the story of how alliances, originally defensive and stabilizing in intent, turned into an aggressive and destabilizing system. Furthermore, the unification of Germany and of Italy, far from marking a halting place, opened up a hornet's nest of nationalist revindications. After 1870 the nationalist movement which had agitated western Europe for 40 years, spilled over into the Balkans; and the struggles of the Balkan peoples for independence inevitably involved the powers who were their supporters or adversaries, particularly Russia and Austria-Hungary, which, after its exclusion from Germany and Italy after 1866, was essentially an eastward-looking Balkan power.

The evolution of the relations between the great powers between 1879, when Bismarck tried to reconcile his sympathies with a conservative Russia with support for Austria–Hungary, and 1914, when the whole precarious balance fell apart, is shown on the map (right). Until the beginning of the new century the system worked reasonably well. Revolts in the Balkans between 1875 and 1878, culminating in Russian intervention and war with Turkey, thoroughly alarmed the powers; and after the Congress of Berlin (1878) Balkan affairs took a secondary place. Checked in Europe, Russia turned to central Asia and the Far East, and during the first half of the period the dominant themes were Anglo–Russian rivalry in Asia and Anglo–French rivalry in Africa. What changed this situation was the decision of Germany under William II, particularly after Bülow became chancellor in 1900, to seek 'a place in the sun'. This was not unreasonable; but by now most places in the sun had been occupied, and German policy was seen as a threat by the established imperial powers. The result was the Anglo–French reconciliation (1904) and the Anglo-Russian reconciliation (1907). German 'world policy' also required a navy, resulting in the naval competition which soured Anglo–German relations between 1906 and 1912. After 1907 the Triple Entente with France and Russia became the lynch-pin of British policy, the only firm assurance against the German 'threat'. Germany, on the other hand, saw itself being 'encircled' by a hostile ring constructed by Great Britain.

The result was that the lines between the Triple Alliance and the Triple Entente were drawn tighter. Also Germany was driven closer to its only dependable ally, Austria–Hungary. When Austria annexed Bosnia–Herzegovina in 1908, Bülow lent full support, and Austro–Russian antagonism in the Balkans, hitherto suppressed, was rekindled. The climax was postponed until the outbreak of the Balkan wars in 1912. The aggrandizement of Serbia which resulted was viewed by Austria as an intolerable threat. Russia, on the other hand, could not leave Serbia in the lurch without losing credibility. The result was the stupendous build-up of armaments as the grinding logic of the system came into play. When in 1914 the murder of the Austrian archduke Franz Ferdinand brought matters to a head, the combustible material was piled up which exploded in the First World War.

european alliance systems, 1882–1914

- frontiers, 1912
- The Triple Alliance, 1882
- The Triple Entente, 1912
- The Balkan League, 1912

NORWAY

Christiania

SWEDEN

Stockholm

Helsingfors

St Petersburg

DENMARK

North Sea

Edinburgh

UNITED KINGDOM

1904: Entente Cordiale (with France)
1907: conciliation of interests with Russia

London

NETHERLANDS

BELGIUM

R U S S I A

1894: Dual Alliance with France
1897: Entente with Austria-Hungary (to 1909)
1907: conciliation of interests with Britain
1909: secret treaty with Italy

1879: Dual Alliance with Austria-Hungary
1882: Triple Alliance with Austria-Hungary and Italy
1883: alliance with Romania

Berlin

G E R M A N Y

LUXEMBOURG

Paris

F R A N C E

1894: Dual Alliance with Russia
1902: neutrality agreement with Italy
1904: Entente Cordiale (with Britain)

SWITZERLAND

AUSTRO-HUNGARIAN

Vienna

Budapest

E M P I R E

1879: Dual Alliance with Germany
1882: Triple Alliance with Germany and Italy
1883: alliance with Romania

Belgrade

ROMANIA

Bucharest

1883: alliance with Germany and Austria

BOSNIA-HERZEGOVINA

DALMATIA

Sarajevo

SERBIA

SANJAK OF NOVIBAZAR

Black Sea

I T A L Y

Corsica

Rome

MONTENEGRO

Cetinje

BULGARIA

Sofia

ANDORRA

Balearics

Sardinia

1882: Triple Alliance with Austria-Hungary and Germany
1902: neutrality agreement with France
1909: secret treaty with Russia

ALBANIA

MACEDONIA

Constantinople

O T T O M A N   E M P I R E

Mediterranean Sea

Sicily

GREECE

Athens

ALGERIA (Fr.)

TUNISIA (Fr.)

MALTA (Br.)

Dodecanese (It.)

CYPRUS (Br.)

1 From the 1890s the system of multi-lateral diplomacy gave way to a system of alliance blocs (map above). At the last great congresses, at Berlin in 1878 and 1884, the Powers had collaborated to settle the future of the Ottoman empire and colonial rivalry in Africa. In 1879 Germany and Austria had already become allies, and in 1882 Italy joined what became the Triple Alliance. Fear of Germany drove France and Russia to form a firm alliance in 1894. Collaboration between the Powers still proved possible as the crises over Morocco, Bosnia and Albania showed between 1905 and 1913, but when Britain reached informal agreements on colonial issues first with France in 1904 and then Russia in 1907, Europe divided into two armed camps. The subsequent arms race created a volatile international order, made worse by the rise of popular xenophobia and a growing fatalism about war.

the **first world war**

When the assassination of the Austrian heir-presumptive, Archduke Franz Ferdinand, by Bosnian terrorists at Sarajevo on June 28, 1914, sparked off the immediate sequence of events that led to the First World War, the European powers were already divided into heavily armed camps, and neither was prepared to risk diplomatic defeat. Germany already had its battle plan prepared: the famous Schlieffen Plan, drawn up in 1905, to annihilate the French army by a great encircling movement through Belgium before France's Russian ally had time to mobilize. The expectation everywhere was for a short war, over by Christmas 1914, and only after this proved false did the search for allies begin in earnest. Germany and Austria were joined by the Ottoman Empire and Bulgaria, the Entente powers by Italy, Romania and Greece, and eventually by the United States.

The German strategy was very nearly successful and brought the German armies within 40 miles (65 km) of Paris. It was frustrated by the unexpectedly rapid mobilization of Russia, which invaded East Prussia and defeated the German 8th Army at Gumbinnen (August 20, 1914). Although the Russians were repulsed at Tannenberg (August 26–29), their offensive drew off German reserves, which helped the French and British armies in the west to halt the German advance in the battle of the Marne (September 5–8), while the Russians simultaneously inflicted a crushing defeat on Austria at Lemberg. The Schlieffen Plan had failed. Germany was forced to despatch troops to the east to prop up the Austrian front, and in the west the war became a war of trenches, artillery, barbed wire and machine–guns. Each side launched offensives, with sickening casualties, but without succeeding in advancing more than a few thousand yards. Railways could bring up reinforcements to the front before slow-moving advancing troops could make good any advantage they might have created. The question for both, by the end of 1915, was how to break the stalemate. The answer of the Entente, sponsored by Winston Churchill, was to attack Germany from the rear by campaigns in the Dardanelles and Mesopotamia, at Salonika and, after Italy entered the war on May 23, 1915, against Austria on the Isonzo. All were failures. The German answer was to bring Great Britain to its knees by crippling losses at sea. The submarine campaign, initiated on February 1, 1917, was nearly successful, and only defeated when Lloyd George introduced the convoy system in May. But its result was to bring the United States into the war on the Entente side on April 6, 1917.

1 The war in Europe was fought on four fronts, but most resources were concentrated on the Western and Eastern fronts (map above right and inset left). In the west the superiority of defensive systems led to a static war of attrition dominated by the machine-gun and the artillery barrage. In the east the larger areas and smaller forces made a more mobile form of warfare possible, but even here by 1916 a stalemate had developed which was only broken by Russian internal collapse in 1917. Not until 1918 could the Allies bring their material superiority to bear on an enemy weakened by the effects of the blockade and now also facing a serious domestic crisis. A German offensive in March–May 1918 in France ground to a halt and over the next six months the Allies pushed back the Central Powers in France, northern Italy and the Balkans.

1 the great war in europe, 1919–18

Even so, the German position was not hopeless. Huge losses in the Brusilov offensive of 1916 and economic chaos at home had broken the Russian fighting spirit, and the Russian revolutions of March and October 1917 enabled Germany to transfer troops from the Eastern to the Western Front in the hope of victory before the United States could mobilize. On March 21, 1918, Hindenburg and Ludendorff launched their great offensive in the west. Once again it was a near success, but the Allied line held, and on July 18 the French commander Foch launched the counter-offensive which was to be the decisive campaign of the war. On September 29 Ludendorff acknowledged defeat. By now Austria and Bulgaria were near to collapse; the British blockade had brought Germany to the edge of starvation; and the German government, fearful of a Bolshevik revolution, sued for an armistice. On November 11, 1918, fighting ceased. Over eight million men had perished, as had three empires, the Tsarist, the Austro–Hungarian and the Ottoman. In retrospect the war of 1914–18 was the great European civil war, which destroyed the old European order, squandered Europe's human and material resources, and jeopardized its future. Few people realized in 1918 what had happened; but the age of European predominance was over and a new age of global politics had begun.

the **russian revolution**

Revolution came to Russia suddenly, but not unexpectedly, in the wake of the unsuccessful Russo–Japanese war of 1904–05. Intensive industrialization since 1890 had created a large, profoundly discontented urban proletariat, and it was they who spearheaded the revolution of 1905, although their revolt sparked off widespread unrest in the countryside. The Tsar was forced to grant a constitution, including a *duma*, or parliament, but by 1907 the government was back in full control. Nevertheless, the 1905 revolution irreparably weakened the old order, and after 1912, following the shooting of strikers in the Lena goldfields in Siberia, a great new wave of social unrest swept the empire.

Internally, Russia was in no position in 1914 to meet the challenge of the First World War; and when in the winter of 1916–17 economic dislocation, hunger and sheer incompetence brought the crisis to a head, the government capitulated almost without resistance. This was the February revolution of 1917, which placed power in the hands of liberal Duma politicians. But the Provisional Government's authority was circumscribed by the powerful Petrograd Soviet (or Council) of Soldiers' and Workers' Deputies, and it was also compromised by its commitment to continue the war. When, in April, Lenin returned from exile in Switzerland, promising peace, land and bread, and demanding all power for the Soviets, its days were numbered. An attempt in September by the Commander-in-Chief, General Kornilov, to seize the capital miscarried when his troops rebelled, and on November 7 (October 25 by the old calendar) the Bolsheviks struck, arrested the Provisional Government, and assumed power in the name of the Soviets. This was the October, or Bolshevik, revolution.

The new government's overriding need was peace, and Lenin insisted, against strong opposition, on accepting the onerous terms imposed by Germany in the Treaty of Brest-Litovsk (March 1918). But immediately the Bolsheviks were faced with civil war and foreign intervention, as White Russian armies, with British, French, Czech and other support, attacked the new republic. Lenin pinned his hope on war-weariness and revolution in the west, but to little avail. In Europe, particularly in Germany, revolutionary currents were strong between 1919 and 1923, but they were met by counter-revolutionary forces, including Hitler's National Socialists. However, foreign intervention and the threat of a White Tsarist restoration rallied support for the Reds, and by 1920 the civil war had been won. But the devastation was immense. Industrial production in 1920 was down to one-seventh of the 1913 level, and shortages provoked a wave of strikes and riots, culminating in the Kronstadt naval mutiny (February 1921). Lenin's answer was the 'New Economic Policy' (NEP), in effect a relaxation of requisitioning and controls. The new policy worked: by the end of 1925 industrial production had regained its pre-war level. Furthermore, the overt hostility of the West relaxed. War with Poland, which had invaded Russia in 1920, was ended by the Treaty of Riga (March 1921), and at the same time a treaty of friendship was signed with Turkey. It was followed by the Rapallo Treaty with Germany (1922) and in 1924 by diplomatic recognition from Britain, France and other European countries.

After Lenin's death in 1924 and a period of disputed succession, Lenin's eventual successor, Stalin, ousted Trotsky, with his policy of 'permanent revolution'. Stalin's policy of 'socialism in one country', implying large-scale industrialization and a re-shaping of agriculture, placed Russia, at a terrible human cost, in the first rank of industrial and international powers. Inaugurated by the first Five Year Plan of 1928, in many respects it marked a sharp break with the revolution of 1917. But it was also a fulfilment of Lenin's work. Even at the time of Lenin's death, Russia was backward and under-developed. By 1939, as Lenin foresaw, Bolshevism had become 'a world force', changing the course of history.

1 Under the pressure of total war the Russian monarchy collapsed in February 1917 (map right). The Provisional Government failed to halt either the Germans at the front or the tide of radical revolution at home. In October (by the old calendar), the Bolsheviks seized power and a bloody three-year civil war followed. Anti-Bolshevik 'White' forces, aided by foreign money and troops, almost destroyed the revolutionary state in 1919 until confronted with a reformed Red Army. By 1920 the war was over and the task of consolidating Communist rule in Russia began.

1 russia in war and revolution

— Russian empire, 1914

--- front between Russia and Central Powers, 12 Mar. 1917

serious Russian mutinies, Aug. 1917

★ principal towns where Bolsheviks took power, Nov. 1917–Feb. 1918 (dates in new calendar)

— boundary of Russian territory occupied by Central Powers following the Treaty of Brest-Litovsk, Mar. 1918

·········· area controlled by the Bolsheviks, Aug. 1918

▲ towns occupied Entente forces, Aug. 1918–19

---- eastern boundary of area controlled by Bolsheviks, Apr. 1919

▢ area controlled by Bolsheviks, Oct. 1919

— areas controlled by anti-Bolshevik forces, May 1920

➡ White Russian armies

➡ non-Russian anti-Bolshevik forces (Entente Powers)

— boundary of Soviet territory, Mar. 1921

— frontiers, 1923

Norwegian
Sea

Entente fleet

Barents Sea

70°

70°

40

Murmansk

NORWAY

Narvik

SWEDEN

White
Sea

British
French
Canadians
Italians
Serbs

Canadians
Americans

Mezen

British
French

Archangel
17 Feb. 1918

FINLAND
independence of
Finland recognized
Dec. 1917

Finns

Onega

60

Stockholm

Åbo

Helsingfors

Lake
Ladoga

Lake
Onega

Petrozavodsk
17 Jan. 1918

Sukhona

Revel
8 Nov.
1917

British/French
naval assistance

Yudenich

ESTONIA

Petrograd
7 Nov. 1917

Vologda
8 Feb. 1918

Vyatka
8 Dec. 1917

Perm
14 Nov. 1917

Nicholas II
and family
shot by
Bolsheviks
July 1918

Baltic
Sea

Riga

Letts

Baltic
Germans

LATVIA

Dvinsk

Novgorod
27 Nov. 1917

Kornilov's attack
on Petrograd
Sep. 1917

Yaroslavl
9 Nov. 1917

Kostroma
15 Dec. 1917

Izhevsk
9 Nov. 1917

Kolchak 1918-19

Yekaterinburg
8 Nov. 1917

RUSSIA

Königsberg

LITHUANIA

Vilna

Pskov
15 Nov.
1917

Tver
10 Nov.
1917

Ivanovo
7 Nov. 1917

Kazan
8 Nov. 1917

Ufa
8 Nov. 1917

GERMANY
(E. PRUSSIA)

Minsk
7 Nov.
1917

Government moved
from Petrograd Mar. 1918

Moscow
15 Nov. 1917

Nizhniy
Novgorod
10 Nov. 1917

60

zig

Vitebsk
9 Nov. 1917

BOLSHEVIK

Smolensk
12 Nov. 1917

Kaluga 11 Dec. 1917

Samara
9 Nov. 1917

Czechs

POLAND

Warsaw

Brest-Litovsk

Mogilev
1 Dec. 1917

Tula
20 Dec.
1917

Trans-Siberian Railway

Orenburg
31 Jan.
1918

Cracow

Lemberg

Gomel
12 Nov .1917

Orel
14 Nov.
1917

Don

Penza
4 Jan. 1918

Volga

Saratov
9 Nov. 1917

Ural

CZECHOSLOVAKIA

Poles

Kursk

Tambov
13 Nov.
1917

50

HUNGARY

Debrecen

Vinnitsa

Zhitomir
22 Jan.
1918

Kiev
8 Feb.
1918

Kharkov
24 Dec. 1917

Voronezh
12 Nov.
1917

Don Cossacks
1917-19

Ural Cossack Army
1918-20

Kolozsvár

Dniester

Denikin
1919

Poltava
19 Jan. 1918

Dnieper

Tsaritsyn
27 Nov. 1917

Temesvár

Brassó

Romanians

Jassy

BESSARABIA

Kishinev
10 Dec. 1917

Nikolayev
27 Jan .1918

Yekaterinoslav
11 Jan. 1918

Don

Novocherkassk
25 Feb. 1918

Astrakhan
7 Feb. 1918

Volga

ROMANIA

Bucharest

Danube

Ruse

Odessa
31 Jan.
1918

Wrangel 1920

Simferopol
26 Jan. 1918

Sea of Azov

Rostov
10 Nov. 1917

Cossacks

Kuma

Caspian

BULGARIA

Sofia

Varna

French

Sebastopol
29 Dec. 1917

Novorossiysk
14 Dec. 1917

Black Sea

French

British

Plovdiv

Burgas

Adrianople

British

40

alonica

Constantinople

Entente fleet

Georgians 1919-20

Caucasus

Mensheviks

Baku
15 Nov. 1917

Sea

GREECE

Athens

Smyrna

TURKEY

Angora

Trebizond

Batum

Tiflis

Erivan

British
1918-19

PERSIA

the **chinese revolution**

By 1911 the imperial government of China was thoroughly discredited, and it only needed an army mutiny at Wuchang to repudiate its authority. But the republic proclaimed in 1912, with Sun Yat-sen as its first president, was overwhelmed by its inherited problems, and within weeks Sun was displaced by Yuan Shih-k'ai, the most powerful general of the old regime. After Yuan's death in 1916 the government in Peking lost control and power passed into the hands of provincial warlords, whose armies caused untold damage and millions of casualties. Compounding this misery were the expansionist policies of Japan, which had secured control of Shantung and Manchuria in 1915, as well as the presence of foreign powers, based in the Treaty Ports, who interfered in Chinese politics and exploited the struggling Chinese economy.

In 1919, when the Paris Peace Conference refused to abrogate Japanese and other foreign privileges, this desperate situation exploded in a massive upsurge of Chinese nationalism, which found vent in the 4 May Movement of 1919, a spontaneous uprising of students and urban workers, which was the real starting point of the Chinese revolution. It provided a new constituency for Sun Yat-sen, who had taken refuge at Canton, and in 1923 Sun reorganized his Nationalist (Kuomintang, KMT) Party, allied with the Chinese Communist Party (CCP, founded in 1921), and prepared to reunite the country. But Sun died in 1925, and it was Chiang Kai-shek, the Moscow-trained general of the KMT army, who led the great Northern Expedition of 1926 which aimed at the elimination of the warlords and the unification of the country. Helped by peasant and workers' uprisings along its route, it was astonishingly successful, and by April 1927 Chiang established his capital at Nanking. But the uneasy alliance of KMT and CCP could not hold, and in 1927 Chiang turned on his allies, massacring the Communists in Shanghai. Furthermore, the warlords were not entirely eliminated, and Chiang's direct rule was limited effectively to the lower Yangtze. Finally, the Japanese, fearing the potential challenge from a reunited China, decided to reinforce their hold in the north. After 1931, when Japan overran Manchuria, Chiang had to meet simultaneously the Japanese threat from without and Communist threat at home.

Chiang's purge had virtually eliminated the Communists in the cities, but peasant disaffection, arising from his failure to carry out land reform, provided them with new possibilities in the countryside. It was Mao Zedong who realized this, and his base at Chingkang Shan in a remote mountainous area was the main, though not the only, seedbed of the revitalized Communist movement. KMT attacks drove Mao to Kiangsi where the most important Soviet was established and where the Communists ruled an area of several million people developing reform programmes as a peasant-based party rather than an urban, proletarian party on the Russian model. Further KMT attacks forced the Communists to abandon Kiangsi and it was on the famous Long March, to Yenan, where Mao gathered widespread support by his reform programmes and by spearheading resistance to the Japanese invasion, that his peasant-based wing of the party gained ascendancy. The result was that large areas of China passed under Communist control, while Chiang's government, which had withdrawn under Japanese pressure to the remote fastness of Chungking, was unpopular and out of touch. This was the situation in 1945 after the defeat of Japan, though other factors, particularly the growing Soviet-American involvement, played a part. Negotiations for a political settlement broke down and in 1947 open civil war broke out. The Communists defeated the Nationalists in Manchuria and took Peking in January 1949. The great battle around Suchow (November 1948–January 1949) opened the way south. On October 1, 1949, the People's Republic was proclaimed, and the Nationalists fled to Taiwan. But the civil war compounded the devastation of the previous decades and China's new rulers were left with a formidable task of reconstruction.

1 After the break with the Kuomintang in 1927 abortive Communist risings took place in Nanchang and Canton (map right). The first Communist regime was established at Hailufeng in 1927–8, though small bases also emerged in remote mountain areas in central China in 1927–30, the most important of them Mao Zedong's base at Chingkang Shan. In 1929 Mao moved to southern Kiangsi where a stable soviet government survived repeated Kuomintang campaigns until 1934, when the Communist forces withdrew from their southern bases and travelled to the north-west on the famous 'Long March'. From 1937 the Chinese Communist regime in Yenan and the Nationalist government in Chungking were at least nominally united in resistance to the Japanese who, by the end of 1938, occupied large areas of north and central China, including all the major industrial centres and ports. However, Japanese control was only fully effective in the cities and along the main rail lines. In many rural areas, Communist-controlled centres of resistance developed, and though only a few had any real territorial control, all were centres of Communist political influence among the rural population. In 1937 China's industries, poor and mostly foreign-owned, centred on the Treaty Ports: Shanghai alone contained about 60 per cent of all the country's industrial plant.

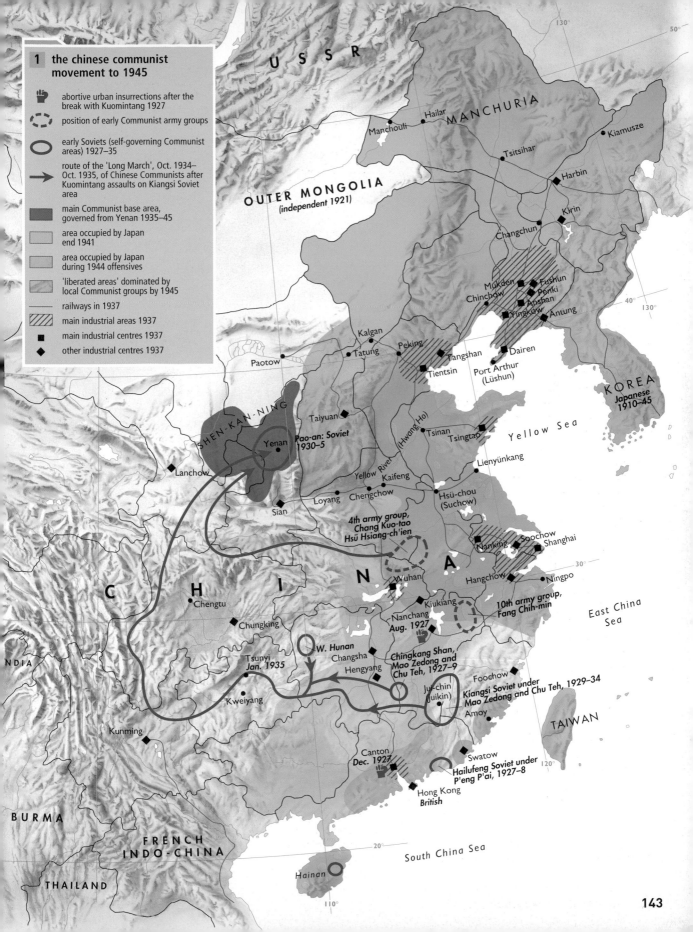

1 the chinese communist movement to 1945

- abortive urban insurrections after the break with Kuomintang 1927
- position of early Communist army groups
- early Soviets (self-governing Communist areas) 1927–35
- route of the 'Long March', Oct. 1934–Oct. 1935, of Chinese Communists after Kuomintang assaults on Kiangsi Soviet area
- main Communist base area, governed from Yenan 1935–45
- area occupied by Japan end 1941
- area occupied by Japan during 1944 offensives
- 'liberated areas' dominated by local Communist groups by 1945
- railways in 1937
- main industrial areas 1937
- main industrial centres 1937
- other industrial centres 1937

U S S R

MANCHURIA

Manchouli   Hailar   Kiamusze

Tsitsihar

Harbin

OUTER MONGOLIA
(independent 1921)   Kirin

Changchun

Mukden   Fushun
Chinchow   Penki
Anshan
Yingkow   Antung

Kalgan

Paotow   Tatung   Peking   Tangshan   Dairen

Tientsin   Port Arthur
(Lüshun)

KOREA
Japanese
1910–45

SHEN-KAN-NING

Taiyuan

Yenan

Pao-an: Soviet
1930–5

Yellow River (Hwang Ho)   Tsinan   Tsingtao   Yellow Sea

Lanchow   Lienyünkang

Yellow River   Kaifeng
Sian   Loyang   Chengchow   Hsü-chou
(Suchow)

4th army group,
Chang Kuo-tao
Hsü Hsiang-ch'ien

C   H   I   N   A   Nanking   Soochow   Shanghai

Chengtu   Wuhan   Hangchow   Ningpo

Chungking   Kiukiang   10th army group,
Fang Chih-min   East China
Nanchang   Sea
Aug. 1927

Tsunyi
Jan. 1935   W. Hunan
Changsha   Chingkang Shan,
Hengyang   Mao Zedong and   Foochow
Chu Teh, 1927–9

INDIA   Kweiyang   Ju-chin   Kiangsi Soviet under
(Juikin)   Mao Zedong and Chu Teh, 1929–34

Kunming   Amoy   TAIWAN

Canton   Swatow
Dec. 1927   Hailufeng Soviet under
P'eng P'ai, 1927–8

Hong Kong
British

BURMA

FRENCH
INDO-CHINA   South China Sea

THAILAND   Hainan

the **ottoman empire**

The Ottoman Empire gradually disintegrated between the beginning of the 19th century and the end of the First World War. Steady European economic and colonial penetration weakened the economy, and the success of the nationalist movements in the latter part of the century caused large areas either to break away or to fall effectively under foreign control.

Austria and Russia had been making inroads into the empire throughout the last decades of the 18th century; they were joined by France, whose expedition to Egypt in 1798 eventually resulted in the end of effective control from Constantinople and the creation of a dynasty by the Ottoman viceroy, Mohammed Ali Pasha, which lasted from 1805 to 1952. His son, Ibrahim Pasha, led expeditions to subdue the Wahabi rulers of Nejd, inaugurated a period of Egyptian rule over the Sudan, and conquered the whole area between what is now Turkey and Egypt between 1831 and 1839.

In the face of this and other challenges, the empire began a series of major reforms, first of its military establishment and then in the fields of law, education and administration. Two major edicts in 1839 and 1856 stressed the subjects' rights to equality and security of life and property. However, especially in the Balkans, the Powers' claims to be able to intervene on behalf of their protegés had the effect of encouraging the nascent nationalist movements; southern Greece, Bulgaria, Montenegro, Romania and Serbia had all become independent   by 1878.

At the same time France was making substantial inroads into North Africa, while Italy invaded Libya in 1911. There were also stirrings of discontent in other Arab provinces, particularly during the long and oppressive reign of Abdul-Hamid II (1876–1909), when ideas of autonomy gradually gained currency, encouraged by the revival of Arabic literature and campaigns to reform the Arab language. Opposition to Abdul-Hamid's rule culminated in the Young Turk revolution of 1908–9, but the policies pursued by the Young Turks alienated much of the Arab population, and contributed substantially to the Arabs' willingness to seek accommodation with Britain in the course of the war. Following Turkish defeat in 1918, the Young Turk regime was overthrown and the sultan briefly restored as an Allied puppet. But in 1920, Turkish nationalists led a war of liberation against the Allied occupying forces. Under the army officer, Kemal Atatürk, and with the support of the emerging Turkish middle classes, the Turkish army reconquered Anatolia. The rest of the former empire was divided up between France and Britain by the League of Nations as mandated territories. By the Treaty of Lausanne (1923), Turkish independence was recognized and Atatürk began the process of building a modern nation state on secular lines.

Similar developments took place in Iran, where the Qajar dynasty (1779–1924) had faced constant Russian and British interference in their internal affairs, culminating in an agreement to divide the country into the spheres of influence of the two powers in 1907. However, the combination of foreign pressures and movements for reform within the country helped to arouse national consciousness and political awareness, and the Constitutional Revolution of 1905–11 marked a major advance in political self-confidence and maturity.

1 The Ottoman empire slowly disintegrated in the 19th and early 20th centuries (map right). Egypt won its autonomy in 1805 while the Balkan nationalities broke away or had their independence confirmed one by one: Greece in 1830, Serbia, Romania and Montenegro in 1878, Bulgaria in 1908, Albania in 1912. Anatolia, the Ottoman heartland, became modern Turkey in 1923.

ITAL

Malta
British

TUNIS
French protectorate 1881

TRIPOLITA
to Italy 1911

ALGERIA
French

F E Z Z A N
to Italy 1911

FRENCH WEST AFRICA

1   **the ottoman empire, 1798-1923**

    Ottoman empire, 1798

    lost by 1886

    lost by 1914

 - - - eastern limit of nominal Ottoman control, 1913

 ——— frontiers, 1914

    lost by 1920

    Ottoman empire under the Treaty of Sèvres, 1920

    Turkey under the Treaty of Lausanne, 1923

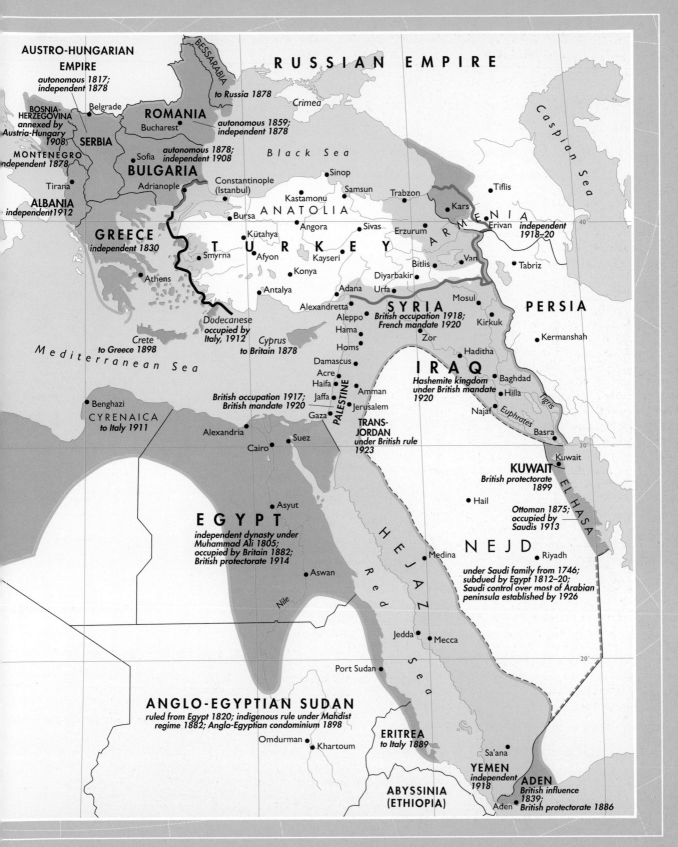

AUSTRO-HUNGARIAN EMPIRE

RUSSIAN EMPIRE

autonomous 1817; independent 1878

BESSARABIA

to Russia 1878

Crimea

BOSNIA-HERZEGOVINA *annexed by Austria-Hungary 1908*

Belgrade

ROMANIA

Bucharest

autonomous 1859; independent 1878

Tiflis

SERBIA

Sofia

autonomous 1878; independent 1908

Sinop

MONTENEGRO *independent 1878*

Black Sea

Samsun

Trabzon

Kars

Tirana

BULGARIA

Constantinople (Istanbul)

Kastamonu

A R M E N I A

independent 1918-20

ALBANIA *independent 1912*

Adrianople

A N A T O L I A

Bursa

Angora

Sivas

Erzurum

Erivan

40°

GREECE *independent 1830*

T U R K E Y

Kütahya

Smyrna

Afyon

Kayseri

Bitlis

Van

Tabriz

Athens

Konya

Antalya

Adana

Urfa

Diyarbakir

P E R S I A

Kermanshah

Dodecanese occupied by Italy, 1912

Crete *to Greece 1898*

Cyprus *to Britain 1878*

Alexandretta

Aleppo

S Y R I A *British occupation 1918; French mandate 1920*

Mosul

Hama

Zor

Kirkuk

M e d i t e r r a n e a n S e a

Homs

Haditha

I R A Q

Damascus

Acre

Haifa

Amman

Jaffa

Jerusalem

P A L E S T I N E

Hashemite kingdom under British mandate 1920

Baghdad

Hilla

Tigris

British occupation 1917; British mandate 1920

Gaza

Najaf

Euphrates

Basra

Benghazi

CYRENAICA *to Italy 1911*

Alexandria

TRANS-JORDAN *under British rule 1923*

Kuwait

KUWAIT *British protectorate 1899*

EL HASA

Cairo

Suez

30°

Hail

Ottoman 1875; occupied by Saudis 1913

Asyut

E G Y P T

independent dynasty under Muhammad Ali 1805; occupied by Britain 1882; British protectorate 1914

H E J A Z

Medina

N E J D

Riyadh

Aswan

Nile

Red Sea

under Saudi family from 1746; subdued by Egypt 1812-20; Saudi control over most of Arabian peninsula established by 1926

Jedda

Mecca

20°

Port Sudan

ANGLO-EGYPTIAN SUDAN

ruled from Egypt 1820; indigenous rule under Mahdist regime 1882; Anglo-Egyptian condominium 1898

ERITREA *to Italy 1889*

Omdurman

Khartoum

Sa'ana

ABYSSINIA (ETHIOPIA)

YEMEN *independent 1918*

ADEN *British influence 1839; British protectorate 1886*

Aden

Caspian Sea

modern **japan**

The Tokugawa shogunate, established in 1609, gave Japan 200 years of peace and prosperity. But a generation before 1868 it was evident that internal tensions were building up and that the *bakufu* (or Shogun's government) in Edo was losing control. Peasant unrest and discontent among impoverished *samurai*, whose position had been undermined by the growth of a money economy, was compounded by British, Russian, French and American pressure for the opening of Japan to foreign trade.

A period of complicated manoeuvring ensued, in which the four western feudal domains (*han*), Satsuma, Choshu, Tosa and Hizen, took the lead. The outcome was the so-called Meiji restoration, when the emperor, supported by dissident elements, moved from Kyoto to Edo, now renamed Tokyo (or eastern capital), displaced the Shogun, and took direct control of government. The Meiji restoration of 1868 was in reality a revolution, carried out with the definite aim of modernization and westernization. The old feudal structure was replaced in 1871 by a modern system of prefectures. Samurai privileges were abolished (1873), though samurai from Choshu had a leading place in the new conscript army. A western-style peerage (1884), cabinet government (1885) and a two-chamber parliament (1889) laid the foundations of political stability; a national education system was instituted (1872) providing teaching for 90 per cent of children by 1900. At the same time economic development was taken in hand. The first railway was opened in 1872, and by 1906 the main network was completed. Industrialization proceeded more slowly, beginning effectively only at the end of the 1800s. By 1889 the number of cotton mills had risen from three in 1877 to 83, and by 1913 Japanese production dominated the home market and had a substantial foothold abroad, particularly in China. Nevertheless, agriculture remained the main employment until after the First World War. The number employed in agriculture fell from 70 per cent of the population in the 1870s to 57 per cent in 1914, but still provided almost all the foodstuffs for a population which rose from 39 million in 1868 to 56 million in 1918.

International recognition of Japan's new status was nevertheless slow in coming. It had been forced in the 1850s to negotiate unequal treaties with the western powers, and it was not until 1894 that foreign consular jurisdiction was abolished and only in 1911 that Tokyo regained tariff autonomy. These concessions were a tribute to Japan's military successes, seen above all in the war with China (1894–95) and in the Russo-Japanese war. The first overseas ventures in the Bonin and Ryukyu islands and in Taiwan were undertaken primarily to still unrest at home, but in 1894 Japan embarked on a full-scale imperialist policy. Even so, it was forced by the European powers to return all its conquests except Taiwan; but the Anglo-Japanese treaty of 1902, inspired by mutual fear of Russia, was a turning point. In the war with Russia (1904–5),

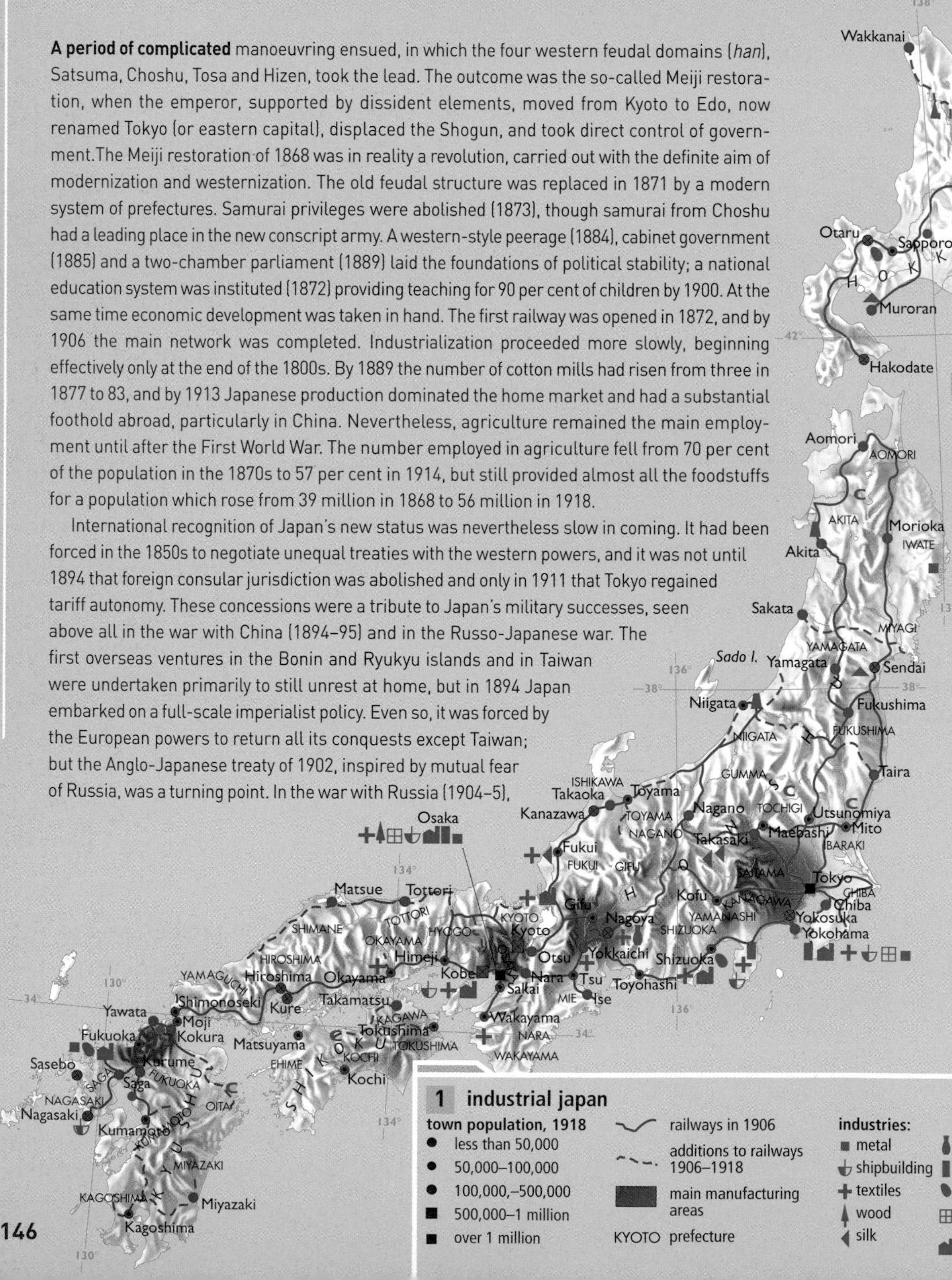

1 By 1918 the first major phase of modern economic growth was completed (map above). Urban population had substantially increased, ports, cities and installations had expanded to meet changes in the scale and structure of foreign trade, and a main railway network connected all major centres. The First World War diverted the energies of all significant competitors and opened large new markets for manufactured exports. Japanese shipping now operated worldwide.

1 industrial japan

town population, 1918
- less than 50,000
- 50,000–100,000
- 100,000–500,000
- 500,000–1 million
- over 1 million

railways in 1906

additions to railways 1906–1918

main manufacturing areas

KYOTO prefecture

industries:
- metal
- shipbuilding
- textiles
- wood
- silk
- ceramics
- chemicals
- food
- machinery
- manufacturing industry

minerals:
- coal
- copper
- iron
- oil

Japan's forces achieved a series of victories culminating in the fall of Port Arthur (January 1905), the battle of Mukden (February–March), and the destruction of the Russian Baltic fleet in the Tsushima Straits (May). After the war the two combatants rapidly reached agreement over a division of spheres of interest, which allowed Japan to annex Korea in 1910. It had embarked on the creation of a Japanese empire on the Asian mainland, and the war of 1914–18 and the Russian revolution enabled it to gain a foot-hold in Shantung and Manchuria. Although once again western pressure compelled it to withdraw, Japan was recognized at the Peace Conference in 1919 as a major power with a permanent seat on the Council of the League of Nations.

During the 1920s Japanese policy veered between cooperation with the west and an inherent anti-foreign feeling, fed by a sense of discrimination. Until 1932 cooperation prevailed, but the impact of the Great Depression swung the balance in the opposite direction, and, beginning with the advance into Manchuria in 1931, Japan set out to carve out an empire in East Asia. In 1934 the nationalist politician Prince Konoye Fukimaro declared the Amau Doctrine, which amounted to a rejection of Western influence in China. After the Japanese attack on the Chinese mainland in 1937 tension grew with the United States. The lines of the Second World War were already being drawn. When Germany defeated France and Holland in 1940, Japan's moment seemed to have arrived, and the advance into South-East Asia began. In spite of astounding initial successes, it was a gamble that failed. But paradoxically the failure, and the subsequent American occupation, propelled Japan even more decisively into the modern world than the Meiji restoratior, socially authoritarian and backward-looking, had done.

2 Growing nationalist and militarist pressure at home pushed Japan into a policy of open imperialism in Asia (map right). In 1931 Manchuria was occupied and over the next six years Japan encroached farther into China, exploiting its political disintegration. In 1932 Japan threatened the port of Shanghai with its large European population. After a restless peace, in 1937 Japan and China became embroiled in a brutal war. Japan then seized much of northern and eastern China.

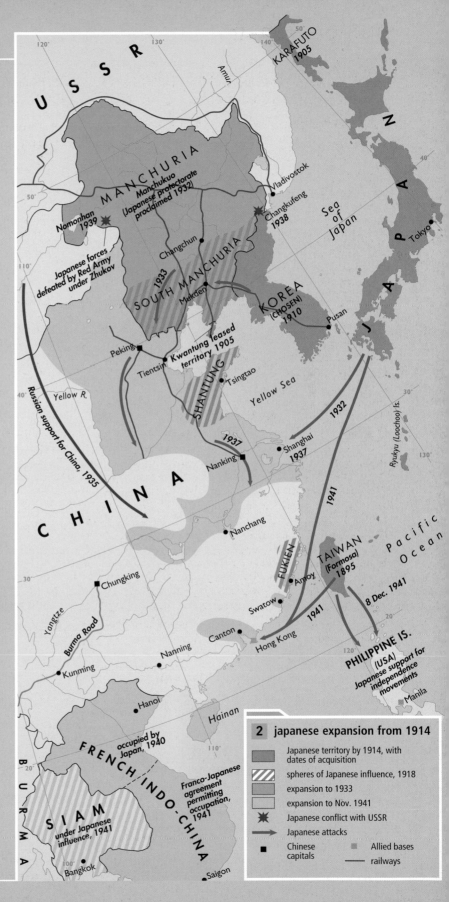

2 japanese expansion from 1914

- Japanese territory by 1914, with dates of acquisition
- spheres of Japanese influence, 1918
- expansion to 1933
- expansion to Nov. 1941
- ✳ Japanese conflict with USSR
- → Japanese attacks
- ■ Chinese capitals
- ▪ Allied bases
- — railways

european **political** problems

The First World War shattered the balance of 1914. The long-term goal after 1918 was a return to 'normalcy', but it was always an illusion. Not merely had the collapse of the Habsburg Empire, the defeat of Germany and the Bolshevik Revolution completely altered the balance of power in Europe, but the pre-war economic equilibrium was also destroyed. All the victorious powers were in debt to the USA, and Great Britain, which had largely financed its allies, never fully recovered.

The dominant fact at the Paris Peace Conference in 1919, was probably fear of the spread of revolution from Russia. This accounts for the relatively lenient treatment of Germany, which suffered only minor territorial losses, except for the restoration to the newly independent Poland of the lands seized in the partitions at the end of the 18th century. The real problem facing the peacemakers was the tangle of nationalities in Europe. Finland, Estonia, Latvia and Lithuania were detached as independent republics from Russia, which was not represented at the Conference, and Russia also lost Bessarabia to Romania and a large part of White Russia to Poland after the Russo–Polish war of 1920. However, the independent republics of White Russia, Georgia, Armenia and Azerbaijan were brought back into the Soviet Union in 1921. The main beneficiary of the peace settlement was Romania, which, in addition to Bessarabia, acquired the Dobruja from Bulgaria and Transylvania from Hungary.

The peace treaties left dissatisfied minorities everywhere, and there were widespread movements of refugees, the most extreme case being the wholesale exchange of populations negotiated after the Greco–Turkish war of 1920-22. More important politically, they also created a lasting sense of injustice and discrimination. It was

2 axis expansion, 1935–39

Germany, 1935
frontiers, 1937

German annexations:
Mar. 1938
Oct. 1938
Mar. 1939
→ Italian campaigns 1935–6

1 At the end of the war the victorious powers tried to redraw the political map of Europe (map above) by creating new states in the east at the expense of the defeated states: Germany, Austria–Hungary, Bulgaria and the Ottoman empire. Though not party to the peace settlement, the Soviet Union also lost extensive territories which had once formed part of the Tsarist empire. Millions of Europeans were expelled or fled from oppression, but there remained many areas where national aspirations were not satisfied, or where national minorities remained under the rule of another nationality. Irredentist conflict and national revolt created an unstable continent, marred by persistent violence and racial tension.

2 Between 1935 and 1939 Italy and Germany began programmes of imperial expansion (map left). In 1936 Italy completed the conquest of Ethiopia and occupied Albania in 1939. Germany under Hitler overturned the Versailles settlement by taking back the Saar (1935), remilitarizing the Rhineland (1936), incorporating Austria (Mar. 1938), compelling Czechoslovakia to cede the Sudetenland (Oct. 1938) and occupying Bohemia and Moravia (Mar. 1939). Hitler's invasion of Poland finally provoked Britain and France to war.

1 plebiscite Feb. 1920: divided between Denmark and Germany
2 occupied by France 1923–5
3 to Belgium 1919
4 to Belgium 1919
5 evacuated 1930, remilitarized 1936
6 League of Nations Mandate by plebiscite to Germany 1935
7 to France 1919
8 divided between Germany and Poland by plebiscite Mar. 1921
9 Allied occupation 1920-3, annexed by Lithuania 1923, autonomous 1924, to Germany 1939
10 to Germany July 1920
11 to Poland Dec. 1918
12 partitioned between Czechoslovakia and Poland 1920
13 to Hungary 1921
14 to Austria 1920
15 occupied by Poland 1920, annexed by Poland following elections 1922
16 to Greece from Bulgaria 1919
17 demilitarized 1924, remilitarized 1936
18 Greek-Bulgarian conflict, 1925

1 national conflicts and frontier disputes, 1919–36

—— German empire, 1914
—— Austro-Hungarian empire, 1914
—— Russian empire, 1914
—— post-settlement frontiers
▲ plebiscites held

new states
areas of dispute
areas temporarily autonomous or independent
areas under armed occupation
areas under League of Nations High Commissioners

inconceivable that either Germany or Russia would ultimately accept a position of inferiority. Thus Europe was divided between revisionists and anti-revisionists, and the only hope for the latter was to support the status quo by a system of military pacts. France, with its alliances with Poland (1921) and Czechoslovakia (1924) was the heart and soul of the security system. When Poland signed a Neutrality Pact with Germany in 1934, it marked the beginning of the collapse of the French security system.

The Locarno treaties (1925), whereby Germany recognized the post-war frontier settlements with France and Belgium, marked the end of the long years of frustration, civil disorder and conflict which had bedevilled Europe since 1918. Germany was welcomed back into the community of nations; so also, after 1925, was Soviet Russia. But the stabilization of 1925-29 was more apparent than real. When the slump in Germany threw up a mass nationalist movement headed by Adolf Hitler, who came to power in January 1933, the post-war settlement came under a direct threat. Germany left the League and in 1936 remilitarized the Rhineland, destroying the Versailles and Locarno agreements. In 1936 civil war broke out in Spain, and Hitler and Mussolini both sent aid to the nationalist rebels of General Franco. Britain and France sought to negotiate away the gathering crisis. But Hitler's annexation of Austria in March 1938, and the threat to Czechoslovakia that followed, undermined European security. At Munich in September 1938 the West agreed to German occupation of the Sudetenland. But Hitler seized the rest of Czechoslovakia in March 1939. A continent-wide war was looming.

the **great depression**

After 1925 it appeared that the disorders of the post-war world had been overcome and a period of relative stability and prosperity had begun. The Great Depression quickly dispelled this illusion. Conventionally its starting point was the financial crash on Wall Street in October 1929; but this was only the manifestation of deeper weaknesses in the world economy.

In the United States business was in trouble long before the crash. Worldwide, commodity prices had been falling since 1926, impairing the capacity of exporters such as Australia to buy products from Europe and the United States. The German economy also was faltering by 1928. However, more important than the causes of the depression were its consequences. These were almost instantaneous, although it was only after 1930 that dislocation reached its peak. Its most arresting manifestation was unemployment which reached record heights in 1932. In many industrial countries over a quarter of the labour force was thrown out of work. Industrial production fell to 53 per cent of its 1929 level in Germany and the United States, and world trade sank to 35 per cent of its 1929 value. Attempts to solve the problem only made things worse. As early as 1930 the United States imposed the Hawley–Smoot Tariff, the highest in its history. The United Kingdom responded in 1932 by negotiating the Ottawa Agreements, a series of preferential tariffs for the Commonwealth. Another expedient was competitive devaluation. After England left the Gold Standard in 1931, country after country followed suit and the result was the development of closed currency blocs, which inhibited international trade still further.

Economic nationalism fostered political nationalism, just as unemployment and the erosion of middle-class living standards fostered political extremism. The fall of the Hamaguchi government in Japan in 1931 marked the end of constitutional democracy and the beginning of Japanese aggression in Manchuria. In Germany, Brüning's deflationary policies, raising unemployment from under three million in 1930 to six million two years later, paved the way for Hitler. Hitler's accession to power in January l933 was followed by Dollfuss's dictatorship in Austria, and eastern Europe, with the exception of Czechoslovakia, quickly followed suit. France remained precariously democratic until 1940, and in the United Kingdom, where a right-wing 'national' government won a huge majority in l931, Mosley's fascist movement made little headway. But even here and in the United States, where F. D. Roosevelt was elected president in 1932 with a promise of a 'New Deal', fascist movements exercised considerable pressure. Only the Soviet Union, isolated from the world economy, was able to sustain economic growth – a fact which was to be of cardinal importance after 1941. Roosevelt's New Deal made initial progress, but faltered after 1936 when a new phase of economic down-turn began. By 1939 the United States had not regained the level of industrial out-put of 1929, and only the Second World War, and the boost it gave to production, pulled it out of depression.

The effects of the depression also hit the primary producing countries of Asia, Africa and Latin America. Here, as the crisis radicalized peasants and workers, nationalist and revolutionary movements gained new bases of support. In this respect, as in many others, the Great Depression was the catalyst of the modern world.

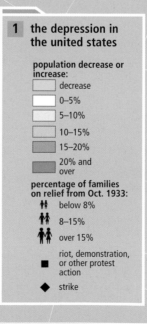

1 the depression in the united states

population decrease or increase:

- decrease
- 0–5%
- 5–10%
- 10–15%
- 15–20%
- 20% and over

percentage of families on relief from Oct. 1933:

- below 8%
- 8–15%
- over 15%
- riot, demonstration, or other protest action
- strike

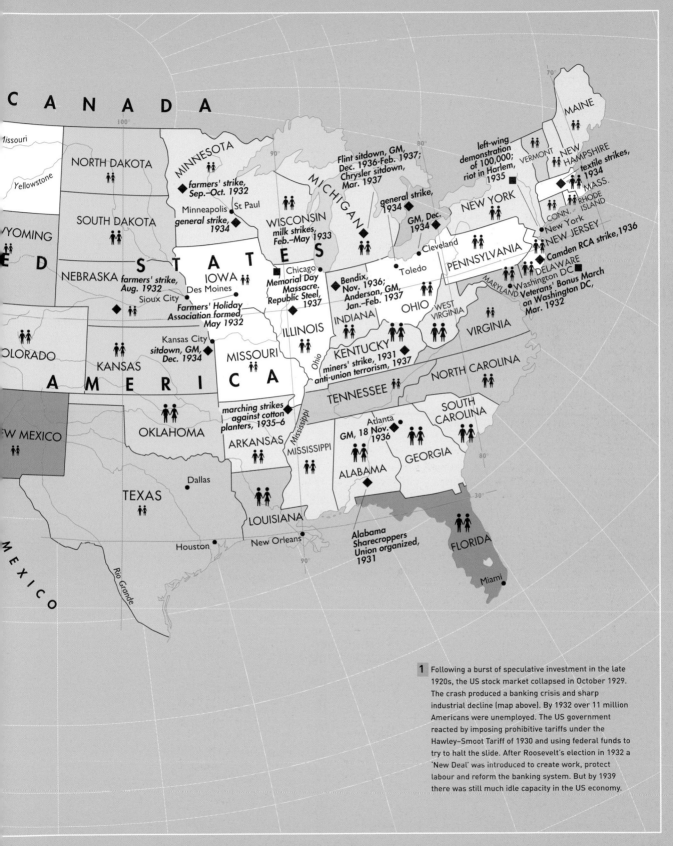

CANADA

Missouri

Yellowstone

NORTH DAKOTA

MINNESOTA

◆ farmers' strike,
Sep.–Oct. 1932

Minneapolis   St Paul

SOUTH DAKOTA

general strike,
1934 ◆

WYOMING

ED   STATES

NEBRASKA   farmers' strike,
Aug. 1932

Sioux City

Farmers' Holiday
Association formed,
May 1932

COLORADO

KANSAS

AMERICA

MISSOURI

Kansas City
sitdown, GM,
Dec. 1934

NEW MEXICO

OKLAHOMA

TEXAS

Dallas

Houston

MEXICO

Rio Grande

New Orleans

LOUISIANA

ARKANSAS

marching strikes
against cotton
planters, 1935–6

MISSISSIPPI

Alabama
Sharecroppers
Union organized,
1931

MICHIGAN

WISCONSIN
milk strikes,
Feb.–May 1933

IOWA

Des Moines

Chicago
Memorial Day
Massacre.
Republic Steel,
1937

ILLINOIS

Ohio

Flint sitdown, GM,
Dec. 1936–Feb. 1937;
Chrysler sitdown,
Mar. 1937

general strike,
1934

GM, Dec.
1934

Cleveland

Toledo

Bendix,
Nov. 1936;
Anderson, GM,
Jan.–Feb. 1937

INDIANA

OHIO

KENTUCKY

miners' strike, 1931
anti-union terrorism, 1937

TENNESSEE

Atlanta
GM, 18 Nov.
1936

ALABAMA

GEORGIA

SOUTH
CAROLINA

NORTH CAROLINA

VIRGINIA

WEST
VIRGINIA

PENNSYLVANIA

NEW YORK

left-wing
demonstration
of 100,000;
riot in Harlem,
1935

VERMONT   NEW
HAMPSHIRE

MAINE

textile strikes,
1934

MASS.

CONN.   RHODE
ISLAND

New York

NEW JERSEY

Camden RCA strike, 1936

DELAWARE

MARYLAND

Washington DC

Veterans' Bonus March
on Washington DC,
Mar. 1932

FLORIDA

Miami

1 Following a burst of speculative investment in the late
1920s, the US stock market collapsed in October 1929.
The crash produced a banking crisis and sharp
industrial decline (map above). By 1932 over 11 million
Americans were unemployed. The US government
reacted by imposing prohibitive tariffs under the
Hawley–Smoot Tariff of 1930 and using federal funds to
try to halt the slide. After Roosevelt's election in 1932 a
'New Deal' was introduced to create work, protect
labour and reform the banking system. But by 1939
there was still much idle capacity in the US economy.

the **war** in the **west**

Hitler's accession to power in 1933 added a new dimension to international politics. He was held back at first by Germany's diplomatic isolation and by the need to put the shattered economy back on its feet. But by 1936 this phase was over. The re-occupation of the Rhineland, the denunciation of the Locarno treaties, the Rome–Berlin axis, and the anti-Comintern Pact with Japan, demonstrated the new thrust of German policy. Nevertheless, Hitler hoped to get his way by threats and bluster rather than by war, and the unopposed annexation of Austria and the dismemberment of Czechoslovakia in 1938 seemed to prove him right. When in the following year he turned against Poland he expected that England and France would once again give way, and believed that the notorious Nazi–Soviet pact of August 23, 1939, would deter the Western powers from intervention. But this time Hitler miscalculated. When German troops invaded Poland (September 1, 1939), England and France declared war, though they did nothing to aid the Poles.

For the first three years the German armies, with their *Blitzkrieg* strategy, were extraordinarily successful. After the fall of Poland Hitler halted, hoping that the Western powers would negotiate a compromise peace. Then, in April 1940, he launched his attack in the West, overran Denmark and Norway, and turned against France, which was knocked out of the war before the end of June. But the new Churchill government in London refused to concede defeat, and Hitler launched a major air offensive, intended to prepare the way for invasion. The victory of the Royal Air Force in the Battle of Britain forced him on September 17, 1940, to call off the projected invasion. Instead, Hitler decided to attack Soviet Russia. The directive for 'Operation Barbarossa' was issued in December 1940, the invasion of Russia launched on June 22, 1941. It nearly succeeded. Before the tide turned, German armies were outside Moscow and Leningrad and had overrun southern Russia to the Black Sea and the Caucasus.

Meanwhile two other events intervened. One was the lack of success of Italy, which had entered the war in 1940, which forced Hitler, in 1941, to divert troops to conquer Yugoslavia and Greece and to reinforce the African front. Secondly the United States, entering the war in 1941, supplied Britain and Russia with much-needed arms and equipment, and also helped to defeat the German submarine campaign in the Atlantic. The British victory at El Alamein (October 1942), the subsequent capitulation of the Italian and German armies in Africa (May 1943), the Anglo–American invasion of Sicily and then Italy, and the fall of Mussolini (July 1943), were major Allied successes. But it was the great Russian victory at Stalingrad (January 1943) that was decisive. The Germans' last major offensive in the east at Kursk failed in July 1943. Thereafter they fought a stubborn defensive war, but after the Anglo–American landings in northern France (June 1944) and the opening of the Second Front, the ring was closed, and the bases were lost for the 'secret weapons' which Hitler hoped would force the British to capitulate. The Ardennes offensive (December 1944) was a final attempt to break out in the west; but by now the Allies held the initiative. A major Soviet offensive against East Prussia opened in January 1945, and by April Berlin was under assault. On April 30 Hitler committed suicide, and on May 7 his successor, Admiral Doenitz, surrendered unconditionally. The costs were appalling: 15 million military and 35 million civilians had perished, 20 million of whom were Soviet citizens. Some six million Jews were exterminated in concentration camps or otherwise. Anglo-American saturation bombing reduced many German cities to rubble, and 25 million Russians were left homeless. Europe was in ruins, and already the differences between the victorious powers, which were to darken the post-war years, were visible.

1 Hitler's failure to defeat Britain by bombing and the Atlantic submarine campaign coupled with the reverse of German fortunes at Stalingrad left Germany fighting a two-front war (map below). While the German army in the east was worn down by Soviet forces in a series of gigantic battles, Anglo–American armies invaded North Africa in 1942, Italy in 1943 and France in 1944. Western air forces undermined the German war effort through bombing, while partisans and resistance movements challenged German occupation.

1 the defeat of germany, 1942–45

- Grossdeutches Reich, 1942
- Axis attacks
- Axis withdrawals
- Allied attacks
- major cities under heavy air attack
- major battle with date
- partisan/resistance movements
- commando raids
- V1 launching sites
- V2 launching sites
- frontiers 1942

1941 to 1945

Japanese expansionism in the 1930s was the product of a desire to achieve economic self-sufficiency, military security and a self-imposed leadership of eastern Asia. Japan after September 1931 overran Manchuria and then set about the reduction of its neighbouring provinces by overrunning much of China north of the Yangtze and sponsoring puppet regimes in its area of conquest. By 1941, Japan, with no possibility of militarily or politically ending the Chinese war, found its ambitions widening to include the European colonial empires in South-East Asia. These offered the raw materials and markets that would free Japan from an economic dependence upon an increasingly unfriendly United States. The latter's re-armament programmes were scheduled to near completion by 1944–45; the prospect of future naval inferiority and the economic blockade imposed upon Japan after its occupation of Indo–China in 1940 prompted Japanese action. The attack upon the US Pacific Fleet at Pearl Harbor in December 1940 was an attempt to forestall American military preparation and thereby buy the time needed to secure and develop South-East Asia.

In challenging the United States Japan sought to fight the world's greatest industrialized power to a stalemate that would result in a negotiated peace which would recognize Japanese hegemony in eastern Asia. Within six months of the start of the Pacific war Japanese forces had conquered American, British and Dutch possessions throughout South-East Asia and had carried the war to the borders of India, to the waters that washed Australia and into the south-west Pacific. Yet in those months Japan failed to inflict a naval defeat sufficient to impair US military capacity and morale: indeed, in attempting to do so the Imperial Navy suffered a reverse in the Coral Sea in May 1942, the devastation of its front-line carrier force off Midway in June and crippling losses in the protracted Guadalcanal campaign of August 1942–February 1943. Thereafter, without the means to end the war that it had initiated, Japanese strategic mobility was rapidly eroded as the Imperial forces became obliged to fight defensively on widely separated fronts against a number of enemies. The United States no less slowly grew into a force that was able to sustain four major efforts: a devastatingly successful campaign against Japanese naval and merchant shipping; an 'island-hopping' strategy with amphibious forces that bypassed the major centres of Japanese resistance; an ultimately overwhelming carrier offensive that was to carry the war to the Japanese Home Islands; and a strategic air offensive, based upon the Marianas, that was to shatter Japanese urban areas in the last six months of the war. By August 1945, when the US atomic bomb attacks upon Hiroshima and Nagasaki and the Soviet offensive in Manchuria enforced their surrender, the Japanese had been utterly exhausted and defeated. However, the brief Japanese colonial adventure had unleashed forces of revolutionary nationalism that were to shape events throughout eastern and South-East Asia over the next three decades.

1 The limits of the Japanese advance were reached in June 1942. A war of attrition followed as Allied forces regained the territories seized in 1941–42. The Japanese fought fanatically but suffered from collapsing air and sea power as America built a vast carrier force and Allied submarines all but destroyed Japan's merchant fleet. In China, Japanese efforts to destroy Nationalist forces in 1944 were followed by renewed Chinese offensives. In August 1945 Soviet forces defeated the northern armies and occupied Manchuria.

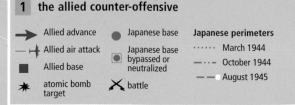

1 the allied counter-offensive

→ Allied advance

—⊩ Allied air attack

■ Allied base

✳ atomic bomb target

● Japanese base

◉ Japanese base bypassed or neutralized

✗ battle

Japanese perimeters

······ March 1944

—·—· October 1944

— —■ August 1945

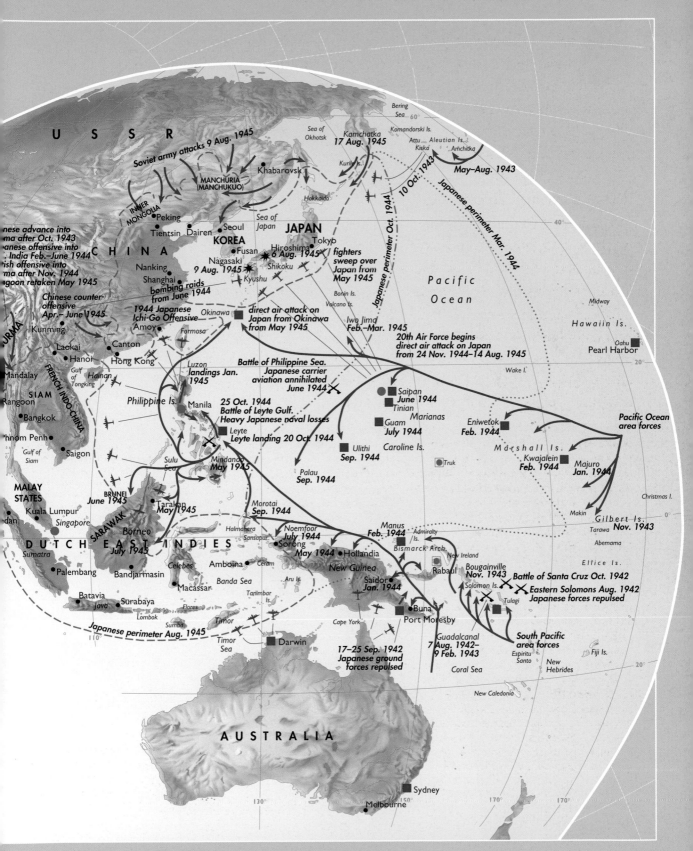

USSR

Soviet army attacks 9 Aug. 1945

Sea of Okhotsk

Bering Sea

60°

Komandorski Is.

Kamchatka 17 Aug. 1945

Attu Kiska *Aleutian Is.* Amchitka

10 Oct. 1943

May–Aug. 1943

Kurile Is.

Khabarovsk

MANCHURIA (MANCHUKUO)

Japanese perimeter Mar. 1944

INNER MONGOLIA

Peking

Hokkaido

Sea of Japan

40°

Tientsin Dairen Seoul **KOREA** Fusan

JAPAN

Tokyo

nese advance into
ma after Oct. 1943
anese offensive into
. India Feb.–June 1944
ish offensive into
ma after Nov. 1944
goon retaken May 1945

CHINA

Nanking

Hiroshima 6 Aug. 1945

Nagasaki 9 Aug. 1945

Shikoku

Kyushu

fighters sweep over Japan from May 1945

Pacific Ocean

Japanese perimeter Oct. 1944

Shanghai

bombing raids from June 1944

Chinese counter-offensive Apr.– June 1945

Amoy

1944 Japanese Ichi-Go Offensive

Okinawa

direct air attack on Japan from Okinawa from May 1945

Iwo Jima Feb.–Mar. 1945

Bonin Is.

Volcano Is.

Midway

Hawaiin Is.

20th Air Force begins direct air attack on Japan from 24 Nov. 1944–14 Aug. 1945

Kunming

Laokai

Hanoi

Canton

Hong Kong

Luzon landings Jan. 1945

Battle of Philippine Sea. Japanese carrier aviation annihilated June 1944

Wake I.

20°

Oahu Pearl Harbor

URMA

Mandalay

Gulf of Tongking

Hainan

Philippine Is.

Manila

25 Oct. 1944 **Battle of Leyte Gulf. Heavy Japanese naval losses**

Leyte

Leyte landing 20 Oct. 1944

Saipan June 1944

Tinian

Guam July 1944

Marianas

Eniwetok Feb. 1944

Pacific Ocean area forces

SIAM

Rangoon

Bangkok

FRENCH INDO-CHINA

hnom Penh

Gulf of Siam

Saigon

Mindanao May 1945

Ulithi Sep. 1944

Caroline Is.

Truk

Marshall Is.

Kwajalein Feb. 1944

Majuro Jan. 1944

Christmas I.

0°

Sulu Sea

Palau Sep. 1944

MALAY STATES

dan

Kuala Lumpur

Singapore

BRUNEI June 1945

Tarakan May 1945

Borneo

SARAWAK

July 1945

Makin

Gilbert Is.

Tarawa Nov. 1943

Abemama

Morotai Sep. 1944

Manus Feb. 1944

Admiralty /Is.

DUTCH EAST INDIES

Sumatra

Palembang

Bandjarmasin

Macassar

Celebes

Halmahera

Sansapur

Noemfoor July 1944

Sorong

May 1944

Hollandia

Ellice Is.

Bismarck Arch.

New Ireland

Rabaul

Bougainville Nov. 1943

Battle of Santa Cruz Oct. 1942

Amboina

Ceram

Banda Sea

Aru Is.

New Guinea

Saidor Jan. 1944

Solomon Is.

Eastern Solomons Aug. 1942 Japanese forces repulsed

Batavia

Java

Surabaya

Lombok

Sumba

Flores

Tarimbar Is.

Timor

Buna

Port Moresby

Guadalcanal 7 Aug. 1942– 9 Feb. 1943

South Pacific area forces

Espiritu Santo

New Hebrides

Fiji Is.

Japanese perimeter Aug. 1945

Timor Sea

Darwin

Cape York

17–25 Sep. 1942 **Japanese ground forces repulsed**

Coral Sea

New Caledonia

110°

20°

AUSTRALIA

Sydney

Melbourne

130°

150°

170°

170°

World War II left Europe politically disorganized and economically prostrate, a situation greatly exacerbated by large-scale population movements. The German collapse released millions of incarcerated prisoners-of-war, refugees and slave-workers. Two more lasting shifts of population also occurred: some 12 million Germans abandoned (voluntarily or forcibly) their pre-war homes in the east, especially in lands annexed by the Nazis after 1938; and over two million Russians moved into the territories annexed by the Soviet Union during its westward advance.

The political frontiers of the new Europe were established at conferences between the victors (USA, USSR, Britain and France) held at Yalta and Potsdam in February and July 1945: the union of Germany and Austria decreed by Hitler in 1938 was dissolved and Germany lost territory to Poland and the Soviet Union; both countries were divided into occupation zones under four-power control. In Austria the system worked relatively smoothly, and in 1955 the country achieved independence; but co-operation between the USSR and her allies in Germany broke down in 1948. Britain and the United States had already amalgamated their zones in 1947 and, in conjunction with France, they now prepared for the formation of a West German government (the Federal Republic: BRD). After an attempt to prevent this by means of a blockade on Berlin, the Soviets prepared their zone for quasi-independence as the German Democratic Republic (DDR): the two states came into existence in 1949.

They immediately took their place in the two political blocs into which Europe had become divided. The eastern republics had all come under communist rule by 1948 and economic growth, though continuous, remained slow thanks to Stalinist methods of production. In the western democracies, thanks largely to lavish American aid (the Marshall Plan from 1947), an economic miracle took place, with smooth and rapid growth year after year. The two blocs had their own military groups – NATO in the west (1949) and the Warsaw Pact in the east (1955) – and their own economic organizations – in the east Comecon (1949) and in the west the

2 During the period 1986–99 the European Economic Community (from 1995 the European Union) expanded beyond western Europe to create a continent-wide structure of full and associated members. The accession, in 2004, of 10 further countries (including eight former communist states in Eastern Europe), will lead to greater difficulties in reaching consensus in the Union's decision-making bodies.

2 the expansion of the european union

- members of the EEC, Jan. 1981
- joined Jan. 1986
- admitted Oct. 1990
- joined Jan. 1995
- countries scheduled for EU accession in 2004, with date of aaplication
- countries scheduled for EU accession in 2007, with date of aaplication
- other countries applying for membership

The European Economic Area (EEA)
- members of the EEA, June 1996

European Community (six members 1957; nine by 1973). However the growth surge suffered a serious check in 1973 when the Arab-led Organization of Petroleum Exporting Countries (OPEC) increased the price of oil by 250 per cent.

In western Europe, the oil crisis encouraged the trend to greater economic integration. By the late 1960s the original six members of the EEC (the EU from 1995) had established themselves as the economic vanguard of the continent. In 1973 Britain, Ireland and Denmark joined, followed in 1981 by Greece, in 1986 by Spain and Portugal, and in 1995 by Austria, Finland and Sweden. Economic, and to an extent political, integration deepened; in 1985 the EU introduced a single market, and in 1991 the Maastricht Treaty committed members to the introduction of a single currency, which became a reality in 2001.

The face of the continent was further transformed by the collapse of the communist regimes in eastern Europe in the late 1980s. In the wake of the collapse of the Soviet Union, no fewer than 15 countries appeared. The nationalist tensions released also led to civil wars in the former Yugoslavia. No fewer than eight of the Soviet Union's former satellites or component republics are due to join the EU in 2004, bringing the membership of the organization to 25 states. Questions about the ability of the expanded EU to take decisions effectively have, therefore, become ever more urgent.

1 post-war population movements and territorial change

Territorial change, 1945–9

- cities divided into four occupation zones
- frontiers, 1949
- Germany, 1937
- Allied control zones of Germany and Austria
- annexed by Soviet Union 1940–45
- states which became Communist, 1945–48
- Yugoslav gains from Italy, 1945
- Federal Republic of Germany from 1949
- German Democratic Republic from 1949

Population movements: peoples resettled, evacuated or expelled (with numbers):

- Germans
- Finns driven from area bordering Russia
- Baltic peoples
- Russians
- Russians forcibly repatriated
- Poles
- Czechs
- peoples settled by International Refugee Organization

1 War and its aftermath drove millions of Europeans from their homelands (map right). An estimated 30 million people became refugees, most of them permanently displaced. Territorially, the Soviet Union emerged as the major victor, its borders shifted dramatically to the west. Politically, it also dominated eastern Europe. Germany, greatly reduced, became two states in 1949, those areas occupied by the Western Allies becoming the Federal Republic, the Soviet zone becoming the German Democratic Republic, a division which endured until 1990.

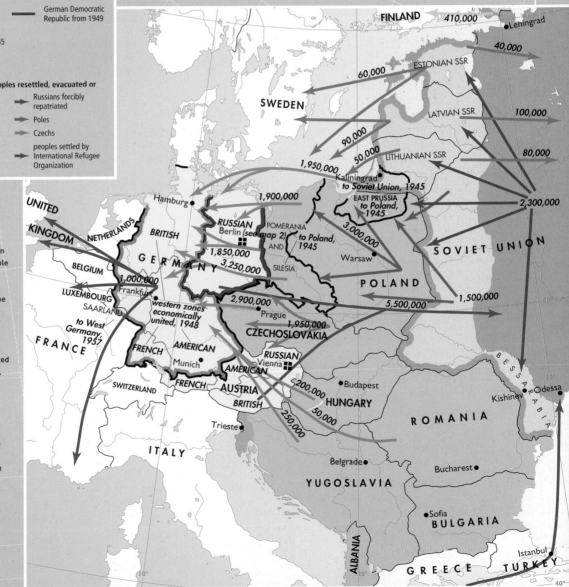

retreat from empire after 1947

The Western empires created in the 19th century remained intact in 1939, though most German and Ottoman possessions had passed to Britain, France and Japan as League of Nations mandates. The United States planned to grant independence to the Philippines, acquired in 1898, and did so immediately after World War II; but none of the seven remaining European colonial powers – Britain, France, Spain, Portugal, Belgium, Italy and the Netherlands – surrendered their empires voluntarily.

Only Britain even conceived of independence as the ultimate goal, albeit with continued membership of the Commonwealth, a goal already attained in 1939 by Canada, South Africa, Australia and New Zealand. The continental colonial powers thought more in terms of evolution towards a common citizenship, with their colonies as overseas parts of the metropolitan territory. Such plans were complicated, however, by

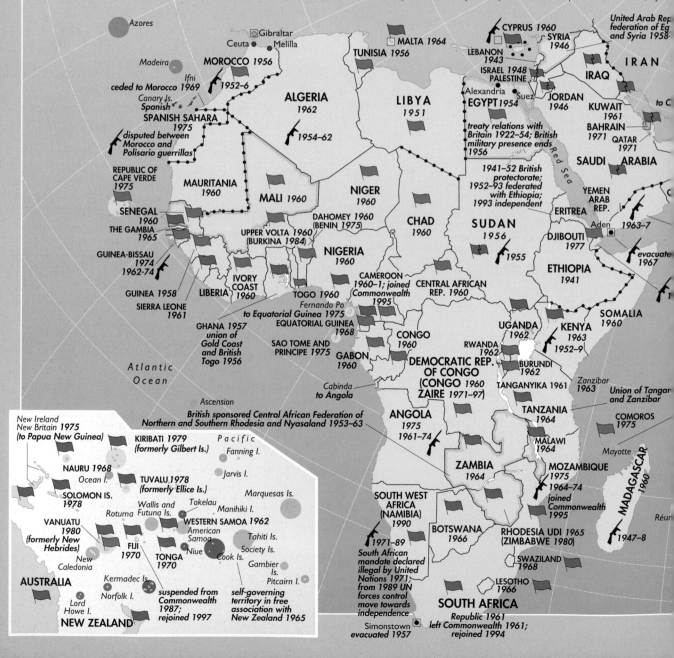

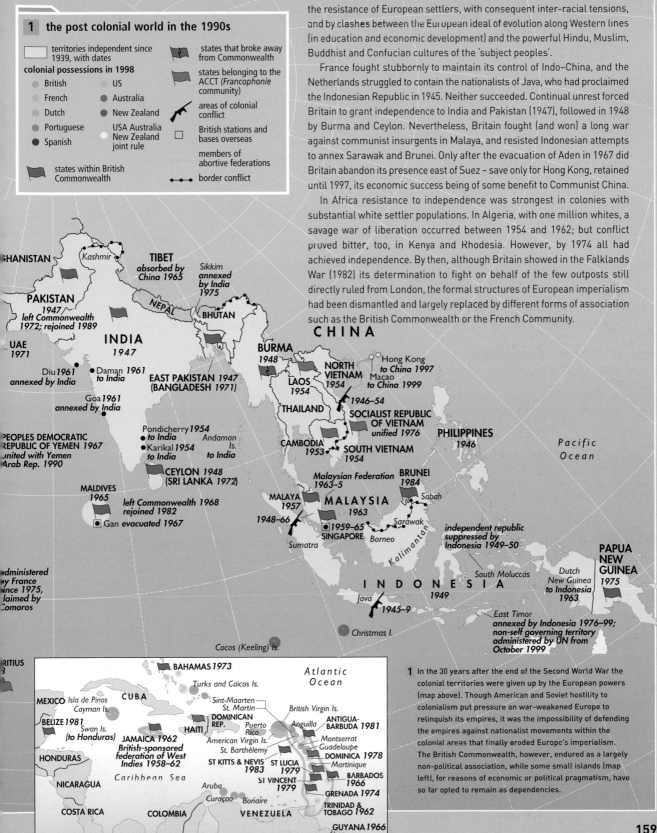

1 the post colonial world in the 1990s

territories independent since 1939, with dates

colonial possessions in 1998
- British
- French
- Dutch
- Portuguese
- Spanish
- US
- Australia
- New Zealand
- USA Australia New Zealand joint rule

states within British Commonwealth

states that broke away from Commonwealth

states belonging to the ACCT (*Francophonie* community)

areas of colonial conflict

British stations and bases overseas

members of abortive federations

border conflict

---

the resistance of European settlers, with consequent inter-racial tensions, and by clashes between the European ideal of evolution along Western lines (in education and economic development) and the powerful Hindu, Muslim, Buddhist and Confucian cultures of the 'subject peoples'.

France fought stubbornly to maintain its control of Indo–China, and the Netherlands struggled to contain the nationalists of Java, who had proclaimed the Indonesian Republic in 1945. Neither succeeded. Continual unrest forced Britain to grant independence to India and Pakistan (1947), followed in 1948 by Burma and Ceylon. Nevertheless, Britain fought (and won) a long war against communist insurgents in Malaya, and resisted Indonesian attempts to annex Sarawak and Brunei. Only after the evacuation of Aden in 1967 did Britain abandon its presence east of Suez – save only for Hong Kong, retained until 1997, its economic success being of some benefit to Communist China.

In Africa resistance to independence was strongest in colonies with substantial white settler populations. In Algeria, with one million whites, a savage war of liberation occurred between 1954 and 1962; but conflict proved bitter, too, in Kenya and Rhodesia. However, by 1974 all had achieved independence. By then, although Britain showed in the Falklands War (1982) its determination to fight on behalf of the few outposts still directly ruled from London, the formal structures of European imperialism had been dismantled and largely replaced by different forms of association such as the British Commonwealth or the French Community.

Map labels:

AFGHANISTAN · Kashmir · TIBET absorbed by China 1965 · Sikkim annexed by India 1975 · NEPAL · PAKISTAN 1947 left Commonwealth 1972; rejoined 1989 · BHUTAN · INDIA 1947 · CHINA · UAE 1971 · Diu 1961 annexed by India · Daman 1961 to India · EAST PAKISTAN 1947 (BANGLADESH 1971) · BURMA 1948 · NORTH VIETNAM 1954 · Hong Kong to China 1997 · Macao to China 1999 · LAOS 1954 · 1946–54 · Goa 1961 annexed by India · THAILAND · SOCIALIST REPUBLIC OF VIETNAM unified 1976 · PHILIPPINES 1946 · Pacific Ocean · PEOPLES DEMOCRATIC REPUBLIC OF YEMEN 1967 united with Yemen Arab Rep. 1990 · Pondicherry 1954 to India · Karikal 1954 to India · Andaman Is. to India · CAMBODIA 1953 · SOUTH VIETNAM 1954 · CEYLON 1948 (SRI LANKA 1972) · MALDIVES 1965 · left Commonwealth 1968 rejoined 1982 · Gan evacuated 1967 · Malaysian Federation 1963–5 · BRUNEI 1984 · Sabah · MALAYA 1957 · MALAYSIA 1963 · Sarawak · PAPUA NEW GUINEA 1975 · 1948–66 · 1959–65 SINGAPORE · Borneo · Sumatra · Kalimantan · independent republic suppressed by Indonesia 1949–50 · administered by France since 1975, claimed by Comoros · INDONESIA 1949 · South Moluccas · Dutch New Guinea to Indonesia 1963 · Java 1945–9 · East Timor annexed by Indonesia 1976–99; non-self governing territory administered by UN from October 1999 · Christmas I. · Cocos (Keeling) Is. · MAURITIUS

Inset map (Caribbean):

BAHAMAS 1973 · Turks and Caicos Is. · Atlantic Ocean · MEXICO · Isla de Pinos · Cayman Is. · CUBA · Sint-Maarten St. Martin · British Virgin Is. · DOMINICAN REP. · Anguilla · ANTIGUA-BARBUDA 1981 · BELIZE 1981 · Swan Is. (to Honduras) · HAITI · Puerto Rico · American Virgin Is. · St. Barthélemy · Montserrat · Guadeloupe · JAMAICA 1962 British-sponsored federation of West Indies 1958–62 · DOMINICA 1978 · ST KITTS & NEVIS 1983 · ST LUCIA 1979 · Martinique · HONDURAS · Caribbean Sea · ST VINCENT 1979 · BARBADOS 1966 · Aruba · NICARAGUA · Curaçao · Bonaire · GRENADA 1974 · TRINIDAD & TOBAGO 1962 · COSTA RICA · COLOMBIA · VENEZUELA · GUYANA 1966

---

1 In the 30 years after the end of the Second World War the colonial territories were given up by the European powers (map above). Though American and Soviet hostility to colonialism put pressure on war-weakened Europe to relinquish its empires, it was the impossibility of defending the empires against nationalist movements within the colonial areas that finally eroded Europe's imperialism. The British Commonwealth, however, endured as a largely non-political association, while some small islands (map left), for reasons of economic or political pragmatism, have so far opted to remain as dependencies.

the **middle east** since 1945

The Middle East has occupied world attention more consistently than any other region since 1945: Israel and its neighbours have engaged in four full-scale wars; Israel has invaded Lebanon twice; two Gulf wars have been fought; military coups have reinforced a regional pattern of internal repression; waves of refugees, from Cyprus to Afghanistan, have been forced to flee their homelands.

> **1** the middle east from 1945
>
> → invasion
> ✸ major conflicts
> ✊ guerrilla activity

1963-74 *Intermittent intercommunal clashes*
1974 *Turkish invasion and occupation of northern part of island*

1969 *Increase in Palestinian guerrilla activity*
1975 *Lebanese civil war breaks out*
1976 *Syrian invasion*
1978 *Israeli invasion*
1982 *Attack on Beirut by Israel*
1985 *Formal withdrawal of Israeli troops*
1992 *Christians boycott first elections for 20 years*
2002 *Israeli forces withdraw buffer zone in South Lebanon*

American support for the state of Israel (founded in 1948), sponsorship of the Baghdad Pact (1955), and intervention in Lebanon (1958) seemed to threaten the USSR's southern frontier, and so it offered assistance to Syria, Egypt and (after 1958) Iraq. The Soviets also championed the Arab states during the Arab–Israeli war of 1967, despite which Israel occupied the west bank of the Jordan, Sinai and the Golan Heights, provoking further large-scale Arab emigration. In 1973 an Egyptian and Syrian attack on Israel met with limited military success, and opened a new phase of negotiation. Egypt and Israel concluded the Camp David Accords (1978) which resulted in the return of Sinai in 1982; but the Israelis refused to return the other territories occupied since 1967, instead installing large numbers of new Jewish settlements. Moreover in 1982, to counter Palestinian guerrilla activity, they invaded and held south Lebanon. Nevertheless, in the wake of a prolonged period of resistance to Israeli rule in the West Bank and Gaza, which excited much outside sympathy, in 1991 the USA succeeded in bringing Israel and its Arab neighbours into extended peace talks, which resulted in limited Palestinian self-rule in 1994–95. Although Israel withdrew from south Lebanon in 2000, hopes for lasting peace foundered in the late 1990s. By 2003, a continuing Palestinian *intifada*, the expansion of Jewish settlements in the West Bank, and a mutual cycle of violent response on both sides had destroyed all sense of trust and left the peace process in tatters.

As open conflict between Israel and her neighbours abated, it began around the Persian Gulf. The replacement of the Shah of Iran by Ayatollah Khomeini in 1979 seemed to President Saddam Hussein of Iraq to offer the chance of territorial gain. He attacked in 1980. However, eight years of attritional warfare achieved virtually nothing and in 1990, in an attempt to gain new resources with which to liquidate his war debts, Saddam invaded and annexed another neighbour, Kuwait. The United Nations, led by the USA, put pressure on Saddam to withdraw and, when he refused, in 1991 used armed force to expel him. Iraq was subject to strict regulations during the 1990s on weapons and military installations. In 2002, his failure to co-operate with UN weapons inspectors led to the invasion of Iraq by a US-led force, without explicit UN support. Saddam's regime crumbled, but the predominantly Anglo–American force struggled thereafter to impose order.

Oil remained the most valuable natural asset of the region. Output and revenue both increased dramatically after the OPEC price-rise in 1973, creating some of the

2 The years immediately before and after the establishment of the State of Israel in May 1947 saw massive movements of populations as Jews entered Palestine and Arabs fled (map right). Subsequent wars saw Israel annex the West Bank, Gaza Strip, Golan Heights and the Sinai Peninsula. The future of the West Bank, nominally now (with Gaza) under Palestinian self-rule, has proved the most intractable.

2 israel and palestine, 1948–95

- ▣ Israel after Arab invasion and War of Independence, 1948
- ▢ Israeli conquests, 1967
- — Egyptian re-conquests, and Israeli conquests, 1973
- → Jewish immigration, 1948–64
- → Arab refugees, 1948
- → Arab refugees, 1967

Sinai, the Israeli withdrawal:
- ----- Egyptian frontline under second Sinai agreement, 1 Sep.1975
- ○ Israeli settlements given up in 1982
- ✈ Israeli military and civil airports given up in 1982
- ⌂ Israeli oil wells given up in 1982

SYRIA
1946 Withdrawal of French troops
1958-61 Union with Egypt (United Arab Republic)
1963 Ba'th Party seizes power
1967 Six Day War; Syria loses Golan Heights
1970 General Hafiz al-Assad seizes power
1973 October (Yom Kippur) War; Syria and Egypt attack Israel; Syrian forces expelled from Golan Heights and Israeli forces occupy Syrian territory
1976 Syrian forces intervene in Lebanese civil war
1980 Treaty of Friendship and Co-operation with USSR
1991 Peace made with Lebanon
2000 Death of President Hafiz al-Asad, succeeded by his son Bashir al-Asad

IRAQ
1955 Anti-Soviet Baghdad Pact
1958 Hashemite dynasty overthrown in military coup, power seized by General Abdel-karim Kassem
1963 Kassem overthrown in military coup
1968 Ba'th Party seizes power
1972-5 Intermittent fighting between Kurds and government
1974-5 Iraq-Iran War; Iran withdraws support from Kurds; Kurdish rebellion collapses
1979 Saddam Hussein becomes president
1980-8 Iraq-Iran War
1990 Invasion of Kuwait by Iraq
1991 UN coalition expels Iraqi army from Kuwait; Shia and Kurdish rebels attempt overthrow of Saddam; massive reprisals ordered by Saddam; Western sanctions imposed; de facto independent Kurdish state established in north
1991-8 Western sanctions remain in place. UN weapons inspectors seek to locate and neutralize Iraqi weapons of mass destruction
1998 UN weapons inspectors withdraw. Operation 'Desert Fox': large-scale airstrikes against Iraq
2002 UN weapons inspectors return to Iraq
2003 US-led forces invade to topple Saddam

IRAN
1941 Abdication of Shah Reza Pahlavi following Anglo-Russian occupation of Iran; his son Mohammed Reza Pahlavi becomes Shah
1951 Nationalization of oil industry; deterioration in relations with UK
1953-4 Prime Minister Mossadeq becomes de facto ruler; the Shah flees but is later reinstated by royalist military forces with covert US support; oil dispute settled
1961 Shah declares 'White Revolution'
1975 Algiers Agreement with Iraq acknowledges Iran's supremacy in Gulf
1978-9 Revolution; the Shah is exiled; Ayatollah Khomeini returns from exile; Iran becomes an Islamic Republic
1980-8 Iran-Iraq War
1989 Khomeini dies, Rafsanjani president
1995 US imposes economic sanctions
1997 Moderate Khatami elected president
2001 Khatami re-elected president

JORDAN
1952 Accession of King Hussein
1970 Attempted destruction of PLO by Jordanian Army (Black September)
1990 King Hussein refuses to join coalition against Iraq
1994 Peace accord and full diplomatic relations with Israel
1999 Death of King Hussein

EGYPT
...8 Leads Arab coalition against Israel
...2 Monarchy overthrown; military government led by Nasser after 1952
...6 Nationalization of Suez Canal Company; tripartite invasion by Britain, France, Israel
...8-61 Union with Syria (United Arab Republic)
...7,1973 Wars with Israel
...0 Nasser dies; Sadat becomes president
...9 Egyptian-Israeli peace treaty
...1 Sadat assassination; Mubarak becomes ...ident
...9 Egypt readmitted to Arab League
...0 Egypt sends troops to Iraq coalition

KUWAIT
1990 Invaded by Iraq; Gulf Crisis
1991 Liberated by UN coalition forces

SAUDI ARABIA
1951 Mutual Defence Assistance Agreement with US
1960 Organization of Petroleum Exporting Countries formed
1981 Gulf Co-operation Council formed (with Bahrain, Kuwait, Oman, Qatar and UAE)
1973 Saudi Arabia embargoes oil exports to USA; oil price soars
1990 Base for UN Coalition attacks against Iraq
1992 Tentative steps towards political openess
1996 King Fahd temporarily steps down

UAE
1971 Created from former British-protected Trucial States after British evacuation

OMAN
1965-75 Marxist insurgency by People's Democratic Republic of Yemen defeated with British and Iranian help
1970 Accession of Sultan Qaboos
1999 'Basic Statues of the State' promulgated; Oman's first written constitution

YEMEN
1948 Assassination of Imam Yahya; his son takes power
1959 Creation of the Arab Emirates of the South (later the Federation of South Arabia)
1962 Civil war and revolution in San'a; Yemen Arab Republic (North Yemen) established
1967 Withdrawal of British forces; declaration of People's Democratic Republic of Yemen (South Yemen)
1990 YAR and PDRY united
1994 Civil war breaks out: Democratic Republic of Yemen declares secession (supressed July)
1999 First direct Presidential elections held; Ali Abdallah Salih elected

SUDAN
1953 Anglo-Egyptian agreement on ending British condominium of 1899
1956 Sudan gains independence
1958 Coup by General Ibrahim Abboud
1963-72 Civil war between Arab Muslim rulers in north and Christian and animist Africans in south
1969 Abboud deposed; Colonel Gaafar Mohammed el-Nimeiri seizes power
1983 Civil war re-erupts; food shortages increase
1985 Military coup ousts Nimeiri
1989 Military coup; National Islamic Front in effective control
1990-1 Famine worsens; reports of military aid from Iran
1994-5 Ceasefire between feuding southern anti-government forces
1998 US attack suspected chemical weapons plant
1999-2001 Parliament suspended
2001 Arrest of Hassan al-Turabi, speaker of parliament and founder of National Islamic Front

YEMEN ARAB REPUBLIC
1962-9 Civil war
1972-9 Intermittent war with Aden

PEOPLE'S DEMOCRATIC REPUBLIC OF YEMEN
1967 Coup by National Liberation Front; civil war; Britain withdraws troops from Aden
1968 Ali Nasar Muhammad overthrown as president by Haidar al Attas

highest per capita incomes in the world in the Arab Gulf states. Their prosperity also attracted massive immigration from Egypt, Jordan, Yemen and the Indian sub-continent, creating a potential problem. The rise of Islamic fundamentalism posed another. After 1979 it became a badge of hostility towards the West in Iran and towards Russia in Afghanistan, and elsewhere toward the regime in power – unless, as in Iran, that regime was an Islamic theocracy. In northern Africa, in the 1990s Islamic fundamentalism stimulated terrorist violence, provoking serious conflict in Algeria and Egypt.

1 Since the countries of the Middle East threw off British and French rule between the 1930s and 1960s, the region has been plagued by instability, partly because of the Arab–Israeli conflict, partly because of its role in the power struggle of the Cold War, and more recently because of the upheavals caused by the rise of militant Islam (map above). In addition, it contains some 65 per cent of the world's oil reserves.

After World War II, although some French and British liberals sympathetic to African claims for advancement initiated programmes of social improvement and political reform, the need to exploit every asset in order to assist metropolitan recovery led to attempts to reassert colonial control. Nevertheless, in the 1950s both Britain and France began to transfer responsibility to elected governments in their West African colonies.

In Muslim North Africa, longer-established nationalist movements received great stimulus from the overthrow of the Egyptian monarchy in 1952 and the rise to power of Gamal Abdel Nasser. In 1956 an Anglo–French–Israeli invasion failed to topple him. Meanwhile France granted independence to Tunisia and Morocco but tried to incorporate Algeria, the colony with the largest white population, into metropolitan France. This sparked a civil war that lasted until France reluctantly granted independence in 1962.

Elsewhere, white settlers strove to maintain their ascendancy. In South Africa, a Nationalist government dedicated to policies of racial separation ('apartheid') came to power; in Kenya, British troops arrived to suppress the Mau-Mau insurrection directed against the settlers; in Central Africa, a federation of Nyasaland and Rhodesia aimed to preserve white dominance. But in 1963 Kenya achieved independence and the Federation collapsed. Southern Rhodesia's white settlers created their own independent state in 1965, but had to accept black majority rule in 1980. Portugal retained its colonies longest, but in all of them guerrilla warfare eventually led to ignominious withdrawal in 1974–5.

Most of the newly independent African states possessed borders drawn by European governments in the 19th century with insufficient attention to ethnic rivalries. Soon after independence, those rivalries began to tear them apart. In 1960, tribal and regional factions in Zaire (formerly the Belgian Congo) led to demands for a federal constitution and, when these were refused, the army mutinied and the mineral-rich province of Katanga seceded. United Nations intervention reunited the country in 1963, but two years later the army seized power and retained it for 34 years. Similarly, in Nigeria the secession of Biafra in 1967 led to a three-year civil war that restored central control, but likewise delivered power to the army. Elsewhere, ethnic violence caused enormous casualties – in the small state of Rwanda, Hutu–Tutsi violence left over 500,000 dead in 1994 – while repeated droughts (compounded by government inefficiency and corruption) caused famine and massive refugee problems in many areas of East Africa. In West Africa, the aftermath of a savage civil war in Liberia from the late 1980s spread instability throughout the region, which by 2003 had engulfed Sierra Leone and Côte d'Ivoire. In Algeria, meanwhile, from 1990 Islamic Fundamentalism challenged government control, leaving tens of thousands dead.

By the 1980s, white supremacy survived only in South Africa where the nationalist regime sought to retain its grip by draconian internal repression, by sending troops against guerrillas in neighbouring states, and by granting spurious independence to some black settlement areas set up under apartheid. Eventually, however, economic crisis and international isolation forced concessions. In 1990, the nationalists released Nelson Mandela, imprisoned leader of the banned African National Congress, and within four years the ANC's victory in the first multi-racial elections in South Africa's history swept away white rule. Despite the problems of healing decades of racial tension, the ANC created a more stable political system than under white rule and preserved the most successful economy on the continent. Mandela retired in 2000. Meanwhile in Zimbabwe (formerly Rhodesia) the Mugabe government's policy from 2000 of confiscating land from white farmers for redistribution to 'war veterans' led to serious economic dislocation.

1976 Western Sahara jointly occupied by Morocco and Mauritania; Polisario guerrilla resistance backed by Algeria
1991 cease-fire between Morocco and Polisario
W. SAH

1976-79 war with Polisario
1978 military rule
1991 multi-party elections

1968 civilian government overthrown
1974-85 border conflicts with Burkina
MAL

1991 RUF launches civil war
1992 military coup
1996 civilian rule restored under Ahmad Tejan Kabbah
1997 military overthrow Kabbah
1998 Kabbah restored
1999 rebels almost capture Freetown
Nov. 2000 RUF call truce
SENEGAL
GA.
GU.

1989 outbreak of civil war
1993 pan-African peace-keeping force (Ecomog) intervenes in attempt to halt civil war
GUIN

1957 first Black African country to gain independence
1966 Nkrumah deposed
1967-85 series of military coups
SIERRA LEON
LIBE

1967-70 Nigerian civil war
1981 civilian rule restored
1984, 1985, 1993 military coups
1993 elections declared void; riots;interim government ousted
1999 civilian ruled restored

1966 military takeover led by Col. Bokassa, crowned emperor 1
1980 republic restored
1981 military coup

1 The years during and after the political emancipation of most of Africa from colonial rule were a period of rapid change and considerable instability (map right). Many civilian governments became one-party states or were swept aside by military regimes. Since the end of the Cold War a wave of democratization has spread through Africa but economic and social progress has been slow as states remain weak, caught in a web of foreign debt and dependency.

1 africa: post-independence wars and revolutions

✸ civil war
➜ invasion
✊ guerrilla activity
✸ border dispute

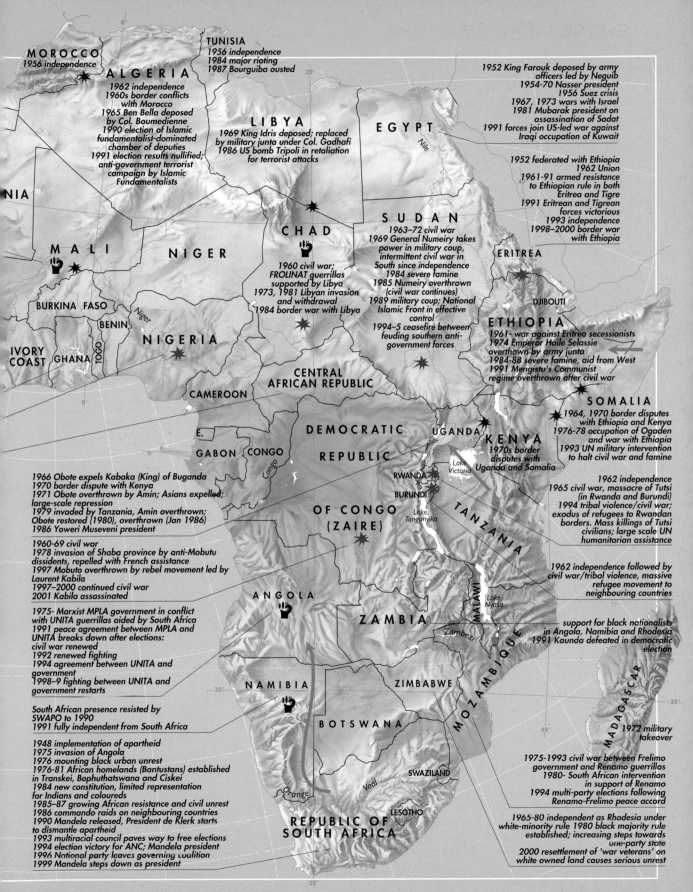

MOROCCO
1956 independence

ALGERIA
1962 independence
1960s border conflicts with Morocco
1965 Ben Bella deposed by Col. Boumedienne
1990 election of Islamic fundamentalist-dominated chamber of deputies
1991 election results nullified; anti-government terrorist campaign by Islamic Fundamentalists

TUNISIA
1956 independence
1984 major rioting
1987 Bourguiba ousted

LIBYA
1969 King Idris deposed; replaced by military junta under Col. Gadhafi
1986 US bomb Tripoli in retaliation for terrorist attacks

EGYPT
1952 King Farouk deposed by army officers led by Neguib
1954-70 Nasser president
1956 Suez crisis
1967, 1973 wars with Israel
1981 Mubarak president on assassination of Sadat
1991 forces join US-led war against Iraqi occupation of Kuwait

ERITREA
1952 federated with Ethiopia
1962 Union
1961-91 armed resistance to Ethiopian rule in both Eritrea and Tigre
1991 Eritrean and Tigrean forces victorious
1993 independence
1998–2000 border war with Ethiopia

MALI

NIGER

CHAD
1960 civil war; FROLINAT guerrillas supported by Libya
1973, 1981 Libyan invasion and withdrawal
1984 border war with Libya

SUDAN
1963–72 civil war
1969 General Numeiry takes power in military coup, intermittent civil war in South since independence
1984 severe famine
1985 Numeiry overthrown (civil war continues)
1989 military coup; National Islamic Front in effective control
1994–5 ceasefire between feuding southern anti-government forces

DJIBOUTI

ETHIOPIA
1961- war against Eritrea secessionists
1974 Emperor Haile Selassie overthown by army junta
1984-88 severe famine, aid from West
1991 Mengistu's Communist regime overthrown after civil war

BURKINA FASO

BENIN

IVORY COAST

GHANA

TOGO

NIGERIA

CAMEROON

CENTRAL AFRICAN REPUBLIC

E. GABON

CONGO

DEMOCRATIC REPUBLIC OF CONGO (ZAIRE)

UGANDA
1966 Obote expels Kabaka (King) of Buganda
1970 border dispute with Kenya
1971 Obote overthrown by Amin; Asians expelled; large-scale repression
1979 invaded by Tanzania, Amin overthrown; Obote restored (1980), overthrown (Jan 1986)
1986 Yoweri Museveni president

KENYA
1970s border disputes with Uganda and Somalia

SOMALIA
1964, 1970 border disputes with Ethiopia and Kenya
1976-78 occupation of Ogaden and war with Ethiopia
1993 UN military intervention to halt civil war and famine

1960-69 civil war
1978 invasion of Shaba province by anti-Mobutu dissidents, repelled with French assistance
1997 Mobuto overthrown by rebel movement led by Laurent Kabila
1997–2000 continued civil war
2001 Kabila assassinated

RWANDA

BURUNDI

1962 independence
1965 civil war, massacre of Tutsi (in Rwanda and Burundi)
1994 tribal violence/civil war; exodus of refugees to Rwandan borders. Mass killings of Tutsi civilians; large scale UN humanitarian assistance

TANZANIA

Lake Victoria
Lake Tanganyika

1962 independence followed by civil war/tribal violence, massive refugee movement to neighbouring countries

ANGOLA

ZAMBIA

1975- Marxist MPLA government in conflict with UNITA guerrillas aided by South Africa
1991 peace agreement between MPLA and UNITA breaks down after elections: civil war renewed
1992 renewed fighting
1994 agreement between UNITA and government
1998–9 fighting between UNITA and government restarts

MALAWI

Lake Nyasa

MOZAMBIQUE

Zambezi

support for black nationalists in Angola, Namibia and Rhodesia
1991 Kaunda defeated in democratic election

NAMIBIA
South African presence resisted by SWAPO to 1990
1991 fully independent from South Africa

ZIMBABWE

MADAGASCAR
1972 military takeover

BOTSWANA

1948 implementation of apartheid
1975 invasion of Angola
1976 mounting black urban unrest
1976-81 African homelands (Bantustans) established in Transkei, Bophuthatswana and Ciskei
1984 new constitution, limited representation for Indians and coloureds
1985–87 growing African resistance and civil unrest
1986 commando raids on neighbouring countries
1990 Mandela released, President de Klerk starts to dismantle apartheid
1993 multiracial council paves way to free elections
1994 election victory for ANC; Mandela president
1996 National party leaves governing coalition
1999 Mandela steps down as president

SWAZILAND

Orange
Vaal

LESOTHO

REPUBLIC OF SOUTH AFRICA

1975-1993 civil war between Frelimo government and Renamo guerrillas
1980- South African intervention in support of Renamo
1994 multi-party elections following Renamo-Frelimo peace accord

1965-80 independent as Rhodesia under white-minority rule 1980 black majority rule established; increasing steps towards one-party state
2000 resettlement of 'war veterans' on white owned land causes serious unrest

The history of southern Asia since independence has been dominated by three factors. First, the seizure of power by military leaders (Pakistan 1958, Indonesia 1967), with the aim – rarely successful – of abolishing corruption and stabilizing the economy; second, the resurgence of long-standing regional, tribal and religious conflicts; finally, intervention by the Great Powers (Russia in Afghanistan; China and the United States in Vietnam).

Wars between states also characterized certain areas. The partition of the Indian subcontinent in 1947 left numerous points of friction between the new states of India and Pakistan, particularly Punjab, Kashmir and Bengal, and these erupted into war in 1965 and again in 1971 (in connection with the secession of East Pakistan to form the separate state of Bangladesh). Indian forces also expelled the Portuguese from their coastal enclaves (1961), fought China over a frontier dispute (1962) and intervened in Sri Lanka to protect the Hindu Tamil minority (1986–90). Civil wars, however, proved far more common. Malaya suffered a communist insurrection, led by ethnic Chinese, between 1948 and 1960; the Philippines experienced rebellions by both communists and Muslims from the 1960s; Cambodia was devastated by the civil war between the communist Khmer Rouge and its non-communist opponents.

The most savage conflict, however, occurred in Vietnam. After the Japanese collapse in 1945 Ho Chi Minh established a communist regime in Hanoi while the French recreated their colonial empire in the south. In 1946 armed conflict began, continuing until a humiliating defeat at Dien Bien Phu in 1954 forced the French to withdraw. Although this left Cambodia and Laos as independent states, Ho was forced to accept a 'temporary' partition of Vietnam at the 17th parallel. An anti-communist regime in the south, backed by the USA, refused to hold elections. In 1959 Ho therefore launched a major attack, and the USA immediately provided munitions and advisers to the south, with regular troops and air strikes after 1965. Despite saturation bombing and the commitment of 500,000 US ground troops, the communists (supported by both Russia and China) held their own and in 1968 negotiations began between Hanoi and Washington. In 1973 American forces withdrew, although the USA continued to supply the south on a massive scale. When the communists launched an orthodox military offensive in 1975, however, the south's army collapsed. Vietnam was now unified, under Hanoi, although its economy was ruined and its invasion of Cambodia in 1978 led to ostracism by the West.

Elsewhere in Asia, however, rapid development occurred. Following the path of Japan, Taiwan, Malaysia, Singapore, Thailand and eventually Indonesia achieved rapid rates of growth from the late 1960s. Even during the world recession of the 1980s, each experienced an annual growth rate of well over five per cent. Various factors were responsible: all except Singapore possessed large pools of cheap labour; all created a substantial industrial base oriented towards export markets throughout Asia, Europe and North America; all the governments sought to attract substantial foreign investment through tax incentives and infrastructural development. A

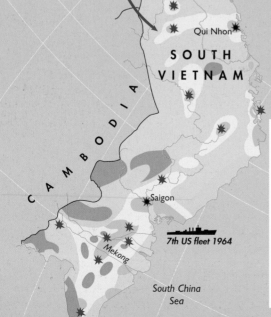

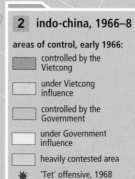

2 indo-china, 1966–8

areas of control, early 1966:

- controlled by the Vietcong
- under Vietcong influence
- controlled by the Government
- under Government influence
- heavily contested area
- ✳ 'Tet' offensive, 1968

7th US fleet 1964

2 From 1957 communist guerrillas waged a war against the pro-Western government of South Vietnam. The government controlled the urban areas, the guerrillas most of the countryside (map left). The Ho Chi Minh trail was the route by which supplies were funnelled from the north to the Viet Cong troops fighting in the south. In 1968 the guerrillas launched the 'Tet' offensive against the cities, which prompted gradual US withdrawal. In 1973 the last US troops left the country. In 1975 the whole country was united under communist rule.

1955 supports Baluchistani separatists in Pakistan
Dec. 1979 invaded by USSR; continued resistance by Islamic guerrillas
1988 USSR withdraws
1992 post Soviet-backed regime defeated by Islamic guerrillas
1997 regime overthrown by radical Islamic Taleban movement

AFGHANISTAN

PAKISTAN

1958 military coup by Ayub Khan
1965 border clashes with India in Rann of Kutch
1965 war with India over Kashmir
1971 war with India over Bangladesh
1972 ceasefire lines established
1977 military coup by Zia ul-Haq
1988 democratic elections;.
Benazir Bhutto prime minister (deposed 1990)
1993 Benazir Bhutto returns as prime minister (deposed 1996)
1998 nuclear tests conducted
1999 military under General Musharraf overthrows government of Nawaz Sharif

1971 secession from Pakistan; civil war followed in 1975 by murder of Sheikh Mujib and military control

C H I N A

TIBET

NEPAL

BANGLADESH

I N D I A

spasmodic unrest among Nagas, Sikhs and Tamils
1961 India occupies Portuguese enclaves
1962 Sino-Indian border war
1975–7 state of emergency proclaimed
1984 Sikh separatist uprising suppressed; Indira Gandhi assassinated
1991 Rajiv Gandhi assassinated
1998 nuclear tests conducted

SRI LANKA

1958, 1961 fighting between Sinhalese and Tamils
1971 government assumes emergency powers after rural guerrilla uprisings; 1983 intercommunal rioting
1986–90 Indian intervention to crush Tamil rebellions
May 1993 President Ranasinghe killed in rebel Tamil attack

1948 Democratic People's Republic of Korea proclaimed
1950 invasion of South Korea
1994 death of Kim Il Sung. His son, Kim Jong Il succeeds

NORTH KOREA

SOUTH KOREA

1948 Republic of Korea proclaimed
1950–3 Korean War
1961 military coup followed by dictatorship of Park Chung Hee (assassinated 1979);
mounting opposition from 1974
1979 martial law (relaxed 1981)

JAPAN

1951 peace treaty with USA and end of occupation
1956 agreement with USSR, ending state of war;
1960 widespread demonstrations against US military bases in Japan and Okinawa
1972 normalization of relations with China
1990 agreements with USSR formally ending 1945 war

Okinawa occupied by US after 1945, reverted to Japan 1972

seat of Chinese Nationalist government since 1949
1958 territorial dispute with China over Quemoy and Matsu
1996 China attempts military intimidations as Taiwan holds first free elections

TAIWAN

1954 French withdrawal; civil war
1956–73 US backed South Vietnam and the communist-backed North engaged in escalating conflict
1973 US withdraws all forces
1976 North and South Vietnam reunified under Viet-Minh rule
1978 invasion of Cambodia and border clashes with China
1979 Chinese invasion

1953–73 civil war
1975 monarchy abolished; Pathet Lao seizes power

BURMA

guerrilla activity since independence (1948)
1958, 1962 military coups
1974 Socialist People's Republic inaugurated
May 1990 pro-democracy protests lend to free elections; military refuse to recognize result
1990 opposition leader Aung San Suu Kyi and her pro-democracy movement suppressed by military

VIETNAM

LAOS

THAILAND

CAMBODIA

Communist and Muslim insurgency since 1968, eruption into civil war 1972–8
1986 Marcos regime ousted following general election. Aquino president
1992 Ramos succeeds as president
2001 President Estrada forced to step down by popular protests

PHILIPPINES

1947 military takeover, guerrilla activity since 1960
1976 border clashes with Cambodia
1978 Cambodian refugee camps in E. Thailand become bases for anti-Vietnamese factions
1987 border clashes with Laos

Mindanao

1970 monarchy abolished
1970–4 civil war; victory of Khmer Rouge who massacre millions of civilians
1978 Vietnamese invasion overthrows Khmer Rouge
1989 Vietnamese forces withdraw
1991 peace agreement leads to May 1993 elections, boycotted by Khmer Rouge which carries on civil war

M A L A Y S I A

Aceh

I N D O N E S I A

1967 Sukarno ousted by military coup; suppression of Communists
1976- resistance to Indonesian rule in E. Timor
1977–99 secessionist rising in Irian Jaya
1989- GAM independence movement in Aceh fights guerilla campaign against government
1998 President Suharto steps down in face of rising protests
1999–2001 intercommunal violence in the Moluccas
1999 UN peace-keeping force enters East Timor after violence following vote in referendum for independence from Indonesia

Irian Jaya

East Timor

1948–60 'The Emergency'- civil war with communist guerrillas
1969 rising by Chinese minority groups
1975–8 Communist guerrilla activity
1978- renewed racial and religious conflict

1 post-independence wars and revolutions

✦ civil war   → invasion   ✊ guerrilla activity

1 Throughout south-east Asia, native communist movements fought against the restoration of colonial rule after 1945 (map above). The communist guerrilla war was defeated in Malaysia in 1960, and communism suppressed in Indonesia and the Philippines in the 1960s. In Indo-China communism achieved power in North Vietnam in 1954, but it took until 1975 before the communists controlled South Vietnam. The same year communist guerrillas, the Khmer Rouge, seized power in Cambodia, and the Pathet Lao took control of Laos.

major part of that investment came from Japan. Finally, political stability – Lee in Singapore; Mahathir in Malaysia; Suharto in Indonesia – underpinned the economic strategy of industrial development and helped to attract foreign investment.

All these economies suffered in the economic turmoil which hit east Asia in 1997, when a currency crisis was transformed into a general crisis of confidence in the Asian economic model. Indonesia was badly hit by a 75 per cent devaluation of the rupiah, again exacerbated by a major political crisis, as the 35-year-old Suharto regime finally collapsed under the weight of nationwide protests. In general the region's economies recovered far faster than expected. Yet Indonesia remained gripped by widespread civil and ethnic unrest (including the withdrawal from East Timor in 1999), which threatened to destabilize the whole country.

china since 1949

The establishment of the People's Republic of China in 1949 marked a fundamental turning point in the modern history of China. After a century of severe internal conflict and disintegration, usually provoked or exacerbated by external aggressors, China was now reunified and strongly governed by leaders who possessed a decisive vision of the society they wished to create. Whatever the excesses and failures since 1949, not least the systematic repression of much of the population, that remains a fundamental achievement.

For a time, China closely followed the Soviet model of directed economic planning and achieved modest progress in developing heavy industries and raising agricultural production. In 1958, however, the communist leader Mao Zedong became impatient and sought to mobilize the revolutionary energies of China's vast population, launching the 'Great Leap Forward'. Rural China was divided into 26,000 communes, each required to abolish private property and meet huge targets in agricultural and industrial production. Some 600,000 backyard furnaces sprang up across the countryside. The experiment proved an unmitigated disaster: production declined sharply, 20–30 million people died from starvation or malnutrition, and the project was abandoned in 1961.

This failure strengthened the hands of moderate communists who preferred a more centrally-planned, Soviet-style development. Mao responded by forming an alliance with the People's Liberation Army (PLA) and with

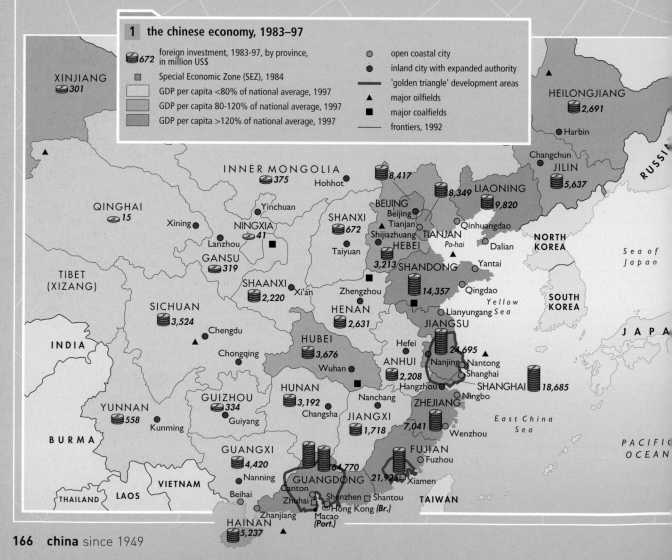

1 the chinese economy, 1983–97

- **672** foreign investment, 1983-97, by province, in million US$
- ▪ Special Economic Zone (SEZ), 1984
- ☐ GDP per capita <80% of national average, 1997
- ☐ GDP per capita 80-120% of national average, 1997
- ☐ GDP per capita >120% of national average, 1997
- ● open coastal city
- ● inland city with expanded authority
- ▬ 'golden triangle' development areas
- ▲ major oilfields
- ■ major coalfields
- ─── frontiers, 1992

1 The world's most populous nation, China developed rapidly after the civil war and communist takeover in 1949 (map left). But the country's industrial and agricultural expansion was slowed by the Great Leap Forward of the late 1950s and the Cultural Revolution of the mid-1960s. From the late 1970s China experienced an economic revolution, following the decision to pursue the 'Four Modernizations' (agriculture, industry, national defence, science and technology). A massive programme of investment produced significant gains in output, but led to high inflation. In the mid-1980s a policy of retrenchment stabilized the economy, before the regime launched more thorough market reforms and a new expansionary wave from 1990. The fruits of this were seen in growth rates regularly in excess of 10 per cent, reaching 13 per cent in 1993 and an economy less affected than most in east and south-east Asia by the economic crisis of 1997–98.

2 In 1966, threatened by growing opposition in the Party and the bureaucracy and impatient of their careerism and autocratic methods, Mao launched the Great Proletarian Cultural Revolution (map right). In July 1966 he set his Red Guards loose. They rampaged through the cities attacking the 'Four Olds' (old ideas, culture, customs and habits) and took over many parts of the establishment. By mid-1968 there was chaos and the PLA was sent in to restore order.

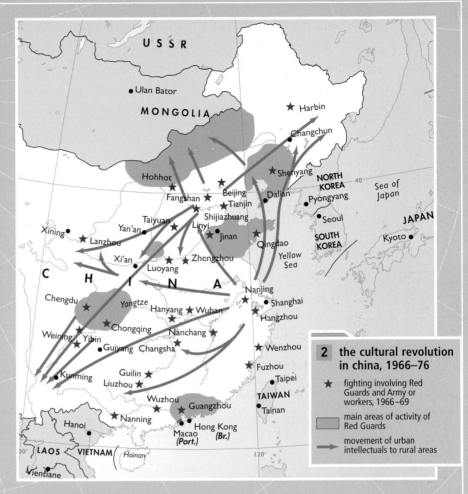

2 the cultural revolution in china, 1966–76
★ fighting involving Red Guards and Army or workers, 1966–69
▨ main areas of activity of Red Guards
➜ movement of urban intellectuals to rural areas

Chinese youth who, as 'Red Guards', faithfully supported his policies. In 1966 Mao launched the Great Proletarian Cultural Revolution. Red Guards were set loose to prevent the development of 'vested interests' and careerism in party and state by establishing permanent revolution. The guards killed thousands and forcibly resettled millions. Chaos followed throughout China, forcing Mao to call on the PLA to restore order.

Mao died in 1976 and his widow Jiang Qing with three allies (later denounced as the 'Gang of Four') tried to seize power; but by this time the PLA and the élite had had enough of revolution. The 'Gang of Four' were arrested, tried and expelled from the Communist Party.

In the late 1970s Deng Xiaoping became the dominant figure in China's politics. Following the visit of United States President Nixon in 1972, which began the process of re-opening China to the capitalist West, Deng launched a policy of economic liberalization. He created special economic zones in areas bordering the foreign colonies of Hong Kong, Macao and Taiwan, and in Shanghai, with inducements to encourage foreign investment. By 1992, $36 billion had been invested. Other reforms followed: peasants were permitted to own land and, by 1984, 98 per cent did so. The communes vanished and agricultural output increased by 49 per cent in five years. Private businesses, also now permitted, grew in number from 100,000 in 1978 to 17 million in 1985.

Economic reforms led to demands for political liberalization. In December 1986, students demonstrated for democracy in 15 cities. Deng responded with repression: he arrested 'troublemakers' and sacked Hu Yaobang, the liberal secretary-general of the Chinese Communist Party. When Hu died in April 1989, students used the occasion to demand democracy, gathering in Beijing's Tiananmen Square, at times numbering over a million, until in June Deng sent in the PLA and the movement was ruthlessly crushed.

After the Tiananmen massacre China swiftly reassured the world that it was a stable economic partner, and most of the world obligingly ignored human rights concerns in return for a share of China's economic boom. Foreign investment soared, and so did China's foreign trade. Further economic liberalization now took place as most of China operated a 'socialist market economy'. Growth rates, which averaged 10 per cent or more for the 1980s and 1990s, were only slightly affected by the economic turmoil which hit most of the rest of east Asia in 1997–98. In 1997, Britain returned its colony of Hong Kong, which retained a degree of self-government, and two years later Portugal surrendered Macao. With growing freedom in many areas of life, the issue of democracy remained the unfinished business of China's 20th-century achievement.

japan and korea since 1945

In the wake of the Second World War, United States support for Japan, South Korea and Taiwan, perceived after 1948 as its first line of defence in east Asia, transformed their economies.

Japan, like Germany, ended the war with its economy in ruins: most towns and industrial plants destroyed; nearly all foreign assets lost; domestic capital run down. Moreover, the victors demanded reparations and occupied the country following its surrender. The Far East Commission, which contained representatives of all the countries that had fought Japan, but remained an American enterprise, sought to demilitarize Japan and create a peaceful, democratic state. It reformed the education system (removing from the syllabus all material that had encouraged military and authoritarian values); abolished the divinity of the emperor and made the Diet (parliament) the highest political authority; established an independent judiciary and free labour unions; introduced a programme of land reform; and sought (with little success) to break up the great concentrations of corporate power. With the advance of the Chinese communists after 1948, however, the United States increasingly came to see Japan not only as the key bulwark of Western power in east Asia but also as one whose effectiveness depended on the reconstruction of its economic power. The occupation formally ended in 1951.

Japan's defeat also ended its harsh colonial rule of Korea (since 1910) and led to the peninsula's occupation by the victors: Japanese forces north of the 38th parallel surrendered to Soviet Russia, those in the south to the United States. The Soviets supported the establishment of a communist state in the north under Kim Il-Sung, a guerrilla leader who had spent considerable time in the Soviet Union; and the Americans retaliated by sponsoring a representative regime under Syngman Rhee, a strong anti-communist. Both new governments entertained strong ambitions to unite the country under their own rule, and in June 1950 the North attacked, pushing the South Korean and remaining United States troops back toward Pusan. The US forces counterattacked in September with a daring amphibious landing at Inchon, leading to a further offensive that promised

2 During the 1970s and 1980s Japan's economic presence abroad expanded dramatically (map below). By 1987 overseas investments were worth $139 billion. Foreign trade totalled only seven billion Yen in 1970 but was 40 billion by 1993. The US trade deficit with Japan reached $60 billion by 1987, over a third of the total trade deficit. The great bulk of Japanese exports was made up of machinery and equipment.

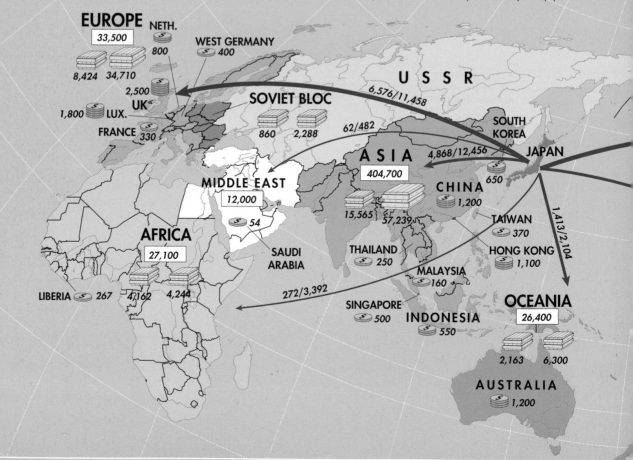

to unify Korea. In November, however, the Chinese committed substantial forces and regained most of the north. A stalemate ensued until an armistice was signed in 1953.

The Korean War boosted the Japanese economy and initiated a period of exceptionally high economic growth – well over 10 per cent a year throughout the 1960s, and over four per cent annually between 1974 and 1985, faster than that of any other OECD country. A key feature of Japan's growth was its flexibility in pursuing economic objectives: in the 1950s it emphasized heavy industry, ship-building and iron and steel; in the 1960s it moved into high-technology consumer manufactures largely for export; from the 1970s it concentrated on technological innovation and higher value-added products while transferring the production of lower value-added goods overseas. Industrial production and exports soared and massive Japanese investment took place in Asia, Europe and North America. In the early 1990s, Japan had the world's strongest economy with the largest per capita GNP and the largest holding of foreign assets and debt.

Korea epitomized the relative success of the communist and capitalist projects. Until 1970 North Korea had the higher GNP per capita, but by the 1990s GNP was declining at five per cent and the state, still communist, came close to economic and humanitarian disaster. From the mid-1960s South Korea embarked on rapid industrialization and by the 1990s boasted the world's 13th largest economy with great strengths in car manufacture, shipbuilding and semi-conductors. Its regime showed little tolerance of political dissent, however, and crushed open protest. The North remained an almost hermetically isolated Stalinist dictatorship into the 21st century, and one whose unpredictability became dangerous once it became clear that it was bent on developing a nuclear weapons capability.

The economic turmoil that hit the east Asian economies in 1997 exposed serious structural weaknesses, particularly in the inefficient and debt-laden finance and banking sectors, putting into question the previously assumed vast underlying strength of the region.

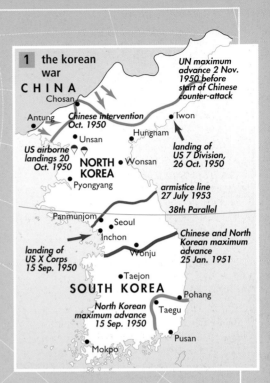

1 the korean war

CHINA
Chosan
Antung
Chinese intervention Oct. 1950
Unsan
US airborne landings 20 Oct. 1950
NORTH KOREA
Wonsan
Pyongyang
Panmunjom
Seoul
Inchon
landing of US X Corps 15 Sep. 1950
Wonju
Taejon
SOUTH KOREA
North Korean maximum advance 15 Sep. 1950
Mokpo
Taegu
Pohang
Pusan

UN maximum advance 2 Nov. 1950 before start of Chinese counter-attack
Iwon
Hungnam
landing of US 7 Division, 26 Oct. 1950
armistice line 27 July 1953
38th Parallel
Chinese and North Korean maximum advance 25 Jan. 1951

1 The Korean War carried the Cold War to the Far East. Occupied in 1945 by Soviet and American forces, the country was already divided *de facto* by 1948. In 1950, after the withdrawal of the occupying armies, the North Koreans attacked the South. The United States and United Nations immediately intervened. After initial North Korean successes, the Americans under General MacArthur counter-attacked and advanced to the Chinese frontier. This resulted in Chinese intervention and stalemate, ended only by the armistice of Panmunjom and the partition of the country along the 38th parallel.

CANADA
$ 650

NORTH AMERICA
83,900

15,357/21,873

USA
14,700

17,170   75,190

BAHAMAS
$ 730

CAYMAN ISLANDS $ 1,200

4,814/6,479

PANAMA
$ 2,300

LATIN AMERICA
128,100

BRAZIL
$ 230

2,024   2,372

2 japanese investment overseas, 1970–96

15,565   57,239   trade with region, 1970–4 and 1985–9 (billion Yen)

6,576/3,392   value of Japanese direct foreign investment in region, 1987/1999 (US$ million)

$ 1,200   value of Japanese direct foreign investment in country, 1987 (US$ million)

404,700   workers in Japanese-affiliated companies, 1980

The Great Depression struck Latin America a shattering blow, cutting off supplies of foreign capital and lowering the price of its primary products in the world markets. Chile's exports fell by over 80 per cent between 1929 and 1933; those of Bolivia and Peru by 75 per cent. Only oil-exporting Venezuela more or less weathered the storm. The economic collapse led to widespread disillusion with middle-class liberal or radical parties: in 1930 and 1931, 11 of the 20 republics south of the Rio Grande experienced revolutionary changes in government. Mexico, where Lázaro Cárdenas (1934–40) revived the land distribution policies of 1911, experienced a shift to the left; but elsewhere the swing was mainly to the right. The new dictators tended to be populists, appealing directly to the masses and cooperating with organized labour and the trade unions. They also introduced programmes of industrialization – following Soviet or, more often, Fascist models – to reduce dependence on overseas markets and hasten economic development.

Manufacturing industry received a further boost during World War II, which cut off imported consumer goods and stimulated the industrial sector. But industrialization made Latin America dependent upon imported capital goods, raw materials, technology and finance – especially from the United States – creating enormous foreign debts. Multinational corporations exploited the cheap labour of Latin America without stimulating economic development. Social tensions arose from income concentration, unemployment, lack of opportunities, and from the intrusion of foreign interests. Social revolutions were attempted but frustrated in Guatemala, Bolivia and Chile, underlining the obstacles to change in economies too narrowly based to sustain welfare programmes, where local élites were prepared to collaborate with the United States.

Cuba after 1959 attempted to achieve social change, economic growth and freedom from the United States simultaneously; but although its revolution led to greater social equality and some improvement in the lot of rural workers, it also brought a repressive regime and dependence on the Soviet Union. Moreover, its attempts to spread revolution in Central and South America all failed.

In the face of revolutionary change, with some support from the upper and middle classes, the military seized power in many areas and combined political repression with economic liberalization. But by the late 1980s their policies too had largely failed and, in the face of economic recession and popular protest, their power gradually weakened. Instead, democratic government resumed in several states of the subcontinent. In 1992 Mexico signed a free trade agreement (NAFTA) with Canada and the United States, creating the largest integrated trading bloc in the world.

2 economic development

direct US investment in Latin America (figures in millions of US dollars)
1929 1943 1960 1979 1995

chief exports of Latin America, 1955–90
coffee chief exports 1955
coffee chief exports 1990
▲ represents over 50 per cent of total exports
● represents over 25 per cent of total exports

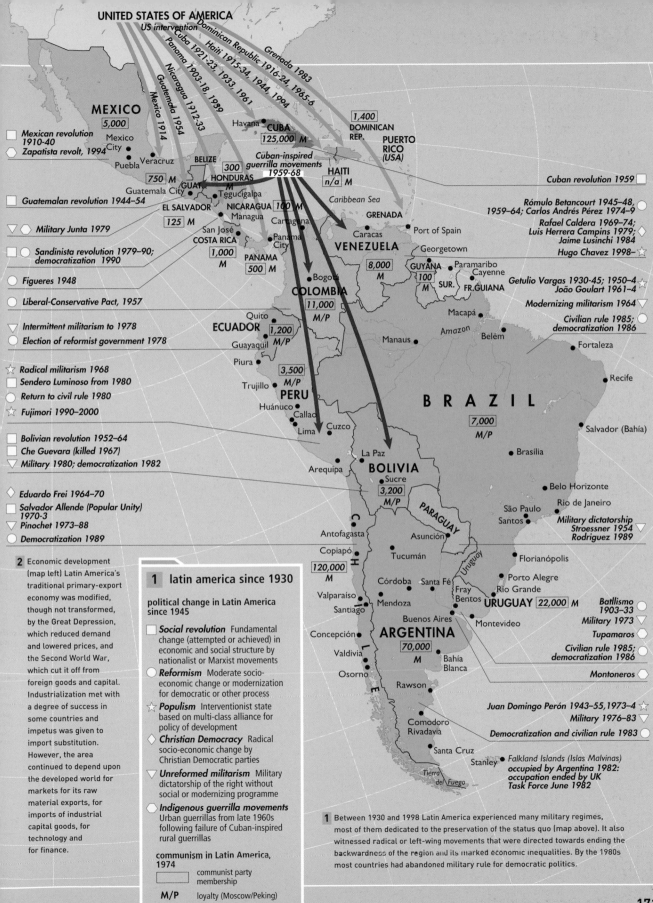

2 Economic development (map left) Latin America's traditional primary-export economy was modified, though not transformed, by the Great Depression, which reduced demand and lowered prices, and the Second World War, which cut it off from foreign goods and capital. Industrialization met with a degree of success in some countries and impetus was given to import substitution. However, the area continued to depend upon the developed world for markets for its raw material exports, for imports of industrial capital goods, for technology and for finance.

1 latin america since 1930

political change in Latin America since 1945

☐ *Social revolution* Fundamental change (attempted or achieved) in economic and social structure by nationalist or Marxist movements

○ *Reformism* Moderate socio-economic change or modernization for democratic or other process

☆ *Populism* Interventionist state based on multi-class alliance for policy of development

◇ *Christian Democracy* Radical socio-economic change by Christian Democratic parties

▽ *Unreformed militarism* Military dictatorship of the right without social or modernizing programme

◇ *Indigenous guerrilla movements* Urban guerrillas from late 1960s following failure of Cuban-inspired rural guerrillas

communism in Latin America, 1974

☐ communist party membership

M/P loyalty (Moscow/Peking)

1 Between 1930 and 1998 Latin America experienced many military regimes, most of them dedicated to the preservation of the status quo (map above). It also witnessed radical or left-wing movements that were directed towards ending the backwardness of the region and its marked economic inequalities. By the 1980s most countries had abandoned military rule for democratic politics.

171

the **united states** since 1945

The requirements of wartime production solved the unemployment problem of the United States at last, and the gigantic output achieved to meet the needs of army, navy, air force and allies demonstrated the economic potential which, when realized, would create an era of unprecedented prosperity for the United States. Gross National Product almost trebled in real terms between 1950 and 1990, while real income per head nearly doubled.

A number of factors brought about the economic surge: rapid population increase (from 132 million in 1940 to 281 million in 2000); technological advances coupled with the emergence of new consumer goods; the sudden spending of wartime savings between 1945 and 1948; and the rearmament programmes connected with the Cold War and the Korean War. Affluence came to seem entirely normal and business confidence was seldom less than buoyant: on this basis of wealth and hope most American people began to transform their entire way of life. The expansion of the suburbs constituted perhaps the most obvious change. Easy credit, cheap fuel (both for homes and cars), mass production of housing and automobiles, and giant road-building programmes (40,000 miles of interstate highways by 1980), all helped encourage Americans in their millions to move off the farms and out of the cities into endless miles of suburbs. So although the population of the central cities grew from 48 million to 79 million between 1950 and 1990, that of their urban fringes also rose from 21 million to 79 million.

By 1990, less than one-third of the US population lived in non-metropolitan areas, but the flight from the farms did not reduce productivity: on the contrary, the number of people fed by one farm worker doubled from 15 in 1950 to 30 in 1970. Thanks to mechanization (by 1990 almost 100 per cent of the cotton crop was harvested by machine, as against only 10 per cent in 1949), improved seeds and fertilizers and government subsidies, the United States provided a significant proportion of the world's staple foods, such as wheat, maize and soya beans. The economy at large grew steadily, with the service sector (as in western Europe) expanding far more rapidly than manufacturing.

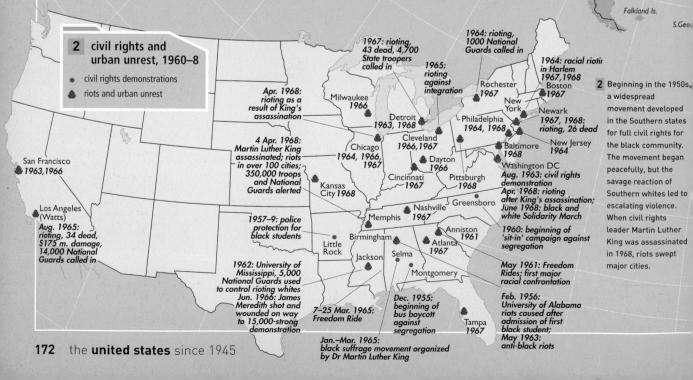

CANADA

USA

Bermuda

Nor
Atlar
Oce

1959
CUBA   DOMINICAN REPUBLIC
1962   1965
MEXICO
JAMAICA
NICARAGUA   GRENADA
1979   1983
VENEZUELA   FRENCH
GUIANA
COLOMBIA

PERU   BRAZIL

BOLIVIA

CHILE

ARGENTINA

Falkland Is.
S.Geo

2 **civil rights and urban unrest, 1960–8**

• civil rights demonstrations
⚑ riots and urban unrest

San Francisco
1963, 1966

Los Angeles
(Watts)
Aug. 1965: rioting, 34 dead, $175 m. damage, 14,000 National Guards called in

Apr. 1968: rioting as a result of King's assassination

Milwaukee
1966

4 Apr. 1968: Martin Luther King assassinated; riots in over 100 cities; 350,000 troops and National Guards alerted

Detroit
1963, 1968

Chicago
1964, 1966, 1967

Cleveland
1966, 1967

Kansas
City 1968

Cincinnati
1967

Dayton
1966

1967: rioting, 43 dead, 4,700 State troopers called in

1965: rioting against integration

Rochester
1967

New
York

Newark
1967, 1968: rioting, 26 dead

Philadelphia
1964, 1968

Pittsburgh
1968

Baltimore
1968

New Jersey
1964

1964: rioting, 1000 National Guards called in

1964: racial riotir in Harlem 1967, 1968
Boston
1967

Washington DC
Aug. 1963: civil rights demonstration Apr. 1968: rioting after King's assassination; June 1968: black and white Solidarity March

Greensboro

Nashville
1967

1957–9: police protection for black students

Little
Rock

Memphis
1967

Birmingham

Jackson

Selma

Montgomery

Anniston
1961

Atlanta
1967

1962: University of Mississippi, 5,000 National Guards used to control rioting whites Jun. 1966: James Meredith shot and wounded on way to 15,000-strong demonstration

7–25 Mar. 1965: Freedom Ride

Jan.–Mar. 1965: black suffrage movement organized by Dr Martin Luther King

Dec. 1955: beginning of bus boycott against segregation

1960: beginning of 'sit-in' campaign against segregation

May 1961: Freedom Rides; first major racial confrontation

Feb. 1956: University of Alabama riots caused after admission of first black student; May 1963: anti-black riots

Tampa
1967

2 Beginning in the 1950s, a widespread movement developed in the Southern states for full civil rights for the black community. The movement began peacefully, but the savage reaction of Southern whites led to escalating violence. When civil rights leader Martin Luther King was assassinated in 1968, riots swept major cities.

NORWAY
WEST GERMANY
EAST GERMANY
UK **B,C,S**
1948
POLAND
CZECH.
US occupation zone, 1945-55
FRANCE **S**
HUNGARY
ROMANIA
BULGARIA
SPAIN
ITALY
GREECE
TURKEY **B,C**
LEBANON *1958,1982*
ISRAEL
1979
B
IRAN *1979* **B,C**
MOROCCO
LIBYA *1969*
EGYPT *1973*
SAUDI ARABIA
OMAN
PAKISTAN **B,C,S**
INDIA
U S S R
MONGOLIA
CHINA
BANGLADESH **B,C,S**
NORTH VIETNAM
BURMA *1964-73*
N. KOREA *1950-3*
S. KOREA
JAPAN *1953*
administered by US under peace treaty with Japan, 1945
Amami-Oshima Is.
Ryukyu Is. 1972
Bonin Is. *1968*
Volcano Is.
Marcus Is.
Parece-Vela I.
1964-73
1962-75
S
LAOS *1975*
1975
CAMBODIA *1970-3*
SOUTH VIETNAM *1975*
PHILIPPINES *independent from US, 1946*
Guam
TRUST TERRITORY OF THE PACIFIC ISLANDS *brought under US control as UN trusteeship, 1947*
NIGERIA
1974
ETHIOPIA
SOMALIA *1977*
Indian Ocean
LIBERIA
Ascension I.
KENYA
ZAIRE
St Helena
ANGOLA
Mayotte
British Indian Ocean Territory
South Atlantic Ocean
Tristan da Cunha
Madagascar
SOUTH AFRICA

1 After 1945 the USA maintained a world presence through a network of military bases and defence pacts in Europe, the Middle East and Asia (map above). The desire to contain the threat of communism forced America into the role of the world's policeman, intervening militarily on numerous occasions. Many states saw America's role as a new imperialism, replacing the defunct colonial empires of Europe. In Iran and Libya rejection of American influence led to popular anti-imperialist revolutions.

AUSTRALIA S

NEW ZEALAND S

But beneath the prosperity lurked tensions. American capitalists tended to spend their profits rather than re-invest them, and industrial workers claimed higher wages and easier conditions of work without regard to the effect such claims (if successful) might have on prices and on the international competitiveness of American industry. The Vietnam War (1965–73) created high inflation and bitter internal divisions. Explicit discrimination against blacks and Asians exploded in urban riots during the 1960s and gave rise to a widespread movement for civil rights led by Dr Martin Luther King . Then came the policies of Presidents Ronald Reagan (1981–89) and George Bush (1989–93), who cut taxes by a third (releasing a flood of spending power on the markets), slashed welfare programmes (turning the inner cities into ghettoes), increased expenditure on armaments (so creating the biggest deficit in history) and failed to remedy the structural defects of American industry (so that the new purchasing power went overwhelmingly into imports, creating an equally unprecedented trade deficit).

Under the presidency of Bill Clinton (1993–2001), Americans rediscovered their national self-confidence. The United States played a decisive role in the conflicts in the Middle East and the Balkans and its economy boomed. Much of this prosperity depended on sales of computers and satellite communications, however, and when demand for these slackened in 2000, recession threatened. The terrorist attacks of September 2001, when Islamic extremists crashed two planes into the World Trade Center in New York, left the nation in shock and precipitated a decline in confidence. But it did not cause America to disengage from the world – the American-led campaigns in Afghanistan (to overthrow the Taliban regime and uproot Al-Qaeda) and in Iraq (to overthrow Saddam Hussein) showed a country both willing and able to assert itself in the international sphere.

1 **the united states and the world, 1945–85**

— anti-communist defensive line under Truman Doctrine, 1947

- - - SEATO anti-communist defensive line, 1954

—·—·— anti-communist defensive line under Formosa Resolution, 1955

······ anti-communist defensive line implied by Eisenhower Doctrine, 1958

- - - - returned to Japan, with date

S SEATO members, 1954-76

B Baghdad Pact members, 1955-8

C CENTO members, 1959-8

NATO and ANZUS members, 1985, including dependencies

Rio Pact (OAS) members, 1985

other US allies, 1985

former allies turned adversaries, with date

former adversaries turned allies, with date

✳ US forces in action, with date

Despite the extensive loss of life and property inflicted on the Soviet Union during World War II, remarkable economic recovery began after 1945.

The output of heavy industry rose steadily and light industry, neglected under Stalin (who died in 1953), also progressed under his successors. The agricultural problems created by collectivization remained – grain production only increased in the late 1950s, and even then the USSR continued to depend on imports – but vast reserves of oil, gas and mineral ores were discovered and exploited in Siberia. Russia's east European satellites were obliged to supply high-quality engineering products and expert personnel (as well as more basic items), which immensely assisted the USSR's economic progress. The development of the atom bomb (1949), of the first satellite (the sputnik: 1957) and of the first manned space flight (1961) all indicated the ability of Russian science to innovate.

After 1945 the Soviet military became a central feature of the state. One-fifth of the budget was devoted to military spending while between 1952 and 1976, 101 military leaders became full members of the Central Committee of the

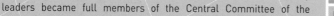

2 communist eastern europe to 1985

- Soviet zone of occupation in Austria, 1945-55
- **C** members of Cominform, 1947
- Iron Curtain, 1948
- ···· frontier incidents, 1950-2
- frontier finalized by GDR-Polish treaty, 1950
- Balkan Pact, 1954 (not functional from 1955)
- Warsaw Pact from May 1955
- → Soviet troop deployments in Hungary, 1956
- participated in invasion of Czechoslovakia, 1968
- ➡ Warsaw Pact troop deployments in Czechoslovakia, 1968
- ⇒ mass exodus of refugees
- • uprisings, 1953
- • uprisings, 1956
- • mass protests, 1968
- • mass protests and strikes, 1970-85
- — frontiers, 1950

2 Between 1944 and 1948 a communist pro-Soviet bloc was created in Eastern Europe. Soviet forces were stationed throughout the bloc, which was bound together by economic agreements (COMECON, 1949) and a military alliance (Warsaw Pact, 1955). In June 1948 Tito's Yugoslavia broke ties with Moscow. All other attempts to challenge Soviet dominance in the 1950s and 1960s – in East Germany, in Hungary and in Czechoslovakia – were crushed.

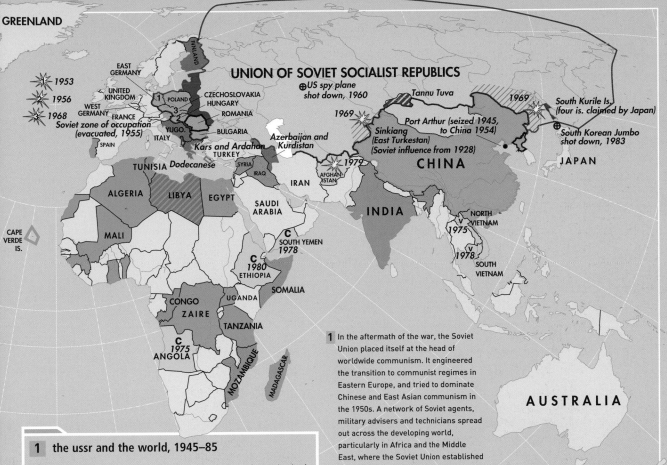

GREENLAND

UNION OF SOVIET SOCIALIST REPUBLICS

⊕ US spy plane shot down, 1960

Tannu Tuva

1953
1956
1968

EAST GERMANY
UNITED KINGDOM
WEST GERMANY FRANCE
Soviet zone of occupation (evacuated, 1955)
ITALY
SPAIN

1 POLAND
3 CZECHOSLOVAKIA
2 HUNGARY
ROMANIA
YUGO.
BULGARIA
Kars and Ardahan
TURKEY
Dodecanese
SYRIA
IRAQ

Azerbaijan and Kurdistan

1969
1979
AFGHANISTAN

IRAN

Port Arthur (seized 1945, to China 1954)
Sinkiang (East Turkestan) (Soviet influence from 1928)

CHINA

South Kurile Is. (four is. claimed by Japan)

⊕ South Korean Jumbo shot down, 1983

JAPAN

1969

TUNISIA
ALGERIA
LIBYA
EGYPT
SAUDI ARABIA

MALI

INDIA

NORTH VIETNAM
1975

V 1978
SOUTH VIETNAM

C SOUTH YEMEN 1978

C 1980 ETHIOPIA

SOMALIA

CONGO
ZAIRE
UGANDA
TANZANIA

CAPE VERDE IS.

C 1975 ANGOLA

MOZAMBIQUE
MADAGASCAR

AUSTRALIA

1 In the aftermath of the war, the Soviet Union placed itself at the head of worldwide communism. It engineered the transition to communist regimes in Eastern Europe, and tried to dominate Chinese and East Asian communism in the 1950s. A network of Soviet agents, military advisers and technicians spread out across the developing world, particularly in Africa and the Middle East, where the Soviet Union established military bases for a brief period.

1 the ussr and the world, 1945–85

USSR and client states, 1938

annexed 1944-5

territorial ambitions thwarted, 1945-6

unsuccessful attempt to gain or maintain control by 1949

control or influence secured by 1954

Warsaw pact, 1955

turned antagonistic to USSR from the early 1960s

acknowledgement demanded from China that 19th-century Russian annexations were by unequal treaties

ties from USSR loosened from mid 1960s

brought into or kept in Soviet sphere in 1970s by military intervention

other allies in 1985

c,v pro-Soviet regime maintained or installed by Cuban or Vietnamese forces, with date

Soviet influence aborted or sought unsuccessfully, 1960-85

Soviet forces in action or deployed in confrontation, with date

⊕ foreign aircraft downed, with detail

frontiers, 1985

Communist Party. The Soviet Union, along with the United States, had become a 'superpower', with a comparable degree of military strength. Although its gross national product fell well short of its rival's, the USSR overtook the USA in the production of iron ore, cement, steel and oil. Nevertheless, the Soviet economy entered a period of crisis in the 1970s. Increasingly, the USSR found the arms-race more costly than did the USA (not least because the latter enjoyed far better credit and so could finance much of its expenditure through loans), and the position became critical when the USA threatened to extend its defence system into outer space (the 'Strategic Defense Initiative'). In 1985 a new Soviet leader, Mikhail Gorbachev, came to power with a programme of reform designed to achieve a 'revolution within the revolution'.

From 1985 to 1990 Gorbachev successfully improved relations with both China and the west in order to provide peaceful external conditions for reconstruction. He introduced *glasnost* (openness) in the media to encourage criticism of deficiencies in the economy and society; but he could not assure an adequate supply of food, and unrest in the cities grew. In desperation, in 1989 he withdrew Soviet forces from eastern Europe, hoping to reduce costs and thus improve the situation at home; but the resurgence of nationalism in many constituent republics began to threaten the entire union. The Soviet Union comprised many different ethnic, religious, linguistic and cultural groups. The majority of the population claimed Slavic origin, including the Russians (53 per cent) and Ukrainians (16 per cent) – by far the largest groups. But the minorities, especially those incorporated by force during the 19th century and the Baltic states, violently annexed in 1945, eagerly anticipated the chance to assert their independence.

from 1947

The defeat of Germany, Italy and Japan and the weakening of Britain and France in World War II left the USA and USSR as the only 'superpowers'. Their ideological and political confrontation expressed itself as the Cold War. Conflict between the two had already appeared before the final victory. The Western Allies had already agreed (reluctantly) at Yalta (February 1945) to allow Soviet control of eastern Europe after the end of the war. By 1949 Stalin had developed an atomic bomb, thus ending the US monopoly of nuclear weapons. In reply, the USA built up the defence of western Europe with the formation of the North Atlantic Treaty Organization (NATO) in 1949. In 1952 the USA tested a thermo-nuclear (hydrogen) bomb; Russia followed suit in 1953.

Although it started as a conflict over central Europe, the Cold War soon developed into a global confrontation. The USA saw the Korean War (1950–53) as evidence of a world-wide communist conspiracy, and American policy now became the 'containment' of Communism by a series of encircling alliances. NATO was followed by the South-East Asia Treaty Organization (SEATO) in 1954 and the Baghdad Pact (1955); the USA maintained over 1,400 foreign bases, including 275 bases for nuclear bombers, in 31 countries around the Soviet perimeter. As long as nuclear devices could only be delivered by aircraft, possession of these bases conferred an enormous advantage on the US. But when in the early 1960s both sides began to deploy ballistic nuclear missiles capable of being launched from land silos and submarines, the odds altered: now, in the event of war, each of the two superpowers could attack the other's cities directly.

In October 1962, this scenario was almost put to the test when, following an unsuccessful US attempt to unseat the communist regime, the USSR established nuclear missile sites in Cuba. President Kennedy proclaimed a 'quarantine' of the island and threatened that, if the missiles were fired, the US would immediately retaliate against the USSR. The Russians then agreed to their removal. In return, Kennedy agreed to remove some of the US missile sites from Turkey.

This crisis, with its real threat of nuclear holocaust, proved a turning point in the Cold War. In practice the Cold War was now conducted at a lower level of confrontation, using conventional weapons, political pressure and propaganda. Already both monolithic blocs had begun to show signs of strain, most seriously on the Soviet side: Hungary and Poland rebelled in 1956, and from 1960 China began to quarrel openly over territory and ideology. In western Europe, France rejected American political leadership after 1958 and left NATO. A desire to limit the spread of nuclear weapons led to the conclusion of a partial test-ban treaty in 1963 and a nuclear non-proliferation treaty in 1968, but not all nuclear or potential nuclear powers signed these agreements (notably France, China and India) while others later reneged on their commitment. The Cold War therefore continued and the superpowers created huge nuclear arsenals.

In the event, the economic and political difficulties of the USSR increased to the point where the Soviet leader Mikhail Gorbachev (1985–91) felt that only a dramatic reduction in the crushing burden of military expenditure could bring relief. First the Soviets withdrew their forces from eastern Europe (1989), then NATO and the Warsaw Pact declared that the other was no longer an enemy (1990), and finally the USSR itself began to disintegrate (1991). Further agreements on the reduction of nuclear and conventional forces soon followed, although the fate of the vast arsenal accumulated by the former USSR gave cause for concern.

1 the age of bipolarity

	USA and allies, 1958
	USSR and allies, 1958
←	Soviet ICBM bases (7000 mile range)
←	other Soviet missile sites, 1961
▲	principal Soviet military airfields
←	US ICBM bases (5000 mile range)
▲	US heavy bomber bases (capable of reaching USSR with airborne refuelling)
■	US nuclear and other major bases (Oct. 1962)
	strategic US fleets
✳	points of conflict in the Cold War
✊	uprisings in the Communist world

1 The world order after 1945 was divided into a bi-polar confrontation between the US-led capitalist states and the Soviet-dominated communist bloc (map above). The NATO system and the Warsaw Pact created an armed camp in Europe either side of an 'Iron Curtain'. A network of bases was set up by the USA to hem in the USSR with the threat of nuclear missile attack, but the subsequent development of intercontinental missiles which could directly attack the enemy's territory created the prospect of mutual assured destruction. This threat prevented the Cold War from slipping into open nuclear conflict, despite conventional wars in the Middle East, Korea, Indo-China and central Asia.

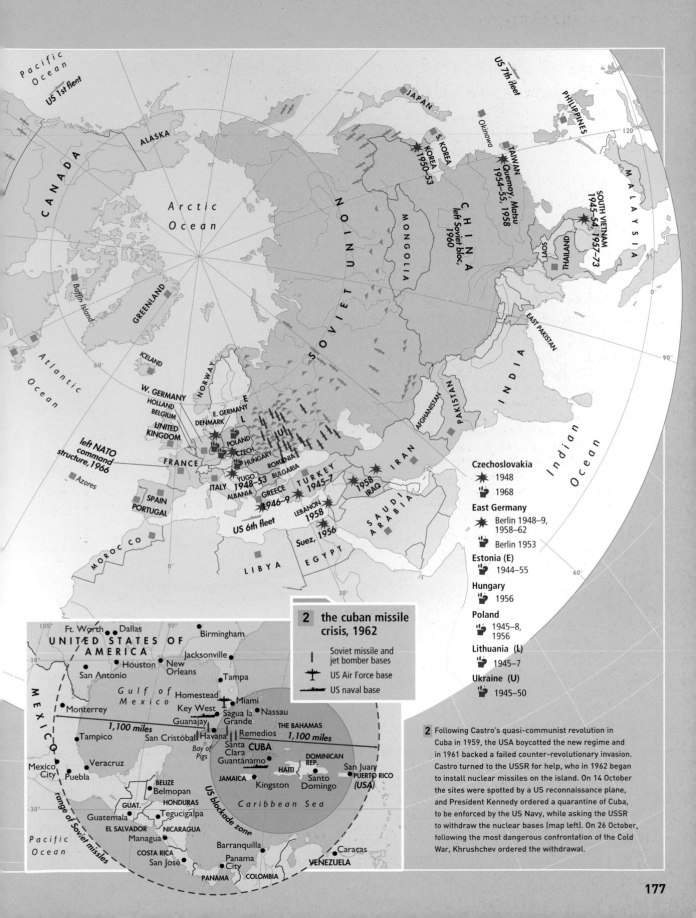

Pacific Ocean

US 1st fleet

CANADA

ALASKA

Arctic Ocean

Baffin Island

GREENLAND

Atlantic Ocean

ICELAND

NORWAY

W. GERMANY
HOLLAND
BELGIUM
DENMARK
UNITED KINGDOM
E. GERMANY
POLAND
CZECH.
HUNGARY
ROMANIA
YUGO.
BULGARIA
ALBANIA
GREECE

left NATO command structure, 1966

FRANCE

Azores

SPAIN
PORTUGAL

ITALY 1948–53

GREECE 1946–9

US 6th fleet

LEBANON 1958

Suez, 1956

MOROCCO

LIBYA

EGYPT

SAUDI ARABIA

TURKEY 1945–7

1958 IRAQ

IRAN

AFGHANISTAN

PAKISTAN

INDIA

EAST PAKISTAN

SOVIET UNION

MONGOLIA

CHINA
left Soviet bloc, 1960

JAPAN

Okinawa

KOREA 1950–53
S. KOREA

TAIWAN
Quemoy, Matsu 1954–55, 1958

PHILIPPINES

US 7th fleet

SOUTH VIETNAM 1945–54, 1957–73

LAOS
THAILAND

MALAYSIA

Indian Ocean

Czechoslovakia
✴ 1948
✊ 1968

East Germany
✴ Berlin 1948–9, 1958–62
✊ Berlin 1953

Estonia (E)
✊ 1944–55

Hungary
✊ 1956

Poland
✊ 1945–8, 1956

Lithuania (L)
✊ 1945–7

Ukraine (U)
✊ 1945–50

2 the cuban missile crisis, 1962

| Soviet missile and jet bomber bases
✈ US Air Force base
🚢 US naval base

UNITED STATES OF AMERICA

Ft. Worth   Dallas
Birmingham
Jacksonville
Houston   New Orleans
San Antonio
Tampa

MEXICO

Gulf of Mexico

Homestead
Key West   Miami   Nassau
Sagua la Grande
Guanajay
San Cristóbal   Havana   Remedios
1,100 miles   Bay of Pigs   Santa Clara   CUBA   1,100 miles
Monterrey
Tampico
THE BAHAMAS

Mexico City   Puebla
Veracruz

Guantánamo
HAITI   DOMINICAN REP.
JAMAICA   Santo Domingo
Kingston
San Juan PUERTO RICO (USA)

BELIZE
Belmopan
GUAT.
Guatemala
HONDURAS
Tegucigalpa
EL SALVADOR
Managua
NICARAGUA
COSTA RICA
San José
PANAMA
Panama City
COLOMBIA
Barranquilla
Caracas
VENEZUELA

Caribbean Sea

US blockade zone

range of Soviet missiles

Pacific Ocean

2 Following Castro's quasi-communist revolution in Cuba in 1959, the USA boycotted the new regime and in 1961 backed a failed counter-revolutionary invasion. Castro turned to the USSR for help, who in 1962 began to install nuclear missiles on the island. On 14 October the sites were spotted by a US reconnaissance plane, and President Kennedy ordered a quarantine of Cuba, to be enforced by the US Navy, while asking the USSR to withdraw the nuclear bases (map left). On 26 October, following the most dangerous confrontation of the Cold War, Khrushchev ordered the withdrawal.

the **collapse** of **communism**

since 1989

The tidal wave that swept away the communist regimes of Eastern Europe arose directly from the changes envisaged by Mikhail Gorbachev, leader of the USSR. Regarding the other communist states as a drain on Soviet resources, he encouraged them to pursue economic and political reform. This policy change came at a difficult time for the Eastern bloc states, whose economic development had been adversely affected by recession in the West and by reductions in trade and aid resulting from renewed Cold War pressures. Economic modernization slowed and provoked growing popular unrest, particularly in Poland, where a military dictatorship arose in 1981 to suppress the democracy movement. In Romania, the isolated and impoverished regime of Nicolae Ceausescu became yet more repressive.

Although few showed enthusiasm for the old regimes, popular opposition remained muted until Gorbachev pressured his communist partners to grasp the nettle of reform in 1989. Without Soviet backing, the regimes crumbled one by one: Hungary legalized opposition parties in January; Poland established the first non-communist government since 1948 in August; demonstrations ended communist rule in Czechoslovakia, East Germany and Bulgaria in November. Violence only occurred in Romania, where an army firing squad shot Ceausescu in December.

Throughout the Eastern bloc, multi-party elections now brought to power coalition governments committed to democratic reform and economic liberalization. In the course of 1990, East Germany voted first for currency union and then for full integration with West Germany; but other former communist countries, exposed to market pressures, soon plunged into economic decline. High unemployment and rural poverty contributed to the revival of deep-rooted ethnic and religious conflicts, conflicts that the communist regimes had only papered over for 40 years. In 1993, tensions between Czechs and Slovaks produced the partition of Czechoslovakia.

2 The Russian Federation, formed in 1991, consisted of 21 republics and 69 other defined areas. Since then several republics have negotiated varying degrees of autonomy from Moscow, and Chechnya fought a war from 1994 in pursuit of independence.

2 the russian federation, 1991–98

— the Russian Federation

☐ constituent republics within the Russian Federation, Mar. 1992

☐ independence declared, Nov. 1991; at war with Russia from Dec. 1994 to 1996 and from Aug. 1999

The Commonwealth of Independent States (CIS)

☐ entered close political and economic union with Russia, 2 Apr. 1996

☐ entered close economic union with Russia, 30 Mar. 1996

☐ other members of the CIS

60% percentage of Russians in other members of the Russian Federation

AD autonomous district

AO autonomous oblast

a KARACHAY-CHERKESSIA 42%
b KABARDINO-BALKARIA 39%
c NORTH-OSSETIA 30%
d INGUSHETIA (from June 1992)
e CHECHENIA } 23% combined

Sep. 1989: mass exodus of politi... refugees reach the West via Hung... Communist leadership in crisis
Oct.–Nov. 1989: widespread demonstrations against leadersh...
9 Nov. 1989: Berlin Wall breached
Mar. 1990: free elections
July 1990: currency union with West Germany
Oct. 1990: reunified with West Germany

Dec. 1989: economic war between Belgrade government and Slovenia
Apr. 1990: free elections
June 1991: independence declare... Yugoslav army attempts to regain... control of Slovenia
July 1991: Brioni Agreement end... fighting in Slovenia; Yugoslav arm... withdraws

Apr.–May 1990: free elections
Dec. 1990: Serb-inhabited areas declare independence
June 1991: independence declared; fighting in Slovenia spreads to Croatia as Serbs attem... to extend territory in Croatia and Bosnia

1987: mass strikes against wage freeze and falling living standards... growing Serb militancy against minorities
July 1990: provincial autonomies abolished
1990–1: increasing tension betwee... Belgrade government and Slovenia and Cro...
Jan.–May 1990: democratic refor... initiated by leadership
Mar. 1991: free elections

178 the **collapse** of **communism**

Meanwhile, in the USSR, nationalist unrest grew as the Russian-dominated republics of the USSR sensed an opportunity to emulate the Eastern European states and break free. The president of the Russian Republic, Boris Yeltsin, elected in 1990, urged Gorbachev to give the Soviet republics more independence. In August 1991, a group of hard-line communists attempted a coup and, although Yeltsin suppressed the revolt, the non-Russian republics soon declared their independence. The USSR was dissolved on 31 December, to be replaced by a Commonwealth of Independent States (the CIS), co-operating on military and economic issues but no longer controlled from Moscow.

With no country left to rule, Gorbachev slipped into obscurity. Russia embraced a form of presidential democracy, with Yeltsin as its first president. In 1993, hard-line parliamentary delegates hostile to further reform tried to depose Yeltsin, but he crushed them too. Yeltsin finally stepped down in 1999 and power transferred peacefully to Vladimir Putin. Meanwhile some republics – Belarus, Uzbekistan, Kazakhstan, Turkmenistan – maintained reformed communist governments while others adopted some form of democracy. In Russia itself local rulers in the constituent republics seized more power and in the case of Chechenia sought to break away from Russia by force. Many of the former Soviet satellites in eastern Europe became firmly oriented towards the western European economic and military structures – eight of them are due to join the EU in 2004, whilst NATO had already welcomed Hungary, Poland and the Czech Republic as members in 1999.

1 Between 1989 and 1991 communist eastern Europe was transformed (map below) from a Soviet-dominated bloc of authoritarian dictatorships to a patchwork of new regimes and states, most of them multi-party democracies. Growing popular dissatisfaction with the absence of civil rights and political freedom coupled with the region's poor economic performance produced widespread popular protest in 1989. Beginning in Hungary and Poland, the protests spread to East Germany. The fall of the East German government, precipitated by a mass emigration through Hungary, was a signal, like the Paris revolution in 1848, for the rest of eastern Europe to follow suit. By 1990, 50 years of Soviet domination of eastern Europe had ended.

1   the collapse of communism, 1985–91

- Soviet-dominated eastern Europe to 1989
- Soviet Union to 1991
- Yugoslavia to 1991
- united with the Federal Republic of Germany, 1990
- achieved independence, 1991
- other former communist states, 1991
- de facto independent states, late 1991, on former territory of the Soviet Union, internationally unrecognized
- overrun by Yugoslav army, July–Dec. 1991
- borders, 1991

SWEDEN

from 1985: Solidarity leads opposition to communism
June 1989: partially free elections
Aug. 1989: Solidarity-led government takes office
Jan. 1990: Communist party dissolved
Oct. 1991: free elections

Baltic Sea

Tallinn
ESTONIA
Mar. 1990: Congress of Estonia formed, declares Soviet rule illegal
Mar. 1991: referendum endorses independence
Aug. 1991: independence declared
Sep. 1991: independence recognized by USSR

Riga LATVIA
1989: mass anti-Communist demonstrations
Mar. 1991: referendum endorses independence
Aug. 1991: independence declared
Sep. 1991: independence recognized by USSR

LITHUANIA
Vilnius
Moscow
1989: mass anti-Communist demonstrations
Mar. 1991: independence declared
Apr.–June 1990: economic embargo imposed by USSR
Sep. 1991: independence recognized by USSR

RUSSIAN FED.

Berlin

POLAND
Warsaw

Prague
CZECHOSLOVAKIA

AUSTRIA
Bratislava

Budapest
HUNGARY

VENIA

TIA

Minsk
BELARUS
June 1989: Popular Front founded
Aug. 1991: independence declared
Dec. 1991: founder member of Commonwealth of Independent States

from 1988: anti-government demonstrations
Nov. 1989: mass demonstrations end Communist rule
Apr. 1990: new constitution adopted; becomes a federation
June 1990: free elections

Kiev

UKRAINE
1989: opposition mass-movements emerge
Aug. 1991: independence declared
Dec. 1991: referendum endorses independence; founder member of Commonwealth of Independent States

from 1987: Communist regime relaxes control
Sep. 1989: allows East Germans to travel to the West
Oct. 1990: Communist rule ends peacefully
Mar.–Apr. 1990: free elections

MOLDOVA

TRANSNISTRIA
June 1989: Popular Front wins 75% of votes in election
Aug. 1991: independence declared

GAGAUZIA

ROMANIA
Bucharest

Belgrade

Sarajevo
YUGOSLAVIA
KOSOVO

Tirana
Skopje

ALBANIA

BULGARIA
Sofia

TATARSTAN

RUSSIAN FEDERATION

Mar. 1985: Mikhail Gorbachev becomes leader of Communist Party; initiates perestroika and glasnost, loosens Soviet control of satellite states
June 1991: Boris Yeltsin elected president of Russian Federation
Aug. 1991: hard-line Communist coup against Gorbachev fails
Nov. 1991: Communist Party declared illegal
Dec. 1991: USSR dissolved

50°

Dec. 1989: mass demonstrations lead to armed uprisings and overthrow of Ceaușescu regime
June 1991: free elections
Nov. 1991: new constitution adopted

Nov. 1989: President Zhivkov removed from office
June 1990: free elections
July 1991: fresh elections following adoption of new constitution

Nov. 1988: mass demonstrations against Russification
Mar. 1991: referendum endorses independence
Apr. 1991: independence declared

Jan. 1990: state of emergency declared; Soviet troops intervene
Oct. 1991: independence declared

Nov. 1991: independence declared

CHECHENIA
Grozny

Sep. 1991: independence declared

GEORGIA

Sep. 1989: economic embargo imposed by Azerbaijan
Sep. 1991: referendum endorses independence; independence declared

AZERBAIJAN
ARMENIA
NAGORNO-KARABAKH

50°

40°

since 1991

The greatest casualty of the collapse of the communist bloc was Yugoslavia. Its six republics (Serbia, Croatia, Macedonia, Bosnia–Herzegovina, Slovenia and Montenegro) were held together by an over-arching communist apparatus and the personal authority of Tito, the founder of communist Yugoslavia. After his death in 1980, internal divisions began to appear. The trigger for conflict was the rise of aggressive nationalism. In 1987, following the choice of Slobodan Milosevic as leader of Serbia, tensions between the republics grew stronger. Milosevic suppressed the Albanian minority in Kosovo, and set out to expand Serbia's influence within the federation.

In 1990 multi-party elections brought nationalists to the fore in Slovenia and Croatia and paved the way for their simultaneous declaration of independence in June 1991. It also provoked a vicious seven-month war when Serb forces intervened, allegedly to protect the ethnic Serb minority in Croatia.

Meanwhile another savage civil war broke out in Bosnia–Herzegovina, where Bosnian Muslims (44 per cent of the population) and Croats (17 per cent) pushed for independence in the face of bitter opposition from the Bosnian Serbs (31 per cent). Each ethnic group sought to 'cleanse' the areas under its control of all opponents until by 1993 the Serbs controlled around 70 per cent of Bosnia and besieged the capital, Sarajevo, held by the Muslim-led government. The war caused the death of at least 100,000 and displaced half of the region's four million inhabitants. In 1995 a renewed Serb offensive provoked NATO intervention, leading to an uneasy peace (the Dayton Accords) which left Bosnia divided among the three ethnic groups and utterly devastated by four years of war.

In 1998, conflict escalated in Serbia's province of Kosovo. Talks brokered by international mediators offered the Kosovo Albanians full autonomy within Serbia, but Milosevic objected.

1 The break-up of the Soviet Union saw widespread ethnic and political conflict in the Caucasus region. Armenia and Azerbaijan fought over the Christian Armenian enclave of Nagorno-Karabakh; Georgia fought to keep South Ossetia within her boundaries and to prevent the independence of Abkhazia, but in both cases was faced with Russian intervention to keep the peace. Chechenia was invaded by Russian forces in December 1994 to prevent its complete independence. After a bitter war lasting two years, a truce was signed in 1996 leaving Chechenia as *de facto* independent. In 1999 the war flared up again as Russian forces once more invaded Chechnya.

1 the caucasus, 1988–2003

- notional extent of Georgia at independence
- advance of pro-Gamsakhurdia forces, Oct. 1993
- Georgian advance into Abkhazia, Aug. 1992
- areas of Georgia under Abkhazian control, Oct. 1993
- evacuated by Georgia, Oct. 1994
- notional extent of Azerbaijan at independence
- Armenia at independence
- limit of Armenian control, May 1992
- Azerbaijani advance into Karabakh, Oct. 1993
- secured by Armenia and Karabakh by Nov. 1993
- Chechenia-Ingushetia at independence
- seceded from Chechenia, joined Rus. Fed., Mar. 1992
- claimed by Ingushetia, 1992
- Russian advance into Chechenia by May 1995
- mass movements of refugees
- autonomous within Russian Federation

Map labels:

Nov. 1991: independence declared
Dec. 1994: Russian troops invade; Grozny largely destroyed;
May 1996: Russian-Chechen ceasefire Russian troops withdraw;
Aug. 1999: Renewed Russian invasion and occupation of most of Chechenia
2000–2: continued sporadic fighting

June 1995: attacked by Chechen forces

Oct. 1992: clashes between Ossetians and Ingush; Russian troops intervene

1989: clashes between Ossetians and Georgians
Dec. 1991 breaks from Georgia in favour of Russian Federation
Jan.-May 1992: clashes with Georgian troops; North Ossetians assist South (Apr. 1992)

Apr. 1991: independence declared
Dec. 1991: President Gamsakhurdia overthrown
1992: Eduard Shevardnadze becomes chairman of State Council
1993: Georgia joins CIS

1990: clashes between Abkhazians and Georgians
July 1992: asserts independence from Georgia; Georgian and Russian troops intervene, North Caucasian Muslims assist Abkhazians (Aug. 1992)
May 1994: ceasefire; Russian peace-keeping troops deployed

Jan. 1990: rioting in Baku: Soviet troops intervene
Oct. 1991: independence declared
Sep. 1992: unsuccessful attempts to subjugate Nagorno-Karabakh and Armenia (to May 1994)

Jan. 1990: independence declared

Sep. 1991: independence declared; Azerbaijani forces intervene; Armenian-supported Karabakh forces clash with Azeris; Armenian invasion of Azerbaijan follows
May 1994: ceasefire

Place names: Terek, Makhachkala, Caspian Sea, Derbent, Kuba, Sumgait, Baku, CHECHENIA, DAGESTAN, Grozny, Chechen, Budennovsk, AZERBAIJAN, Nazran, Ingush, Vladikavkaz, Kura, Lenkoran, Kuma, Nalchik, NORTH OSSETIA, KABARDINO-BALKARIA, Cherkessk, SOUTH OSSETIA, Tbilisi, Kura, Armenians, NAGORNO-KARABAKH, Stepanakert, KARACHAY-CHERKESSIA, Mestia, Tskhinvali, Azeris, Shusha, Lachin Corridor, Kodori Gorge, GEORGIA, Georgians, Lake Sevan, Kelbadzhar Corridor, IRAN, Zugdidi, ARMENIA, Samtredia, NAKHICHEVAN (Azer.), ABKHAZIA, Sukhumi, Poti, AJARIA, Yerevan, Nakhichevan, Gudauta, Araks, Batumi, TURKEY

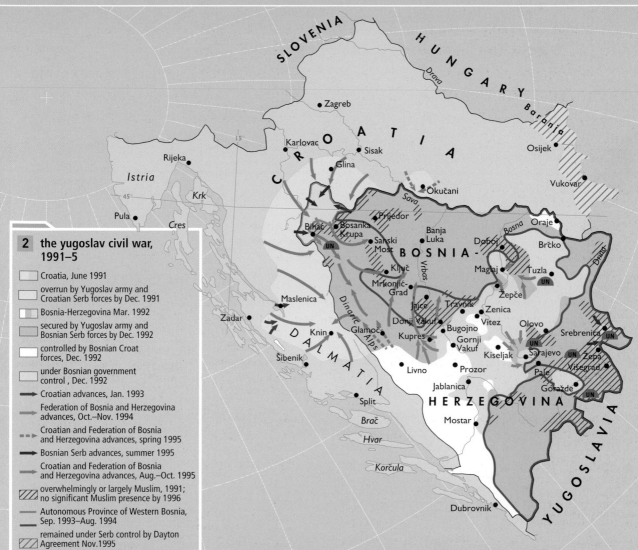

2 the yugoslav civil war, 1991–5

Croatia, June 1991

overrun by Yugoslav army and Croatian Serb forces by Dec. 1991

Bosnia-Herzegovina Mar. 1992

secured by Yugoslav army and Bosnian Serb forces by Dec. 1992

controlled by Bosnian Croat forces, Dec. 1992

under Bosnian government control , Dec. 1992

→ Croatian advances, Jan. 1993

→ Federation of Bosnia and Herzegovina advances, Oct.–Nov. 1994

→ Croatian and Federation of Bosnia and Herzegovina advances, spring 1995

→ Bosnian Serb advances, summer 1995

→ Croatian and Federation of Bosnia and Herzegovina advances, Aug.–Oct. 1995

overwhelmingly or largely Muslim, 1991; no significant Muslim presence by 1996

— Autonomous Province of Western Bosnia, Sep. 1993–Aug. 1994

— remained under Serb control by Dayton Agreement Nov.1995

returned to Croatian control in Jan. 1998 under Erdut agreement of Nov. 1995

UN-designated 'safe areas'

2 After 1989 the Yugoslav Federation began to break up into its constituent parts. In 1991 Croatia and Slovenia declared their independence. Though the Serb-dominated rump of Yugoslavia tried to force both states to remain in the federation, they became fully independent in 1992. When Bosnia tried to assert its independence a bitter civil war broke out between Serbs, Muslims and Croats which lasted until 1995, when NATO compelled Serbia to accept a ceasefire. The subsequent agreement divided Bosnia into two separate states, one Serb and one Croat/Muslim.

NATO responded with air strikes against Yugoslavia in March 1999 to force Belgrade to sign the peace agreement and to stop the repression of Kosovo Albanians. The Serbian security forces instead accelerated a programme of 'ethnic cleansing' against Kosovo Albanians. After more than two months of NATO bombing, Milosevic agreed in June 1999 to a peace plan that incorporated most of NATO's demands and a NATO-led peace implementation force entered the province.

Tensions within the Yugoslav Federation continued as the pro-western government of Montenegro sought to assert its independence from Belgrade until Milosevic fell from power in December 2000, after massive popular protests following his false claim of victory in presidential elections. His successor, Vojislav Kostunica, made overtures to the West and promised a return to democratic rule, but, especially following the assassination of Prime Minister Djindjic in March 2003, the future of the Federation remained uncertain.

The break-up of the Soviet Union, too, saw widespread ethnic and political conflict, particularly in the Caucasus region. Armenia and Azerbaijan fought over the Christian Armenian enclave of Nagorno–Karabakh; Georgia fought to keep South Ossetia within her boundaries and to prevent the independence of Abkhazia. The worst conflict occurred in Chechenia, which Russian forces invaded in 1994 and 1999 to prevent secession. Russia suffered heavy casualties in both cases and, despite occupying virtually the whole province, could not stifle a vigorous Chechen resistance.

the **21st-century** world

The 1990s saw progress in spreading democracy, in ending conflicts, in superpower disarmament and in stabilizing economic development. Yet many critical issues remained. Ecological crisis and the threat of regional wars challenged the mood of optimism in the West as it celebrated the new millennium.

The absence of global confrontation after the Cold War did not prevent regional disputes, many of which dragged in the major powers as arbiters. In 1990, Iraq invaded Kuwait, only to be expelled by United Nations' forces in 1991. Thereafter, tensions persisted as Iraq and the UN argued about the terms set for the inspection and elimination of Iraqi weapons of mass destruction, leading to another American-led invasion in 2003 which overthrew Saddam Hussein, but left a country teetering on the brink of chaos. In Chechnya, Russian forces fought a grim civil war against Chechen nationalists, which left the region desolate. The largest war of all involved the states that emerged from the collapse of former Yugoslavia in 1991. In 1995 NATO imposed a settlement on the warring groups, but three years later fighting broke out again between Serbs and Albanian separatists in Kosovo.

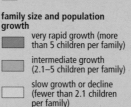

1 world population towards the millennium

family size and population growth

▓	very rapid growth (more than 5 children per family)
▒	intermediate growth (2.1–5 children per family)
□	slow growth or decline (fewer than 2.1 children per family)

fastest-growing populations (% per annum)

4.5%	1980–98
4.0%	1998–2015 (projection)
48.6	% of population under 15

slowest-growing populations (% per annum)

-4.5%	1980–98
-4.0%	1998–2015 (projection)

MACAO 25,880 countries with over 200 people per km² (with population density)

● world's largest cities, 1995 with population (in millions)

2 By the 1960s religion seemed to be in decline across the world. But in the last quarter-century it has revived remarkably, and religious conflict and violence has returned with it. A search for traditional Islamic values has led to widespread conflict between modernizers and fundamentalists. Inter-communal violence has also flared up in India and Yugoslavia.

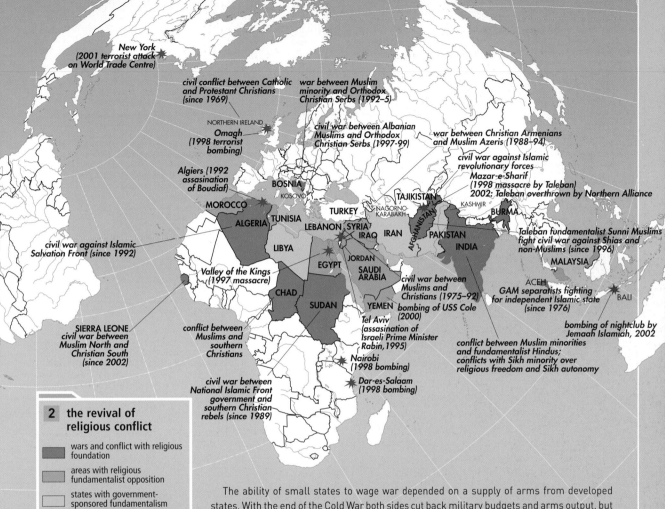

New York
(2001 terrorist attack
on World Trade Centre)

civil conflict between Catholic
and Protestant Christians
(since 1969)

war between Muslim
minority and Orthodox
Christian Serbs (1992-5)

NORTHERN IRELAND
Omagh
(1998 terrorist
bombing)

civil war between Albanian
Muslims and Orthodox
Christian Serbs (1997-99)

war between Christian Armenians
and Muslim Azeris (1988-94)

Algiers (1992
assasination
of Boudiaf)

civil war against Islamic
revolutionary forces
Mazar-e-Sharif
(1998 massacre by Taleban)
2002: Taleban overthrown by Northern Alliance

BOSNIA
KOSOVO

TAJIKISTAN

MOROCCO
TUNISIA
TURKEY
NAGORNO-
KARABAKH
KASHMIR
BURMA

ALGERIA
LEBANON
SYRIA
IRAQ
IRAN
AFGHANISTAN
PAKISTAN
INDIA

civil war against Islamic
Salvation Front (since 1992)

LIBYA

Valley of the Kings
(1997 massacre)

EGYPT
JORDAN
SAUDI
ARABIA

Taleban fundamentalist Sunni Muslims
fight civil war against Shias and
non-Muslims (since 1996)

MALAYSIA

ACEH
GAM separatists fighting
for independent Islamic state
(since 1976)

BALI

CHAD

SUDAN

YEMEN

civil war between
Muslims and
Christians (1975–92)

bombing of USS Cole
(2000)

SIERRA LEONE
civil war between
Muslim North and
Christian South
(since 2002)

conflict between
Muslims and
southern
Christians

Tel Aviv
(assasination of
Israeli Prime Minister
Rabin, 1995)

bombing of nightclub by
Jemaah Islamiah, 2002

conflict between Muslim minorities
and fundamentalist Hindus;
conflicts with Sikh minority over
religious freedom and Sikh autonomy

Nairobi
(1998 bombing)

Dar-es-Salaam
(1998 bombing)

civil war between
National Islamic Front
government and
southern Christian
rebels (since 1989)

**2 the revival of
religious conflict**

- wars and conflict with religious foundation
- areas with religious fundamentalist opposition
- states with government-sponsored fundamentalism
- ✳ sites of religious terrorism

9.0 MARSHAL

TUVALU
400

1 The population boom which began
in the 1960s showed signs of slowing
in the 1990s. It is now expected that by
the middle of the next century world
population will stabilize at around
nine billion. The slow-down has been
caused partly by improved contraception
and efforts by states to restrict family
size. Disease and famine have also
played their part, particularly in Africa.
Smaller family sizes will also produce
stable population growth. There are
now 51 nations with a small average
family size (2.1 children or less).
By 2016 that number is expected
to rise to 88.

NEW
ZEALAND

The ability of small states to wage war depended on a supply of arms from developed
states. With the end of the Cold War both sides cut back military budgets and arms output, but
weapons sales to the developing world became ever more vital. Between 1990 and 1995, the
major arms producers sold $120 billion of weapons ($62 billion by the USA). While defence
spending in the USA fell to 4.3 per cent of GDP by the mid-1990s, Middle Eastern states spent
up to eight to ten per cent. In east and south Asia, where countries confronted the massive
military weight of China, defence spending rose steadily in the 1990s, reaching around three to
five per cent of GDP. The trade in arms also led to an illicit trade in technology to support the
development of weapons – chemical and biological warfare and nuclear devices – which the
West tried to limit. In 1998 India and Pakistan both tested nuclear bombs, while other states
(such as Israel and North Korea) have nuclear expertise and, probably, nuclear weapons.

Some of the tensions in the Middle East and in south and south-east Asia arose from rapid
population growth. In these areas, people under 25 sometimes make up half the total population. Indeed, students and schoolchildren played a conspicuous part in protests in India,
Indonesia, Burma and in Tiananmen Square in Beijing in 1989. Young South Africans, too,
played a central part in achieving democracy in 1990–94. The image of the peasant-soldier
typical of the liberation movements of the 1960s gave way to chilling images of pre-teenage
boys with modern weapons in their hands.

Population growth has threatened to destabilize the world system for decades. In the late
1990s the growth began to slow, though not fast enough to avert famine and the impoverishment
of many developing states.

the global economy

By the 1990s electronic communication and world-wide investment and marketing had created a genuinely global economy. Giant transnational companies dominated finance and production. However, world economic development still depended in part on the central management of key economic factors by groups of states, and on collaboration between them. Representatives of the largest industrial economies met regularly as the Group of Seven to co-ordinate financial and trade policies. Additionally, regional agreements sought to expand trade between small groups of states.

The most successful of these groupings was the European Union, which grew from the original six members of the EEC in 1957 to embrace 15 states by 1996 (to increase to 24 in 2004). Gradual economic integration culminated on 1 January 1999 in the introduction of a single currency, the euro. Economic groups elsewhere were looser associations aiming to enhance regional economic integration. In 1994, for example, the USA, Canada and Mexico joined in the North American Free Trade Association (NAFTA).

The world's top ten trading nations in 1996 provided 61 per cent of the world's imports and 63 per cent of exports. A high proportion of that trade took place between the top traders, rather than trade between the developed and developing world; and an increasing proportion occurred within free-trade blocs.

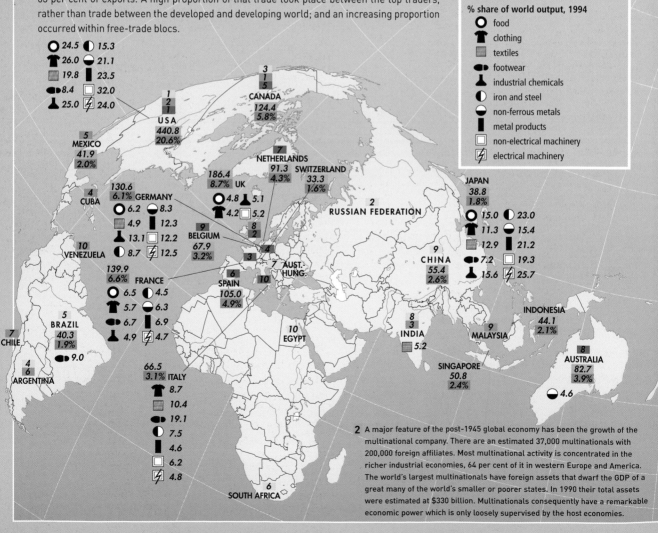

2 multinationals and transnational investments

leading 10 FDI hosts by rank

3	in 1914
5	in 1929
7	in 1993

leading FDI host countries in 1993

105.0	in US$ bn
4.9%	as % of total

% share of world output, 1994

- ⭘ food
- clothing
- ▦ textiles
- footwear
- industrial chemicals
- ◐ iron and steel
- ⊖ non-ferrous metals
- ▮ metal products
- ☐ non-electrical machinery
- ⚡ electrical machinery

2 A major feature of the post-1945 global economy has been the growth of the multinational company. There are an estimated 37,000 multinationals with 200,000 foreign affiliates. Most multinational activity is concentrated in the richer industrial economies, 64 per cent of it in western Europe and America. The world's largest multinationals have foreign assets that dwarf the GDP of a great many of the world's smaller or poorer states. In 1990 their total assets were estimated at $330 billion. Multinationals consequently have a remarkable economic power which is only loosely supervised by the host economies.

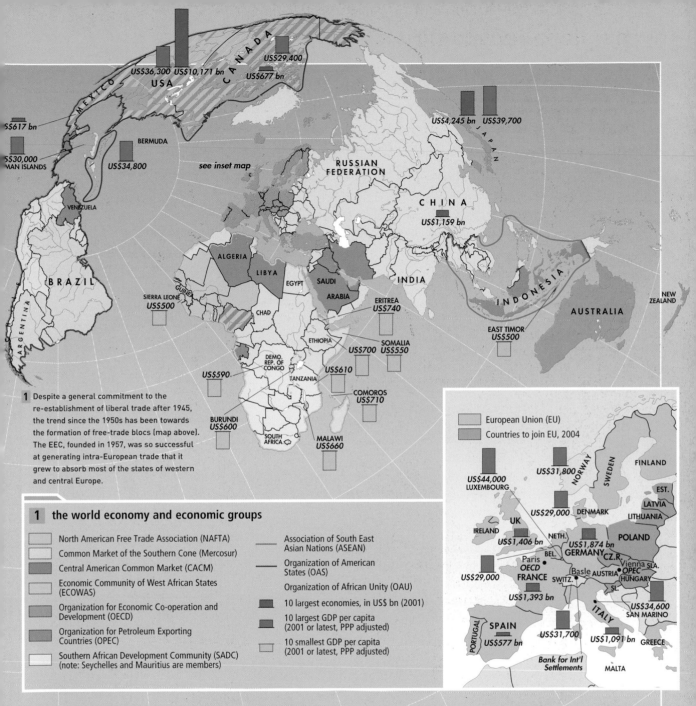

USA US$36,300 US$10,171 bn

CANADA US$29,400 US$677 bn

MEXICO

US$617 bn

US$30,000
CAYMAN ISLANDS

BERMUDA

US$34,800

VENEZUELA

BRAZIL

ARGENTINA

see inset map

RUSSIAN FEDERATION

CHINA US$1,159 bn

INDIA

ALGERIA

LIBYA

EGYPT

SAUDI ARABIA

SIERRA LEONE
US$500

GUINEA

CHAD

ETHIOPIA

ERITREA
US$740

SOMALIA
US$550

US$700

DEMO. REP. OF CONGO

TANZANIA

US$590

US$610

COMOROS
US$710

BURUNDI
US$600

SOUTH AFRICA

MALAWI
US$660

INDONESIA

EAST TIMOR
US$500

AUSTRALIA

NEW ZEALAND

JAPAN US$4,245 bn US$39,700

1 Despite a general commitment to the re-establishment of liberal trade after 1945, the trend since the 1950s has been towards the formation of free-trade blocs (map above). The EEC, founded in 1957, was so successful at generating intra-European trade that it grew to absorb most of the states of western and central Europe.

1 the world economy and economic groups

North American Free Trade Association (NAFTA)

Common Market of the Southern Cone (Mercosur)

Central American Common Market (CACM)

Economic Community of West African States (ECOWAS)

Organization for Economic Co-operation and Development (OECD)

Organization for Petroleum Exporting Countries (OPEC)

Southern African Development Community (SADC) (note: Seychelles and Mauritius are members)

Association of South East Asian Nations (ASEAN)

Organization of American States (OAS)

Organization of African Unity (OAU)

10 largest economies, in US$ bn (2001)

10 largest GDP per capita (2001 or latest, PPP adjusted)

10 smallest GDP per capita (2001 or latest, PPP adjusted)

European Union (EU)

Countries to join EU, 2004

US$44,000
LUXEMBOURG

US$31,800

NORWAY

SWEDEN

FINLAND

US$29,000 DENMARK

EST.

LATVIA

LITHUANIA

UK
US$1,406 bn

IRELAND

NETH.

BEL.

Paris
OECD

US$29,000
FRANCE
US$1,393 bn

GERMANY
US$1,874 bn

CZ.R.

POLAND

Vienna SLA.
Basle AUSTRIA OPEC
SWITZ. HUNGARY

SL.

US$34,600
SAN MARINO

ITALY
US$1,091 bn

GREECE

PORTUGAL

SPAIN
US$577 bn

US$31,700

Bank for Int'l Settlements

MALTA

The fruits of the global economic success were spread very unevenly. In 1995, Europe possessed almost 33 per cent of the world's wealth, and North America a further 30 per cent. Sustained expansion in Asia, Europe and the United States contrasted with economic decline in Africa, Latin America and the former Soviet bloc. The Russian economy in particular faced serious crisis by 1998 as the rush for capitalism failed to generate the wealth to sustain employment and welfare at the level achieved under communism. Even in east Asia, which grew faster than anywhere else in the world from the 1960s to the mid-1990s, the boom turned sour in 1997. Burdened with debt, high population growth and excessive dependence on a cluster of manufacturing exports, the new Asian economies generated a financial crisis that threatened the health of the whole global economy.

Outside the growth areas, there was persistent reliance on aid and investment from the developed world, much of it supplied by the International Monetary Fund (IMF) or the Organization for Economic Co-operation and Development (OECD). The per capita Gross Domestic Product (GDP) of the poorest states in the late 1990s was less than $300, while per capita GDP in the USA was almost $27,000. For many sub-Saharan African states, aid represented more than half of the value of total GDP. This pattern of aid-dependence altered little over the 1990s, and the gulf between the poverty of the developing world and the vast wealth of the developed industrial core remained one of the unresolved issues of global economics.

the global environment

Until the 20th century, natural changes largely determined the environment. Now, industrialization, modern communications and mass consumption have combined to produce damaging man-made environmental change. Ecological disasters have become urgent global problems.

The onset of large-scale population growth and industrialization in the 19th century stimulated a parallel rapid increase in man-made damage to the world's environment. Before 1945, this damage was largely localized, though very visible; the spread of industry worldwide after 1945 produced new threats to the environment which, if less visible, were nonetheless more deadly.

1 Rapid industrial development since the Second World War has led to high levels of water pollution in the world's major rivers and shorelines (map below). The reliance on oil as fuel contributed to this crisis with a series of sinkings of giant oil tankers. Population growth has also taken a toll of the world's rainforests, which are vital to maintaining the chemical balance of the atmosphere. Latest estimates suggest that the largest single forest, in the Amazon basin, will die through rapid loss of forested area to agriculture. This would be an unparalleled environmental disaster.

1 the crisis of the environment

**deforestation:
rainforests under threat**

- tropical rainforest
- edge of rainforest undergoing the most rapid deforestation
- ★ threatened area with large concentrations of endemic species

**ocean and river pollution:
oil slicks and tar balls**

- high occurrence
- low occurrence

oceanic pollution

- frequent and severe
- partial and intermittent
- major oil tanker disaster
- oil rig blowout
- natural seepage

river pollution

- severe
- background

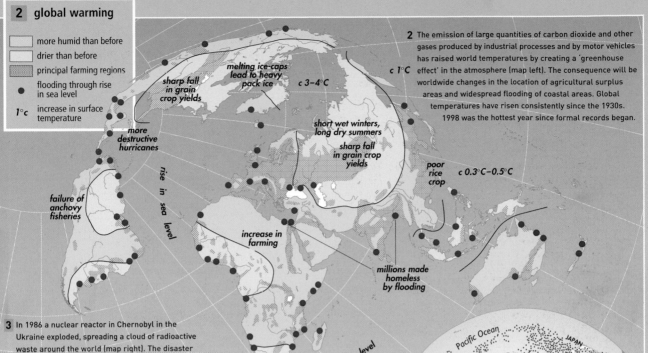

2 global warming

- more humid than before
- drier than before
- principal farming regions
- ● flooding through rise in sea level
- 1°c increase in surface temperature

2 The emission of large quantities of carbon dioxide and other gases produced by industrial processes and by motor vehicles has raised world temperatures by creating a 'greenhouse effect' in the atmosphere (map left). The consequence will be worldwide changes in the location of agricultural surplus areas and widespread flooding of coastal areas. Global temperatures have risen consistently since the 1930s. 1998 was the hottest year since formal records began.

sharp fall in grain crop yields

melting ice-caps lead to heavy pack ice

c 3-4°C

c 1°C

more destructive hurricanes

rise in sea level

short wet winters, long dry summers

sharp fall in grain crop yields

poor rice crop   c 0.3°C-0.5°C

failure of anchovy fisheries

increase in farming

millions made homeless by flooding

rise in sea level

3 In 1986 a nuclear reactor in Chernobyl in the Ukraine exploded, spreading a cloud of radioactive waste around the world (map right). The disaster was the most spectacular of many accidents in the production of nuclear power, which have given rise to growing protests against the use of nuclear fuel. As a proportion of energy generated worldwide, nuclear power has been falling since the mid-1980s.

3 radioactive fallout from the chernobyl accident, 1986

- .·.: pattern of fall-out

Acid rain from waste in the atmosphere destroyed forests and eroded buildings. Pollutants in rivers and seas poisoned wildlife.

High levels of carbon dioxide released from the burning of fossil fuels raised global temperatures, while other chemicals began to weaken the ozone layer in the earth's atmosphere. Between 1800 and 1900 the level of carbon dioxide in the atmosphere increased by only four per cent; in the 20th century it increased by 23 per cent, with most of the change occurring since the 1950s. This raised world temperatures significantly: the 1990s were the warmest decade of the millennium.

Global warming stemmed in part from a massive increase in energy consumption, most of which consisted of fossil fuels (oil, coal and natural gas). Between 1970 and 1990 energy consumption grew by 60 per cent, despite efforts to find more efficient ways of generating power and to reduce emissions. Fossil fuels released a range of chemicals into the atmosphere which blocked the natural loss of heat and created the so-called 'greenhouse effect', leading to a global rise in temperatures.

The search for alternative sources of energy produced other types of disaster, however. In 1986, a nuclear reactor at Chernobyl in the Ukraine exploded, spreading a cloud of radioactive waste around the world. This catastrophe was the most spectacular of many accidents in the production of nuclear power, eventually causing a reduction in its use.

Environmental issues became a central concern of the 1990s and state action produced some positive results. In Brazil, deforestation fell from a rate of 21,000 square kilometres in 1988 to only 1,000 square kilometres by 1993. At Rio de Janeiro in 1992 an assembly of world leaders agreed to reduce harmful pollutants and emissions, a decision reaffirmed at a further meeting in Kyoto in 1997. The richer states also promised to subsidize industrial and agricultural projects in the developing world that respected environmental interests. In European states, political movements developed based entirely on issues of the environment, and in 1998 the environmentalist Green Party won a share of power in Germany. The future of the world eco-system depended on the willingness of the world's richest states to accept substantial changes in consumption patterns.

187

Index